PREDICTIVE ASTROLOGY

♑

♒   ↗

♓   ♏

♈ PREDICTIVE ♎

♉   ♍

♊   ♌
     ♋

Frances Sakoian
& Louis S. Acker

ASTROLOGY

Understanding Transits as the Key to the Future

HARPER & ROW, PUBLISHERS

NEW YORK, HAGERSTOWN, SAN FRANCISCO, LONDON

1817

To
SARK
husband and friend
without whose patience, encouragement,
and able assistance
this book would
be but a dream

FIRST EDITION

Designed by Sidney Feinberg

Library of Congress Cataloging in Publication Data

Sakoian, Frances.
  Predictive astrology.
  Includes index.
  1. Astrology. I. Acker, Louis S., joint author. II. Title.
BF1708.1.S246 1977   133.5   77-3768
ISBN 0-06-013744-4

77 78 79 80 81 10 9 8 7 6 5 4 3 2 1

Contents

PART II
INTERPRETING TRANSITS

Introduction

This book contains valuable material for both the astrological beginner and the professional astrologer. The contents have grown out of many years of study, research, and experience on the part of both authors. All the materials presented here are based on the fundamental principles and significance of the planets, signs, aspects, and houses.

This volume falls into two major parts. Part I presents the basic astrological principles that underlie transit analysis. It explores the basic question of what a horoscope is and goes on to expand upon some of the lesser known factors in astrological interpretation. The main emphasis, however, is on the factors inherent in the natal chart that are periodically stimulated by the transiting planets—a transit cannot bring any event into the life of the individual which the natal horoscope has not promised.

Part II is a handbook for transit interpretation. It delineates the actual planetary transits and their significance.

This volume is the third in a series that has analyzed three major areas of Astrology. It deals with predictive Astrology, which is, in many ways, the most challenging part of astrological study and practice. Taken together, these three volumes, *The Astrologer's Handbook, The Astrology of Human Relationships,* and *Predictive Astrology: Understanding Transits as the Key to the Future,* cover all of the basic materials necessary to the training of a well-rounded and competent astrologer.

Astrology is a vast field, and no set of writings, regardless of size or scope, could hope to cover all astrological subjects of interest or importance. However, these three volumes do provide the essential materials for gaining competence in Astrology, and they can be used as a springboard for further research and development. It is our hope that eventually these volumes will provide the basis for an organized course of university studies.

An understanding of the unfoldment of individual destiny is more important now than ever before, because of the fast-moving times. Foreknowledge of upcoming trends can be an invaluable aid to the use of latent opportunities and to the intelligent direction of life.

How to Use This Book

Whether you determine the transits on your own with the aid of an Ephemeris or use our computer service, Part II of this book provides you with a guide to interpretation. All the major transits are listed and delineated.

If you do not want to get involved with the mathematical procedures of determining transits, a computer service providing an accurate birth horoscope and a complete listing of all the planets transiting your birth horoscope is available. The dates of these transits will be listed in a readout. The transits themselves will be correlated to the pages in this book that explain their significance. If you wish to use this service, complete the order blank in the back of this book.

If you wish to determine transits on your own, first find the positions of the planets given in an Ephemeris* on a given date. Next, ascertain if angles of 0°, 60°, 90°, 120°, or 180° are formed by these planets to any of the natal planets in the birth horoscope. (Minor aspects are not treated in this volume.) The next step is to look up the period of time during which these angles are formed within an allowable orb of 1°. If the Sun or Moon is involved, an orb of 2° is allowed.

After you have determined the aspect or angle, look it up in Part II of this book under the section devoted to the transits of that particular planet. Transits of the houses are also treated under the individual planets.

* An Ephemeris is a book giving the positions of the planets for Greenwich noon or midnight for each day of a year.

PART I

ASTROLOGICAL PRINCIPLES

1 What Are Transits?

Transits are the key to the psychology of human events. They indicate the unfolding pattern of a person's relationship to his or her environment. Transits stimulate the individual's latent psychological tendencies, and this makes transit analysis, in our opinion, the major and most important technique of predictive Astrology.

Transits have important guidance value in making decisions and handling times of crises. They are useful in understanding the psychological reactions of others and in the timing of actions and attitudes that affect important personal relationships.

The basic psychological pattern with which an individual begins life is revealed by the birth horoscope, often referred to as the natal horoscope. The natal horoscope gives the positions of the planets at the exact time and place of an individual's birth. As the individual grows older, the planets change their positions in the Zodiac and thus move into new relationships to each other and to their positions in the birth horoscope. These movements of the planets in the heavens with respect to the planets in the natal horoscope are called transits.

Transits are, by definition, the aspects formed between the positions of the planets in the heavens at any given time in relationship to the positions of those planets in the natal or birth horoscope. Aspects, transiting or natal, are specific angular relationships that exist between planets in the heavens at any given time. The most important of these angular relationships are called major aspects. These include the conjunction (0°), the sextile (60°), the square (90°), the trine (120°), and the opposition (180°). A transiting planet can form any of these angles to the planets in the birth horoscope at various times. When one of these angles is formed, the planet is making a specific transiting aspect to a specific natal planet. Suppose that an individual has natal Saturn in 2°03' of Taurus. At the time of this writing (October 14, 1975), the planet Uranus is transiting the sign Scorpio at 2°03', forming an exact transiting opposition to that individual's natal Saturn. Transiting Saturn at 2°04' of Leo is forming a transiting square to its own natal position at the same time. On October 27, 1975, transiting Mars will be at 2°03' of Cancer, forming an exact transiting sextile to natal Saturn.

Also of significance in the delineation of transits is the natal house position or department of life through which the transiting planet is moving.

The transits that have the most noticeable and powerful effects are those that reinforce aspects of a similar nature in the birth horoscope. The power of a transiting planet is dependent on the power and significance of the same planet in the natal horoscope. All transits produce some effect, so the discerning astrological practitioner should know which influences are of major significance and which are secondary or minor.

The transits of the slower-moving planets—Jupiter, Saturn, Uranus, Neptune, and Pluto—indicate long-range trends which can be of major significance.

The faster-moving planets and lights—Sun, Moon, Mercury, Venus, and Mars—indicate day-to-day changes in mood and attitude. They act as timing factors in determining the significant events indicated by the slower-moving planets.

During stationary and retrograde periods, transits of the faster-moving planets can act in much the same manner as those of the slower-moving planets.

It is important to note the overall cyclic motion of transiting planets as they move through the hemispheres and quadrants of the horoscope. These cycles indicate periods of personal versus social and objective versus subjective activity.

When a planet transits the Eastern Hemisphere, the sector of the horoscope that includes the Tenth, Eleventh, Twelfth, First, Second, and Third houses of the horoscope, the activities governed by the planet making the transit of that hemisphere will be personal and self-determined.

When a planet transits the Western Hemisphere, the sector of the horoscope that includes the Fourth, Fifth, Sixth, Seventh, Eighth, and Ninth houses, the activities governed by that planet will be influenced by others in some manner.

When a planet transits the Southern Hemisphere, the sector of the horoscope that includes the Seventh, Eighth, Ninth, Tenth, Eleventh, and Twelfth houses, the affairs governed by that planet will be large-scale issues that go beyond immediate personal concerns.

When a planet transits the Northern Hemisphere, the sector of the horoscope that includes the First, Second, Third, Fourth, Fifth, and Sixth houses, the activities governed by the planet making the transit will be subjective and of immediate personal concern.

Retrograde and direct periods of the planets must also be taken into consideration. In many cases, the retrograde motion of a transiting planet will cause it to repeat the same aspect to a natal planet two or three times. This pattern of repeated contacts almost always occurs in the transits of the slower-moving planets to natal planets.

The first contact is made when the planet is direct in motion; usually, it remains direct in motion until it reaches a stationary position beyond the orb of aspect to the natal planet. When the transiting planet becomes retrograde in motion, it moves backwards (as seen from the Earth) and forms the same transiting aspect to the natal planet. Then, in most cases, it retrogrades out of orb of aspect to the natal planet, becomes stationary, and then resumes direct motion again, moving forward and re-establishing the same transiting aspect for the third and last time.

There are occasions when only two contacts are made to a natal planet: this occurs when the aspect is formed and completed during the stationary period of the transiting planet. These stationary transits are of particular significance because they are of longer duration than the same transit of the particular planet would normally be and they mark an important turning point in events and personal attitudes.

At the time of the first contact of a transiting planet to a natal planet, the event indicated by the transiting planet is often in a gestation period. The second, usually retrograde, contact indicates a time when the attitudes, circumstances, or events gather strength and momentum. When the third and last contact is made, the die is cast and events related to the nature of the transiting aspect are forthcoming—either during the contact period or shortly thereafter.

Because of the precession of the equinoxes, the event indicated by the transit may be delayed, especially in the case of middle-aged or older people. This is because the tropical Zodiac shifts its position at the rate of fifty seconds of arc each year, creating a discrepancy between the positions of planets in Ephemerides of different years. In the life of a seventy-year-old individual, for example, the natal planet must be moved forward a full degree to compensate for this factor. This is especially important in the horoscopes of nations, cities, or corporate entities whose life spans are longer than that of the average individual.

Transits of Uranus, Neptune, and Pluto often bring peak experiences and expand the consciousness when they make important contacts to natal planetary positions or the Angular houses—the First, Fourth, Seventh, and Tenth houses.

All transiting aspects are allowed a one degree orb unless the Sun or Moon is involved, in which case an orb of two degrees can be used.

Other predictive techniques, such as progressions, are significant. Progressions, however, are more subjective. They deal with inner inclinations and attitudes, and because these do not necessarily manifest themselves in objective experience, usually because of a lack of opportunity for realization in the external environment, they play a secondary role. *Only* when progressions and other similar techniques are *reinforced by transits* do they result in actual events and circumstances in the individual's life.

Solar and lunar returns are cyclical charts based on important transits and can be considered as adjuncts to the transit technique of prediction.

2 Steps in Transit Analysis

Transits are determined by comparing the positions of the planets in the heavens on a given date to those of the natal horoscope.

The transits that have the most dramatic and marked influences are those which reinforce natal aspects and involve the same planets. For example, a natal square between Mars and Mercury indicates a tendency toward irritability and mental vehemence; thus, whenever transiting Mars or Mercury makes a square, conjunction, or opposition to natal Mars or Mercury, the individual experiences unusual irritation and mental annoyance. This is because transiting Mercury or Mars is reinforcing a natal stress aspect involving these two planets.

The meaning of a transit depends upon the position of the transiting planet in relation to the natal horoscope, the aspects it makes to the natal planets, and its position in the natal houses.

To interpret a transit, first look to the sign and house position the planet is transiting. These indicate the practical affairs of life to be directly activated by the transiting planet. The natal houses ruled by the transiting planet should also be considered, as well as the house or houses of which the planet is the exalted ruler.

Next, consider the aspects made by the transiting planet to any natal planet during its transit through a house. The affairs ruled by the natal planet receiving the transit will influence the affairs of that house.

The type of aspect being made, the signs and houses ruled by the transiting planet, and the natal planet that is being aspected, along with the signs and houses the natal planet rules, must be considered in determining the effects of a transit.

The exalted rulerships of the transiting and natal planets and the houses holding the signs of these exalted rulerships must also be considered. Exalted rulerships indicate where the power behind an event or action signified by the transit originates or is generated. For example, if Venus is transiting the natal Fifth House, the individual will experience pleasurable social, romantic, and esthetic activities. To determine the source of these romantic or social stimulations, look to the houses where Taurus, Libra, and Pisces are found in the natal horoscope. (Venus rules Taurus and Libra and is exalted in Pisces.)

Furthermore, if Venus is making a trine aspect to natal Mars while transiting the natal Fifth House, consider the sign and house position of natal Mars and the houses where Aries, Scorpio, and Capricorn are placed, for Mars rules Aries and Scorpio and is exalted in Capricorn. The duads and decanates involved in the transit must also be considered. (See *The Zodiac Within Each Sign* by the authors.)

Thus, the following factors all require consideration in this single example of transiting Venus in the natal Fifth House trine natal Mars.

1. Venus—the transiting planet.
2. The house being transited and the sign on the Fifth House cusp.
3. The Seventh House, natural house ruled by Venus.
4. The Second House, natural house ruled by Venus.
5. The Twelfth House, the natural house of Venus's exaltation.
7. Libra, sign ruled by Venus.
8. Pisces, the sign where Venus is exalted.
9. The house where Taurus is placed.
10. The house where Libra is placed.
11. The house where Pisces is placed.
12. The Sun, natural ruler of the Fifth House.
13. Leo, sign ruled by the Sun.
14. The house where Leo is placed.
15. Mars—the natal planet being aspected by transiting Venus.
16. Mars's house position.
17. Mars's sign position.
18. Aries, sign ruled by Mars.
19. Scorpio, sign ruled by Mars.
20. Capricorn, the sign where Mars is exalted.
21. The First House, natural house ruled by Mars.
22. The Eighth House, natural house ruled by Mars.

23. The nature of the trine aspect—Fifth and Ninth House connotation.
24. Natal aspects of Venus.
25. Natal aspects of Mars.
26. Planets natally disposited by Venus.
27. Planets natally disposited by Mars.
28. The sign positions of these disposited planets.
29. The house positions of these disposited planets.
30. The decanate and duad placements of transiting Venus and natal Mars.

The synthesis of this information comprises the skill and art of Astrology. These factors could be overwhelmingly confusing unless their relative importance is considered.

The most important consideration is that Venus is transiting the natal Fifth House and is making a trine to natal Mars.

Next in importance is the nature of the trine aspect, which has a harmonious, creative, expansive quality derived from Leo and the Sun and from Sagittarius, Jupiter, and Neptune in the natural Zodiac. The trine is based on the signs and houses that correspond to the trine aspect in the natural Zodiac, beginning with Aries.

The next consideration is the sign that Venus is in while transiting the natal Fifth House and trining natal Mars. This may or may not be the same sign as that on the cusp of the natal Fifth House.

Next, consider the natal sign and house position of Mars, the planet receiving the trine from transiting Venus.

Then, determine if there is a natal aspect between Mars and Venus that would indicate a similar potential for actualization by this transit.

These are the primary factors to be considered, the factors that will have the most obvious impact on the individual.

The other points listed provide background data for understanding the relationships of this influence as it is integrated into the overall life of the individual. This background information provides an understanding of the psychology of the individual with respect to romantic, social, and pleasurable activities, as represented by the planet making the transit. This background information also provides an understanding of the fundamental nature of Venus, Mars, and the Fifth House as it functions on a universal scale, as well as how it is integrated into the psychology of the individual's character.

Now, let us analyze these data.

First, Venus represents the principle of attraction, beauty, harmony, and grace. Through Venus's rulership of Libra and the Seventh House in the natural Zodiac, she is also concerned with relationships and harmonious cooperation. In addition, through Venus's rulership of Taurus and the Second House in the natural Zodiac, the individual attracts possessions and people who can be instrumental in providing material security, beauty, and comfort. Venus's exaltation in Pisces, the position of Pisces in the natal chart, and the Twelfth House all show the understanding that may be gained through the experiences that make such refinements and cooperation possible.

The houses where Libra, Taurus, and Pisces are placed in the natal horoscope and the activities assigned to these houses show the specific areas where the individual's ease of cooperation, refinement, and ability to attract the things represented by Venus are expressed. These houses provide both the content and the means of contacting the romantic, social, and pleasurable activities indicated by Venus's transit of the natal Fifth House.

Second, the Fifth House is the natural house of Leo and the Sun and has a harmonic relationship with Leo and the house where Leo is placed, as well as with any planets placed in Leo. It is well to remember when considering this relationship that the Fifth House and the house carrying the sign Leo are places of power and creative self-expression. The trine aspect itself is related to Leo and the Fifth House in the natural Zodiac, and, thus, there would be a reinforcement of the Fifth House characteristics in this transiting trine situation.

Third, in this particular situation, another factor is added—Mars, as ruler of Aries, and the First House's natural trine-aspect affinity for Leo and the Fifth House.

Since Mars is the planet receiving the transiting trine from Venus in the natal Fifth House, the nature of the Fifth House and the trine aspect is amplified. This is because the transiting planet is the activating principle; the natal planet receiving the transit experiences the effects of this action.

In the case of transiting Venus through the natal Fifth House and trine natal Mars, Venus, as the activating planet, instigates social overtures to the individual through the signs ruled by Mars in the horoscope. Because Mars is basically an action-oriented planet, the individual responds instinctively to these overtures.

Let us examine the background information on Mars. Mars rules the principle of energy expended in action and motivated by desire. Mars, as ruler of Aries and the First House in the natural Zodiac, deals with competitive, self-initiated action and self-expression based on the need to survive as an individual.

The house where Aries is found in the natal horoscope shows the affairs that are of immediate concern to personal survival. These are the affairs in which the individual must personally initiate action and creative self-expression without waiting for encouragement from others.

Mars, as ruler of Scorpio and the natural Eighth House, is concerned with the use of collective resources, represented by the Eighth House, and the destruction and elimination of that which no longer serves a useful purpose, all in preparation for new creative efforts. Mars has much to do with the sex drive through its rulership of Scorpio. This is of particular interest in the case of this transiting aspect because Venus is also related to sex. Venus corresponds to the receptive, feminine sex principle. This combination, when related to the Fifth House of romance, strongly suggests sexual attraction. The invitation on the part of transiting Venus to start a relationship will meet with a quick, aggressive response on the part of Mars. Transits involving these particular planets are usually objectively realized as romantic attractions.

Because Mars is exalted in Capricorn, such a relationship could be sought as a means of achieving status, professional opportunities, or security. This is also indicated by Mars's accidental exaltation in the Tenth House of the natural Zodiac.

Fourth, planets disposited by Mars and Venus, and the houses and signs in which they fall, will show the affairs of life that are related to the activities associated with this transit of Venus.

Further insights will be provided through study of the decanate and duad positions of both transiting Venus and natal Mars.

All of this information is pertinent to an accurate description of the significance and probable result of this transit. Similar methods should be used in studying all transits, as well as in the interpretation of the natal horoscope.

The delineation of this sample transit points out why a comprehensive understanding of the basics of Astrology is necessary to achieve accurate and worthwhile results. The use of these basic techniques should become so thoroughly ingrained in the practitioner as to become almost instinctive.

3 What Is a Horoscope?

Because space is filled with many types of subtle energies, and because these energies influence life on Earth, it is reasonable to suppose that heavenly bodies, such as the Sun, Moon, and planets, absorb and redistribute such energy. It is also reasonable to suppose that distant stars can emanate energy and that this energy may influence life on our small planet. The energies emanated by these heavenly bodies are modified, and in some cases intensified, according to the angular relationships of their sources.

The scientific explanation for this is provided by wave mechanics in physics and paraphysics. Some of these subjects are in the forefront in the evolution of scientific thought, and they are beyond the scope of this presentation.

Experience has shown the horoscope to be an accurate and detailed guide to understanding human character and potential.

A horoscope is a diagram of the heavens as they appeared at the time and place of an individual's birth. It shows the positions of the Sun, Moon, and planets with respect to Earth's surface or the horizon, to the Zodiac, and to each other.

The Zodiac is the belt in which the positions of the planets are measured. It is a division of the ecliptic (the plane of Earth's orbit around the Sun) into twelve segments of equal arc of 30°, called signs. The Zodiac begins with the vernal equinox. The vernal and autumnal equinoxes constitute a line where the plane of the ecliptic and the plane of the Earth's equator intersect.

The Cardinal Ingresses

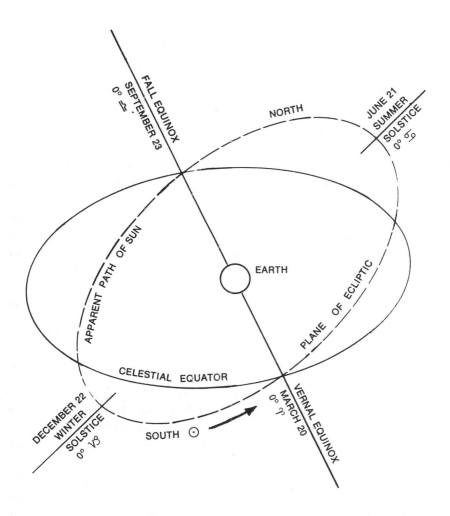

A cardinal ingress is the entry of the Sun into one of the signs of the cardinal grouping or quadruplicities. The signs are Aries, Cancer, Libra, Capricorn, indicating the beginning of the four seasons which are demarcated by the vernal equinox, the summer solstice, the fall equinox, and the winter solstice.

4 The Houses

The houses are divisions of the ecliptic or circle of the Zodiac into twelve segments with respect to the horizons and the time and place for which a horoscope is cast. These twelve divisions are not necessarily of equal arc, unlike the signs of the Zodiac, which consist of 30° each.

The most important houses are the Angular houses, beginning with the Ascendant or First House cusp, the Nadir or Fourth House cusp, the Descendant or Seventh House cusp, and the Midheaven or Tenth House cusp.

The Ascendant is the point where the ecliptic crosses the Eastern horizon at the time and place for which the chart is cast.

The Nadir is the place where the ecliptic crosses the meridian below Earth (the meridian is a great circle around Earth passing from north to south through the zenith and the opposite point to the zenith).

The Descendant or Seventh House cusp is the point at which the ecliptic or plane of Earth's orbit around the Sun crosses the western horizon at the time and place for which the horoscope is cast.

The Midheaven (M.C.) or Tenth House cusp is the point at which the ecliptic crosses the meridian overhead.

The Second and Third, Fifth and Sixth, Eighth and Ninth, and Eleventh and Twelfth House cusps are divisions of the spaces between the Angular house cusps. These spaces are called quadrants. There are three divisions for each quadrant. This makes twelve houses in all.

There are several systems for determining these subdivisions of the quadrants. The most commonly used system in Western Astrology is the Placidean, upon which this work is based. For a more detailed explanation of this subject, see page 20.

The Second, Fifth, Eighth, and Eleventh houses are called Succedent houses, and the Third, Sixth, Ninth, and Twelfth houses are called Cadent houses.

The Angular houses, like the Cardinal signs of the Zodiac, indicate situations in life which demand immediate attention. The Succedent houses, like the Fixed signs of the Zodiac, indicate future goals. The Cadent houses, like the Mutable signs of the Zodiac, indicate an adaptability based on past experience.

The following sets of phrases provide a shortcut to understanding what each of the houses represents:

First House—Basic quality of consciousness—self-image—self-awareness—personal action—personal self-expression—beginning of new cycles of experience—personal will power —physical appearance—vitality and resistance to disease—personal mannerisms—early environment.

Second House—Attitude toward money—personal wealth and property —need for material security—business activities—dealings with banks and other financial institutions—personal values—earning capacity—how one meets financial obligations—personal credit or lack of it—desire for material status—resources necessary for self-expression— financial expenditures—stewardship of material resources.

Third House—Thinking capacity—personal ideas and communications —planning of self-expression—ideas for handling of personal resources—sensory perceptions—study—communication of all kinds—short trips—relationships to siblings, neighbors, and others in the immediate environment— choice of mental focus of attention—reasoning, logical mind—daily exchange of ideas—practical decision-making—mental alertness—expression of intellectual curiosity—thinking processes.

Fourth House—The home environment—conditioned emotional habit patterns—ingrained emotional attitudes which determine our responses—family affairs—relationship with the mother—matters related to food and diet (along with the Sixth House)—activity in the home—concerns related to the land or the earth itself (ecology, geology, farming, building, and real estate)—emotional attitudes instilled in childhood—last half of life—final resting place.

Fifth House—Creative self-expression—social activity—romantic activity—sexual involvements—pursuit of pleasure—dealings with children and their education—financial speculation —stock market activity—gambling—entertainment activity involving the performing arts—self-dramatization— desire to be noticed and appreciated—sports—social popularity or lack of it—pregnancy and childbirth—primary education—primary schools.

Sixth House—Work or services rendered—employees—detailed responsibilities—involuntary service—health or lack of it—dietary habits and personal hygiene—work methodologies —mental awareness of practical problems and how to solve them—dealings with doctors or medical personnel —conditions in work environment—communication and conditions in the working environment—occupational hazards—clothing.

Seventh House—Marriage, business partnerships, and other close personal relationships—responsibility toward others—law suits—desire or need to cooperate with others—reaction of others to personal action—attitudes and actions of others—social awareness and interest in psychology— personal sense of justice and fair play—need for cooperation—social activity connected with business or public relations—condition of marriage relationships—general awareness of the public.

Eighth House—Death and affairs of the dead—other people's values— joint finances and corporate business activity—financial transactions—insurance, joint monies, inheritance, taxes, alimony, and goods of the dead—end of old conditions in preparation for the new—transformation of personal motivation, for better or worse—recycling of old, discarded or outworn items and resources—handling of waste products—sexual energies—need for spiritual regeneration and interest in reincarnation—life after death —parapsychology and occult subjects—clairvoyance and other paranormal abilities.

Ninth House— Higher education—personal cultural, religious, philosophic, and educational ideals and principles—legal and moral codes—long journeys and contact with foreigners and foreign cultures—religious attitudes—all codification of cultural thought and tradition—prophetic awareness of future cultural trends and conditions—publishing—personal conscience based on philosophic and religious values and cultural conditioning.

Tenth House— Profession—public status and reputation—political activities and ambitions—desire for power and status—fall from position, if power is misused—administrative responsibilities and duties—relationships with employers, bosses, authority figures, and governmental authorities—enforcement of laws and cultural standards—established authoritative figures in the individual's life—father—personal authority, status, and reputation.

Eleventh House— Friends, groups, and organizations—group creativity—personal goals and objectives—intuitive contact with the Universal Mind—occult, scientific, and humanitarian interests—sense of universal brotherhood—revolt against abuse of power—detached mental outlook—awareness of universal laws and principles.

Twelfth House— The unconscious mind—escapist tendencies—private affairs of life—meditation, mysticism, and intuitive awareness—imagination—dream state—quiet appreciation of beauty—self-deception—unconscious distortions—neurotic tendencies—self-undoing—hidden support—subconscious memory—memory of previous lives—secret enemies—places of confinement or seclusion.

As planets transit these houses, the affairs ruled by them will be stimulated or activated, for better or worse, depending upon the natal planets placed in these houses and aspects made to them. The transits of the individual planets through the houses are delineated in detail in Part II.

Triplicities, Quadruplicities, and Polarities

The Triplicities or Elements denote basic types of temperament.

Fire signs—Aries, Leo, and Sagittarius—indicate leadership potential, enthusiasm, creativity, and energy.

Earth signs—Taurus, Virgo, and Capricorn—indicate practicality, con-

Signs of the Zodiac: Their Astrological Nature and Rulers

| SIGN | DATE (Approx.) | RULERS | | NATURE | | |
		RULER / CO-RULERS*	EXALTED RULER	QUADRU-PLICITY	TRIPLICITY	MASCULINE/ FEMININE
ARIES ♈	March 21- April 20	MARS/ PLUTO ♂♇	SUN ☉	Cardinal	Fire	Masculine
TAURUS ♉	April 21- May 20	VENUS ♀	MOON ☽	Fixed	Earth	Feminine
GEMINI ♊	May 21- June 21	MERCURY ☿		Mutable	Air	Masculine
CANCER ♋	June 22- July 22	MOON ☽	JUPITER/ NEPTUNE ♃ ♆	Cardinal	Water	Feminine
LEO ♌	July 23- Aug. 23	SUN ☉	PLUTO ♇	Fixed	Fire	Masculine
VIRGO ♍	Aug. 24- Sept. 22	MERCURY ☿		Mutable	Earth	Feminine
LIBRA ♎	Sept. 23- Oct. 23	VENUS ♀	SATURN ♄	Cardinal	Air	Masculine
SCORPIO ♏	Oct. 24- Nov. 22	PLUTO/ MARS ♇♂	URANUS ♅	Fixed	Water	Feminine
SAGITTARIUS ♐	Nov. 23- Dec. 21	JUPITER/ NEPTUNE ♃ ♆		Mutable	Fire	Masculine
CAPRICORN ♑	Dec. 22- Jan. 19	SATURN/ URANUS ♄ ♅	MARS ♂	Cardinal	Earth	Feminine
AQUARIUS ♒	Jan. 20- Feb. 18	URANUS/ SATURN ♅ ♄	MERCURY ☿	Fixed	Air	Masculine
PISCES ♓	Feb. 19- Mar. 20	NEPTUNE/ JUPITER ♆ ♃	VENUS ♀	Mutable	Water	Feminine

*The predominent sign appears first.

cern with concrete results, and, usually, an occupation with financial, business, and professional affairs.

Air signs—Gemini, Libra, and Aquarius—indicate intellectuality, mental agility, and communicativeness. They are primarily concerned with the communication of ideas and with human relations.

Water signs—Cancer, Scorpio, and Pisces—indicate emotion and are primarily concerned with feeling and intuitive awareness.

It is important to note the predominant distribution of planets in these Elements. If four or more planets are found in one Element, the characteristics of that Element will predominate in the character of the individual. If the planets are more or less evenly distributed among the Elements, the characteristics ascribed to these Elements will be evenly balanced in the personality. If there are no planets in one or more Elements, the characteristics of those Elements will be lacking and compensation must be made in some manner.

An excessive predominance of planets in one Element or a total lack of planets in an Element can cause an imbalance in the character. The presence of the Ascendant or Midheaven in an Element that has no planets can offset the imbalance to some extent.

The Quadruplicities indicate modes of human activity and behavior.

The Cardinal Quadruplicity is made up of Aries, Cancer, Libra, and Capricorn. This influence inclines one toward constant activity, with concern for immediate present circumstances.

The Fixed Quadruplicity is made up of Taurus, Leo, Scorpio, and Aquarius. This influence inclines the individual toward future goals and persistent, unwavering efforts to achieve them.

The Mutable Quadruplicity consists of Gemini, Virgo, Sagittarius, and Pisces. This influence deals with memory and utilization of past experience. It is adaptable and inclines one to work around obstacles rather than confronting them directly.

A predominance of five or more planets in a particular Quadruplicity will emphasize the qualities of that Quadruplicity in the individual's personality.

The masculine-positive and feminine-negative Polarities concern themselves with the basic active versus passive, radiant versus reflective, generative versus receptive nature of human behavior.

Individuals born under the masculine-positive signs—Aries, Gemini, Leo, Libra, Sagittarius, and Aquarius—take the initiative in the affairs of life which these signs influence, without waiting for an outside stimulus to motivate them into action.

Individuals born under the feminine-negative signs—Taurus, Cancer, Virgo, Scorpio, Capricorn, and Pisces—take action only when stimulated to do so by an outside influence. Often, they attract the things which they need, rather than actively seeking them.

If a majority of the planets are in masculine-positive signs, the individual initiates action without awaiting outside motivation. Therefore, he or she manifests leadership abilities and tends to be a self-starter in the departments of life ruled by the houses where these planets are found.

If a majority of the planets are in feminine-negative signs, the individual acts and makes decisions in response to outside stimuli. This does not mean that these individuals are not just as strong and forceful as those whose planets fall into masculine-positive signs, but merely that they wait to act until they are confronted with circumstances that require it. Often, they attract that with which they must deal, instead of actively seeking it.

Domification

A great deal of confusion in Astrology has been generated by the matter of domification or division of the house cusps. In most systems, the Angular house cusps remain the same. However, the Succedent and Cadent house cusps change from system to system. In addition, all but one of the systems in current use break down completely at extreme northern or southern latitudes.

The only system which does not break down at such extremes of latitude is an equal house system that uses the Midheaven as a reference point. The Midheaven and Nadir are the only house cusps that do not change along with latitude changes. This is because the Midheaven is defined as the point at which the meridian (a great circle passing from north to south through the zenith) crosses the ecliptic or the plane of Earth's orbit around the Sun.

When the Midheaven–Nadir axis and degree are the point of reference in an equal house system, the same degree of each succeeding sign is placed on the succeeding house cusp, and a system of domification is produced which is simple to use and dependable at all latitudes. In simple terms, the degree of the Midheaven will be the degree of all twelve house cusps even though each house will have a different sign on each cusp.

The Ascendant is the degree of the Zodiac where the ecliptic crosses the eastern horizon. The Descendant is the degree of the Zodiac where Earth's orbit around the Sun crosses the western horizon at the time and place for which the chart is cast. These points do vary with latitude changes, and they should be treated as sensitive points in the horoscope, much as a planet or node would be. However, the Ascendant and Descendant need not be treated as house cusps, for their significance is not diminished by dissociation from the house cusps and domification. The Ascendant would then represent a point of selfhood; and the Descendant, a point of relationship with others. Any interpretation should be based on sign positions and aspects only.

Such a system of equal houses based on the Midheaven may be the key to resolving the difficult area of domification.

Astrology as it was practiced in ancient civilizations where astrological tradition had its origin dealt with individuals born and events occurring at latitudes that were equatorial, or nearly so. Hence, no distinction between the Ascendant and Descendant and the First and Seventh house cusps was ever made.

This equal house system of domification certainly warrants more research and investigation on the part of serious astrologers. One approach would be to note house changes of planets when comparing this system of domification with the traditional Placidean system, and then, by examining what is known about the individual, determine the credibility of each. Such differences should be particularly noted with respect to Succedent and Cadent houses, though changes of house positions of the First and Seventh houses should also be evaluated.

We use the Placidean system and find it adequate for most purposes. However, we have obtained very good results with the system of equal houses based on the degree of Midheaven, especially in extreme northern or southern latitudes. This equal house system of domification is impressively simple and logical, whereas other systems, with the possible exception of an equal house system based on the Ascendant, suffer from inherent flaws and untidy aspects which are never entirely resolved, especially in extreme northern or southern latitudes.

Signs on the House Cusps

The nature of the sign on a house cusp is an important factor in horoscope delineation. The Triplicity, Quadruplicity, and masculine/feminine nature of the sign in question must be considered.

Each house represents a specific department of the practical affairs of life, and the individual's approach to handling these affairs is indicated by the type of sign found on the cusp of the house, as well as by the planets in the house, the planet ruling the house, and aspects made to this ruler by other planets.

If a Fire sign—Aries, Leo, or Sagittarius—is found on a cusp of a house, the affairs ruled by that house are energetically and enthusiastically handled by the individual. They bring out his leadership ability.

If an Earth sign—Taurus, Virgo, or Capricorn—is found on a house cusp, the affairs ruled by that house are handled by the individual in a practical way. Such affairs are often related to money-making activities or professional endeavors. Material goods are of consequence to these affairs in some way.

If an Air sign—Gemini, Libra, or Aquarius—is found on a house cusp, the affairs of that house are handled by the individual in an intellectual manner. The ideas and mental deliberations concerning these matters are of primary concern. The person communicates about them and studies them in an intellectual framework, and the attitude toward them is likely to be detached or dispassionate.

If a Water sign—Cancer, Scorpio, or Pisces—is found on a house cusp, the affairs of that house are handled emotionally. The individual's decisions on matters ruled by that house are based on feelings, emotional considerations, and intuitive perceptions.

If a Cardinal sign—Aries, Cancer, Libra, or Capricorn—is found on the cusp of a house, the individual is decisive, active, and sometimes impulsive in handling the affairs ruled by that house. The present circumstances of these affairs, rather than their past or future ramifications, are of primary concern. The person feels a need for action in these affairs and is likely to be opportunistic in dealing with them.

If a Fixed sign—Taurus, Leo, Scorpio, or Aquarius—is found on the cusp of a house, the individual is determined and goal-oriented in regard to the affairs ruled by that house. The future development of these affairs, rather than their past or present ramifications, is of primary concern.

If a Mutable sign—Gemini, Virgo, Sagittarius, or Pisces—is found on the cusp of a house, the individual's approach to the affairs of that house is mental and adaptable. Past experience is used as a guide in handling them and the person is not particularly concerned with their present and future ramifications. However, care must be exercised not to become trapped in memories of past misfortunes regarding these matters, as this may interfere with present and future success.

If Cardinal signs are found on the Angular house cusps, the individual's approach to life is basically active, initiatory, and opportunistic.

If Fixed signs are found on the Angular house cusps, the individual's approach to life is purposeful, determined, and goal-oriented.

If Mutable signs are found on the Angular house cusps, the individual's approach to life is basically adaptable, mental, and introspective.

When a masculine-positive sign—Aries, Gemini, Leo, Libra, Sagittarius, or Aquarius—is found on a house cusp, the individual will initiate action in the affairs ruled by that house. If the individual is unhappy with the circumstances ruled by a house with a masculine-positive sign on the cusp, he or she will, on their own initiative, take action to change or improve those conditions.

Conversely, when a feminine-negative sign—Taurus, Cancer, Virgo, Scorpio, Capricorn, or Pisces—is found on a house cusp, the individual awaits opportunities to make a move that will change conditions ruled by that house. He or she is more likely to accept the status quo regarding those matters. However, he can be just as forceful as those with a masculine-positive sign on the cusp when dissatisfied enough with the conditions of affairs ruled by that house. Because feminine-negative signs are receptive, the individual is able to attract the people and circumstances necessary to further his desired ends in such matters.

It is possible to have both a positive and a negative sign in a house. This condition occurs when the house contains an intercepted sign. The sign on the house cusp is always the predominant influence in determining the approach to handling the affairs of that house. However, both qualities can manifest alternately.

5 The Sun, Moon, and Ascendant —Basic Principles

In most social astrological conversations, the first question asked is: "What is your Sun, Moon, and Ascendant?" The questioner often seems to assume that these factors are almost interchangeable. In reality, they are three important, distinct, and noninterchangeable influences. They *are*, however, interrelated. Let's examine them, one at a time, and ascertain the true implications of each.

The Ascendant represents the most spiritual aspect of the individual; it deals with the individual's self-awareness or awareness of awareness. Any student of psychology can tell you of the importance of self-image in determining character. A person can only be what he or she is honestly capable of conceiving himself to be, and, until the self-image is changed, the person cannot change. Before there can be personal possessions, thoughts, a real home, creative self-expression, work, partnerships, joint resources, a philosophy, a profession, friends, or an awareness of past memories, there must be selfhood or self-awareness. This awareness of self and determination to survive is directly related to the Ascendant.

The Ascendant also determines how a person views reality. It indicates the fundamental capacity for awareness from which self-expression springs. The Ascendant, in traditional Astrology, is said to influence physical appearance, and this is true. More important, however, is its influence on the basic consciousness, which *is* the individual.

Some older astrological texts state that the Sun in the horoscope represents the real spiritual essence and the Ascendant the outer personality. However, in our experience, the view set forth in the writings of Alice Bailey seems closer to the truth. Since a new degree of the Zodiac rises over the eastern horizon every four minutes, as compared to the approximate one degree per day of the Sun's motion, it is apparent that the Ascendant is associated with the *now*ness of each new moment. Therefore, it is associated with awareness or consciousness itself. Assuredly, the Sun and the Ascendant are closely related. The Sun, which is exalted in Aries and accidentally exalted in the First House, gains its power of creative self-expression from the pure beingness or "I am"-ness inherent in Aries and the First House.

The Sun in the horoscope is the channel for the expression of active, creative energy. Through this creative activity and the expression of the will, an individual realizes his or her creative potential.

The Sun rules the dynamic expression of energy in the process of creation, and the Sun sign determines the manner in which this energy is expressed. Aspects to the Sun indicate the channels for its expression and the degree of harmony or disharmony which accompanies it.

The house position of the Sun, the Fifth House, and the house(s) on whose cusps(s) Leo is found indicate the practical affairs of life that are directly influenced by creative activity.

If the Sun is weak in the horoscope, the individual may lack the dynamic drive and will power for creative self-expression. If the Sun is heavily aspected, elevated, or Angular by placement, the necessary drive and will power to bring about dynamic activity will be in evidence. If many squares and oppositions, inconjuncts or exact minor aspect afflictions are evident, conflict, discord, obstacles, and ego confrontations may accompany such efforts. Generally speaking, it is better to have afflictions to the Sun than to have a weak, unaspected Sun, because, even if mistakes are made, something is accomplished and the individual grows by experience.

People usually do not begin to fully realize their Sun's potential until they reach astrological adulthood, or twenty-nine years of age. Until that time, their typical behavior is often characterized by their Moon sign, its house position, and its aspects.

The Moon's position in the horoscope represents those aspects of human behavior that depend upon automatic responses, whether they be the familiar motions of driving a car or irrational stimulus-response based on past experiences which the individual cannot consciously remember. The Moon represents inertia of character or the tendency to go on behaving and living in the manner to which one is accustomed and familiar. A consciously directed effort of the will is required to change these automatic response patterns. Often, these patterns are inappropriate, and even dangerous, and serve only to impede the individual's success and progress. This is especially true if the Moon is afflicted. Then, such response patterns are apt to be irrational and aberrant. Usually, they are based on past experiences that have been restimulated without the individual's conscious, rational awareness. Hence, the Moon in the horoscope represents something to be outgrown and overcome through a conscious awareness of all the reasons for choosing a particular path of self-expression.

The Moon has a great deal to do with everyday affairs, family and domestic matters, food and eating habits. When one stops to consider the extent to which most people's eating habits are dictated by irrational emotional needs, rather than by what is good for health and vitality, it becomes apparent that irrational responses to past emotional conditioning can dictate dietary habits that are actually detrimental to health and well-being.

The sign position of the Moon indicates the manner in which the individual's habitual responses are expressed. The house position of the Moon shows what department or affairs of life will be directly influenced by such responses (as will the Fourth House and the house(s) on whose cusp(s) Cancer is found in the horoscope).

6 The Planets
—Basic Principles

Mercury—Key to the Mind

Next to the Sun, Moon, and Ascendant, Mercury is the most important factor in the horoscope. This is because Mercury's position by sign, house, and aspects to the other planets indicates the individual's degree of intelligence, mental attitudes, and ability to think and communicate.

The closest major aspect to Mercury indicates the predominant mental interest and intellectual focus of the individual. This is because Mercury itself is a neutral planet.

If Mercury is found in a Fire sign—Aries, Leo, or Sagittarius—the individual is capable of mental leadership and tackles intellectual problems with energy and self-confidence. However, egocentric mental attitudes can be a danger.

If Mercury is found in an Earth sign—Taurus, Virgo, or Capricorn—the individual is mentally concerned with matters of practical value and application. He or she evaluates ideas on the basis of their practical usefulness. The danger here is an excessively materialistic outlook.

If Mercury is found in an Air sign—Gemini, Libra, or Aquarius—the individual is interested in ideas and intellectual pursuits for their own sake. These people's communications are often concerned with social relationships, psychology, and group endeavors. There is the danger of an overly theoretical, impractical mental outlook. The individual must remember that the best idea is of no use unless it is put into action.

If Mercury is found in a Water sign—Cancer, Scorpio, or Pisces—the individual's thinking is colored by emotional factors. Decisions are often based on intuitive feelings. These individuals are capable of communicating their emotions and are receptive to the feelings of others. However, emotional biases, distorted reason, or inaccurate perception of reality must be guarded against when Mercury is found in this Element.

If Mercury is found in a Cardinal sign—Aries, Cancer, Libra, or Capricorn—the individual is decisive in following a course of action and in drawing conclusions. If this decisiveness is carried too far, however, it can result in impulsive decisions.

If Mercury is found in a Fixed sign—Taurus, Leo, Scorpio, or Aquarius—the individual is slow and deliberate in making decisions and usually unwilling to change them once they are made. If this tendency is carried too far, irrational, stubborn, fixed attitudes can result.

If Mercury is found in a Mutable sign—Gemini, Virgo, Sagittarius, or Pisces—the individual is adaptable and flexible in making decisions and draws upon past experience for guidance. If the tendency to rely on past experiences is carried too far, however, the individual may make decisions that are irrational in terms of his present circumstances.

If Mercury is found in a masculine-positive sign—Aries, Gemini, Leo, Libra, Sagittarius, or Aquarius—the mind is curious and aggressive.

If Mercury is found in a feminine-negative sign—Taurus, Cancer, Virgo, Scorpio, Capricorn, or Pisces—the mind deals with that which confronts it rather than reaching out aggressively.

Although so-called adverse aspects made to Mercury can cause mental conflicts and problems, they do tend to activate the intelligence. Therefore, it is better to have an afflicted Mercury than a Mercury without any aspects.

For transits made to or by Mercury, see Chapter 21.

Venus—Key to Social Relationships

Venus is the key to the individual's financial, romantic, artistic, musical, and social activities. The sign and house placements of Venus and aspects made to Venus by other planets indicate how the individual considers and handles these affairs.

Venus, as a feminine planet, rules the principle of attraction. It rules the desire for things of refinement and beauty, as well as the things themselves. In addition, the Venus individual has the ability to attract because of beauty and desirability. This is a very definite and real power. It can be more effective than the action of Mars, which causes aggressive personal desires.

As ruler of Taurus and the natural Second House, Venus attracts money and possessions. As ruler of Libra and the natural Seventh House, it attracts people and partners. In both cases, the Venusian principle of attraction is at work.

Venus rules the principle of love, especially in terms of romantic relationships. Consequently, its sign and house position indicate how the individual attracts a romantic partner; important aspects made to Venus and the sign and house positions making these aspects are additional clues.

In a woman's horoscope, Venus indicates what the woman is able to give a man. In a man's horoscope, Venus indicates the type of woman the man would like to attract, but not necessarily the type of woman he will marry. The Seventh House and its ruler must be taken into consideration in determining the propriety and strength of a marriage.

The strength of Venus in the horoscope indicates the extent of an individual's artistic, creative ability and capacity to create beauty and refinement. The sign, house placement, and aspects of Venus in the horoscope are more specific indicators of the individual's approach to art and beauty.

Venus also affects the ability to understand and empathize with others emotionally. This is due to the exaltation of Venus in Pisces. A weak or afflicted Venus indicates a lack of social refinement, diplomacy, and consideration in relating to others.

If Venus is found in a Fire sign—Aries, Leo, or Sagittarius—the individual actively seeks romantic and social fulfillment. These people show a sense of color and drama in artistic expressions and initiative and leadership in money-making endeavors.

If Venus is found in an Earth sign—Taurus, Virgo, or Capricorn—the individual combines a practicality and sensuousness in artistic, financial, social, and romantic affairs. These people demand quality and durability in their personal possessions and artistic creations. They use lovely personal possessions as a means of achieving status and comfort. They often have business ability in matters related to art, music, or social activity.

If Venus is found in an Air sign—Gemini, Libra, or Aquarius—the individual has a strong sense of social interrelations and a great interest in the feelings and psychology of others. These individuals seek to establish intellectually stimulating friendships and romantic partnerships, and they usually possess social charm and savoir-faire.

If Venus is found in a Water sign—Cancer, Scorpio, or Pisces—the individual takes an emotional approach to art, music, social activity, and, especially, romantic partnerships. These people are able to empathize, sympathize, and exhibit depth of feeling, but they can become emotionally distraught over romantic disappointments and difficulties as a result. Their feelings can be easily hurt by social mistreatment or neglect.

If Venus is found in a Cardinal sign—Aries, Cancer, Libra, or Capricorn—the individual takes an active approach to money-making, social activity, and romantic relationships. The present circumstances of these individuals' social and romantic affairs are their primary concern.

If Venus is found in a Fixed sign—Taurus, Leo, Scorpio, or Aquarius—the individual adopts a determined attitude toward making money. These individuals are thorough in handling artistic and social endeavors and will see them through to completion. Their affections are steadfast once a friendship or romantic relationship has been established. However, if the relationship is seriously betrayed, they will not reinstate it on the same basis.

If Venus is found in a Mutable sign—Gemini, Virgo, Sagittarius, or Pisces—the individual is adaptable in handling social, artistic, and romantic affairs. These individuals draw upon past experiences to adjust to all types of social circumstances. If the Mutable tendencies are carried too far, however, there can be inconstancy and fickleness in romantic relationships, especially with Gemini and Sagittarius, least so with Pisces. In artistic endeavors, they possess a high degree of ingenuity and a keen imagination. Venus in a Mutable sign also indicates diverse ways of making money.

If Venus is found in a masculine-positive sign—Aries, Gemini, Leo, Libra, Sagittarius, or Aquarius—the individual takes the initiative in new friendships, social activities, and romantic relationships.

If Venus is found in a feminine-negative sign—Taurus, Cancer, Virgo, Scorpio, Capricorn, or Pisces—the individual is more passive and waits for romantic and social opportunities to arise, rather than seek them out.

For transits made to or by Venus, see Chapter 22.

Mars—Key to Desire and Action

Mars indicates the individual's capacity for direct action. This action is always based on desire of some sort, and Mars rules the principle of desire. Because Mars is the ruler of Aries and of the natural First House, the actions it rules are largely based on the survival instinct and the expending of energy to acquire that which is essential to survive or to defend one's life and property. This applies to the preservation of the ego as well as to physical survival.

If this basic survival drive becomes distorted by mental aberrations and neurotic or psychotic tendencies of the subconscious mind, the Mars energy often becomes destructive. This is why Mars is considered to be a malefic planet in traditional Astrology. The Mars influence, more than that of any other planet, needs guidance, tempering, and alloying with other factors. When the Mars energy is disciplined and properly channeled, it brings practical accomplishment.

Mars is exalted in the Earth sign Capricorn, reflecting the essential relationship between action and practical results. The best intentions or ideas are useless without action, even though it is equally true that misguided action can be destructive. The manner in which action is taken and the affairs affected by the action are indicated by the sign and house positions of Mars in the horoscope. Aspects made to natal Mars indicate the degree of harmony and positive results or disharmony and negative results associated with such action.

If Mars is found in a Fire sign—Aries, Leo, or Sagittarius—the individual has abundant energy and natural leadership qualities. Whether the individual is a man or woman, there will be strong masculine traits in the character. These individuals generally have a dynamic will and take positive action whenever necessary.

If Mars is found in an Earth sign—Taurus, Virgo, or Capricorn—actions and desires are motivated by practical considerations. The individual does not take action unless there is an opportunity to acquire wealth, property, or material benefit.

If Mars is found in an Air sign—Gemini, Libra, or Aquarius—the individual can become intellectually vehement about ideas and concepts. There is a tendency to identify the ego with personal opinions and points of view. The desire and actions of these individuals are based on intellectual considerations, and consequently they are guided by reason and intelligence rather than by impulse or emotional promptings. Mars in an Air sign can express itself through intellectual debate or contest.

If Mars is found in a Water sign—Cancer, Scorpio, or Pisces—the individual's actions and desires are based on emotional considerations. If the emotions are subject to distortions by subconscious mechanisms, the individual can act self-destructively. Emotional tirades, jealousy, and hurt pride are the result of an afflicted Mars in a Water sign. On the positive side, the individual can be motivated to action by compassion, love, and empathy for others.

If Mars is found in a Cardinal sign—Aries, Cancer, Libra, or Capricorn —the individual acts decisively, and sometimes impulsively, to make the most of existing circumstances, as he or she understands them. Motivation for action is based on present circumstances rather than on past experiences or future goals. There is a need for continuous activity or change, and if these are not in evidence, a Cardinal Mars becomes bored.

If Mars is found in a Fixed sign—Taurus, Leo, Scorpio, or Aquarius— the individual is motivated primarily by future goals. These individuals can be determined, and often stubborn, in adhering to a course of action that will give them what they want.

If Mars is found in a Mutable sign—Gemini, Virgo, Sagittarius, or Pisces—the individual is adaptable and changeable in his actions. Motivation to action is based primarily upon past experiences rather than future goals or present circumstances. These individuals desire to repeat pleasant experiences from their past and avoid painful ones. If their actions are motivated by neurotic tendencies, their irrational behavior can propel them into trouble. A well-aspected Mars in a Mutable sign can indicate a highly skilled, adaptable, and versatile capacity for action. These individuals know how to get around difficulties by periodically changing their tactics.

If Mars is found in a masculine-positive sign—Aries, Gemini, Leo, Libra, Sagittarius, or Aquarius—the individual fights offensive battles and actively seeks what is desired. Mars in the masculine-positive signs does not need the influence of others to motivate action.

If Mars is found in a feminine-negative sign—Taurus, Cancer, Virgo, Scorpio, Capricorn, or Pisces—the individual fights or springs into action only when prodded to do so by others or by outside influences. These people are not ineffective in accomplishing what they want; they merely wait for suitable circumstances before taking action.

For transits made to or by Mars, see Chapter 23.

Jupiter—Key to Cultural Values

Jupiter indicates the individual's awareness of morals and of religious, ethical, social, cultural, and educational values, traditions and goals. The extent to which the individuals are aware of these things and how much they aspire to a more noble way of life is determined by the position of and the aspects to Jupiter in the horoscope. Since social traditions and values can vary widely, the individual's cultural, social, religious, and economic background must be considered when Jupiter's influence in the horoscope is evaluated. What is socially and morally acceptable in one culture may not be in another. However, because certain basic precepts of justice and spiritual truth are universally accepted, such differences are generally superficial.

The sign position of Jupiter shows the manner in which individuals express their values and beliefs, and the house position of Jupiter indicates the practical affairs of life influenced by these beliefs.

Jupiter in the horoscope also shows in what ways the individuals can grow and expect greater enrichment in the affairs of their lives, to the extent that their karmas allow. They can achieve this growth and enrichment only to the extent to which their actions are just and well motivated. Because life is a cooperative endeavor, all growth and expansion depends on the good will and cooperation of others, and this can only be gained through ethical behavior on the individual's part. Thus, the principle of growth and expansion is linked to the individual's relations with the social order, and both come under the rulership of Jupiter. The large endeavors of a civilization must be concerned with and support the overall well-being of society as a whole, and these large, expansive endeavors come under Jupiter's influence.

Jupiter also rules the institutions and professions concerned with cultural rules and traditions, such as universities, churches, charitable institutions, and the legal profession. Jupiter rules all codification of thought and rules of conduct. The way in which these affect the life of a particular individual is shown by the sign and house positions and aspects made to Jupiter.

If Jupiter is well aspected in the horoscope, the individual will benefit from his cultural traditions and be well adjusted. If Jupiter is afflicted in the horoscope, these individuals will be in conflict with the traditional social order, or insincere and hypocritical in their relations to it.

If Jupiter is found in a Fire sign—Aries, Leo, or Sagittarius—the individual can become a leader in cultural affairs. The self-confidence of these people enables them to attempt large-scale endeavors. However, their egos can prevent their taking an objective and unbiased view of reality or blind them to the whole truth of a situation. These individuals can inspire enthusiasm and confidence in others. Should an endeavor fail, they always manage to find a new field for growth and expansion. They are seldom daunted by disappointments or defeats.

If Jupiter is found in an Earth sign—Taurus, Virgo, or Capricorn—the individual takes a practical approach to religion, philosophy, education, and social tradition. These people judge these matters by their practical results: unless there is measurable benefit, they will not be interested. If this tendency is carried to extremes, material things can become an end in themselves rather than a means to an end, and thus thwart the spiritual purpose of the individual's life.

If Jupiter is found in an Air sign—Gemini, Libra, or Aquarius—the individual adopts an intellectual approach to philosophy, education, and social traditions. These individuals are generally well informed and knowledgeable about these matters. They have a desire to circulate widely in order to experience as many life styles, traditions, and cultural ideas as possible. As a result, they are well informed in making choices for themselves. They are fond of philosophical discussion and debate. If the intellectual tendencies of these Jupiter placements are carried to extremes, these individuals are apt to have an impractical, theoretical approach to life. They tend to pay lip service to exalted ideals, but neglect to put them into practice.

If Jupiter is found in a Water sign—Cancer, Scorpio, or Pisces—the individual is likely to have strong emotional ties to family traditions and the values of the culture in which he was raised. These individuals have deep feelings, compassion, and understanding for others. However, their moral and social values can be biased in favor of the familiar and emotionally comfortable. They must be careful not to let their feelings interfere with a balanced picture of any social or moral issue.

If Jupiter is found in a Cardinal sign—Aries, Cancer, Libra, or Capricorn—the individual is socially and culturally active. Moral and ethical judgments are based on present circumstances more than on past conditioning or future expectations. These individuals seek to grow through some kind of social or cultural activity.

If Jupiter is found in a Fixed sign—Taurus, Leo, Scorpio, or Aquarius—the individual has rigid ideas about religion, philosophy, education, ethics, and correct social behavior. These individuals aspire to definite and fixed educational and cultural goals. They are not likely to compromise their principles. On the negative side, this can result in inflexibility and a refusal to see others' points of view. Their cultural and ethical values are dictated by future goals, rather than by present circumstances or past experiences.

If Jupiter is found in a Mutable sign—Gemini, Virgo, Sagittarius, or Pisces—the individual's ethical, religious, educational, and social values are based on past experience and conditioning. These people can adapt readily to a changing social context, though past conditioning may interfere with accurate perception of present and future cultural possibilities.

If Jupiter is found in a masculine-positive sign—Aries, Gemini, Leo, Libra, Sagittarius, or Aquarius—the individual will take the initiative in religious, educational, social, or cultural activities, or in arranging for long-distance travel.

If Jupiter is found in a feminine-negative sign—Taurus, Cancer, Virgo, Scorpio, Capricorn, or Pisces—these individuals are likely to accept and follow prevailing religious, social, educational, and cultural views. They rely on outside people or influences to instigate action along these lines or to encourage them to travel.

For transits made to or by Jupiter, see Chapter 24.

Saturn—Key to the Capacity for Discipline and Patience

Saturn indicates the individual's capacity for self-discipline, organization, and perseverance in pursuit of long-range goals.

Saturn deals with the serious purposes of life. It is better to have an afflicted Saturn than a weak Saturn without aspects or a Saturn without a prominent place in the horoscope (Angular house placement, singleton, dignity, exaltation, or final dispositor). If Saturn is weak, the individual usually does not achieve importance or prominence in life, regardless of potential talents shown in the horoscope. The individual will lack the ambition, discipline, and sense of purpose necessary to accept responsibility and achieve significant goals. If Saturn is afflicted, however, the individual is able to achieve success and prominence, although serious obstacles may have to be overcome in the process.

The square and opposition aspects are harmonious to the basic nature of Saturn because of Saturn's exaltation in Libra, which corresponds to the opposition aspect in the natural Zodiac, and because of Saturn's rulership of Capricorn, which corresponds to the square aspect in the natural Zodiac. Squares and oppositions of Saturn act as spurs to higher professional, business, or scientific goals. A large number of presidents of the United States have had squares between the Sun and Saturn in their natal horoscopes.

Saturn's influence confers the ability to pursue a discipline over an extended period of time. It enables the individual to gradually perfect innate skills and establish a reputation and professional standing. Saturn gives us only what we earn through our own efforts, and if the Saturnian principle becomes perverted, status, power, and material wealth can become ends in themselves. The perversion of the Saturnian energy can cause the individual to become ego-centered, with the rigid, crystallized mental patterns and attitudes which are indicated by the adverse aspects to Saturn. When these individuals take themselves too seriously and do not measure up to their own or others' expectations, they can become depressed. There can be a tendency to impose hard restrictions or regimentations on others. Such restrictions, however, can be useful and constructive if they are tempered with compassion, wisdom, and the desire to do what is best for all concerned. Because constructive discipline will always be necessary, Saturn's influence is an essential and indispensable part of life.

The sign position of Saturn shows the manner in which the individual expresses discipline and builds structure into his or her life.

The house position of Saturn indicates the practical affairs of the individual's life that will be directly affected by such structuring and discipline. It also reveals the area of the individual's major responsibilities. For instance, if Saturn is found in the natal Fifth House, the individual's major responsibilities are often the care and raising of children. However, this Saturn-Fifth House combination can also indicate that an individual who desires children is denied them. In any event, there will be a responsibility for giving birth to some creative idea or project and bringing it to fruition.

Aspects to Saturn indicate the individual's capacity for discipline, organization, patience, and hard work. Favorable aspects to Saturn indicate capacities developed in the individual's evolutionary experience. Adverse aspects to Saturn indicate that the individual is developing new skills and capacities by overcoming current obstacles.

Saturn is a more positive influence in Earth and Air signs than in Water and Fire signs.

If Saturn is found in a Fire sign—Aries, Leo, or Sagittarius—the individual has a natural capacity for leadership and the ability to initiate new projects in business and professional spheres of activity. However, authoritarian, egotistical attitudes in regard to these matters can be a danger.

If Saturn is found in an Earth sign—Taurus, Virgo, or Capricorn—the individual possesses excellent practical, professional, business, and organizational abilities. There is a natural capacity for handling and organizing practical tasks and responsibilities. However, the individual may develop an excessively materialistic outlook.

If Saturn is found in an Air sign—Gemini, Libra, or Aquarius—the individual has a natural intellectual, organizing ability and the capacity to give concrete expression to abstract concepts. These individuals are capable of mental discipline and organization in literary, educational, and scientific fields, especially in terms of mathematical ability. If these intellectual tendencies are carried too far, however, the individuals can seem intellectually detached, cold, aloof, and, at times, insensitive to feelings.

If Saturn is found in a Water sign—Cancer, Scorpio, or Pisces—the individual is likely to show great depth of feeling, though, at times, can become emotionally depressed and morose.

If Saturn is found in a Cardinal sign—Aries, Cancer, Libra, or Capricorn—these individuals are decisive in handling business and professional affairs. They will organize opportunities offered by present circumstances to achieve career advancement.

If Saturn is found in a Fixed sign—Taurus, Leo, Scorpio, or Aquarius—the individual organizes business and career efforts toward the achievement of long-range goals. Although this may not become evident until Saturn has returned to its natal position when the individual is approximately twenty-nine, there is great staying power in this placement of Saturn. However, if it is afflicted, the individual can have stubborn, fixed, unyielding attitudes.

If Saturn is found in a Mutable sign—Gemini, Virgo, Sagittarius, or Pisces—the individual relies on past experience and accumulated knowledge to organize business and professional affairs. If Saturn is afflicted, fear, based on painful memories of the past, can inhibit self-confidence and stand in the way of success.

If Saturn is found in a masculine-positive sign—Aries, Gemini, Leo, Libra, Sagittarius, or Aquarius—the individual will take the initiative in organizing business and professional affairs.

If Saturn is found in a feminine-negative sign—Taurus, Cancer, Virgo, Scorpio, Capricorn, or Pisces—the individual is more apt to manage existing enterprises than to initiate new ones.

For transits made to or by Saturn, see Chapter 25.

Uranus—Key to Freedom of Expression

Uranus indicates the manner in which the individual seeks new friendships and group and organizational associates, as well as new experiences. Uranus brings new, sudden, and often unexpected experiences and changes into the individual's life. It also indicates the way in which the individual goes about seeking freedom and independence.

The individual uses scientific proof or direct experience to test his or her ideas and opinions on the matters ruled by Uranus's position in the horoscope. He refuses to blindly accept doctrines based on traditions or authority. Uranus has much to do with scientific experimentation and work that deals with technological, corporate enterprises, especially those that relate to scientific technology. Uranus indicates how the individual can tap his intuitive level of inspiration by going beyond the limitations of personal ego and forming a link with the Universal Mind. For this reason, Uranus has much to do with occult and astrological ideas and practices.

Uranus also deals with the motivation behind the individual's goals and objectives. Because Uranus rules universal brotherhood, this planet is always kind to those whose motives are honest and unselfish. If the individual's motives are selfish and destructive to others, sudden and seemingly inexplicable occurrences thwart him and bring him misfortune.

The action of Uranus often seems mysterious. This is because Uranus rules the principle of transference of conditions out of subjective manifestation into objective manifestation. The conditions previously existed only in the realm of thought or the Universal Mind.

Through its exaltation in Scorpio, Uranus is closely linked with Mars and Pluto, which are also agents of change and transformation. The means by which change is brought about depends upon the sign position and aspects of Uranus. The departments of life most directly influenced by these changes are indicated by the house position of Uranus and the houses where Aquarius and Scorpio are found.

According to the theory of the Ladder of the Planets, we suspect that Uranus is also linked to Capricorn. This makes sense when one considers the amount of scientific research and development carried on by governments and large corporate enterprises. (See *Ladder of the Planets,* by the same authors, for more on this concept.) Uranus, through its exaltation in Scorpio and possible co-rulership of Capricorn, thus, has much to do with the use and management of large-scale collective financial resources, such as stocks, or resources provided by taxes.

If Uranus is found in a Fire sign—Aries, Leo, or Sagittarius—these individuals are strong-willed and highly independent in their expression of original, creative drive. They are able to initiate new enterprises and have the vision and insight to find new ways of doing things. They also are able to inspire others to support such projects. If Uranus is afflicted in a Fire sign, headstrong pride and egotism make cooperation difficult.

If Uranus is found in an Earth sign—Taurus, Virgo, or Capricorn—these individuals have the ability to find new and more efficient ways of handling financial, business, and professional affairs. They can put their original, creative ideas into practical use. If Uranus is afflicted, they may have an overly materialistic attitude toward friendships and group associations, and their attitudes toward business affairs could be erratic, eccentric, and, at times, impractical.

If Uranus is found in an Air sign—Gemini, Libra, or Aquarius—these individuals have inspired and unusual intellectual abilities. They demonstrate ease in establishing new friendships and group associations. Many unique ideas come to them through sudden flashes of illumination. However, if Uranus is afflicted in an Air sign, mental concentration may be scattered and they may be too easily distracted by new ideas and experiences.

If Uranus is found in a Water sign—Cancer, Scorpio, or Pisces—these individuals usually have strong intuitive abilities. They empathize with others and understand people from all walks of life. However, if Uranus is afflicted, their sudden changes of mood can confuse and upset associates.

If Uranus is found in a Cardinal sign—Aries, Cancer, Libra, or Capricorn—these individuals are quick and decisive in adjusting to new circumstances and changing conditions and have a knack for turning seemingly chaotic conditions to advantage. There is a strong need for constant, new, exciting activity wherever Uranus is placed by sign, house, and aspects. If Uranus is afflicted in a Cardinal sign, the individuals tend to be impatient with routine, and thus find it difficult to bring projects to conclusion.

If Uranus is found in a Fixed sign—Taurus, Leo, Scorpio, or Aquarius—these individuals are able to follow through on original ideas and concepts with great energy and determination. They are determined to express their creative independence and will not be deterred in their course of action. If Uranus is afflicted in a Fixed sign, however, they may be obstinate in pursuing personal objectives, even when they are impractical.

If Uranus is found in a Mutable sign—Gemini, Virgo, Sagittarius, or Pisces—these individuals are adaptable and versatile in adjusting to changing conditions. This is accomplished through utilization of past experience. There is an ability to break away from old attitudes and habit patterns that is not true of other planets in Mutable signs. There is also an ability to bring to light and utilize old, forgotten ideas or concepts. Should Uranus be afflicted in a Mutable sign, however, painful memories can cause the individuals to act irrationally and unpredictably.

If Uranus is found in a masculine-positive sign—Aries, Gemini, Leo, Libra, Sagittarius, or Aquarius—these individuals are likely to initiate unusual ideas, projects, friendships, and group associations.

If Uranus is found in a feminine-negative sign—Taurus, Cancer, Virgo, Scorpio, Capricorn, or Pisces—these individuals are apt to wait until outside stimuli necessitate sudden change and the utilization of unique new ideas before taking action along these lines.

For transits made to or by Uranus, see Chapter 26.

Neptune—Key to the Subconscious Mind

Neptune indicates the manner in which the individual's imagination and aesthetic and intuitive faculties work. Neptune rules the picture-making faculties of the mind.

Neptune, as ruler of Pisces and the natural Twelfth House, deals with the storehouse of memory in which the individual's entire past history as a spiritual being is recorded in detail. Most people do not have conscious access to this information, but this does not mean that it does not exist in a deeper level of awareness. Those memories which the individual is able to recall consciously are like the tip of an iceberg visible above the surface of the water—the rest of the iceberg belongs to those levels of the mind which are generally called the unconscious. However, the word *un-conscious* is really a misnomer, since these deeper levels of recorded experience are always present, even when the individual is asleep or literally unconscious. The fact that a person cannot recall all of these past memories and experiences does not mean that his outlook on life and behavior are not influenced by them. These memories predispose many of the individual's likes, dislikes, abilities, and personal limitations. Painful or unpleasant past experiences are the most likely to be suppressed from conscious recall, and their effect upon the individual from a subliminal level of awareness can stand in the way of the individual's abilities. In extreme cases, they can cause neuroses and psychoses.

In Astrology, Neptune gives us a major key to understanding irrational and inexplicable behavior. The sign position of Neptune and adverse aspects made to it show the manner in which such mental distortions are expressed. The house position of Neptune and the houses where Sagittarius, Pisces, and Cancer are found show the affairs of life most directly affected by such difficulties. Many of these subconscious distortions are related to previous incarnations, not just to early childhood experiences.

Neptune confers creative talent in musical and artistic fields of expression. It is also helpful to designers, architects, and others whose professions require a good imagination.

Neptune gives intuitive and telepathic ability. Psychics and clairvoyants almost always have a strong Neptune in their horoscopes. (A strong Neptune is one which is in an Angular house or in its own sign or sign of exaltation and has many aspects.) A strong Neptune enables a person to draw upon past experience to find solutions to present problems. The sign position and aspects to Neptune describe the manner in which a person is able to express his imaginative faculties and intuitive abilities.

The house position of Neptune and the houses where Cancer, Sagittarius, and Pisces are found show the practical affairs of life that are directly influenced by such imagination and intuition.

If Neptune is found in a Fire sign—Aries, Leo, or Sagittarius—the individual is able to express intuitive and imaginative abilities dramatically and forcefully and, through these abilities, may even become a cultural leader in some capacity. If Neptune is afflicted in a Fire sign, however, egotistical tendencies may lead to delusions of grandeur.

If Neptune is found in an Earth sign—Taurus, Virgo, or Capricorn—the individual is able to apply intuitive and imaginative faculties to the solution of practical problems. However, if Neptune is afflicted in an Earth sign, there is the danger of prostituting spiritual, intuitive abilities for financial gain.

If Neptune is found in an Air sign—Gemini, Libra, or Aquarius—the individual will be able to express intuitive and imaginative abilities intellectually. Air sign placements are favorable for those engaged in professions related to creative writing. If Neptune is afflicted in an Air sign, however, undisciplined imagination and mental wanderings can lead to neglect of practical responsibilities.

If Neptune is found in a Water sign—Cancer, Scorpio, or Pisces—the individual has the ability to empathize with and intuitively sense other people's moods and feelings. Neptune is at home in the Water Element, and the intuitive abilities associated with this planet are intensified when it is found in a Water sign. However, if Neptune is afflicted in a Water sign, the individual can be emotionally drawn into the problems of others and be overly susceptible to negative psychic conditions and subliminal suggestions.

If Neptune is found in a Cardinal sign—Aries, Cancer, Libra, or Capricorn—the individual is intuitively sensitive to the immediate surrounding conditions. This responsiveness gives an intuitive awareness of what is needed in any situation as it occurs. However, if Neptune is afflicted in a Cardinal sign, the individual can be constantly thrown off balance by the psychic and emotional impact of daily crises.

If Neptune is found in a Fixed sign—Taurus, Leo, Scorpio, or Aquarius—the individual is intuitively drawn to the possibilities of the future. These individuals have staying power in the pursuit of their visionary goals. If Neptune is afflicted in a Fixed sign, the individual can stubbornly adhere to distorted religious, cultural, and psychic beliefs.

If Neptune is found in a Mutable sign—Gemini, Virgo, Sagittarius, or

Pisces—the individual's intuitive and creative imagination is strongly influenced by past experiences. These individuals are able to tap the vast resources of their "soulic" memory. If Neptune is afflicted in a Mutable sign, the individual can easily become trapped in painful subconscious memories which, in turn, can cause neurotic or psychotic behavior.

If Neptune is found in a masculine-positive sign—Aries, Gemini, Leo, Libra, Sagittarius, or Aquarius—the individual is able to initiate creative, imaginative, artistic activities without any need for outside stimuli. This also applies to religious and cultural activities.

If Neptune is found in a feminine-negative sign—Taurus, Cancer, Virgo, Scorpio, Capricorn, or Pisces—the individual will exercise imaginative and intuitive faculties in response to the influence of people and conditions in the immediate environment.

For transits made to or by Neptune, see Chapter 27.

Pluto—Key to the Need for Regeneration

Pluto indicates the manner in which fundamental and irrevocable changes come into the individual's life.

The planet Pluto has much to do with the power of the will and with the faculty of attention—that is, the ability to consciously observe and choose the focus of one's attention, selecting the thoughts to be entertained by the conscious mind. To the extent that people can consciously choose their thoughts, they have free will; all action originates in thought, and everyone is bound by the consequences of their actions.

Pluto represents a principle that goes beyond the mind and its mental image-recordings and memories: the principle of awareness of awareness. Pluto deals with the faculty of consciousness.

Memory and mental habits tend to persist in the same patterns. Because the mind is composed of a highly subtle level of matter and because all matter has its own rate of vibration, the mind tends to go on vibrating in the same pattern in which it was originally set into motion. A conscious effort of the will is required to redirect or change these patterns, and this is only possible when people realize that they are pure spiritual consciousness or spiritual being. They must learn to observe and control their minds. Only then can they free themselves from mechanical conditioning by past experiences and from the automatic control of mental and emotional response mechanisms.

If Pluto is powerfully placed and aspected in a horoscope, this self-awareness/self-determinism is more highly developed than that of the average person and indicates an advanced level of spiritual evolvement. (Pluto is powerful when it is in the sign of its rulership or exaltation, in Angular houses, conjunct or aspecting Angular house cusps, in its accidental rulership or accidental exaltation by house position, powerfully aspected by other planets or any combination of the above.) Conversely, if Pluto is weak by placement and lacking in aspects, self-awareness and self-determinism are not highly developed.

Pluto also rules the process of recycling. All things in the material universe undergo a process of creation, evolution, and dissolution except the spirit itself; that supersedes the material universe. In other words, the only thing not subject to this process is pure consciousness, the creative principle behind all manifestation. This pure consciousness is infinite in its speed and, therefore, occupies an infinite amount of space in an infinitely short period of time. This makes it omnipresent, still and static, and thus it creates time, space, and energy. It is through interaction of vibrations or energy pulses in time and space that matter is brought into being. When a material form is destroyed, the fundamental energy which organized the structure is redirected into another pattern which creates a new and different material form. The fundamental energy responsible for material manifestation is redistributed but not destroyed, and the new form generated can either be useful or destructive.

The spiritual principle of consciousness directs the destruction of old forms and the creation of new ones as a means of creating order and gaining mastery over the material universe. Through this evolutionary process, perfected forms are created through which life can express itself more fully and creatively.

Each individual being is responsible for his or her own use of the recycling process. This pertains to all levels of creative manifestation, be they physical, emotional, or mental.

The residue of old conditions must not be allowed to poison the ongoing process of life. Failure to obey this law is evident in our modern industrial/ecological crisis. Unresolved thoughts and emotions of the past can poison the psyche in a similar manner, interfering with perception and distorting reason.

Because Pluto rules the elimination and recycling of waste products, Pluto's position in the horoscope shows how and where people must clean up and recycle the residues in their physical, emotional, and mental environments. Only when this transmutation is accomplished can the individual go on to higher levels of creative expression, indicated by Pluto's co-rulership of the sign Aries, the sign of new beginnings.

If Pluto is afflicted in the horoscope, these individuals can be tempted to use collective resources for self-aggrandizement. They will attempt to coerce or force others, on some level, to carry out their personal desires, often done through self-righteousness or the attitude that they know what is best for others. It should be remembered that Pluto, as ruler of Scorpio and the natural Eighth House, is concerned with corporate money and collective resources.

Through the one-pointed concentration which Pluto makes possible, spiritual forces can be focalized to generate power.

The sign position of Pluto indicates the manner in which people express transforming will-power. Aspects to Pluto indicate how they focus their attention and direct their will-power.

The house position of Pluto and the houses where Aries, Scorpio, and Leo are found show the practical affairs of life which need regeneration, and where the individual is likely to express his or her will to change and transform conditions.

If Pluto is found in a Fire sign—Aries, Leo, or Sagittarius—the individual has a positive, dynamic will. Because it takes approximately fifteen to thirty-two years for Pluto to transit a sign, these Pluto sign characteristics apply to a whole generation. However, by using decanates, duads, and degrees (see *The Zodiac Within Each Sign* by the authors), particular individual characteristics can be noticed and observed. (The same applies to sign positions of Neptune and Uranus, whose placements also denote generational differences.)

A generation which has Pluto in a Fire sign is likely to bring about dramatic, revolutionary changes in life styles, sexual mores and economic, political, and educational conditions. This has certainly been true of the generation born with Pluto in Leo. The negative characteristics of these Fire sign placements of Pluto are egotism, revolutionary attitudes lacking in constructive improvement, and automatic rejection of old traditions.

The generation with Pluto in an Earth sign—Taurus, Virgo, or Capricorn—brings about important transformations in business, labor, financial, professional, and political institutions. Major changes may be made in the structure and style of commonly used manufactured items, such as clothing, furniture, and appliances. Medical and dietary practices may also undergo major changes. A negative characteristic of this placement is a materialistic trend in social values and customs.

The generation that has Pluto in an Air sign—Gemini, Libra, or Aquarius—has penetrating intellectual abilities and talents in the literary, scientific, and sociological fields. A negative characteristic of these Pluto placements is fanatical adherence to intellectual dogmas.

The generation with Pluto in a Water sign—Cancer, Scorpio, or Pisces—is concerned with emotional, psychological, and psychic issues. This generation experiences a general need to clean up and regenerate emotional habit patterns, both individual and social. Negative characteristics of these Pluto placements are undue vehemence in the expression of personal emotions or the destructive use of psychic powers.

The generation with Pluto in a Cardinal sign—Aries, Cancer, Libra, or Capricorn—is inclined to actively and constantly pursue social change, with major emphasis on immediate crises affecting humanity. In general, they feel a need for constant change, improvement, and new activity. The negative expression of Cardinal placements of Pluto is an over-reaction to situations as they arise, and this may lead to undesirable long-range consequences.

The generation with Pluto in a Fixed sign—Taurus, Leo, Scorpio, or Aquarius—is relentless and determined in efforts to bring about necessary large-scale changes in civilization. The negative expression of these Fixed placements of Pluto is a fanatical adherence to fixed ideologies.

The generation with Pluto in a Mutable sign—Gemini, Virgo, Sagittarius, or Pisces—is concerned with cleaning up and regenerating the mental and emotional residues of past experiences. This generation can draw upon the vast knowledge and experience of Man's spiritual being. The negative characteristics of these Pluto placements are entrapment in past habit patterns and vacillation of purpose.

The generation with Pluto in a masculine-positive sign—Aries, Gemini, Leo, Libra, Sagittarius, or Aquarius—has the ability to bring about major changes and transformation through their own initiative.

The generation with Pluto in a feminine-negative sign—Taurus, Cancer, Virgo, Scorpio, Capricorn, or Pisces—brings about major changes and social transformation in response to necessity dictated by existing conditions.

For transits made to or by Pluto, see Chapter 28.

7 The Moon's Nodes

The nodes of the Moon indicate the individual's attitudes toward and reactions to prevailing cultural trends and popular beliefs.

The North Node deals with expansion and with the way good fortune comes to the individual. It has a Jupiterian significance, and its position in the horoscope indicates the mode and degree of the person's harmony with prevailing cultural trends and ability to utilize them for self-advancement and development. The affairs ruled by the house and sign positions of the North Node are furthered and benefited through the activities and values inherent in the prevailing social and cultural order.

The South Node tends to restrict and isolate the individual in some way. Its nature is individualistic and self-reliant in contrast to that of the North Node. The South Node individual does not receive support and recognition from the surrounding culture. The South Node has the advantage, however, of giving the person a more critical point of view toward prevailing cultural attitudes. In the matters affected by the position of the South Node, the person is less apt to be subject to the limitations, mistakes, and foolishness of prevailing cultural trends. Individualism and integrity will be expressed and the individual will not be swayed by others. All this is usually the result of wisdom gained through past experience, and of a long-range, comprehensive understanding of cause-and-effect relationships. The affairs of the house and sign in which the South Node is placed generally show a significant degree of organization and discipline, unless other factors in the horoscope are contradictory.

The Nodes in the Houses

North Node in the Natal First House

With this placement, self-expression conforms, more or less, to prevailing social and cultural patterns. These people are generally outgoing, popular, and well liked. In addition, they are gifted with an innate sense of how to blend with and utilize their social surroundings. In many cases, they are tall and slender.

South Node in the Natal First House

Individuals with this nodal position tend to be reserved, cautious, and conservative in manner. They may be short in physical stature and may have a speech difficulty of some sort. These people evaluate current fads and social beliefs by relating them to their own experience and practical common sense. If they do not agree with the current vogue, they will refuse to compromise their personal convictions, even at the risk of forfeiting personal popularity.

Women with this nodal position are generally slow to accept new styles and trends; they want to be certain that the style or trend is more than just a passing fancy. In general the individual tends to identify with conservative traditional cultural values and mores.

North Node in the Natal Second House

This placement indicates that the individuals make money easily because of their expansiveness and optimism, and their ability to appeal to current social trends and fads. However, they are likely to spend in a big way, or find that their money dissipates quickly; this placement inclines them to spend money on frivolous nonessentials.

South Node in the Natal Second House

This nodal position indicates the adoption of a more conservative attitude toward money and possessions. The individuals spend money cautiously and seek possessions that have lasting value. They feel that they work hard for their money, and they refuse to squander it foolishly.

North Node in the Natal Third House

This nodal placement indicates an ease of speech and communication in relating to the prevailing social context. The individuals tend to use currently popular expressions and colloquialisms.

There is a great deal of social activity. These people's ideas and mental attitudes are strongly conditioned by current social trends and popular beliefs. There can be a strong intellectual awareness of the cultural context of current events. Often, this awareness arises through conversations with or interaction between the individuals and their brothers, sisters, or neighbors.

South Node in the Natal Third House

This position of the South Node indicates the adoption of a conservative attitude toward currently popular ideas and beliefs. The individuals are inclined to accept those concepts that have stood the test of time. They tend to be reserved and individualistic in their intellectual ideas and attitudes.

North Node in the Natal Fourth House

This position of the North Node indicates that the individuals adhere to currently acceptable social and cultural values in their family and domestic affairs. The home is often used as a meeting place for social and cultural activities. This position favors good fortune and peacefulness in the domestic environment.

South Node in the Natal Fourth House

This position of the South Node indicates an adherence to traditional cultural and social values and mores in family and domestic life. The individuals can tend to be recluses in their homes, and to use the home as a place of personal retreat and privacy.

North Node in the Natal Fifth House

This position of the North Node indicates an adherence to current tastes in entertainment, social activity, art, and attitudes toward romance and sex. The individual is likely to enjoy social popularity and to have many opportunities for social involvement, romance, and pleasure-seeking.

South Node in the Natal Fifth House

This position of the South Node indicates an adherence to traditional values with respect to social activity, pleasure-seeking activities, sex, and romance. These individuals may appear somewhat stiff, formal, and proper in social situations. They may consider themselves too busy to be bothered with trivial social and pleasurable activities. This position sometimes indicates a lack of romantic opportunities and frustration in seeking romantic fulfillment.

North Node in the Natal Sixth House

This placement of the North Node indicates that the individuals probably enjoy a socially pleasant working environment. Health can also be benefited by this position of the North Node. When these individuals become ill, they make certain that they receive proper medical attention. This position favors popularity with the "boss," and with fellow workers.

South Node in the Natal Sixth House

This placement of the South Node indicates a "loner" where work is concerned. These individuals do not necessarily enjoy popularity or pleasant conditions in their working environment. They must work very hard to achieve even moderate results. On the positive side, their accomplishments are worthwhile, lasting, and practical. They are inclined to exercise discipline where health and diet are concerned.

North Node in the Natal Seventh House

This position of the North Node indicates skill in public relations and psychology through insight into cultural conditionings and current attitudes.

These individuals possess a natural understanding of the diplomacy and tact needed in social situations. They are outgoing, especially in seeking partnerships and associations with others, and they benefit and are benefited by others in cooperative endeavors.

South Node in the Natal Seventh House

The South Node's placement here indicates that the individuals are cautious when entering into close personal relationships. However, because the North Node is in the opposite or First House, they appear to be outgoing and friendly.

These individuals are interested in what can be personally gained through a relationship. They are cautious and astute in handling public relations and diplomatic affairs. Often, they marry older, serious-minded individuals or those who are financially established.

North Node in the Natal Eighth House

The North Node in the Eighth House indicates an ease in establishing or promoting financial endeavors. This ease is the result of an innate awareness of current attitudes regarding business ventures. Their attitude toward the occult tends to be orthodox and conformist.

South Node in the Natal Eighth House

This position of the South Node indicates a cautious and conservative approach to corporate money and joint finances. These individuals must exercise care when dealing with tax matters, alimony, and inheritances if they are to avoid financial losses and possible legal difficulties. They should take a responsible and unselfish attitude in handling affairs that concern other people's money. The South Node in this house can also indicate a cautious and conservative attitude toward occult practices.

North Node in the Natal Ninth House

The North Node in the Ninth House indicates adherence to current cultural norms where religious, educational, philosophic, and legal attitudes are concerned. These individuals are inclined to travel to increase their awareness of what is going on in the world. They will express an interest in whatever imported philosophies, religions, and art forms are in vogue.

South Node in the Natal Ninth House

The South Node in the Ninth House indicates a cautious and conservative appraisal of currently popular educational, philosophic, and religious ideas. These individuals do not blindly adhere to imported cultural ideas simply because they are currently popular. They are likely to adhere to traditional values where philosophy, education, and religion are concerned. They may feel a responsibility to teach these traditional values or to help others to a deeper understanding of moral values.

North Node in the Natal Tenth House

The North Node in the Tenth House indicates an ability to use currently popular trends and fads for professional advancement. If the individuals are involved in politics, administration, or business, they can play on the current public mood to advance their cause. These individuals are usually popular and well liked in the community. More cautious observers may regard them as opportunistic. In some cases, this placement of the North Node indicates a rise to fame and popularity in early life and relative obscurity in later years.

South Node in the Natal Tenth House

This placement of the South Node indicates a struggle to attain a position of importance in the world. The individual's professional interests and activities are not always in harmony with the prevailing mood. These individuals are not likely to compromise professional principles or long-range ambitions to accommodate current trends. In the long run, they often achieve success and distinction of lasting value and meaning in contrast to those with the North Node in the Tenth House.

This position of the South Node indicates power and prestige in a previous incarnation and, consequently, no interest in status and prestige as ends in themselves. These individuals are free to pursue quality and excellence in their work for its own sake. The authors, of course, cannot prove that this is so; however, through our own experience and observations, and through the experience of other serious astrologers, it would appear to be the case.

It is generally considered that the North Node represents the direction in which the individual can expand into new experience, whereas the South Node deals with past experience. There is danger, with the South Node in the Tenth House, of a fall from high position and public disgrace if dishonest means have been used. These individuals have an innate awareness of this danger, and are usually scrupulous about their professional conduct and very cautious about accepting responsibility.

North Node in the Natal Eleventh House

The North Node's placement in the Eleventh House indicates an ease in establishing friendships and finding a niche in groups and organizations. These individuals' awareness of current trends and beliefs makes it easy for them to establish a rapport with others on their terms. On the negative side, they can be easily influenced and led by their associates to participate in activities that are not in their best interests. These individuals are usually friendly, with a sense of brotherhood with all mankind.

South Node in the Natal Eleventh House

The South Node in the Eleventh House indicates a sense of responsibility toward friends and group associates. Individuals with this placement choose their friends carefully, and are loyal once a friendship has been established. They do not go along with the group merely for the sake of popularity or acceptance. They must be convinced that the group's intent or purpose is meaningful. Their reserve, their experience, and their objectivity in dealing with people often make these individuals astute judges of character. They often feel alone, however, even in crowds, because they are so discriminating in choosing their associates.

North Node in the Natal Twelfth House

The North Node in the Twelfth House indicates individuals who are psychically attuned to the moods and attitudes of their culture. This can give them an inner sense of belonging. At the same time, the interference of others in their private affairs can cause problems. At times these individuals find it difficult to shut out unwanted psychic impressions of their cultural environment. Current attitudes and beliefs may have a strong subconscious, psychological effect on them. On the positive side, the North Node in this house gives a universal empathy, understanding, and compassion for others.

South Node in the Natal Twelfth House

The South Node in the Twelfth House indicates individuals who are subconsciously out of sympathy with prevailing attitudes and trends. There is a sense of isolation and loneliness, either by choice or necessity. They can even become recluses or hermits, if the rest of the horoscope reveals a similar trend. They may find themselves accepting unsuitable responsibilities out of a sense of social obligation. Individuals with this placement may also be subconsciously burdened by the trouble of the world.

8 Hemispheric Emphasis: Natal and Transiting

Division by Midheaven/Nadir Axis—East and West

If the majority of the natal planets are in the eastern sector of the natal horoscope—that is, in the Tenth, Eleventh, Twelfth, First, Second, and Third houses—these individuals tend to choose their own paths in life. They are largely self-determined and able to choose their own life styles and the set of social and business conditions in which they move.

If the majority of the transiting planets are in the eastern sector of the horoscope—that is, in the Tenth, Eleventh, Twelfth, First, Second, and Third houses—these individuals are in a phase of initiating new endeavors and entering into new experiences. They will experience freedom in making decisions and choices rather than feeling bound by obligations to others.

If the majority of the natal planets are in the western sector of the natal horoscope—that is, in the Fourth, Fifth, Sixth, Seventh, Eighth, and Ninth houses—the needs and wishes of others play an important part in determining how the individual functions. This is not to imply that the individual does not have free will; personal creativity is expressed in handling and utilizing the surrounding circumstances or conditions.

Superficially, it would appear that people who have most of their natal planets in the western sector would be at a disadvantage; however, individuals with most of their planets in the eastern sector often experience a sense of loneliness or isolation. They tend to feel that nothing worthwhile happens unless they make it happen. They must reach out to establish relationships and create conditions which would automatically be provided for those with a predominantly western emphasis. Thus, the freedom of choice associated with the eastern emphasis has its liabilities.

If the majority of the transiting planets are in the western sector of the horoscope—that is, in the Fourth, Fifth, Sixth, Seventh, Eighth, and Ninth houses—the individual's activities are conditioned by obligations to others, and the opportunities for new experience arise through activities and circumstances related to other people.

Division by Ascendant/Descendant Axis—North (Below) and South (Above)

If the majority of the planets are above the horizon in the natal horoscope—that is, in the Seventh, Eighth, Ninth, Tenth, Eleventh, and Twelfth houses—these individuals have an objective and impersonal attitude toward life, especially toward what is happening around them on a large scale, whether or not it affects them directly.

If the majority of the transiting planets are above the horizon—that is, in the Seventh, Eighth, Ninth, Tenth, Eleventh, and Twelfth houses—the activities of the individual tend to be apparent and concerned with outer, practical activities and with affairs that go beyond personal considerations. The individual is likely to achieve some kind of public recognition during this phase of life.

If the majority of the planets are below the horizon in the natal horoscope—that is, in the First, Second, Third, Fourth, Fifth, and Sixth houses —where Earth obscures the direct view, these individuals have a subjective view of life, based upon a visceral level of response to those things which directly affect their personal lives.

There are modifications of this. For instance, a preponderance of Air signs or signs ruled by Mercury would indicate a somewhat objective viewpoint; however, they still would tend to be intellectually interested in that which is of personal concern to them.

If the majority of the transiting planets are below the horizon—that is, in the First, Second, Third, Fourth, Fifth, and Sixth houses—these individuals' activities are primarily concerned with personal affairs. During this time period, they are apt to work in obscurity and be less in the public eye. Although their work may concern public affairs, a great deal of it will be done in private, in the background.

9 The Psychology of Your Scout Planet

Transiting planets move through the signs and houses of the natal horoscope in a counter-clockwise direction. On the other hand, the signs and planets move clockwise through the twelve houses of the horoscope in a cycle which is completed approximately every twenty-four hours. In the course of a twenty-four-hour period then, a planet, while remaining in a particular degree of a sign, will pass through all twelve houses of the horoscope. The Sun, for example, at 3:00 A.M. will be in the Second House of a chart, while at 7:00 A.M. the Sun, still in the same degree of the Zodiac, will be in the Twelfth House of a chart. This is due to the rotation of Earth and should not be confused with the counter-clockwise progress of the planets as they transit through the signs of the Zodiac.

Once a natal horoscope is erected, the positions of the signs on the cusps of the houses are considered fixed for interpretive purposes. In interpreting transits, the primary concern is the sequence in which transiting planets make aspects to the natal planets.

According to Marc Edmund Jones, the Moon, Mercury, Venus, and Mars are determinators of vocation. According to his system, whichever of these four planets precedes the Sun in a clockwise direction is the vocational indicator.

We have done considerable research on the rest of the planets and found them to be important indicators of the direction of self-expression. We have found that using the Scout planet (or the Oriental planet, as it is sometimes called) in a more general sense gives us important insights into the individual's self-expression. Transits made to the Scout planet are highly significant in understanding the future direction of an individual's self-expression. Any planet that makes a transiting aspect to the Sun first makes the same transiting aspect to the Scout planet—that is, a transiting planet will always make a specific aspect to the Scout planet before it makes the same aspect to the Sun.

We have found that this first planet ahead of the Sun in a clockwise direction from the Sun has a special significance in astrological interpretation. The psychological and experiential impact of this planet modifies and qualifies the creative potential of the Sun.

Usually, the Scout planet has a lower degree of longitude, with respect to 0° of Aries, than the degree of the Sun. The exception to this rule occurs when 0° of Aries intervenes between the Scout planet and the Sun; usually, in such a case, the Sun would be in Aries, while the Scout planet would be in Pisces.

The affairs ruled by the planet preceding the Sun indicate the affairs of life that are constantly brought to the fore, demanding a response of some kind. These matters must be dealt with and handled effectively before individuals can freely express themselves and use the power potential of their Sun. As a result of this constant confrontation, they develop an acute awareness of these matters. They also develop unusual abilities of the type associated with the planet that rises ahead of the Sun. This planet deals with immediate pertinencies and its influence eventually makes individuals more proficient in realizing their Sun potential.

In studying the Scout planet, consider the distance between it and the Sun—that is, the longitudinal arc. This planet may be anywhere from conjunct to many signs away. The greater the distance, the more time the individual has to make adjustments before attempting a major personal effort.

If the Scout planet is close to the Sun or conjunct the Sun, circumstances indicated by the Scout planet force the individual to respond immediately.

Consider the sign and house position, aspects, duad, decanate, and quadrant placement of the Scout planet as keys to the way in which the affairs ruled by this planet will be brought into focus.

If the Moon is the Scout planet, rising ahead of the Sun, everyday business, domestic, and practical affairs are brought to attention and demand a response. Individuals often deal with these circumstances automatically or instinctually, in accordance with cultural and family upbringing, as well as their emotional conditioning. Women often play a large part in daily activities. Financial concerns and practical affairs of life are often of uppermost concern. This is because the Moon is exalted in Taurus and derives its power from Taurus, and Taurus is the Second House sign in the Zodiac, dealing with possessions, values, and money.

Because the Moon is a receptive, neutral planet, these instinctual, emotional reactions will be colored by the sign and house position of the Moon and the aspects made to the Moon, especially major aspects.

If Mercury is the Scout planet, these individuals base their course of action on information gathered daily from books, communications media, and conversations with friends and those in the immediate environment, especially brothers, sisters, and neighbors. They are likely to plan their actions rationally and ahead of time. Their planning will be influenced by the sign, house position, and important aspects to Mercury. This is because Mercury is a neutral planet that takes on the coloring of whatever strongly influences it.

Work, health, clothes, personal appearance, friendships, and communications will demand attention, as will comings and goings and short trips.

If Venus is the Scout planet, social activities, aesthetic values, business affairs, and romantic or marital relationships will be dominant influences on the major actions and decisions of these individuals. They will want to attract people who can help them bring about the conditions of life that they wish to create. Because Venus rules the principle of attraction, these individuals have special ability for dealing with the circumstances of life in a very diplomatic, socially harmonious way. They attract the special favors and consideration from others that help them to accomplish what they want.

Venus is a benefic planet and, even if Venus is afflicted as the Scout planet, the activities it influences will not be without some worthwhile results.

If Mars is the Scout planet, the experiences that come about through direct action will guide and determine major life efforts. There will be skirmishes in the preparation of major advances in creative efforts. There is also liable to be some strife and consternation.

These individuals tend to challenge the obstacles in their path. They may have a chip on the shoulder: "I'm a little bit bigger than you are, and I can flex my muscles," muscles of whatever kind—physical, mental, or emotional. Through such testing and challenging, they gain a sense of what is required to overcome the major obstacles that confront them.

Mars, as the Scout planet, gives a strong strategic sense in planning and carrying out personal creative endeavors and ambitions. If Mars is afflicted in the natal horoscope, there is a tendency to be continually involved in battles and confrontations.

If Jupiter is the Scout planet, cultural, religious, educational, and moral precepts are used to pave the way for major life expressions. This makes possible much creative expansion and improvement. A generous, optimistic attitude will inspire confidence in others, and make them willing to help in the realization of the goals and objectives of the individual.

If Saturn is the Scout planet, these individuals have a cautious, systematic approach to organizing and planning major creative self-expressions. Much advanced guidance comes to them through their profession and other serious responsibilities.

An older, mature, or well-established person often plays an important role in guiding their careers and the development of their creative potential. When these individuals reach a mature and responsible stage in life, they are likely to similarly guide members of the younger generation.

Those that have Saturn as their Scout planet must take care of the immediate, serious responsibilities in their lives if they are to achieve the status and freedom of creative expression that they want. If they properly discharge these responsibilities, they will build a solid foundation for further growth and unfoldment. These people are ambitious and often achieve status and position of power and responsibility. They have a strong grasp of the practical necessities of immediate situations, especially if Saturn is well placed by sign and house and well aspected.

If Uranus is the Scout planet, the immediate affairs of these people are constantly subject to sudden changes and unusual occurrences, and they are forced to learn to adapt quickly. Occult influences, unusual friendships, group associations, and scientific and humanitarian concepts and activities can change the course of the life in very unusual and unexpected ways. These individuals often become citizens of the world, with a unique and broad outlook on life. Because of their unusual breadth of experience, they can employ unique ways of achieving their goals and objectives. Often, their actions seem eccentric or incomprehensible to others; they are a little bit difficult to understand.

If Neptune is the Scout planet, these individuals often use their intuitive abilities and perceptions to guide their course through life. They will be subject to subliminal impressions from the immediate environment, and these cause responses that are peculiar and not easily understood by others.

If Neptune is well aspected, these people can be successful and avoid many difficulties by following intuitive perceptions. But if Neptune is afflicted, responses to the circmstances of life may be faulty or confused because of subconscious aberrations or neurotic tendencies. These individuals need a lot of understanding from others.

If Pluto is the Scout planet, an in-depth, X-ray-like perception of surrounding circumstances often guides these individuals. Their plans and actions will be carried out in secret. They will seek to find a better way of doing things in order to achieve their purposes and creative self-expression. If Pluto is afflicted, they may try to improve others instead of refining their own ways of doing things.

Three sample charts are presented to demonstrate the operative influences of the Scout planet.

Chart A has the Moon moving ahead of the Sun, ascending toward the Midheaven of the chart. Thus, the Moon is the Scout planet and the vocational indicator. According to Marc Edmund Jones's concept, the Moon as the vocational indicator shows that the individual's work is oriented toward the public in a service capacity. This is especially true in this case, because the Moon is the ruler of the natal Tenth House of the profession and public activity.

Let us look at the Moon as the Scout planet in a more general sense and examine how it affects the self-expression. We have the Moon in Virgo in the natal Twelfth House; it is also co-ruler of the natal Tenth House. Cancer is intercepted, and Gemini is on the Midheaven. All this indicates that this person enters into professional activities and dynamic expression with intuitive awareness. She is also psychically aware of the practical details of life because the Moon is in an Earth sign and posited in the natal Twelfth House, a very psychic house, and it rules Cancer in the natal Tenth House. Women, because the Moon rules women, play an important part in this individual's self-expression in some manner. Because Virgo rules service, service and practical awareness of what goes on behind the scenes is a very important factor.

This behind-the-scenes activity often comes about through a practical implementation of the individual's philosophic, religious, cultural, and educational ideas, which are indicated by the Moon in this chart because it is the exalted ruler of the natal Ninth House (we have Taurus on the natal Ninth House cusp). The Moon gets its power from Taurus and, in this case, Taurus is located in the house of higher education, philosophy, and the cultural aspects of a person's life. With the Moon as exalted ruler of the natal Ninth House, the Moon's position in Virgo in the natal Twelfth House is reinforced. This suggests a keen awareness of details that escape the notice of most people (Virgo is the sign of details).

CHART A

Female
10/8/12
41N22.4; 81W54.1
4:40 AM TLT

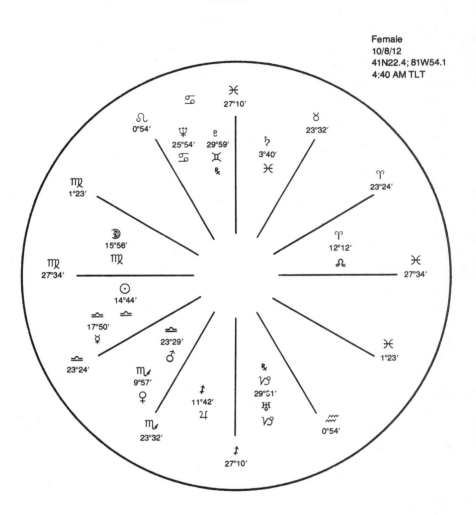

The Moon's position in the natal Twelfth House suggests that the individual's awareness or intuition is brought over from a past life, and could be related to behind-the-scenes activity. The approaching semi-sextile (see page 80) of the Moon to the Sun and Mercury suggests an ability to draw upon the resources of the subconscious mind and the resources of the past to plan and conduct self-expression along intellectual lines. These resources are suggested by the presence of the Sun and Mercury in intellectual, Air signs.

The approaching semi-sextile aspect has a Twelfth House connotation, which is further emphasized by the Moon's position in the natal Twelfth House and in the Pisces duad of Virgo. This, again, indicates a strong, intuitive link with the subconscious mind. The Moon sextile to Venus indicates social acuteness and refined taste in respect to personal possessions. Venus's position in the natal Second House, combined with the approaching sextile of the Moon, indicates a tendency to share a lovely home and domestic environment with friends and group associates. However, the individual's aesthetic values and personal possessions must communicate some kind of intellectual ideals. Venus derives her power from her exaltation in Pisces on the natal Sixth and Seventh house cusps. Venus also rules the sign Taurus, and Taurus is found on the natal Ninth House cusp. Venus also disposits the Sun, Mercury, and Mars, all found in Libra. All this also indicates a refined home environment, and this kind of environment is very important to the person's self-expression, as are marriage and partnerships (Venus is exalted ruler of the natal Seventh House) and cultural activities (because Venus rules the natal Ninth House and makes a sextile to the Moon, exalted ruler of the natal Ninth House). This individual then is concerned with cultural, aesthetic values in the home.

The Moon is also square to Jupiter in Sagittarius, and both Jupiter and Sagittarius are found in the natal Third House, indicating a daily concern with practical, ethical, cultural, and educational matters. Jupiter's co-rulership of the natal Sixth House (Pisces on the cusp), combined with the Moon's position in Virgo in the natal Twelfth House, indicates delicate health that is easily influenced by emotional factors that are related to moral issues. Emotional factors often relate to the subconscious memory of past injustices, indicated by the Moon's placement in the natal Twelfth House. Because the Moon and Jupiter are both placed in Mutable signs and Cadent houses, which deal with the experiences of the past, Jupiter's co-rulership of the natal Seventh and Fourth houses indicates the involvement of family and close personal relationships in these emotional matters. Because this square is a separating square, these past experiences will become less of a problem with maturity.

CHART B

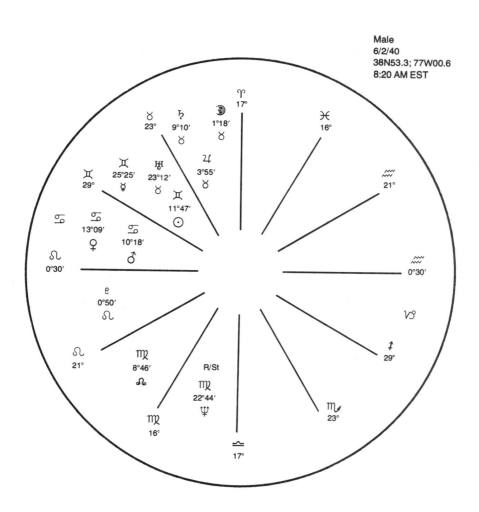

Male
6/2/40
38N53.3; 77W00.6
8:20 AM EST

Chart B has Uranus as the Scout planet, indicating something unusual about the individual's contact with friends, groups, and associates. These contacts are of a scientific or occult nature and draw out his self-expression. Uranus is posited in the house of its natural rulership, the natal Eleventh House. It is trine to Neptune in the natal Third House, and Neptune rules the natal Ninth House, indicating that intuitively inspired ideas are a major determining factor in self-expression.

A less obvious, but significant, factor is Uranus's placement in the Aquarian duad of Taurus, which reinforces its natural Eleventh House placement. Because Uranus rules the natal Seventh and Eighth houses, partnership and cooperation in business and the presentation of unusual ideas are very important. Uranus is semi-sextile to Mercury in the Aquarian decanate of Gemini, which further suggests the expression of unusual ideas and communication with friends concerning these ideas. This is also confirmed by Mercury's natural and actual rulership of the natal Third House.

Chart C, like Chart A, has the Moon as the Scout planet, in the sign Libra in the natal Third House. This position of the Moon indicates that the individual's self-expression is guided by continual day-to-day social communications, continual comings-and-goings involving friends and group activities, again indicated by the Moon, exalted ruler of the natal Eleventh House of friends, where Taurus is found on the cusp. These friends play a major part in setting up the situation for the individual's creative self-expression. Friends and group associations demand attention and communication. This is further indicated by the Moon applying (see page 80) to a square to Uranus, the natural ruler of friends and groups.

Because Uranus is placed in the natal Twelfth House in Cancer (the sign of the home), the home becomes the meeting place for those who wish to confide their emotional problems, or for friends who need a home for a while. Because Uranus is in the natal Twelfth House and rules the natal Eighth House, where Uranus is accidentally exalted, the individual must consider whether he feels that others are using him without consideration for his own emotional needs. On the positive side, there is a continual sense of excitement and immediacy in the contact with these changing experiences of people's lives. But the situation can interfere with the realization of his own long-range goals and objectives.

The Moon is semi-sextile to Mercury and Saturn, indicating a serious, penetrating view of intellectual and political issues as they affect the individual's day-to-day life. This is further indicated by the presence of the Moon and Uranus in Cardinal signs. The Cardinal signs are concerned

CHART C

Male
10/1/48
42N07.0; 75W58.2
11:55:08 PM EST

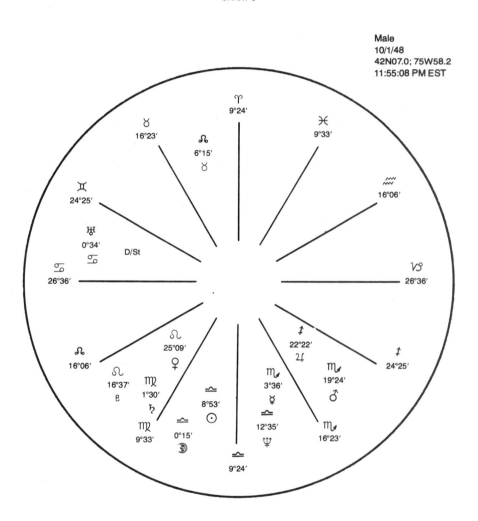

with constant activity and what is going on at the present time.

Because the Moon's position in the natal Third House is semi-sextile to Mercury, the natural ruler of the Third House and actual ruler of the natal Third House, in an applying aspect, the individual may eventually write about these experiences. This is further indicated by the Moon's role as vocational indicator and by its placement in the natal Third House.

Uranus is the exalted ruler of the natal Fifth House, and the exalted dispositor of Mercury and Mars, suggesting that relationships with unstable women can cause frustration in the individual's romantic and sexual relationships. If this individual is a male (as is the case), he tends to attract emotionally unstable and flighty women through this combination.

The Moon is semi-sextile to Saturn, ruler of the natal Seventh House. This could indicate a professional partnership or working relationship with an older, more mature woman. Such contact could be of financial benefit to the individual because of Saturn's placement in the natal Second House of money.

10 The Cutting Planet

The cutting planet is the planet facing, in a clockwise direction, the largest open space between two planets in the horoscope.

According to Marc Edmund Jones, the cutting planet is one of the major indicators of the important characteristics of the individual. It shows the manner in which the person enters into new experiences.

Any planet transiting through the largest open space in the horoscope will first make a conjunction to the cutting planet before it makes a conjunction to any other natal planet. For example, a new series of conjunctions of a transiting planet to natal planets begins with a conjunction to the cutting planet. The quality associated with the cutting planet sets the tone for later activities, as they are indicated by the transiting planet's subsequent conjunctions.

For example, if Saturn is the cutting planet, as in Chart A, then all future aspects made by transiting planets to other natal planets are colored by serious, purposeful, and long-range goals and objectives, as indicated by Saturn in Gemini in the natal Ninth House. These contacts include all of the planets which follow the cutting planet in a counterclockwise direction. In Chart A, the other natal planets would be conjuncted in this order, following Saturn: Pluto, Neptune, the Moon, the Sun, Mercury, Mars, Venus, Jupiter, and Uranus. In Chart B, the Moon is the cutting planet, followed by Jupiter, Saturn, Uranus, the Sun, Mercury, Mars, Venus, Pluto, and Neptune.

When a transiting planet makes a series of a specific kind of transiting aspect, such as a series of transiting sextiles, squares, trines, or oppositions, the natal planets are always contacted in the same order, beginning with the cutting planet. Basically, the cutting planet begins a series of aspects of a specific type and sets the stage for later experiences that are associated with the cutting planet and with the particular type of transiting aspect.

Considering only the five major aspects, the following types set a series of contacts to natal planets, starting with the cutting planet:

Conjunctions
Approaching Sextiles
Departing Sextiles
Approaching Squares
Departing Squares
Approaching Trines
Departing Trines
Oppositions

Each of these aspects constitutes a series of contacts to natal planets for each transiting planet, starting with the cutting planet.

We can now see the logic behind the importance of the cutting planet because the cutting planet sets the tone at the beginning of each of these cycles for each kind of aspect.

The largest space between two planets in a horoscope occurs between the cutting planet, which faces clockwise into this empty space, and the trailing planet, which faces counter-clockwise into the same space (only planets and lights are considered in this determination). The space between the cutting planet and the trailing planet is called the largest empty zone in the horoscope.

The empty zone defined by the cutting and trailing planets is shifted forward in the Zodiac in the case of departing aspects and backward in the case of approaching aspects by the number of degrees of the aspect under consideration. For example, in Chart A, in the case of the conjunction aspect, the empty zone is between Uranus at 29°34′ of Capricorn and Saturn at 3°40′ of Gemini; thus, any transiting planet making an approaching sextile to the natal planets will go through the empty zone where no approaching sextiles can be made to natal planets between 29°34′ of Scorpio and 3°40′ of Aries. In this case of the approaching sextile, the empty zone is shifted backward into the Zodiac 60°, as indicated in the above formula.

Let us take the departing sextile as another example. Here, the empty zone is moved forward 60° in the Zodiac, and the empty zone consists of the space between 29°34′ of Pisces and 3°40′ of Leo. Any planet transiting between these two positions in the natal horoscope cannot make a departing sextile to any natal planet.

In the case of the approaching square (Chart A), the empty zone occurs between 29°34′ of Libra and 3°40′ of Pisces. In the case of the departing square, it occurs between 29°34′ of Aries and 3°40′ of Virgo.

In the case of the approaching trine, it occurs between 29°34′ of Virgo and 3°40′ of Aquarius. In the case of the departing trine, it occurs between 29°34′ of Taurus and 3°40′ of Libra.

In the case of the opposition, it occurs between 29°34′ of Cancer and 3°40′ of Sagittarius.

This largest empty zone for each type of transiting aspect brings about a period of inactivity where that type of aspect is concerned for each transiting planet.

When a transiting planet enters the empty zone for a particular type of transiting aspect, it makes its last transiting aspect of that type to the trailing planet. No more aspects of that type are made by that planet until it reaches the end of the empty zone for that type of aspect and, once again, begins a new cycle of activity. Therefore, the cutting planet begins new cycles of activity for a particular transiting planet making a particular type of aspect, and the trailing planet ends old cycles of activity for a particular transiting planet making a particular type of aspect.

Each type of aspect has its own specific attributes (see page 80). Briefly, these are as follows:

Conjunction—Power of self-expression—dynamic expression of energy—new beginnings and personal initiative—qualities akin to Aries and the First House.

Departing Sextile—Intellectual curiosity—ideas—communication—opportunity through increased practical mental awareness and perception of the environment—qualities akin to Gemini and the Third House.

Approaching Sextile—Intuitive thought—scientific understanding of universal laws and principles—opportunities through friendship and group activity—qualities akin to Aquarius and the Eleventh House.

Departing Square—Need to overcome negative habit patterns based on family upbringing and environmental conditioning —crisis situations in everyday family and domestic affairs—need to understand automatic emotional reactions—impulsive reaction to changing daily conditions—qualities akin to Cancer and the Fourth House.

Approaching Square—Obstacles to ambition—hard work—professional responsibility—conflict with authority figures—struggle to overcome difficulties—increased ambition—need for discipline and organization—qualities akin to Capricorn and the Tenth House.

Departing Trine—Creative self-expression—enjoyment of social, artistic, and romantic activity—personal charisma and self-confidence—matters related to children and their education—speculative activity—self-dramatization—qualities akin to Leo and the Fifth House.

Approaching Trine—Expansion, travel, increased cultural awareness—cultural, ethical, philosophical, and religious values—contact with foreign cultures and traditions—cultural leadership—benefit through higher education—good will—philosophic outlook—karmic reward of past good actions—qualities akin to Sagittarius and the Ninth House.

Opposition—Need for either cooperation or separation in relationships—people's challenges or negative reactions to personal action and self-expression—interest in psychology and understanding other people—responsibility in relationships—companionship and sharing—conflict in relationships—qualities akin to Libra and the Seventh House.

The specific quality of each type of aspect, when combined with a specific planet, gives a unique combination. For example, approaching sextiles of Venus have the quality of universal intuitive, intellectual understanding of what is needed to achieve harmony in human relationships; they indicate beauty and material prosperity expressed in a constructive way. The complete sequence of approaching sextiles of Venus to all of the natal planets, beginning with the cutting planet and ending with the trailing planet, constitute a cycle of experience in the enlightened expression of Venusian qualities. The same pattern is true for all the other types of aspects combined with specific planets.

The importance of the cutting planet in beginning and setting the tone for these cycles, and the importance of the trailing planet in ending and summarizing their experience, becomes readily apparent. Many important insights can be gained by considering the sequence in which the other natal planets are contacted by transiting planets.

For those who do not wish to get involved in the detailed theory of the importance of the cutting and trailing planets and their aspects, the use of these planets in horoscope interpretation can be stated simply: The cutting planet sets the tone for new cycles of experience, and the trailing planet summarizes and synthesizes such cycles of experience, much as do the planets of lowest and highest degree.

If the Sun is the cutting planet, the individual's initial contact with new experiences of life comes through creative self-expression. The individual tends to enter into new activities through a show of personal power, initiative, and creative activity. The affairs ruled by the sign and house in which the Sun is found can play a significant part in the contacts with new experiences. The houses where Leo and Aries are found also play an important part. It should be remembered that the houses where the Sun and Leo are found and the Fifth House are places of power. The house carrying Aries, representing the exaltation of the Sun, shows where the individual makes new beginnings.

If the Moon is the cutting planet, everyday occurrences, family and domestic affairs, daily business activities, and daily contacts with the public provide the means through which the individual enters new experiences. Women may also play an important part in the new experiences. The individual tends to play a maternal guiding role in daily affairs. The individual's emotional reactions to these daily occurrences can set the stage for events that follow, as the other planets in the horoscope contact the same sensitive point that the Moon has just occupied.

If Mercury is the cutting planet, the individual's first contact with new conditions is made through communications and mental evaluation. The individual examines situations intellectually before becoming involved. Schooling, reading, and other intellectual pursuits will inaugurate new conditions in the individual's life. Brothers and sisters, neighbors, friends, those in the working environment, and those in the immediate environment also tend to introduce the individual to new conditions. The individual, too, is often drawn into new interests through curiosity.

If Venus is the cutting planet, these individuals become involved in new conditions through business, social, romantic, and artistic activities. A charming manner enables these people to enter into situations unavailable to those with less savoir faire. If Venus is afflicted, they must guard against allowing their emotions to get them into undesirable situations against their better judgment.

If Mars is the cutting planet, these individuals tend to enter into new situations because of their own desire, drive, and initiative. It is the desire for new experiences or for some form of personal gratification that propels them into these situations. They have the initiative and courage to tackle new ventures that open new avenues for self-expression. If Mars is afflicted, impulsiveness can get them involved in activities and circumstances that can become dangerous or undesirable.

If Jupiter is the cutting planet, these people enter into new experiences through educational, religious, philosophic, and cultural activities. A confident and optimistic attitude enables them to proceed with enthusiasm. If Jupiter is afflicted, unrealistic optimism can get them into trouble; they are apt to get involved with more than they can adequately handle. Often, past karma sets the stage for new expansive experiences.

If Saturn is the cutting planet, these individuals have a systematic, organized, disciplined approach to new endeavors. They are cautious about committing themselves until they have sized up a situation. If Saturn is afflicted, fear of some kind can stand in the way of opportunities for new expression and experience, or they may take on too much responsibility and find themselves overloaded with work.

If Uranus is the cutting planet, these people enter into new experiences through unexpected events and sudden occurrences. These are often brought about through the agency of friends, groups, organizations, corporate affairs, or the pursuit of personal goals and objectives. These new experiences may be related to scientific, occult, or humanitarian activities and endeavors. If Uranus is afflicted, a desire for freedom at any cost may involve them in circumstances that may be dangerous or detrimental to their wellbeing.

If Neptune is the cutting planet, these individuals enter into new experiences through intuitive feelings and hunches. Often, their initial actions are carried on secretly or behind the scenes. The new activities and experiences may involve educational, religious, medical, or philosophic institutions. If Neptune is afflicted, they can be confused or deceived in their involvement with these new conditions. As with Jupiter, karmic circumstances would involve them in these new experiences.

If Pluto is the cutting planet, these individuals tend to enter into new experiences through efforts at improving or regenerating the status of current conditions. They will have a great deal of courage and resourcefulness in dealing with new experiences. These experiences may involve corporate money, secret activities, or scientific or occult endeavors. If Pluto is afflicted, they may display a reckless, autocratic attitude in attempts to influence or remake others. These new experiences may also come about through efforts to remake or reconstruct old, discarded items or outmoded conditions.

If the Sun is the trailing planet, the individual concludes the cycles of experience through acts of creative self-expression, personal leadership, and a greater sense of self-confidence and will power.

If the Moon is the trailing planet, the individual concludes the cycles of experience with a changed sense of values about the seemingly unimportant daily activities of life.

If Mercury is the trailing planet, the individual concludes the cycles with a more logical and scientific understanding of what he or she has experienced, and greater knowledge with which to guide himself in life. He will be made aware of many avenues of communication and gaining knowledge.

If Venus is the trailing planet, the individual concludes the cycles with a greater understanding of human psychology and what is needed to achieve harmony in human relationships. This is accompanied by an improved sense of values and a greater appreciation of the beauties which life has to offer.

If Mars is the trailing planet, the individual concludes the cycles with a greater sense of self-reliance and self-confidence and is thus able to attain higher levels of business and professional achievement.

If Jupiter is the trailing planet, the individual ends the cycles with a greater philosophic understanding of the overall spiritual and evolutionary purpose of life and the need for generosity of spirit. The individual may also place a higher value on cultural, educational, and philosophic values.

If Saturn is the trailing planet, the individual concludes the cycles by achieving a greater awareness of the need for discipline and organization in achieving security and worthwhile accomplishments.

If Uranus is the trailing planet, the individual concludes the cycles with a greater understanding of universal laws and principles and of the need for spiritual detachment, which brings ultimate freedom and the possibility for realizing worthwhile goals and objectives.

If Neptune is the trailing planet, the individual concludes the cycles with a greater intuitive understanding of life's experiences as they relate to the overall spiritual, evolutionary unfoldment of both the individual and humanity. Thus, the individual can achieve a greater degree of compassion and universal understanding.

If Pluto is the trailing planet, the individual concludes the cycles with the awareness that death is a daily experience and is part of a rebirth to a higher level of creative expression, thus, learning to die and be reborn daily.

11 The Role of the Aspects

Aspect Predominance

When one type of aspect—conjunctions, sextiles, squares, trines, oppositions, or inconjuncts—is more in evidence than any other, the nature of that predominant aspect becomes a character trait.

For example, a predominance of conjunctions indicates a strong, self-aware, action-oriented individual. A predominance of sextiles indicates a friendly, communicative person with strong intellectual traits. A predominance of squares indicates an ambitious, career-oriented person who is faced with continual crisis situations in professional, political, and family affairs and with a series of obstacles to be surmounted. A predominance of trines indicates harmonious self-expression in creative, artistic pursuits and in educational, religious, and philosophical affairs, as well as an ease in constructive efforts to implement personal desires and ideas, particularly in the cultural context. A predominance of oppositions indicates a continual concern with relationships and with the resolution of interpersonal difficulties. A predominance of inconjuncts indicates a need for constant improvement and regeneration of existing conditions.

The basic significance of any type of aspect can be derived by relating it to the signs and houses of the natural Zodiac—that is, taking the number of degrees of the aspect and counting that distance both clockwise and counter-clockwise around the Zodiac from the natural First House or the sign Aries. The houses and signs of the natural Zodiac, determined by the above means, and their relationship to the natural First House and the sign Aries reveal the basic significance of any type of aspect.

The conjunction is related to Aries and the natural First House; therefore, it concerns the expression of self-awareness and power through action.

The sextile (60°), two signs away from Aries in the natural Zodiac and the natural First House, involves the natural Third House and Gemini on one side and Aquarius and the natural Eleventh House on the other side. Thus, the sextile aspect partakes of the intellectual nature of these two Air signs. There is a particularly strong Mercury influence with the sextile aspect, because Mercury rules Gemini, the Third House sign, and is exalted in Aquarius, the Eleventh House sign. The sextile is also influenced by Saturn and Uranus, co-rulers of Aquarius. It is concerned with communication and with ideas, especially the intuiting and organization of ideas. It is an aspect of opportunity because of the awareness of alternatives for life expression that it provides. If this awareness is utilized in a practical way, the opportunity can be fulfilled in terms of the goals and objectives indicated by the Eleventh House.

The square aspect (90°) is related to the signs Capricorn and Cancer and to the natural Tenth and Fourth houses. It indicates a need to overcome the negative habit tendencies of the past indicated by the Moon's rulership of Cancer. It also indicates a drive to achieve professional success and status. This can be accomplished by overcoming obstacles through discipline, organization, and hard work, as indicated by Saturn, ruler of Capricorn.

Mars, the exalted ruler of Capricorn, and Jupiter and Neptune, the exalted rulers of Cancer, are also factors in the influence exerted by the square aspect. Energy and action, represented by Mars, are required to achieve ambitions, represented by Capricorn. Psychological habit patterns based on past experience and family and cultural conditioning are important factors in the formation of psychological patterns, and these must be dealt with in order for the limitations of past conditioning to be overcome. Therefore, the square represents the uphill climb.

The trine aspect (120°) relates to the signs Leo and Sagittarius (which are, respectively, four signs counter-clockwise and clockwise from the starting point of Aries in the natural Zodiac). The trine aspect has the enthusiastic self-expressive, expansive qualities of the Sun, ruler of Leo, and of Jupiter and Neptune, co-rulers of Sagittarius. There is also a Pluto influence in the trine aspect, encouraging renewal and regeneration through its exaltation in Leo.

A trine does not always produce the beneficial effect inherent in it. It must be acted upon by exerting the will if a higher rung of expression or regeneration, represented by the Sun, Jupiter, Neptune, and Pluto, is to be achieved.

The opposition aspect (180°) corresponds to the sign Libra, to the natural Seventh House, and to the planet Venus, ruler of Libra. It is primarily an aspect of relationships. It indicates the positive qualities of companionship and complementary points of view. It has the reputation of being malefic. Saturn's exaltation in Libra indicates that discipline, justice, and fair play must be emphasized if relationships are to produce positive results. Once a degree of maturity has been developed, the Venusian qualities of love, beauty, and companionship become part of the expression of the opposition aspect. The opposition requires either cooperation or separation. The planets involved in the opposition represent opposing psychological drives which must be brought into harmony before balance and happiness can be achieved. Only through awareness of the need for balance and cooperation can justice be served and progress be made.

The inconjunct, a minor aspect of 150° allowed half the effective orb of a major aspect, is influenced by the qualities of Virgo, Scorpio, Mercury, Pluto, Uranus, and the natural Sixth and Eighth houses. These signs are five signs away from the starting point of Aries in the Natural Zodiac.

The inconjunct, through its relationship to Scorpio, often brings about the termination of old conditions in preparation for a new start. It demands constant improvement and regeneration of existing conditions. Through its relationship to Virgo, it is concerned with health, work, and detailed methodologies. Often, the inconjunct brings about a situation where one is stymied by circumstances beyond one's personal control.*

Aspect Configuration

Aspect configurations are aspect combinations involving three or more planets in a geometric pattern. There are several well-known types of aspect configurations, each of which has its own special interpretation based on the combination of aspects of which it is composed.

The Stellium or Multiple Conjunction

If three or more planets form an unbroken series of conjunctions, the affairs ruled by the house and sign positions of these planets will be a

* For a more thorough treatment of the inconjunct aspect, see *That Inconjunct Quincunx: The Not-So-Minor Aspect*, by Frances Sakoian and Louis S. Acker.

central focus of activity in the life of the individual. Strong will power, self-awareness, and impetus to action will be manifested in these affairs.

The Grand Trine

The grand trine occurs when three planets are placed an equal distance apart, approximately 120° from each other. Usually, these planets are found in the same Triplicity or Element, unless there is a hidden aspect, in which case there is a mixture of Elements.

The grand trine indicates a harmonious flow of energy and shows that the individual has karmically earned many special advantages. At times, the grand trine confers too much stability and leads to inertia and a lack of motivation to dynamic action. As a rule, if Mars or Saturn is included in the grand trine, this difficulty does not exist.

The grand trine strongly emphasizes the potential for creative self-expression and spiritual self-unfoldment that is characteristic of the trine aspect. The grand trine indicates talents, which are expressed through the Element or Elements in which the trine is found.

The set of houses in which the grand trine is found is highly influential. If the grand trine is found in houses corresponding to all of the signs of a particular Element in the natural Zodiac, then abilities associated with that Element are emphasized. For example, if a grand trine involves planets in the Second, Sixth, and Tenth houses, which correspond to the Earth Triplicity, the individual finds it easy to achieve monetary security, employment, and professional status. He is also adept at handling practical affairs.

The potential of the grand trine must be acted upon and used in creative self-expression and efforts toward spiritual self-improvement. Otherwise, it will lie dormant.

The T-Square

The T-square occurs when two planets oppose each other and both are squared by a third planet. The T-square has a strong Saturnian connotation because Saturn is not only exalted in Libra, which corresponds to the opposition aspect in the natural Zodiac, but also rules Capricorn, which corresponds to the square aspect in the natural Zodiac.

The T-square usually indicates the need to overcome obstacles, and a strong, driving ambition to do so, as indicated by its Saturnian nature.

The tension and awareness of the opposition must be resolved through the planet square the opposition. Marc Edmund Jones refers to this as the planet in "point focus." The point-focus planet is the nexus of powerful, directed activity. Because of its Saturnian connotation, this activity, whether constructive or destructive, is generally purposeful.

When the T-square's energy is directed by a mature individual, it often leads to significant accomplishment. The T-square is an impetus to success, and many famous people have it.

The Quadruplicity (Cardinal, Fixed, or Mutable) in which the T-square is found will be strongly emphasized, as will the set of houses (Angular, Succedent, or Cadent) in which it is found. If the T-square contains a hidden aspect, the strong Quadruplicity emphasis will be eased somewhat.

Should one of the planets be found in an Anaretic Degree, the 29th degree of a sign, the native will have to contend with acute crises, especially if one or more of the planets is in an Angular house or Cardinal sign.

Like the Cardinal signs, the T-square indicates immediate crisis situations, and this quality is greatly accentuated if the T-square is found in Cardinal signs and/or Angular houses.

The Grand Square or Grand Cross

The grand square configuration consists of four or more planets spread at intervals of approximately 90°. This configuration can best be visualized as two oppositions square to each other—it must contain at least two oppositions and four planets square to each other.

This configuration differs greatly from the T-square configuration; it diffuses energy, while the T-square focalizes it. This is because any one of the planets in a grand square can be considered a point focus—a focalized energy outlet demanding attention. Any attempt to resolve the problem associated with a single planet aggravates the problems associated with the other planets involved in the configuration. The individual is thus forced to hurry from one crisis situation to another, without being able to concentrate on any one situation long enough to really find a permanent solution. He or she finds himself in a continuous cycle of crises, working with each of the planets in the grand square, yet unable to fully resolve the problems and challenges represented by each. Should all of the planets of this configuration be found in one Quadruplicity (Cardinal, Fixed, or Mutable) or one set of houses (Angular, Succedent, or Cadent), the qualities and problems of that Quadruplicity or set will be dominant in the individual's life.

The best approach to handling this difficult configuration is to work with the planet having the greatest number of benefic aspects to planets not involved in the grand square. This enables the individual to redirect energy for easier flow.

If this configuration is found in Cardinal signs or Angular houses, it indicates a life of constant and continuous crisis situations. If it is found in Fixed signs or Succedent houses, the individual is constantly struggling to overcome stubborn, unyielding problems that obstruct the fulfillment of needs and goals. Individuals with this configuration often feel constantly thwarted in achieving their objectives. If this configuration is found in Mutable signs or Cadent houses, they tend to be nervous and mentally depressed; reminders of unpleasant past experiences can keep them in a constant state of agitation and unrest. It is essential to forget the past and deal with the present.

If the configuration is found in *both* Cardinal signs *and* Angular houses, Fixed signs *and* Succedent houses, or Mutable signs *and* Cadent houses, the characteristics described above are more strongly accentuated. However, if hidden aspects are involved in the above configuration, such tendencies will be less pronounced.

The Y-Configuration

The Y-configuration consists of two planets sextile to each other, both inconjunct a third planet. The Y-configuration brings about dramatic, irrevocable changes in the life of the individual. This is because the inconjunct aspect is related to the sign Scorpio, ruled by Mars and Pluto with Uranus as the exalted ruler, and to the sign Virgo, ruled by Mercury.

The sextile aspect contained in the Y-configuration is a Mercurial aspect. This is due to Mercury's rulership of the sign Gemini and its exaltation in the sign Aquarius, which corresponds to the sextile aspect in the natural Zodiac. The qualities of Saturn and Uranus, co-rulers of Aquarius, are also incorporated in the sextile. The sudden, dramatic changes brought about by the Y-configuration result from the qualities of Uranus, brought into play by Uranus's rulership of Aquarius and exaltation in Scorpio. These signs correspond, respectively, to the sextile and inconjunct aspects.

The Y-configuration demands intelligence (Mercury), originality (Uranus), and decisive action toward the improvement and regeneration of existing conditions. These requirements arise from circumstances beyond the individual's control. If the individual is successful in meeting the challenge posed by these circumstances, awareness and the circumstances of life are elevated to higher and more universal levels. This requires renouncing the past and entering into an entirely new phase of life experience. If a natal Y-configuration is activated by important transits, and if these transits are accompanied by progressions and other directions, major changes along these lines will occur in the individual's life.

If the missing Element or Elements of a Y-configuration are provided by transiting planets, unavoidable external circumstances may alter the course of the individual's destiny, for better or worse. Such occurrences are often related to large-scale changes affecting society as a whole.

The intellectual awareness generated by the sextile aspect in the Y-configuration alerts the individual to possibilities for action through the planet which forms the inconjuncts. At times, this produces a reaction in the sign, houses, and possible planetary placement opposite the planet forming the inconjuncts. Because of the Virgo influence of the inconjunct aspect, the Y-configuration also provides the opportunity for significant accomplishment through work that can produce results with far-reaching consequences.

If willing to work, the individual with this configuration can achieve positive results, rather than becoming a victim of circumstances.

The Double Sextile

The double sextile occurs when two planets are in trine aspect, with a third planet sextiling both. The intellectual energy of the planet making the double sextile to the trining planets provides the knowledge and awareness of how to release the creative, expansive energy of the trine aspect. If the individual is willing to put this creative awareness into action, worthwhile goals and objectives can be achieved. The energy in this configuration flows freely and easily, but only if the individual is willing to utilize it.

The Double Semi-Sextile

The double semi-sextile configuration involves two planets in sextile aspect, with a third planet between them that is semi-sextile to both. The two planets forming the sextile will be approximately 60° apart, with the third planet between at approximately 30° from each of the sextiling planets.

The intellectual nature of the sextile aspect is focused through the central planet making the double semi-sextile. It provides the individual with the understanding and the ability to communicate whatever is needed to utilize the central planet to amass resources and to make use of past experience to achieve goals and objectives.

The semi-sextile partakes of the nature of Pisces and the Twelfth House, which indicate past experience, and Taurus and the Second House, which indicate resources. Because Venus is exalted in Pisces and rules Taurus, the semi-sextile also has a Venusian connotation, which gives individuals with the double semi-sextile configuration the ability to attract wealth, social contacts, and romantic opportunities. Individuals with this configuration often have unusual artistic talent, business ability, and social refinement in communication. The strong Mercurial nature of the sextile, combined with the Venusian nature of the semi-sextile, can give literary ability, wit, and a refined and precise manner of communication.

This configuration provides the opportunity to realize goals of self-expression and the rewards and values connected with them. However, it demands that the individual systematically take advantage of every opportunity.

The Double Semi-Square

The double semi-square occurs when two planets are in square aspect to each other (90° apart) with a central planet between them that is semi-square (approximately 45°) to each of the planets involved in the square aspect.

The semi-square aspect is considered an aspect of irritation. It relates to the Eleventh and Second houses. Irritations are aroused through frustration in realizing goals and objectives. The obstacles presented by the square aspect are focused in the irritations and psychological stresses of the planet forming the semi-square aspects. The dissatisfaction which this configuration engenders can spur the individual to greater effort, or it can result in a sense of futility. In any event, the configuration represents a challenge worthy of anyone's mettle.

Approaching/Departing, Applying/Separating Aspect Analysis, Orb, and Upper/Lower Aspects

Approaching and Departing Aspects

All aspects, with the exception of the conjunction and opposition, relate to two signs and houses in the natural Zodiac. The positions of the planets forming the aspects determine which of the two signs in the natural Zodiac is accentuated when the aspect is interpreted.

A departing aspect occurs when a planet that is faster in motion is moving away from the conjunction with and toward the opposition with the slower-moving planet at the time of the formation of an aspect (other than the conjunction or opposition). Departing aspects always partake of the nature of one of the first six signs of the natural Zodiac—Aries, Taurus, Gemini, Cancer, Leo, or Virgo. They also partake of the nature of the First, Second, Third, Fourth, Fifth, or Sixth House. Departing aspects have a somewhat subjective, personal significance and are related to things which are of immediate personal concern to the individual.

If the planets are forming an aspect other than a conjunction or opposition, and are positioned in such a manner that the faster-moving planet is moving from the opposition with the slower-moving planet toward a conjunction with it, then the aspect is an approaching aspect. Approaching aspects relate to one of the last six signs of the natural Zodiac—Libra, Scorpio, Sagittarius, Capricorn, Aquarius, or Pisces. They also partake of the nature of the Seventh, Eighth, Ninth, Tenth, Eleventh, or Twelfth House. Approaching aspects always have an impersonal, objective significance beyond the scope of what is of immediate concern to the individual. They are more concerned with relationships than are departing aspects.

For example, if Saturn is in 5° of Aries and Mercury is in 5° of Leo, then we have a departing trine aspect, because Mercury is moving away from the conjunction to Saturn in Aries toward the opposition that would occur in 5° of Libra. This is called a Fifth House/Leo-Sun trine aspect. If Mercury were in 5° of Sagittarius and Saturn in 5° of Aries, then we would have an approaching trine aspect, with a Ninth House/Sagittarius-Jupiter significance (see Aspect Rulerships, page 82).

Planetary and Luminary Orbs

All aspects have an allowable tolerance of exactness, called the *orb* of the aspect. The orb is the permissible degree to which an aspect can vary from the exact number of degrees characteristic of that aspect. Major aspects—that is, conjunctions, sextiles, squares, trines, and oppositions—are allowed an orb of up to 6° in natal Astrology. If the Sun or Moon is involved in the aspect, an orb of 10° is allowed for major aspects, and if the planets are Angular, a slightly larger orb can be allowed, at the discretion of the astrologer/interpreter.

ASPECT RULERSHIPS

Type/Glyph	Phase	Sign (Glyph)	House	SIGNIFICANCE Planetary (Rulers/Exalted Rulers)
CONJUNCTION ☌	Approaching	ARIES (♈)	1st House	Mars (♂)–Pluto (♇)/Sun (☉)
	Departing	ARIES (♈)	1st House	Mars (♂)–Pluto (♇)/Sun (☉)
SEMI-SEXTILE ⚼	Approaching	PISCES (♓)	12th House	Neptune (♆)–Jupiter (♃)/Venus (♀)
	Departing	TAURUS (♉)	2nd House	Venus (♀)/Moon (☽)
SEXTILE ✶	Approaching	AQUARIUS (♒)	11th House	Uranus (♅)–Saturn (♄)/Mercury (☿)
	Departing	GEMINI (♊)	3rd House	Mercury (☿)
SQUARE □	Approaching	CAPRICORN (♑)	10th House	Saturn (♄)/Mars (♂)
	Departing	CANCER (♋)	4th House	Moon (☽)/Jupiter (♃)–Neptune (♆)
TRINE △	Approaching	SAGITTARIUS (♐)	9th House	Jupiter (♃)–Neptune (♆)
	Departing	LEO (♌)	5th House	Sun (☉)/Pluto (♇)
INCONJUNCT QUINCUNX ⚻	Approaching	SCORPIO (♏)	8th House	Pluto (♇)–Mars (♂)/Uranus (♅)
	Departing	VIRGO (♍)	6th House	Mercury (☿)
OPPOSITION ☍	Approaching	LIBRA (♎)	7th House	Venus (♀)/Saturn (♄)
	Departing	LIBRA (♎)	7th House	Venus (♀)/Saturn (♄)

Minor aspects—quintiles, biquintiles, deciles, septiles, etc.—are allowed a maximum orb of 2°. Intermediate aspects—such as the semi-sextile, semi-square, sesquiquadrate, and inconjunct aspects—can be allowed a 3° orb, or a 5° orb if the Sun or Moon is involved.

Major transiting or progressed aspects are allowed a 1° orb, unless the Sun or Moon is involved, in which case 2° can be allowed. Minor transiting or progress aspects are permitted a ½° orb.*

Applying and Separating Aspects

An aspect is applying when the faster-moving planet is closing in on the exact orb of the aspect to the slower-moving planet, and thus completing the exact aspect. When an aspect is applying, the trends or tendencies which it indicates are becoming more powerful. The aspect is moving toward its completion, building up to a decisive event or circumstance.

In a natal horoscope, applying natal aspects indicate karmic conditions which have not reached full fruition. In a horary chart, they indicate events that have not yet taken place. An applying transiting aspect signifies a condition which is increasing in power, building toward a decisive event or decision.

Retrograde motion, especially by the faster-moving planet involved in an aspect, must always be considered in determining whether an aspect is applying or separating.

A separating aspect occurs when the faster-moving planet is receding from exact orb of the aspect made to the slower-moving planet. A separating aspect is, generally, less important than an applying aspect because it represents a condition or influence on the decrease. The decisive event inherent in the aspect has already occurred, unless, in the course of a transit, the effects of retrograde motion cause the aspect to recur.

In a natal horoscope, a separating aspect signifies a condition that decreases in importance as the individual's life progresses. In a horary chart, it signifies an event that has already occurred. In a transiting aspect, provided it is the last contact of that transit, it indicates the diminishing of an event or condition.

Minor Aspects

Family groupings of minor aspects, such as the decile, quintile, tridecile, biquintile, and vigintile, are based on multiples of fractions of a circle.

* These are the orbs used by the authors and The New England School of Astrology.

The viginitile aspect (18°) is the only exception. However, it is one-half of one-tenth, or one-twentieth, of a circle. The decile aspect (36°) is one-tenth of a circle; the quintile aspect (72°) is two-tenths, or one-fifth, of a circle; the tridecile aspect (108°) is three-tenths of a circle; the biquintile aspect (144°) is four-tenths, or two-fifths, of a circle.

The angles of these minor aspects are the same angles found in the pentagram or five-pointed star, a symbol of humanity's will and mastery over the four elements. It represents the quintessence or refined synthesis of the elements, and people who have these aspects in their horoscopes possess special talents and unusual abilities that allow them to synthesize and combine many diverse situations in a purposeful way.

These angles are also found in the pentagonal dodecahedron and icosahedron, which contain and synthesize the tetrahedron, the cube, and the octahedron, which contain the major aspects of Astrology and form the geometric basis for the standing wave patterns behind all manifestation.

In delineating these minor aspects, an orb of not more than two degrees should be allowed, with the exception of a one-degree orb for the vigintile.

If the Sun or Moon is involved in one of these aspects, a four-degree orb is permissible. However, only two degrees should be allowed for vigintiles involving the Sun or Moon.

The vigintile aspect (18°) indicates a subtle self-refinement and utilization of past experience, based on the aspect's First and Twelfth House connotation.

The decile aspect (36°) deals with the expression of the will, and is related to the development of group resources. It confers special insight and intuitive ability. The individual is able to grasp ideas and relationships that are not readily apparent. The nature and scope of such perceptions will be dependent upon the planets forming the decile and the affairs which they rule in the horoscope. This aspect will enable the individual to relate seemingly isolated sets of information and combine them to achieve a definite purpose or result. This is because of the decile aspect's Second and Eleventh house connotation.

The quintile aspect (72°) relates to the Third and Tenth houses, and it indicates special talent in the utilization of ideas and communication to further career or professional goals. Like the decile aspect, it confers the ability to interrelate and combine many seemingly isolated sets of information that can help the individual to realize goals and objectives. It is an aspect of special talent or genius.

Inherent in both the decile and the quintile aspect is an excellent capacity for visualization and creative imaginative ability.

The tridecile aspect (108°) has many of the same qualities as the decile aspect. It relates to the Ninth and Fourth houses and, therefore, deals with the individual's cultural background and development. It has a strong Jupiter-Neptune nature because of the exaltation of these planets in Cancer and their co-rulership of Sagittarius. Thus it confers intuitive insight, imagination, prophetic ability, and a capacity to understand the subtle forces shaping cultural destiny.

The biquintile aspect (144°) has a Fifth and Eighth house connotation. Many of the same qualities accorded the quintile aspect are inherent in this aspect. It confers special insight into utilizing creative self-expression and improving existing conditions.

The semi-square and the sesquiquadrate are members of a group of aspects which includes two major aspects, the square and the opposition. The semi-square and sesqui-quadrate are allowed a three-degree planetary orb, which increases to five degrees if the Sun or Moon is involved.

The semi-square aspect (45°) relates to the Second House and the Eleventh House. It indicates frustrations and irritations in relation to possessions, earning ability, resources, and the pursuit of goals and objectives. A lack of resources, money, and wherewithal can make these individuals feel thwarted in their attempts to achieve goals and objectives. If a semi-square is exact, its influence will be stronger than a loose square or opposition.

The sesquiquadrate aspect (135°) relates to the Fifth and Eighth houses and indicates irritations, frustrations, and difficulties in child-rearing and in seeking creative self-expression, romantic fulfillment, and pleasure. The Eighth House connotation of this aspect can give rise to difficulties in business, joint finances, insurance, taxes, inheritances, and goods of the dead. There is also the danger of misuse or misapplication of sexual or occult practices.

The septile aspect (51$\frac{3}{7}$°) is allowed a planetary orb of one degree, or two degrees if the Sun or Moon is involved. The septile belongs to a family of aspects that includes multiples of one-seventh of a circle or fifty-one and three-sevenths degrees, such as 102$\frac{6}{7}$° or 154$\frac{2}{7}$°. These aspects have a subtle occult significance which introduces an element of randomness and unpredictability. The affairs ruled by planets linked by one of these aspects are subject to subtle, unexpected ramifications that tend to recur in a similar, but never identical, manner. These aspects also confer originality and intuitive ability. They can also bring important and irrevocable changes in the personal destiny.

The nonagon aspect (40°) is one-ninth of a circle. It belongs to a family of aspects that includes 80°, the trine (120°), and 160°. The nonagon aspect also has an occult significance, with strong harmonic implications. It confers the ability to understand the working relationship between affairs of a similar nature that exist on different planes or levels of manifestation.

Much research remains to be done on this aspect series. The nine-pointed star used in the teachings of Gurdjieff is based on this series of angles and would be a good source for investigation. This family of aspects contains far more significance than is apparent. A two-degree planetary orb should be used, expanding to three degrees in cases where the Sun or Moon is involved. We suspect that this series of angles is related to interdimensional transformations.

The semi-sextile aspect (30°) relates to the Twelfth and Second houses. It deals with the utilization of past experience and the accumulation of resources necessary for further growth and unfoldment. The semi-sextile confers artistic ability, because Venus is exalted in Pisces and rules Taurus. A three-degree orb is allowed for the semi-sextile aspect. If the Sun or Moon is involved, this orb can be increased to five degrees.

The inconjunct aspect (150°) relates to the Sixth and Eighth houses. It is concerned with the perfection of work procedures and methodologies, health, and the simultaneous termination of old conditions and creation of new ones. It is also related to corporate business affairs. Inconvenient situations that seem to be beyond the individual's personal control are often indicated by this aspect. Because of Uranus's exaltation in Scorpio, and Mercury's rulership of Virgo and its exaltation in Aquarius, these difficulties often arise from sudden, unexpected occurrences. Sudden changes can also come about through work or health-related situations. Patience, thoroughness, and attention to detail are needed to surmount and benefit from such situations.

12 Retrograde Planets

A planet is retrograde when it appears to be moving backward in the Zodiac, as seen from Earth. When a planet is retrograde in a horoscope, the affairs ruled by that planet are slowed down and the individual is more introspective concerning them. Because of this slowed motion, the individual is able to profit from all the fine details that would otherwise be missed. This introspection may not be obvious on a conscious level; however, deep psychological processes are at work.

Retrograde planets indicate that the individual will eventually become engaged in resolving unfinished business related to the retrograde planet, the house and sign in which it is found, the house(s) it rules, and the aspects made to it. This unfinished business represents unresolved or unfinished situations and unfulfilled objectives from previous lifetimes.

The affairs ruled by retrograde planets are often conducted in a behind-the-scenes manner until the planet resumes its forward motion by progression. Often, the experiences, tendencies, and affairs related to a retrograde planet remain in a latent state until the planet resumes its forward motion. Certain of the individual's abilities also lie temporarily dormant. When the planet moves forward by progression, these abilities and the past experiences related to the retrograde planet are recapitulated and expressed openly.

The Sun and Moon never experience retrograde motion. All of the other planets have retrograde periods from time to time.

About three times a year, Mercury turns retrograde, stationary, and direct again. These motions of Mercury have profound significance in terms of the flow of communication and the unfoldment of plans and ideas.

When Mercury is retrograde in the natal horoscope, these individuals tend to be slow and deliberate in their thinking processes and cautious in communications. They make decisions only after long deliberation, and are likely to continue to reconsider and revise decisions already made. These people appear to be slow learners during this period because of their subjective recapitulations of past experiences and ideas. However, through this process, deep insights are often gained. Conditions of work and health often undergo a process of revision and improvement.

There is a personal slowing down of communications, which is often accompanied by confusion, changes of plans, indecisiveness, and unexpected factors which make work and communication go awry. These can take the form of mail slowdowns, telephone breakdowns, transportation problems, misprints, late shipments in industry which result in production slowdowns, and so on. This is especially true in the electronics industry—where the unavailability of small parts can hold up a whole production line—because of Mercury's exaltation in Aquarius, ruled by Uranus, the ruler of electronics.

Illnesses, labor strikes, equipment breakdowns, and failures of negotiations can hold up progress during retrograde periods of Mercury. This is a poor period for signing contracts or launching new projects. Important decisions, signing contracts, or handling important negotiations should be held off until Mercury is direct and has passed the degree at which it went retrograde.

Retrograde Mercury will have a greater impact upon individuals ruled by this planet, or those engaged in such Mercurial professions as teaching, writing, lecturing, negotiating, communications media, medicine, or travel.

During Mercury's stationary periods, there is usually a mulling over of important decisions and a gestation of new plans and ideas. The results of this are not immediately apparent, and may not become so until Mercury has passed the position in the Zodiac in its forward motion at the degree which it went retrograde.

Should Mercury make an important aspect to a natal planet during its stationary period, that aspect will have profound significance in the future development of the individual's plans. This significance will not be immediately apparent, however, because the effects of the retrograde and stationary period of Mercury are not fully realized until Mercury returns to direct motion and reaches the position in the Zodiac at which its retrograde motion began.

During the retrograde and stationary period, the individual can go into an introspective state to draw knowledge and guidance from the deeper levels of consciousness. The retrograde and stationary periods of Mercury make it possible to carefully consider, at leisure, all of the possible ramifications of actions and decisions. During these periods, many factors can come to light which enable the individual to make wiser choices or decisions in the long run. Retrograde periods of Mercury can be utilized to take care of unfinished tasks and business affairs that were started while Mercury was direct in motion. The seemingly frustrating experience of retrograde and stationary periods of Mercury can be a blessing in disguise.

When Mercury is direct in motion, communication, travel, decisions, and business affairs proceed rapidly. The individual can proceed with confidence in planning new activities and endeavors.

Retrograde Venus in the natal horoscope often indicates emotional frustration and loneliness. The emotional, social, and romantic affairs of these individuals are subjective, and their feelings about them are not obvious to others. Retrograde Venus often makes them feel unloved and leads to romantic frustration. These people often have deep feelings of love, strong affections, and a need for social belonging which again is not readily apparent. Retrograde Venus also can cause a slowing down or restriction in financial affairs or in the acquisition of desired possessions. This situation will persist until Venus goes direct by progressed motion. Then, these submerged feelings will openly manifest themselves, and the individuals will enter into circumstances that will enable expression of them.

If Mars is retrograde in the natal horoscope, desires and impulses to action can be delayed or frustrated by inner uncertainties, a lack of opportunity, or unfavorable circumstances. These individuals are apt to be cautious and circumspect in taking action. They want to be certain of what they are going to do before committing themselves, and this trait can save them from unpleasant results of ill-considered, impulsive action. There may be a tendency to repress anger and other desires, often with negative psychological consequences. These emotional attitudes can be bottled up and have a disintegrating effect upon the attitude toward life. If retrograde Mars is handled properly, valuable lessons in organization, thoroughness, perseverance, and patience can be learned and they can realize constructive accomplishments. These individuals are more determined and, sometimes, more angry than appears on the surface.

If Jupiter is retrograde in the natal horoscope, these individuals tend to be introspective about educational, philosophic, cultural, and religious interests and activities. They often have a mystical approach to religion and philosophy. Their introspective nature tends to make them cautious about accepting current cultural and religious attitudes and standards. There can be an unusual degree of psychological involvement with the past conditions of the family and social upbringing. While this can give an in-depth understanding of the inner feelings of others, it indicates neurotic tendencies in family affairs if Jupiter is afflicted. These people will have stronger moral, religious, and cultural convictions than is apparent on the surface. Retrograde Jupiter enables them to gain understanding, wisdom, and depth through a careful review of the moral lessons of past experience.

Retrograde Saturn in the natal horoscope indicates that efforts toward status and professional prominence are based on past experience. Often, these people are resolving unfinished business or completing work that has been left undone or has never reached full fruition. Professional activities undergo constant refinements and revisions. The retrograde motion of Saturn often emphasizes the patience, caution, and conservatism normally associated with Saturn. They may be so concerned with old business that they could fail to act decisively when new opportunities arise.

If Uranus is retrograde in the natal horoscope, old unfinished business may come up for review suddenly and unexpectedly. Friends, group associations, and the direction of goals and objectives often have their roots in the past. Personal freedom is gained by revising behavior in the light of past experience.

If Neptune is retrograde in the natal horoscope, these individuals are introspective and inclined to evaluate and reflect upon their intuitive, emotional feelings. Deceptive or mysterious circumstances often cause a continuous revision and re-evaluation of psychological attitudes. Such tendencies can make these people even more sensitive to internal, intuitive perceptions. If Neptune is afflicted, idle dreaming can keep them out of touch with present reality.

If Pluto is retrograde in the natal horoscope, these individuals tend to act secretively and mysteriously. They will probably take an indirect approach to corporate affairs and matters related to insurance, taxes, and inheritance. Their efforts at self-improvement are not obvious, but, nonetheless, they are active below the surface.

When a planet that is retrograde in the natal horoscope is retrograde in its transiting motion, the individual is more involved in the affairs of that planet than would normally be the case.

If a retrograde planet stays retrograde throughout an individual's life, the affairs which it rules may be held in abeyance so that other evolutionary lessons can be learned during the present lifetime. The affairs ruled by the retrograde planet may be experienced second-hand by the individual through observing or watching others, rather than through direct personal involvement.

When a planet that is natally retrograde becomes stationary by progression, the individual openly expresses what has been assimilated in the introspective, retrograde phase of that planet.

When a planet that is retrograde at birth becomes stationary, and then becomes direct in motion by progression, the individual expresses what has been learned during the period of introspection indicated by the initial retrograde motion. This makes possible the active re-experiencing of lessons reviewed in the introspective phase.

When a planet that is retrograde at birth becomes stationary, goes direct, and reaches its initial retrograde position, the individual begins a new cycle of experience with regard to things ruled by that planet. This new experience begins when the progressed motion of the planet brings it to the position in the Zodiac at which it became retrograde.

A planet that is stationary at birth is a planet that is neither direct nor retrograde in Zodiacal motion as viewed from Earth. It is either changing from direct to retrograde motion, or from retrograde to direct motion.

There are two types of stationary planets. The first occurs when a planet that has been direct is about to turn retrograde. Movement in the affairs of life ruled by this planet slows down in preparation for an introspective phase of experience. The second occurs when a planet that has been retrograde is about to go direct. The individual, who has been in an introspective phase regarding the affairs ruled by this planet, is preparing to move out into new experience.

If a planet is stationary in a natal horoscope, its effects are felt in a constant and unchanging way, unlike those of a moving planet. A stationary planet focuses its energy in one spot and in one way and thus produces an indelible impression on the individual. Until this stationary planet becomes direct or retrograde by progression, the influence is stamped on the individual's consciousness.

13 Anaretic Degrees

If a planet is found in the final degree of any sign, that is from 29° to 30° of the sign, it is posited in an Anaretic Degree, commonly labelled a "Fate Degree." The matters influenced by a planet in this degree have reached a critical phase of development and must be dealt with.

The affairs ruled by a planet in an Anaretic Degree must be handled at the appointed times—when the planet is activated by major predictive factors, such as transits and eclipses. The individual will feel a sense of urgency when the planet is activated. Any attempt to ignore or delay dealing with the affairs indicated results in serious failure and frustration where they are concerned. To understand the details involved in these affairs, consider the sign and house position of the planet, the house or houses it rules, the sign and house of which it is the exalted ruler, the aspects made to it, and the planet which disposits it. When this planet is set off by major transits—that is, by Saturn, Uranus, Neptune, or Pluto—major events are brought into focus that teach important karmic lessons and make a deep impression upon the individual.

In considering the influences of a planet in an Anaretic Degree, the houses which the planet rules, its dispositing planet, and its decanate and duad should also be considered.

If the Sun is posited in an Anaretic Degree, these individuals have to deal with a major unfulfilled drive for self-expression each time the Sun is set off by Saturn or any of the outer planets. Jupiter is instrumental in this process, stimulating past memories and karmic conditions that must be dealt with if these people are to expand in self-expression. Jupiter and Saturn transits stir them to an awareness of the ego's demand for self-expression through the ambitions and through the practical circumstances of life which these planets activate. The outer planets—Uranus, Neptune, and Pluto—can subject these individuals to the effects of large-scale cultural changes that demand a creative effort on their part to bring about practical realization of what is required of them in the larger scheme of things.

The Moon posited in an Anaretic Degree indicates that the established emotional habit patterns and automatic responses require thorough revision and are periodically brought up for review. These individuals must be willing to surrender prejudiced and preconceived notions inherent in their family and cultural backgrounds, especially if the Moon is afflicted, if they are to make further progress in life, particularly in regard to business, family, and domestic affairs.

Major transits of Jupiter, Saturn, Uranus, Neptune, and Pluto bring about emotional crises that force this realization. Fundamental emotional prejudices and conditionings are often shaken to the roots and they enter a phase of more expanded awareness and growth. This process can be particularly painful for those with an afflicted Moon in a Fixed sign. Critical circumstances may arise through relationships with women or through interactions with family members. The type of situation experienced is determined by the sign and house positions of the Moon.

If Mercury is posited in an Anaretic Degree, important issues arise in relation to work, health, education, ideas, intellectual attitudes, and communications with friends and those in the immediate environment. These important issues often concern brothers, sisters, neighbors, and others with whom there is daily contact. These individuals can influence or be influenced by these people in significant ways. They are often faced with decisions of major consequence. Negotiation of legal documents and agreements should be taken seriously and handled with caution. In determining what decisions should be made, the sign and house position of Mercury and the natal and transiting aspects to it must be considered.

If Venus is posited in an Anaretic Degree, critical issues will arise in relation to sex, money, business partnerships, romantic relationships, marriage, and other close personal relationships. Handling these issues requires great psychological understanding and diplomacy. The house and sign placements of Venus and natal and transiting aspects should be considered.

If Mars is posited in an Anaretic Degree, these individuals' desires and impulses to action bring about critical events and circumstances of major consequence. Crisis situations that demand immediate and effective action often arise and can keep them in a continual state of emotional tension and upset. Precipitous action can have undesirable results. It is wise to exercise wisdom and moderation when Mars is placed in an Anaretic Degree. These individuals should learn to avoid all-or-nothing attitudes and extremist tendencies. Dangerous situations should be avoided when Mars is set off by adverse transits. Patience and deliberate action must be employed. Often, they are forced to understand and change the level of expression of their desires through realizing that these desires can lead to personal, even physical, danger.

If Mars is well aspected, these people have a strong strategic sense born out of experience, which enables them to be highly effective in their endeavors. The house and sign positions of Mars and natal and transiting aspects should all be considered in determining the wisest course of action and its probable outcome.

If Jupiter is posited in an Anaretic Degree, there is a strong sense of cultural awareness based on rich past experience. However, if Jupiter is afflicted, past conditioning may cause narrowmindedness or prejudice. These individuals may be faced with serious moral choices when Jupiter is set off by important transits. Critical situations arise, and a far-sighted and broad outlook must be adopted to achieve results beneficial to all concerned and to their own long-range well-being. These critical situations often relate to higher education, religion, philosophy, legal affairs, or cultural institutions. The house and sign positions of Jupiter and natal and transiting aspects to it will describe these situations and provide guidance in making the proper choices.

If Saturn is posited in an Anaretic Degree, critical situations can arise in the financial, professional, legal, political, and organizational affairs. When Saturn is activated by important transits, these individuals are usually required to handle serious and grave responsibilities, usually of a professional nature, or related to older people or to those in established positions of power and authority. Often, unfinished business or responsibilities that have not been properly handled in the past will demand attention. They must consolidate their positions and organize the affairs of their lives to achieve maximum security and stability. Practicality, organization, discipline, and common sense are demanded when important transits activate this placement of Saturn. The nature of these responsibilities can be determined by the sign and house positions of Saturn and the natal and transiting aspects made to Saturn.

If Uranus is posited in an Anaretic Degree, sudden and unexpected circumstances demanding immediate attention arise in the individual's life. It is necessary to adjust rapidly to changing circumstances and adopt new methods of coping with them. Often, these sudden changes are brought about by scientific, occult, corporate business and group, and organizational associations, and by friends. Because of Uranus's exaltation in Scorpio, the sudden death of people important to these individuals can drastically alter their lives. These events will come into focus when Uranus is set off by transits or other predictive phenomena. The nature of these events will be indicated by the natal sign and house positions of Uranus and natal and transiting aspects.

If Neptune is posited in an Anaretic Degree, psychological tendencies of the past will be forced into critical evaluation. If Neptune is afflicted and these individuals have neurotic or psychotic tendencies, crisis situations can arise. They must either deal with them or succumb to them completely. Private affairs and secrets in the past can be brought into the open when Neptune is activated by important transits. These people are forced to rely on intuitive faculties. Ultimately, they attain a spiritual level of guidance on which they can rely to sustain themselves. In this way, progress can be made toward the resolution of subtle and difficult problems. If they are lacking in spiritual awareness, they may be self-deceptive or lay themselves open to deception by others. The nature of the psychological tendencies expressed depends upon the sign and house positions of Neptune, as well as natal and transiting aspects made to Neptune.

If Pluto is posited in an Anaretic Degree, situations arise in the individual's life which demand regeneration and improvement. These individuals may be forced to assume a role of authority or leadership. Failure to handle these critical situations can result in undesirable and even drastic consequences. However, penetrating insights and profound realizations can arise from coping with such situations. They can refine the pure essence or value from these experiences and transform it into something of large-scale value. How this is accomplished depends upon the sign and house positions of Pluto, as well as natal and transiting aspects.

14 Singletons

A singleton is one planet isolated from the other planets in the horoscope. This particular planet stands alone in the hemisphere in which it is found—it is the only planet east or west of the Midheaven/Nadir axis, or the only planet above or below the horizon. (See Chapter 8 for a discussion of the significance of hemispheric placement.)

The singleton planet is a very significant factor in interpreting the natal horoscope. Because it stands alone, it acts as a focusing terminal in the hemisphere in which it is found. The affairs ruled by the house in which a singleton is found are subject to intensive activity characterized by the singleton planet.

If the Sun is a singleton in the Eastern Hemisphere, and the other nine planets are in the Western Hemisphere, the individual's life circumstances are molded by the influence of other people (as indicated by the nine western planets). The focus is on intense, individual self-awareness and will power. The individual struggles to maintain personal freedom and independence.

If the Sun is a singleton in the Western Hemisphere, the individual clings to an independent life style (as indicated by the nine eastern planets). There is an intense involvement in activities with other people and a tendency to associate with strong-minded individuals.

If the Sun is a singleton above the horizon, in the Southern Hemisphere, and the other nine planets are below the horizon (or Earth), the subjective, personal affairs of life, indicated by these nine planets, are expressed in intense personal leadership and exercise of will power in public affairs.

If the Sun is a singleton below the horizon, in the Northern Hemisphere, and the other nine planets are above the horizon, the individual's will power and dynamic creativity are expressed privately through the subjective, personal affairs of life.

If the Moon is a singleton in the Eastern Hemisphere, the individual has a strong involvement in the activities of others (as indicated by the nine Western planets). This involvement is expressed in an intense emotional awareness of personal family, domestic, and financial matters. A need for personal emotional and material security dictates the nature of the individual's involvement with others.

If the Moon is a singleton in the Western Hemisphere, with the other nine planets in the Eastern Hemisphere, the individual's concern with freedom and personal expression in the life style is directed and focused through a strong emotional dependence on others, especially family members and those who represent emotional and material security to the individual.

If the Moon is a singleton above the horizon or in the Southern Hemisphere of the chart, and the other nine planets are below the horizon or in the Northern Hemisphere, the individual's personal and subjective tendencies (indicated by the nine planets below the horizon) are expressed through an intense emotional involvement in public affairs, especially as these relate to financial and family security.

If the Moon is a singleton below the horizon or in the Northern Hemisphere, and the other nine planets are above the horizon or in the Southern Hemisphere, the public concerns of the individual (indicated by the nine planets in the Southern Hemisphere or above the horizon) are focused through intense emotional involvement in personal subjective issues related to emotional, family, and financial security.

If Mercury is a singleton in the Eastern Hemisphere, the individual's involvement in other people's lives and circumstances (indicated by the nine planets in the Western Hemisphere) is expressed in initiating communications and making decisions. Decision-making and the formulation of ideas are achieved independently of the opinions and dictates of others. The individual maintains an attitude of independence where the affairs of others are concerned.

If Mercury is a singleton in the Western Hemisphere, the individual's independence of action and life style (indicated by the nine planets in the Eastern Hemisphere) is conditioned by others' influence on ideas, decisions, and opinions. There is frequent communication with others that influences the individual's work, health, daily contacts, travels, ideas, and mental attitudes.

If Mercury is a singleton above the horizon, in the Southern Hemisphere, the individual has an objective and impersonal outlook on life and on subjective, personal affairs (indicated by the nine planets in the Northern Hemisphere).

If Mercury is a singleton below the horizon, in the Northern Hemisphere, the individual's point of view toward the objective, impersonal public affairs that affect the life (indicated by the nine planets in the Southern Hemisphere) is largely intellectual.

If Venus is a singleton in the Eastern Hemisphere, the placement of the other nine planets in the Western Hemisphere represents the individual's involvement in the circumstances of other people's lives and their activities. This involvement is focused in the individual's exercise of free will in choosing social, business, and romantic contacts and initiating social, business, and romantic activities. The individual knows that once involved with others, the activities will be circumscribed by their affairs. Hence, caution is used in making commitments.

If Venus is a singleton in the Western Hemisphere, the placement of the other nine planets in the Eastern Hemisphere represents the individual's freedom of choice and self-determinism. This singleton of Venus indicates that freedom of choice is focused and expressed through an emotional and psychological awareness of other people and the affairs of their lives. Because of this strong awareness, the individual expresses self-determinism (indicated by the nine planets in the Eastern Hemisphere) in seeking out and utilizing business, artistic, social, and romantic relationships.

If Venus is a singleton above the horizon, in the Southern Hemisphere, the placement of the other nine planets in the Northern Hemisphere indicates a concern with the private, personal affairs of life. However, these personal concerns are focused and expressed through an objective, impersonal awareness of the social, artistic, and romantic attitudes and activities of the larger social environment. Participation and cooperation in these activities will become a focus and provide an outlet for the private, individual concerns of the person's life.

If Venus is a singleton below the horizon, in the Northern Hemisphere, the objective, impersonal, public-oriented activities of the individual (indicated by the nine planets in the Southern Hemisphere) are expressed through personal concern with social, romantic, and artistic expression. This expression is the motivation for much of the person's public activity.

If Mars is a singleton in the Eastern Hemisphere, the individual seeks to balance dependence on the actions and circumstances of other people's lives (indicated by the nine planets in the Western Hemisphere) through aggressive, personal action. Individuals with this arrangement are apt to seek gratification of personal desires overtly and aggressively, primarily as a defense against the conditioning influence of the nine planets in the western sector of the natal chart. This will be true even if Mars is in a feminine-negative sign, in which case they will resort to more subtle activities in the aggressive pursuit of their desires. These people will always consider the rights of others and, at the same time, protect their own personal dignity and autonomy against unreasonable encroachment.

If Mars is a singleton in the Western Hemisphere, the individual's freedom of choice (indicated by the nine planets in the Eastern sector) is focused in aggressive efforts at involvement in the affairs of others. If Mars is afflicted, the individual should guard against such intrusion in the affairs of others and, instead, develop an awareness of their needs, feelings, and rights.

If Mars is a singleton in the Southern Hemisphere, personal interests (indicated by the nine planets in the Northern Hemisphere) are translated into aggressive action through public activity or public affairs (represented by Mars in the Southern Hemisphere) to achieve the desired results.

If Mars is a singleton in the Northern Hemisphere, these individuals express an impersonal view of public activities (represented by the nine planets above the horizon) by aggressively pursuing personal interests. They must be careful not to use public responsibilities and privileges as a means of merely satisfying personal desires and concerns. They should develop a sense of responsibility to the larger social order and adhere to strict moral principles to avoid public disgrace and unpopularity.

If Jupiter is a singleton in the Eastern Hemisphere, and the other nine planets are in the Western Hemisphere, then the personal cultural, ethical, religious, social, and educational beliefs of these individuals are of great importance in determining how they respond to the people around them. They accept or reject opportunities offered by others on the basis of personal principles.

If Jupiter is a singleton in the Western Hemisphere, the individual's drive for personal independence (indicated by the nine planets in the

Eastern Hemisphere) is conditioned by an acute awareness of cultural and moral issues.

If Jupiter is a singleton above the horizon, in the Southern Hemisphere, and the other nine planets are in the Northern Hemisphere, then the personal, subjective experiences associated with the nine planets below the horizon are expressed publicly as concern for educational, moral, religious, and cultural issues.

If Jupiter is a singleton in the Northern Hemisphere, then the public-related activities of these individuals (indicated by the nine planets above the horizon) affect them personally through their moral, educational, and cultural values.

If Saturn is a singleton in the Eastern Hemisphere, involvement in the lives and activities of others (indicated by the nine planets in the Western Hemisphere) is focused through strict adherence to a sense of ethics, justice, and personal responsibility. Because of their strong sense of responsibility, these individuals generally have a significant influence upon others. They remain true to their principles, even if it means unpopularity. However, there is danger of a calculated misuse of group involvement for personal advantage.

If Saturn is a singleton in the Western Hemisphere, the individual's self-determinism and freedom of choice (indicated by the nine planets in the Eastern sector) are expressed through a planned and purposeful involvement in the affairs of others. These affairs are usually professional, business, or legal. The individual has a strategic sense in dealing with others, and, often, associations are with older individuals or those in established positions of power and authority.

If Saturn is a singleton in the Southern Hemisphere, the individual's concern with the personal and private interests of life (indicated by the nine planets in the Northern Hemisphere) is focused through an acute awareness of the professional and political aspects of life (represented by Saturn's presence in the Southern Hemisphere). This is furthered by careful planning and manipulation of professional and public responsibilities.

If Saturn is a singleton in the Northern Hemisphere, the individual's concern with the impersonal public and professional affairs of life (indicated by the nine planets in the Southern sector) is focused through a strong ambition to achieve private, personal ends (indicated by Saturn's presence in the Northern Hemisphere).

If Uranus is a singleton in the Eastern Hemisphere, involvement in the lives and activities of others (indicated by the nine planets in the

Western sector) is paralleled by an intense need for personal freedom (indicated by Uranus in the Eastern Hemisphere). These individuals demand freedom of choice in the way they involve themselves with others, especially in personal friendships and group associations. Their approach to such involvement is often unusual, and includes many seemingly surprising accidents of "Fate."

If Uranus is a singleton in the Western Hemisphere, the individual's self-determinism and freedom of choice (indicated by the nine planets in the Eastern sector) will be expressed in sudden, unexpected or unusual involvement in the affairs of others (indicated by Uranus in the Western Hemisphere). This involvement is often related to corporate business, friends, groups, and organizations, and may lead the individual to be regarded as an eccentric.

If Uranus is a singleton in the Southern Hemisphere, and the other nine planets are in the Northern Hemisphere, these individuals express concern with private and personal activities through an open-minded, universal approach to large-scale impersonal issues. They show a high degree of freedom and originality in dealing with the impersonal, large-scale social, political, economic, and cultural issues that confront them.

If Uranus is a singleton in the Northern Hemisphere, involvement in impersonal public affairs (indicated by the nine planets in the Southern Hemisphere) is expressed through a unique approach to personal interests. These people will use unusual methods and choose unpredictable times to assert their rights to a private life. Often, this results in periodic rebellion against the stereotyped roles that they are expected to play in the outside world.

If Neptune is a singleton in the Eastern Hemisphere, involvement in the affairs and circumstances of other people's lives (indicated by the nine planets in the Western sector) is focused through an intense, subjective, intuitive awareness of personal preferences. When it comes to choosing a life style, these individuals insist upon exercising personal freedom of choice. This often takes the form of subtle, psychological rebellion against or evasion of control by others, especially in the inner, psychological life. Individuals with this arrangement often have a strong, but subtle, controlling influence on others. They should be honest and open about their real feelings and intentions; otherwise, they are likely to experience a conflict between a subjective desire for independence and outer servitude.

If Neptune is a singleton in the Western Hemisphere, freedom of choice and self-determinism (indicated by the nine planets in the Eastern sector) are focused and expressed through an intense psychic attunement to others and the circumstances of their lives. Although these individuals appear to be psychically independent, they can be easily influenced by conscious or subconscious telepathic influences emanating from those around them. Consequently, they should be careful in choosing their friends and associates. Often, these individuals are regarded as mysterious, uncanny, or just difficult to understand.

If Neptune is a singleton in the Southern Hemisphere, the individual's involvement with subjective, personal interests (indicated by the nine planets below the horizon) is focused through an intuitive awareness of the workings of the larger and more impersonal issues of life. This awareness can guide the individual in handling business, professional and organizational affairs. If Neptune is well aspected and well placed by sign and house, the individual may become known as a psychic healer or intuitive guide of some sort. Talent may be evident in art, music, photography, and the entertainment field. The individual's fortunes in life may be enriched by past experiences, or hindered by neurotic tendencies based on the past. Neptune as a singleton in this hemisphere induces an acute psychic awareness of the changes going on in the world. The individual's adaptation to these changes, however, depends upon the purity and clarity of intuitive responses, as indicated by the presence or absence of neurotic or psychotic tendencies.

If Neptune is a singleton in the Northern Hemisphere, the concern of these individuals with the larger issues of life (indicated by the nine planets in the Southern sector) is expressed through a subjective, intuitive, and personal response to them. The woes of the world will be a heavy burden on the personal psyche. They must strive to maintain a realistic attitude, evaluate their personal positions in the world, and determine what is needed to secure their survival, while making a practical contribution to the universal whole. Failure to achieve this results in a dissipation of time and opportunities with little to show for it. Thus, these individuals must be selective in choosing fields in which they can be effective in a practical way, for it is almost impossible to physically realize all that the imagination can conceive.

If Pluto is a singleton in the Eastern Hemisphere, involvement in the affairs of others (indicated by the nine planets in the Western sector) is focused through a desire to exercise authority in these affairs and improve or regenerate them. These people defend their personal freedoms, and may assume an aggressive role in wielding authority, primarily as a defense against being reduced to anonymity or circumscribed by others. In immature individuals, this will be manifested as rebellion against any control, good or bad. These individuals often exhibit great personal magnetism and charisma, which they use to defend their personal autonomy. Unfortunately, their tendency to throw their weight around can arouse resentment. It is just because this is a powerful pattern that they should seek to regulate the affairs of life by cooperating with the universal, impersonal principles of justice. If they can accomplish this, they can transform the conditions of their own lives, as well as the lives of others.

If Pluto is a singleton in the Western Hemisphere, freedom of choice and self-determination (indicated by the nine planets in the Eastern sector) are focused through relationships with powerful, dynamic people, and involvement in their activities. Effects upon these individuals can be destructive or regenerating, depending upon the motivations and type of activity of those with whom they are associating. Because of the far-reaching consequences of such associations, these people must carefully choose their associates.

If Pluto is a singleton in the Southern Hemisphere, involvement with personal, subjective interests (indicated by the nine planets in the Northern sector) is expressed through a desire to transform the outside, larger environment to suit personal desires and inclinations. Because the world is not changed in a day, these individuals often become revolutionaries or dissidents. On the positive side, if they are mature and purely motivated, they can have a meaningful impact on the world as reformers or initiators of constructive change. This pattern confers leadership potential. Often, these people feel in conflict with prevailing, established traditions and institutions.

If Pluto is a singleton in the Northern Hemisphere, the approach to the larger, impersonal issues of life (indicated by the nine planets in the Southern sector) is based on a desire to change existing conditions according to subjective feelings and insights. Intuitive impressions, impulses, and even compulsions, arise within the psyche and bring about far-reaching changes in the way these individuals conduct their public affairs. They often rebel against their inner worlds' being controlled or dominated by outer circumstances.

15 Planetary Cycles Through the Natal Horoscope

All transiting planets subject the individual to cycles of inner-subjective and outer-objective expression. These cycles are based on the motion of the transiting planets through the quadrants and hemispheres of the natal horoscope. When a planet moves from the Midheaven toward the Nadir on the eastern side of the chart, the affairs ruled by that planet gradually become more personal and subjective in scope once the Ascendant has been contacted.

When a transiting planet moving toward the Nadir reaches the natal First House cusp, individuals enter into a more private phase of their lives. They will use whatever is on hand to deal with the affairs ruled by that transiting planet: by the time the transiting planet contacts the natal Ascendant, they have gathered about them enough material to assimilate and enough work to absorb them until the planet hits the Nadir. Thus, while a planet is transiting this first quadrant, from the natal First House cusp to the natal Nadir, these people should fully utilize the things about them to further the affairs of that planet. This is not the time to seek public recognition, especially for the things related to that planet, but a time to establish the groundwork for a new cycle of activity. This is like a gestation period for a phase of expression that will later reach full maturity. The seed that was planted when the planet transited the natal First House cusp will break through ground into the sunlight when the planet transits the natal Nadir. It reaches its full maturity and flowering when it reaches the natal Midheaven. This mature stage will involve matters of a universal and impersonal nature. It is then that the experience makes its contribution to the greater whole.

When a transiting planet reaches the natal Nadir, individuals experience a period of personal struggle that can affect deep-seated attitudes and beliefs. From that point on, they emerge into increasing recognition; first in terms of their family, then in terms of social and romantic activities, then in terms of contacts made through work and service, and, finally, as the planet crosses the natal Descendant, they emerge into open mutual partnerships or cooperative efforts with others.

From that point on until the planet reaches the natal Midheaven, these individuals assume an increasingly public role with respect to the affairs ruled by that planet. If they have performed well, they reach a crest of recognition and status as the planet reaches the natal Midheaven or Tenth House cusp. From that point on, the fruits of these achievements will bear seeds in friendship, group associations, and accumulated experience which, in turn, give rise to a new cycle as the planet reaches the natal First House cusp.

The cycle described above is most commonly associated with the planet Saturn, whose ebb and flow (trough and crest, height and depth) of material status, fame, and political and professional achievements has such a significant impact on daily life.

It should be remembered that this cyclic trek can be applied to any of the planets with respect to the affairs ruled by that planet:

Cycles of the Sun moving through the natal horoscope indicate cyclic changes in creative self-expression with respect to art, social and romantic activity, personal authority, leadership, and physical vitality.

Cycles of the Moon moving through the natal horoscope indicate cyclic changes in everyday family, domestic, and financial affairs.

Cycles of Mercury moving through the natal horoscope indicate cyclic changes in communication, the exposure of personal ideas, work, and health.

Cycles of Venus moving through the natal horoscope indicate cyclic changes in financial affairs, art, music, and romantic and social activities.

Cycles of Mars moving through the natal horoscope indicate cyclic changes in personal desires, physical activities, business and professional activity.

Cycles of Jupiter moving through the natal horoscope indicate cyclic changes in cultural affairs, philosophical and religious beliefs, higher education, law, publishing, and cultural recognition.

Cycles of Saturn moving through the natal horoscope indicate cyclic changes in career, success, status, public recognition, political fortunes, and the achievement of material status and security.

Uranus takes 84 years, the average life span, to go around the Zodiac. Consequently, its cyclic changes cover a whole lifetime and are related to the spiritual motivations, goals and objectives of the incarnating spirit of the individual. Uranus's cycle is concerned with the contribution the incarnation makes to humanity as a whole, usually through friends and group goals and objectives.

Neptune takes the average life span to move through only half the houses of the natal horoscope. Hence, the cyclic changes associated with it concern spiritual unfoldment beyond the scope of a single incarnation.

Pluto moves through even less than half of the houses of a natal horoscope in an average lifetime. Hence, its cyclic changes are related to the development of the spiritual will and encompass more than one incarnation.

These cycles should be used to raise the individual to a higher rung on the spiral of evolutionary unfoldment. Each new cycle should yield increased experience and understanding of an innate ability and should eventually lead to mastery.

16 The Psychology of Sequential Experience by Planets of Earliest Through Latest Degrees

The planets of earliest and latest degrees in a natal horoscope have special significance. They make up a psychological fingerprint of personal response patterns to planetary stimuli. The order of the degrees of the planets is also important.

The planet of latest degree (also called the planet of highest degree) in a natal horoscope is especially significant because this is the last planet to be aspected by a transiting planet before it departs one sign and enters a new one. The transiting planet makes a conjunction, semi-sextile, sextile, square, trine, inconjunct, or opposition to that planet. These aspects are all even multiples of 30°, and thus represent the pure Zodiacal impact of each sign in relation to the natural Ascendant of 0° Aries. For example, the square aspect has a natural 0° Capricorn to 0° Aries and 0° Aries to 0° Cancer connotation (note here that 0° of any sign, by sign, decanate and duad, constitutes the purest expression of that sign in relationship to 0° of any other sign, where natural aspect connotations, 0° of Aries, are concerned).

Before the planet of latest degree receives a transit, the transiting planet aspects in sequence each of the other planets in the horoscope, in the order of their degrees. This establishes a cycle of unfoldment of the principle of each planet as it transits each sign.

The transiting of one sign by a planet corresponds to one set cycle of unfoldment. The sequential order in which the natal planets are aspected establishes an individual pattern of unfoldment or dharma. This pattern is further individualized by the sign and house positions of the natal planets as they are touched off, one by one, by the transiting planet.

The planet of latest degree is concerned with the conclusion or the termination of a particular cycle of experience, with the accumulated understanding and experience that has been brought about by a transiting planet after its contact with each of the natal planets.

By the same logic, the planet of earliest degree (also called the planet of lowest degree) reveals how the individual enters into a new cycle of unfoldment, associated with a transiting planet moving through the signs. The planet of earliest degree is concerned with the first impression that the individual makes on others, and that others make on the individual. The phase of experience that was begun by a transiting planet's contact to the planet of earliest degree will be concluded by and stamped with the quality of the planet of latest degree, and a new cycle of experience is then begun.

The house and sign positions of the planets of earliest and latest degrees strongly affect the attitudes and circumstances with which the individual begins and ends a cycle of experience. Also significant are the signs and houses ruled by the planets of earliest and latest degree, and those of which they are the exalted rulers.

Additional insight can be gained by examination of the decanate and duad placements of these planets, as well as the important aspects made to them.

For example, by applying astrological laws and procedures to Chart A,* Pluto and Uranus are in 29° of Gemini and Capricorn, respectively. Consequently, this individual ends cycles of experience through the large-scale social issues related to these planets. Pluto is posited in 29°59′ of Gemini, and Uranus, in 29°31′ of Capricorn. Hence, technically speaking, Pluto is the planet of latest degree. However, in terms of the allowable one-degree orb of a transiting aspect, both planets would play a part in the conclusion of cycles of experience. In this chart, Saturn is found in 3°40′ of Gemini; it is the planet of earliest degree and thus concerns the initiation of new cycles of experience (it is also the cutting planet).

In Chart B,† the planet of latest degree is Mercury at 25°25′ of Gemini, and the planet of earliest degree is Pluto at 0°50′ of Leo.

In Chart C, the planet of latest degree is Venus at 25°09′ of Leo, and the planet of earliest degree is the Moon at 0°15′ of Libra, though Uranus's placement at 0°34′ of Cancer, as in Chart A, lends some impact to any cyclical initiation.

* Refer to page 60.
† See page 62.

The complete pattern of this cycle of unfoldment needs to be studied because it establishes a basic sequential set of responses that are uniquely characteristic of the individual.

Individuals who are consciously working with their evolutionary development should endeavor to follow the sequential order in which their natal planets are contacted and seek to actively express the positive qualities of the planets contacted by the transiting planets. The decanates and duads of each of these planets, as well as the sign and house positions, should be considered in order to gain an understanding of the individual's characteristic response to the influences of each of these planets. Let us take Chart A as an example:

Chart A

The first planet to be aspected by a transiting planet is the planet of earliest or lowest degree—in this case, Saturn in 3°40' of Gemini. This indicates that the individual enters into a new cycle of experience with cautious structuring and planning. Because Saturn is in the natal Ninth House, the individual utilizes her religious, cultural, philosophic, and educational experience in evaluating new situations. She takes a cautious approach, with keen awareness of the work involved and the responsibilities entailed. Saturn's position in Gemini shows that the individual applies logic, communication, and practical mental organization to this evaluation. Cautious curiosity then would characterize this individual's involvement in a new cycle of experience. Saturn is in the first (Gemini-Mercury) decanate and second (Cancer-Moon) duad of Gemini, indicating an intellectual concern with how the new circumstances will affect home, family finances, and daily activities.

The next planet to be contacted is Venus in 9°57' of Scorpio in the natal Second House. Having analyzed the situation and established an overall plan through Saturn, the individual next seeks to involve others, as Venus indicates. Venus's position in Scorpio in the natal Second House suggests that this involvement may be related to business and joint finances, as represented by the Second House and Scorpio. The individual seeks to bring refinement, prosperity, and harmonious cooperation into the new set of circumstances. Venus is in the first (Scorpio-Pluto) decanate of Scorpio and the fourth (Aquarius-Uranus) duad of Scorpio. There is a triple Uranus influence because of Uranus's exaltation in the sign Scorpio, the Scorpio decanate, and its rulership in the Aquarius duad. Hence, occult influences and unexpected factors enter into the picture at this time. Because Venus disposits the Sun, Mercury, and Mars in

Libra, this phase of the developing situation is of vital importance to the individual's self-expression as a Libran.

The next planet to be contacted is Jupiter in 11°42′ of Sagittarius. The partnership and cooperation indicated by the previous planet, Venus, will be expressed on an expanded cultural scale. The individual now seeks to incorporate the elements of the new cycle of experience into the practical utilization of religious, educational, philosophic, cultural, and travel-oriented ideas and principles. Jupiter's position in the natal Third House in a creative, positive Fire sign indicates the expression of these ideas through lecturing, teaching, writing, publishing, and so on. Because Jupiter rules the natal Fourth House, the home is often used for these activities. Work and partnerships are also involved in these affairs, as indicated by Pisces' placement on the natal Sixth and Seventh house cusps and Cancer's interception in the natal Tenth House. (These cusps are included because of Jupiter's co-rulership of Pisces and its exaltation in Cancer.) Jupiter is in the second (Aries-Mars) decanate and fifth (Aries-Mars) duad of Sagittarius, indicating an air of authority and a crusader's zeal in the individual presentation of religious, philosophic, and educational ideals and values. Because the Sun is exalted in the Aries decanate and duad, where Jupiter is found, it has a natural Fire sign affinity for this placement of Jupiter. Jupiter in its own sign, combined with the double Sun influence of the Aries decanate and duad (through its exaltation) gives vitality and creative enthusiasm to the presentation.

The next planet to be contacted is the Sun in 14°44′ of Libra in the natal First House. The religious, philosophic, educational, and cultural activities developed through Jupiter become a means of creative self-expression. There is a natural carry-over from Jupiter (in this case) because the Sun is exalted in the Aries decanate and duad in which Jupiter is found and, thus, has a natural affinity for the Fire sign placement of Jupiter. The Sun is placed in the First House, which corresponds to Aries in the natural Zodiac and where the Sun is exalted. Hence, the cultural activities developed under Jupiter become a field of dynamic self-expression. The individual assumes a role of leadership among friends (the Sun is the ruler of the Eleventh House) in social activities and in groups and organizations. She exhibits social grace and personal charm, as indicated by the Sun's placement in Libra in the natal First House. The Sun's placement in the second (Aquarius-Uranus) decanate and sixth (Pisces-Neptune) duad of Libra indicates intuitive ability and originality in creative expression.

The next planet to be contacted is the Moon in 15°56′ of Virgo in the natal Twelfth House. This indicates service and emotional involvement with those in need of help, especially women. There is concern for the practical details that form the supportive background for creative self-expression. Because the Moon rules the natal Tenth House (where Cancer is intercepted), a great deal of professional activity and work goes on behind the scenes. The Moon is in the second (Capricorn-Saturn) decanate and seventh (Pisces-Neptune) duad of Virgo, indicating a sense of duty and responsibility in the profession, as well as toward others. The Moon is the dispositor of Neptune and is placed in the natal Twelfth House in the Pisces-Neptune duad of Virgo, reinforcing other contacts that indicate strong imaginative and intuitive abilities. The Moon square to Jupiter, co-ruler of the natural Twelfth House, further expands the idea of service along the lines of the individual's philosophic, cultural, and educational values. The Moon semi-sextile to the Sun in the natal First House shows that good works behind the scenes support the individual's self-expression.

The next planet contacted is Mercury in 17°50′ of Libra, dispositor of the Moon. Here, again, a natural carry-over indicates that the behind-the-scenes activities associated with the Moon are given further impetus through the individual's intellectual self-expression indicated by Mercury in the natal First House in an Air sign and conjunct the Sun. Because Mercury disposits Saturn in Gemini in the natal Ninth House, much of this intellectual activity involves serious philosophical teaching, lecturing, and publishing. Mercury's position in Libra, where Saturn is exalted, is linked with the Moon's position in the Capricorn-Saturn decanate of Virgo. Mercury is in the second (Aquarius-Uranus) decanate and eighth (Taurus-Venus) duad of Libra. Mercury's exaltation in the sign Aquarius gives it added strength in this decanate, and its position in the Taurus duad reinforces the Venusian influence in the individual's intellectual self-expression. Mercury is conjunct the Sun in an Air sign, which indicates that intellectual activity is fundamental to the individual's creative self-expression. Mercury's conjunction to Mars shows that the individual will defend her intellectual values and viewpoints. That she can be vehement when basic issues of justice are involved is indicated by Mercury conjunct both Mars and the Sun in Libra.

The next planet to be contacted is Mars in 23°29′ of Libra, which indicates that the ideas of Mercury are put into action through Mars in Libra, conjunct the natal Second House cusp, to achieve financial gain through cooperative enterprises. Because of the Taurus significance of the natural Second House, the individual's actions are directed toward lasting practical accomplishments. Mars is in the third (Gemini-Mercury) decanate and tenth (Cancer-Moon) duad of Libra. This indicates a carry-over from the previous contact of Mercury through this Mercury-ruled decanate of Libra and the loose conjunction of Mars and Mercury. The Cancer-Moon duad indicates that the individual may become emotionally upset by injustice in cooperative financial dealings. Mars forms a T-square, involving Neptune and Uranus. This indicates possible intrigues and dangers of deception involving financial issues. The ambitious, driving nature of the T-square and the action orientation of Mars makes the individual work hard to get ahead financially.

The next planet to be contacted is Neptune in 25°54′ of Cancer in the natal Tenth House. This indicates a psychic awareness of factors influencing professional dealings and the work involved in them. Neptune's square to Mars creates an awareness of political intrigues on whatever scale they occur; those may involve the individual's work and partnerships, because Neptune rules the natal Sixth and Seventh houses. Neptune is in the third (Pisces-Neptune) decanate and eleventh (Taurus-Venus) duad of Cancer. Venus rules Taurus and is exalted in Pisces, indicating an artistic imagination. Neptune, ruling the natal Seventh House, gives a strong intuitive insight into the motivations of others.

The next planet to be contacted is Uranus in 29°31′ of Capricorn in the natal Fourth House. This brings about sudden changes and unusual modes of creative self-expression that may affect domestic activity, financial investments, and groups and organizations. This is because Uranus rules the natal Fifth House, and Uranus is the decanate dispositor of the Sun. The individual's self-expression is stimulated by unusual ideas and by friends and group activities in the home. Uranus is the exalted ruler of the natal Third House, indicating sudden intuitive insights into both the potential and the outcome of any situation. The activities associated with this contact are related to the individual's profession through Uranus's inconjunct aspect to Pluto and the natal Midheaven. Uranus has almost exactly the same degree as Pluto, with an 18′ difference; hence, these planets tend to act concurrently. Uranus is in the third (Virgo-Mercury) decanate and twelfth (Sagittarius-Jupiter) duad of Capricorn; hence, the individual gains unusual insights by noticing small environmental changes that are indicative of the workings of large-scale cultural forces.

Technically speaking, Pluto is the planet of latest degree, at 29°59′ of Gemini in the natal Tenth House. The individual concludes a cycle with actions that have transforming and far-reaching consequences and that build her a reputation as an important person, especially in her profession. The ultimate aim of this individual's life's endeavors is to improve and transform existing political, business, and power structures and institutions. Pluto's placement in the third (Aquarius-Uranus) decanate and twelfth (Taurus-Venus) duad of Gemini indicates an unusual, original, and yet practical approach to improving existing conditions.

Because both Uranus and Pluto are in anaretic degrees, the consequences of this individual's endeavors are particularly intense, and simultaneously influence and are influenced by large-scale cultural changes. The involvement of Uranus and Pluto in an approaching (Eighth-House/Scorpio) inconjunct partile aspect to each other, and the fact that both relate to the sign Scorpio (through Pluto's rulership of Scorpio and Uranus's exaltation there) and to the house where Scorpio is found, is particularly important in determining how the cycle of experience is concluded. Scorpio is found here on the natal Third House cusp, indicating that the individual concludes a cycle of experience with penetrating, practical, intellectual analysis and observation. Because Pluto and Uranus are both linked to Venus (found in the natal Second House in Scorpio), cooperative financial affairs often play a part in this cyclic conclusion.

Let us now take the example of a specific transiting planet (or light) to demonstrate what can be drawn from the above analysis. Since the Moon is the fastest transiting body, we shall use it for this example. Because the Moon usually takes approximately two and one-half days to transit a sign, the psychology of the cyclic experience through the order of planetary degrees, from the earliest to the latest, can be easily recognized and followed. This sequence begins when the Moon enters any sign. We shall begin with Pisces.

Since 1°23' of Pisces is on the natal Sixth House cusp and 27°34' of Pisces is on the natal Seventh House cusp, most of this cycle, while the Moon is transiting Pisces, will occur in the natal Sixth House, though the conclusion will involve the natal Seventh House. In this chart, the Moon transiting Pisces will involve the individual in service and finally in cooperative partnerships.

Let us now follow the transiting Moon as it makes the sequential aspects from the planet of earliest degree through to the planet of latest degree and observe the pattern of psychological reactions that the individual will experience.

The first contact the Moon makes is an approaching square to Saturn, the natal planet of earliest degree. This indicates a phase of emotional letdown and depleted vitality that can affect the individual's health and emotional well-being. Hard tasks and practical work are demanded for handling business, educational, cultural, and domestic responsibilities. Because the natal Moon is in the natal Twelfth House in Virgo, the individual will wish for privacy in handling these matters but may not get it. However, an elevated Saturn in the sign of communication will militate against such privacy. There is a tendency to view this cycle of experience with a jaundiced eye. The individual is aware of the work it entails. Because Saturn represents the defense mechanism, the experiences of this cycle will appear too difficult or unpleasant to contemplate, and the individual may become emotionally indisposed or physically ill.

The Moon's next contact is a trine to Venus in Scorpio in the natal Second House. The individual seeks to enlist the aid of others in handling practical money-making responsibilities and cultural activities. This is done through an emotional (Venus is a Water sign) appeal. The individual points out the value and improvement potential of such work and the profit in mutual involvement. Because the aspect is a trine and the endeavors genuinely worthwhile, cooperation is usually forthcoming. Because this is a departing (Leo/Fifth-House) trine, this cooperation is creative and, to some extent, socially enjoyable.

The Moon's next contact is a departing square to Jupiter in Sagittarius in the natal Third House. The projects that arise out of this contact usually involve much more than initially was anticipated, even with the help of others. Unwanted communications, such as telephone calls and visits, interfere with work, as indicated by Jupiter's position in the natal Third House. Because Jupiter co-rules the natal Seventh House, the individual's associates may make untimely demands that may interfere with her work. Jupiter is the exalted ruler of Cancer, intercepted in the natal Tenth House. Thus, it is necessary for the individual to combine professional endeavors and domestic activities within manageable limits. The tendency to let one thing lead to another may expand a project to the point where it becomes too complicated to deal with. The individual should realistically evaluate her emotional sympathies to avoid being taken advantage of by unreasonable demands. Because the natal Moon is square natal Jupiter, misguided sympathy is another danger, and discipline must be exercised if it is to be avoided.

The Moon's next contact is an inconjunct aspect to the Sun in Libra in the natal First House. This indicates the possibility of frustration by petty annoyances that interfere with creative self-expression and work. Because this is a departing (Virgo/Sixth-House) inconjunct aspect, the individual may feel physically indisposed.

The next contact made by the Moon is its opposition to its own place in

Virgo in the natal Twelfth House. Emotional problems of women, or even of the public in general, may demand the individual's attention. It is important during this transit to take proper care of health and not overdo expenditures of energy. Petty environmental annoyances can distract the individual and make accomplishments difficult. Because the natal Moon is in Virgo, and the transiting Moon is in the natal Sixth House, details of work demand time and attention.

The next contact made by the Moon is an inconjunct to natal Mercury in Libra in the natal First House. This indicates that the individual tries to analyze the difficulties inherent in the situation. Because Mercury rules the natal Tenth, Twelfth, and First houses, professional affairs and subconscious and conscious personal reactions can play an important part in these difficulties. These hidden factors must be recognized and understood. Ideas often need revision in the light of practical experience, as indicated by Mercury's rulership of the natural Sixth House (in the natural Zodiac) and its dispositing the Moon in the natal horoscope.

The Moon's next contact is an inconjunct to Mars in Libra in the natal Second House. Lack of cooperation in handling material resources can annoy and irritate the individual. Because Mars rules the natal Eighth House, joint finances and business dealings with others may be affected. What the individual considers to be a lack of initiative on the part of others in handling practical affairs may also be an irritation.

The next contact made by the Moon is a trine to Neptune in Cancer in the natal Tenth House. This brings a strong intuitive awareness of the psychological factors involved in a situation. Neptune's rulership of the natal Sixth and Seventh houses indicates a strong intuitive awareness of the feelings, thoughts, and motives of others during this contact. This may also take the form of a prophetic awareness of what is coming next or an uncanny ability to know factors that are completely hidden to others. This awareness can be advantageous in furthering professional plans and purposes. It also enhances the individual's public appeal and reputation.

The next planet to be contacted by the Moon is Uranus in Capricorn in the natal Fourth House. The transiting Moon, which is now in the natal Seventh House, makes a sextile to natal Uranus. The individual now has the opportunity to employ unusual insights in developing close personal relationships and implementing ideas, creative self-expression, and matters that affect the home and family life, as indicated by Uranus in the natal Fourth House, exalted ruler of the natal Third House and ruler of the natal Fifth House.

The next and last contact made by the Moon before it leaves Pisces is a transiting square to Pluto in Gemini in the natal Tenth House. This indicates a final effort to improve and regenerate existing conditions. This improvement and regeneration extends to professional affairs, the expression of ideas, and the handling of close personal relationships and business partnerships. Large-scale factors beyond the individual's control can bring obstacles into her path. Since Pluto is in the anaretic 29th degree of Gemini, these circumstances are often preordained. Because Pluto is the most highly elevated planet and conjunct the natal Midheaven, this concluding set of circumstances may have important and far-reaching consequences for the individual's career and reputation. They make for a dramatic ending of the cycle. The individual is left with the feeling that there is much more to be accomplished, and in a better way.

The next cycle of experience begins with the Moon's entry into the sign Aries. The first contact is a sextile from the transiting Moon in the natal Seventh House to natal Saturn in the natal Ninth House. The Moon then makes an inconjunct to Venus, a trine to Jupiter, an opposition to the Sun, an inconjunct to its own place, and so on.

A Planet-by-Planet Interpretation

The Planet of Latest Degree

If the Sun is the planet of latest or highest degree, the individual finishes cycles of experience with an assertion of personal creative expression, authority, and leadership. When a transiting planet conjuncts the Sun, the individual concludes cycles of experience with direct, aggressive expression and a surge of creative self-expression and personal leadership, expressed through the affairs ruled by the sign and house in which the natal Sun is placed and colored by the natal signs and houses influenced by the planet transiting the Sun.

If the Moon is the planet of latest degree, the individual finishes cycles of experience with family, domestic, and business activities. He is left with strong subconscious, emotional impressions that could influence him for some time to come.

If Mercury is the planet of latest degree, the individual finishes cycles of experience with greater understanding of how to handle future cycles. The experiences associated with a cycle are looked upon as valuable lessons. The individual's rational and analytical approach to these experiences enables an understanding of their cause-and-effect relationships and insight into the significance of their details.

If Venus is the planet of latest degree, the individual finishes cycles of experience by seeking to achieve beauty in the surroundings and harmony in important relationships. Understanding the human psychology involved in recent experiences will be of particular concern. If all has gone well, the individual will have arrived at greater harmony and material prosperity, and will share this with others.

If Mars is the planet of latest degree, the individual finishes cycles of experience by taking dynamic action to end old conditions and make way for new ones. In some cases, if Mars is afflicted, this process may seem explosive or violent. In any event, the individual will end old cycles by preparing for the new in a dynamic and energetic way, often through physical action or business activities of some kind.

If Jupiter is the planet of latest degree, the individual finishes cycles of experience with a broad cultural, philosophic overview of what has been experienced. The moral, philosophic lessons of these experiences are sought. This process often involves cultural, religious, educational, or legal activities of some kind. As a result of this cycle, the individual may seek to make some kind of cultural contribution.

If Saturn is the planet of latest degree, the individual finishes cycles of experience with an effort to organize and structure the conditions associated with the cycle. Some business or career advancement or status will be sought in the process. These experiences will leave a practical and realistic sense of what it takes to be successful and fulfilled.

If Uranus is the planet of latest degree, the cycles of experience leave the individual with a desire for freedom from crystallized conditions. The experiences encountered can provide a universal and scientific understanding of life, along with a greater appreciation of universal laws. If the individual has utilized these experiences constructively, a greater degree of personal intuitive insight and freedom will be attained. The ending of the cycle often takes an unexpected turn, because of the "sudden" nature of Uranus's influence. The benefit received from this cycle will be in proportion to the purity of motivations.

If Neptune is the planet of latest degree, the individual finishes cycles of experience with introspection and meditation. Privacy and seclusion are usually sought for this purpose. Intuitive insights are gained into the meaning of these experiences, along with greater compassion and philosophic understanding.

If Pluto is the planet of latest degree, cycles of experience conclude with decisive and irrevocable events. They bring about the death of old conditions and prepare for new and improved circumstances. In winding up old cycles, the individual will have to deal with issues of profound and far-reaching consequences. A strong exercise of the will is usually required.

The Planet of Earliest Degree

The planet of earliest degree shows how the individual enters into a new cycle of experience as any transiting planet moves into a new sign, makes its first transiting aspect from that sign to the planet, and thus starts a new cycle of experience encompassing the principles of that planet and the sign it is transiting.

If the Sun is the planet of earliest degree, the individual begins new cycles of experience with a dynamic show of personal creative initiative and leadership. He or she exercises his will to get the new conditions under way. However, if the natal Sun receives stress aspects, self-centeredness and egotism may interfere with fulfillment of objectives. Because the planet of earliest degree has much to do with the impressions we make upon others, the individual should avoid egotistical attitudes that may alienate others. On the positive side, the individual's self-confidence can inspire confidence.

If the Moon is the planet of earliest degree, the individual begins new cycles of experience with seemingly inconsequential, everyday experiences. A receptive attitude gives an awareness of new opportunities. However, if the Moon receives stress aspects from other planets, emotional hypersensitivity may prevent the individual from taking advantage of those opportunities. Women, family, and domestic affairs often play an important part in these cycles. Emotional issues and business and financial affairs may motivate the experiences associated with the cycle.

If Mercury is the planet of earliest degree, the individual begins new cycles of experience with intellectual curiosity, communication, and the expression of ideas. New cycles of experience are entered into by means of information gained through newspapers or any type of communication, including short trips. New activities are begun by acquiring as much practical information as possible. These activities are usually related to brothers and sisters, neighbors, co-workers, the job, or the services the individual renders. If Mercury receives stress aspects from other planets, the individual may impair chances of success by scattering his attentions and getting involved in affairs which should not be of concern to him.

If Venus is the planet of earliest degree, the individual begins new cycles of experience with social activities, marriage, partnerships, and business affairs. Relationships with others play a key role in bringing about a new set of circumstances to be dealt with. These circumstances often involve close personal relationships or contact with the public in some way. Women often play an important role in opening up new possibilities for the individual. If Venus receives stress aspects from other planets, inertia or hedonistic tendencies may interfere with the individual's progress.

If Mars is the planet of earliest degree, the individual begins new cycles of experience through aggressive, dynamic personal initiative, often with an element of competition and struggle. Activities may involve physical exertion and professional and business activities. If Mars receives stress aspects from other planets, the individual may have a "me-first" attitude or a chip on the shoulder which can interfere with the attributes necessary to achieve success.

If Jupiter is the planet of earliest degree, the individual begins new cycles of experience with educational, religious, philosophic, cultural, or legal activities. These activities may arise through travel or contact with people in faraway places, and a broader cultural understanding gained from them can open up new possibilities for the individual. An optimistic attitude will inspire confidence in others and lead to support and cooperation for the individual's endeavors. If Jupiter receives stress aspects from other planets, unrealistic optimism, overexpansion, and moral hypocrisy can undermine success.

If Saturn is the planet of earliest degree, the individual begins new cycles of experience with a careful, organized appraisal of what is required to achieve success. The cycle's activities are often motivated by professional, political, or business ambitions, in addition to other long-range goals. The individual can start the cycle's activities with discipline and organization. If Saturn receives stress aspects from other planets, selfish ambition or negative attitudes and fears on the part of the individual or others could interfere with success.

If Uranus is the planet of earliest degree, the individual begins new cycles of experience through unexpected events, new friendships, and organizational associations. Intuitive guidance and unusual methods are often associated with new activities. If Uranus receives stress aspects from other planets, unexpected difficulties and lack of an organized approach could interfere with progress.

If Neptune is the planet of earliest degree, the individual begins new cycles of experience through intuitive guidance and behind-the-scenes activities. Use of past experience stored in the unconscious, plus creative imagination, often play an important part in determining the individual's approach. Karmic influences and other conditions from the past often are important factors in these cycles of experience. If Neptune receives stress aspects from other planets, confusion, deception, and distortions arising from the individual's unconscious mind can interfere with success and fulfillment.

If Pluto is the planet of earliest degree, the individual begins new cycles of experience with efforts to improve existing conditions and a dynamic expression of the will. Intuitive insights and scientific, occult or business interests may play a part in these cyclic experiences. The way in which the individual starts this cycle can have important and far-reaching consequences. If Pluto receives stress aspects from other planets, the individual could impair success through headstrong coercive tactics.

In Chart A, then, since Saturn is the planet of earliest degree, placed in Gemini in the natal Ninth House, the individual starts new cycles of experience through carefully thought-out and organized cultural and intellectual endeavors. Pluto is the planet of latest degree, placed in Gemini in the natal Tenth House, conjunct the natal Midheaven (Tenth House cusp), indicating that cycles of experience conclude with efforts to improve professional activity, and that the success or lack thereof has important and far-reaching consequences.

17 Planetary Ages

The normal human life span can be divided into seven periods from birth to old age and death. These correspond to the seven traditional planets of Astrology. The trans-Saturnian planets, Uranus, Neptune, and Pluto, are not included.

The First Age

The first four years of life are ruled by the Moon. The emphasis is on physical growth and development. During this period, the baby is under the care of parents. Hence, a strong emotional and psychological conditioning is established that later influences the individual's general emotional outlook and automatic habit responses. During this period, the individual must submit to the immediate physical environment and the care of those to whom he is entrusted.

The Second Age

The second period, from age five to fourteen, a span of ten years, comes under the rulership of Mercury. During this period, the individual learns basic practical skills and gains a fundamental education and practical knowledge of the physical environment. Skills of communication and rational understanding are developed.

The Third Age

The third period, from age fifteen to twenty-two, a span of eight years, is ruled by Venus. During this period, the sex organs develop and romantic issues become a major concern. Social activities and related emotional issues preoccupy people during this period of their lives.

The Fourth Age

The fourth period, from age twenty-two to forty-one, a span of nineteen years, is ruled by the Sun. Full maturity, vitality, and creativity are developed and expressed. Individual autonomy and authority is brought into play. Individuals assume a role of responsibility and leadership in their chosen fields. Because of the Sun's natural rulership of Leo and the Fifth House, this period is usually accompanied by the responsibilities of parenthood—it takes approximately nineteen years to raise a child.

The Fifth Age

The period from age forty-two to fifty-six, fifteen years, is ruled by Mars. During this period, people seek power, status, and authority. Material ambition reaches its highest peak. This is easily understood in terms of Mars's exaltation in Capricorn and rulership of Scorpio, a sign which has much to do with business affairs. The competitiveness of Aries is also in evidence.

The Sixth Age

The sixth age, from age fifty-seven to sixty-eight, a span of twelve years, is ruled by Jupiter. During this age, the status and security that they have achieved enables individuals to become philosophic and reflective. Social values and long-range cultural issues take on greater interest. The individuals' gains are often shared with the larger community through their support of cultural, educational, and religious institutions and activities.

The Seventh Age

The seventh age, from age sixty-eight until the end of life, is ruled by Saturn. During this period, the forces of crystallization set in, and ultimately result in death. The consequences of the kind of life the individual has lived are realized and fully experienced at this time, and a chapter in the pattern of karmic unfoldment is closed. Reputation and social standing have reached their final stage, and cannot be revoked.

The planets Uranus, Neptune, and Pluto deal with larger cycles of unfoldment, whose significance spans more than one incarnation.

Uranus, which is exalted in Scorpio, following Saturn, may be viewed as the means of final liberation from physical incarnation, which would automatically bring about a spiritual expansion of consciousness and a transition to a subtler dimension of existence.

Neptune represents the ongoing accumulation of karmic experience from lifetime to lifetime. Neptune rules the unconscious mind and the storehouse of the soul's memory. Therefore, it concerns the continuity of the subtler tendencies of character from one incarnation to the next. (Neptune is exalted in Cancer, the sign of birth.)

Pluto is concerned with the drive toward evolutionary perfection, which is the purpose of the spiritual entity in repetitive incarnation.

The significance of planetary ages should not be underestimated, especially when the planet ruling the planetary age which the individual is experiencing is retrograde or turns retrograde or direct by progression during the period of life corresponding to the planetary age ruled by that planet.*

* See Chapter 12.

18 Fixed Stars

Fixed stars can be a significant factor in horoscope and transit interpretation. The fixed stars are part of the constellations of the sidereal Zodiac and, as such, move forward in the tropical Zodiac at the rate of fifty seconds of arc per year. This forward motion is due to the precession of the equinoxes.

The vernal equinox, which is used as a reference for the beginning of the tropical Zodiac, moves backward through the sidereal Zodiac at the rate of fifty seconds of arc per year. This brings about the forward shifting of the fixed stars in the tropical Zodiac and must be taken into account when the position of a fixed star in the natal horoscope is being determined. Positions for the fixed stars are given in such books as *Science and the Key of Life,* by Alvidas, and *Astrology: Mundane and Spiritual,* by S. R. Parchment. The positions are given for a specific year, so they must be pressed forward, or backward, to the particular time for which the chart is constructed. If the birth occurs after the year given, fifty seconds of arc for each year of difference must be added to the fixed star positions as given for a particular year. If the birth occurs before the year given in the book, fifty seconds of arc must be subtracted for each year of difference.

Let us take the fixed star Aldebaran as an example. According to S. R. Parchment's *Astrology: Mundane and Spiritual,* the position of Aldebaran, as of 1927, was 8°46′ of Gemini. The elapsed time from 1927 to 1975 is 48 years; thus, to obtain the precession and correct the position of Aldebaran for 1975, simply multiply forty-eight years by fifty seconds of arc motion per year, then divide the result by sixty to convert it into minutes. This yields a motion of forty minutes. Add this forty minutes to 8°46′ of Gemini to obtain 9°26′ of Gemini, which is the position of Aldebaran for 1975.

The fixed stars are especially important if they are conjunct or opposing a natal planet or Angular house cusp. For this factor to be a significant influence in interpretation, the orb of aspect should be less than two degrees, and the fixed star making the aspect should be a first- or second-magnitude star.

Magnitudes are a scale for the measurement of the brightness of stars. The twenty brightest stars in the heavens belong to the first magnitude; second- and third-magnitude stars are not as bright, though they are easily visible. Fourth- and fifth-magnitude stars are less visible, and sixth-magnitude stars can barely be seen by an unaided eye, even under the best conditions.

In traditional astrological texts, the influence of a particular fixed star is generally classified by ascribing it to the nature of one or two planets. For example, Sirius is presently at 13° of Cancer and is ascribed the combined nature of Mars and Jupiter. Most of these rulerships have been handed down from medieval times and modern research and investigation may be needed for greater, and possibly more accurate, insight into their true meaning.

The celestial latitudes of fixed stars can vary considerably from the ecliptic, due to the fact that they do not belong to our solar system. It may be necessary to use spherical trigonometry or more advanced mathematical techniques to accurately determine aspects to these fixed stars. This is a virgin field for research by a mathematically inclined astrologer.

When spherical trigonometry is used to formulate aspects between planets and fixed stars, the significance of these fixed stars may turn out to have more importance than we realize. This is especially true if the nature of the fixed star corresponds to the nature of the planet it contacts.

For the average astrologer, it is useful to note exact conjunctions and oppositions to fixed stars. In general, they tend to act as step-up transformers or higher-octave influences on the planet that contacts them. For instance, if Venus conjuncts Sirius, her influence could exhibit higher intuition akin to Neptune.

PART II

INTERPRETING TRANSITS

19 Transits of the Sun

Transit Sun Through the Houses

Transiting Sun Through the Natal First House

Increased vitality and greater self-confidence and will power characterize the Sun's transit through the natal First House.

There is an increased drive to achieve personal significance and authority. Ambition, positive and dramatic modes of self-expression and personal leadership are usually associated with this drive.

Transiting Sun Through the Natal Second House

An increased determination to acquire wealth and achieve material status characterizes this transit. Individuals with this transit tend to assume leadership roles in business and financial affairs. They are likely to become interested in the stock market and in financial speculation.

Money is used to enhance personal status and social distinction. The individual tends to spend on romance and social activities during this period. Funds are also used for children and their education and for entertainment or artistic expression, and the individual can become involved in business matters related to these things.

Transiting Sun Through the Natal Third House

Pride in one's own ideas, and an assertion of personal authority in speech, writing, and communication characterize this transit. The individual may experience a psychological need to be an intellectual authority in some field.

Ideas and communications during this period involve romance, social activity, artistic self-expression, children and their education, or financial speculation.

Social activities and communications with brothers, sisters, neighbors, and friends are likely to be intensified during this transit. Much short-distance traveling is also likely, especially for pleasure.

Transiting Sun Through the Natal Fourth House

Personal initiative and leadership in domestic and family affairs characterize this transit. Domestic activity is dynamic and likely to involve romance, social activity, artistic self-expression, and children.

The individual takes an active approach to understanding and dealing with deep-seated emotional attitudes and habit patterns.

Transiting Sun Through the Natal Fifth House

Romantic, artistic, and social expression all characterize this transit. Educational activities are likely to be pleasurable. Social contacts are frequently made with people of power and importance. The individual's activities involve games, sports, and entertainment. This transit is also a sexual stimulus and often brings about sexual encounters. Pregnancy or childbirth is a real possibility at this time for the individual, or for someone with whom he or she is dealing, as is responsibility for the personal supervision of children and for their education.

Transiting Sun Through the Natal Sixth House

This transit triggers the expression of personal authority in the individuals' own work or in their supervision of the work of others. They are likely to enjoy their work and may receive promotion or recognition of some kind if this transit is combined with other favorable astrological indications. Work is often a means of creative self-expression and provides social or romantic opportunities. Many individuals become involved in work related to art, music, and entertainment.

They may have to deal with the health of children or be involved with helping children in some way. They are likely to become interested in health and dietary regimes to improve personal attractiveness, and in dramatic clothing and personal adornment. They enjoy good recuperative powers and resistance to disease.

Transiting Sun Through the Natal Seventh House

Involvement with dynamic authoritative individuals characterizes this transit. Partnerships and close personal relationships become a means of creative self-expression. There is a desire to be noticed and appreciated by others.

Public relations, legal activities, and possibly promotional or political affairs tend to occupy these individuals' attention. A sense of competition often arises in important relationships. If reinforced by other similar indications in the horoscope, this transit indicates a marriage opportunity.

Transiting Sun Through the Natal Eighth House

Dynamic personal involvement in business, joint finances, corporate affairs, and financial speculations characterizes this transit. Individuals with this transit will probably have to deal with taxes, insurance, inheritance, alimony, and joint finances. They are likely to become involved in making financial provisions for children and their education or in business activities related to art, music, or entertainment.

Often, the individual takes a personal interest in the occult and the study of reincarnation and life after death.

There is likely to be increased resourcefulness in recycling waste products or in finding new uses for discarded items. An increased sex drive or sexual involvement is also likely at this time.

Transiting Sun Through the Natal Ninth House

Positive self-expression and an increased interest in the areas of higher education, religion, and philosophy characterize this transit. The individual will probably take part in cultural, educational, religious, or philosophic activities. In general, there is a desire to be a cultural authority in some field. This is a favorable time to apply for admission to a university or have dealings with educational, religious, or cultural authority figures. An interest in foreigners, foreign countries and their cultures may develop at this time. The individual may embark on a journey for educational or religious purposes or simply take time off for pleasure.

Transiting Sun Through the Natal Tenth House

The increased professional ambition and desire for worldly status, power, and authority that characterize this transit tend to bring about involvement in business speculation, politics, or social activities related to professional affairs. Romantic or social opportunities often arise through the individual's profession. Professional concern with children, art, music, or entertainment is also likely. This is a good period for dealing with one's boss or with other authority figures. This transit brings personal fame or recognition if it is combined with other similar indications in the horoscope.

Transiting Sun Through the Natal Eleventh House

Positive self-expression in scientific, humanitarian, or occult group or organizational activities characterizes this transit. The individual may assume a role of personal leadership in these affairs. Friendships with dynamic or important people are frequently established at this time. Friendships and group activities can involve powerful or important people, children, or romantic partners. The individual is apt to gain a more universal outlook on life during this transit.

Transiting Sun Through the Natal Twelfth House

Intuitive inspiration in art and music and an appreciation for beauty characterize this transit. Many individuals become interested in the intuitive and mystical side of life.

Leadership tends to be behind the scenes during this transit. In some cases, personal activities, too, are carried on in secret or behind the scenes —love affairs or private pleasurable pursuits. If the individual's clandestine activities involve drinking or drug abuse, they can have an undermining effect. Gambling and speculation may also bring about the individual's undoing.

During this transit, the individual is apt to be very sympathetic to the emotional needs of children.

Transit Sun Conjunctions

Transiting Sun Conjunct the Natal Sun

This transit occurs on or close to the birthday of the individual. The festive activity associated with this occasion is associated with the Sun's rulership of the Fifth House and Leo—the Fifth House deals with social activities and pleasurable pursuits. This transit sets the cyclic pattern for the ensuing year. A chart erected for the exact conjunction of the transiting Sun to the natal Sun—called a solar return—is sometimes used by astrologers for predictive purposes, as it sets the tone for the period between one birthday and the next. This birthday transit is especially important for children because they come under the domain of the Sun, Leo, and the Fifth House.

Transiting Sun conjunct the natal Sun indicates enjoyment of educational, social, and romantic activities. Dealing with children is usually a source of pleasure for the individual.

In general, the individual is happy and optimistic. Increased vitality, self-confidence, and personal leadership are evident. This is a favorable time for beginning new enterprises and personal endeavors and for approaching those in positions of power and authority. However, if this conjunction is afflicted natally or by other transiting planets, pride and egotism can be displayed.

Transiting Sun Conjunct the Natal Moon

This transit indicates increased personal initiative in family and domestic affairs. It brings dynamic business, social, and domestic interaction, especially with members of the opposite sex. It is a good period for family gatherings and social activities in the home and for improving the domestic environment by making it more artistic and beautiful. Concerns related to children are apt to surface at this time. Women desiring pregnancy will find this period favorable for conception. Greater emotional self-expression is evident during this transit.

Business activities related to the home, real estate, farming, domestic products and services, toys, and speculative financial investments will be triggered.

When the transiting Moon conjuncts the natal Sun, the significance is much the same. However, the duration of the influence is much shorter; it lasts only a few hours, whereas the transiting Sun is conjunct with the natal Moon for approximately four days.

Transiting Sun Conjunct Natal Mercury

Individuals with this transit experience increased self-confidence and assertiveness in the expression of their personal ideas. Their intellectual interests are stimulated. They take a special interest in games, such as chess, that involve mental skill.

There are increased communications with children and with romantic partners, and social contacts, in general, are increased. There is frequently an active involvement with the education of children. Social and romantic activity often leads to short trips.

This transit indicates dynamic communication with brothers, sisters, neighbors, and co-workers. It is a favorable period for communicating with those in power or authority. It provides inspiration for writers, teachers, lecturers, scientists, and those whose work requires a creative intellectual acuteness. It is favorable for the purchase of dramatic clothing. Increased interest in dietary regimens is likely.

If other planets make adverse aspects to this conjunction, ego identification with one's personal viewpoints can distort one's perception of truth.

When transiting Mercury conjuncts the natal Sun, the effects are the same, but of shorter duration, unless Mercury is stationary or retrograde. New perceptions or communications will spark the activities mentioned above.

Transiting Sun Conjunct Natal Venus

Personal involvement in social, artistic, and romantic activity characterizes this transit. There is a happier, friendlier, and more optimistic outlook and a greater desire to cooperate with and to please others. It is a good period for planning or taking part in social activities or gatherings and for approaching those in positions of power and authority. The individual may be especially kind and considerate toward children and vice versa. It is an excellent period for all types of artistic self-expression and for business activities related to art, music, entertainment, and luxury items.

If this conjunction is adversely aspected by other transits, extravagance and dissipation in pursuit of pleasure, as well as narcissism, can develop.

Transiting Venus conjunct the natal Sun produces the same effects; however, its influence may be activated by other people, especially by women, rather than by one's own actions.

Transiting Sun Conjunct Natal Mars

This transit is characterized by dynamic self-assertion in action, often of a physical nature. The individual is likely to become involved in sports, physical activities with children, and competitive games. The sex drive is stimulated, and this often results in aggressive pursuit of romance.

Competition for power and supremacy in some important area of the individual's life is manifested under this transit. Ambition and initiative are likely to be expressed in business and professional affairs. Self-confidence, aggressive self-assertion, desire for power and authority, and greater will power result from the increased personal energy this transit indicates. Decisive actions of some kind are often precipitated by this transit, but danger can result from rash impulsive action.

If the conjunction is adversely aspected natally or by other transits, impatience, anger, overly aggressive behavior, and lack of consideration for the rights of others can cause problems. Aggressive sexual behavior may also be a source of problems.

Transiting Mars conjunct the natal Sun has the same significance as the transiting Sun conjunct natal Mars, although the former last somewhat longer.

Transiting Sun Conjunct Natal Jupiter

Greater personal optimism and a generous benevolent attitude both toward and from others characterize this transit. Individuals with this transit are usually inclined to help those less fortunate than themselves. There is a genuine interest in the well-being and happiness of others, which brings good fortune.

Personal interest or leadership in educational, cultural, religious, or philosophic pursuits also comes into the foreground. This is an excellent time to approach those in positions of power and authority. It is also favorable for seeking admittance to a college or university or for undertaking any kind of postgraduate studies. This is a favorable time for dealing with legal, educational, cultural, or religious organizations or activities.

Reasonable financial investments and speculation, romance and social activities, artistic pursuits, and other creative endeavors are also favored. The individual may use art as a means of conveying religious, educational, or philosophical ideas.

This is a favorable time for dealing with children and their spiritual guidance and education. Pregnancies or childbirth are often associated with this transit. During this period, women find it easier to get along with and benefit from associations with men.

Commerce and long-distance business transactions are also favored. Long-distance travel can be especially pleasurable, educational, and profitable during this transit.

The individual is apt to put on weight during this period.

If the conjunction is adversely aspected natally or by other transits, the individual is apt to take too much for granted or to entertain inflated notions of his or her own importance.

The effects of transiting Jupiter conjunct the natal Sun are the same as those of transiting Sun conjunct natal Jupiter, but of much longer duration. Transiting Jupiter conjunct the natal Sun marks an important period of positive personal growth and expansion. It occurs once every twelve years, whereas the transiting Sun conjunct natal Jupiter occurs yearly.

Transiting Sun Conjunct Natal Saturn

During this transit, professional and political ambitions are stimulated; the individual feels an increased personal responsibility toward business, professional, legal, and political affairs, and an increased capacity for self-discipline, organization, and career advancement. There is an increased concern with the serious long-range responsibilities of life. This transit often brings honor and recognition for work well done.

However, lowered vitality, burdensome responsibilities, and difficulties in dealing with government agencies or with those in positions of power and authority can also accompany this transit. Egotistical or dogmatic attitudes may show themselves in the individual's behavior if this conjunction is afflicted.

This transit tends to make one cautious, reserved, and prone to self-doubt. Creative self-expression can be frustrated if this conjunction is adversely aspected. Professional responsibilities can interfere with social or romantic enjoyment. These responsibilities are likely to involve older or established individuals. Social or romantic involvement with such individuals is also a possibility. Children may also become a heavy responsibility during this transit.

If the natal horoscope shows business ability, this transit could indicate shrewdness in business dealings. If it is afflicted, however, this is not a favorable time for financial speculation.

The individual's strength, patience, and endurance will be tested during this transit. Whether frustrations to personal ambitions discourage the individual or increase his or her resolve depends on the natal horoscope.

Transiting Saturn conjunct the natal Sun has the same significance as the transiting Sun conjunct natal Saturn. However, it is of longer duration and much more significant to the individual's development. Transiting Saturn conjunct the natal Sun occurs once in twenty-nine years and marks a major milestone in the development of individual maturity. It also brings about whatever a person has merited through past work and actions—

whether the result is favorable or not, a valuable lesson is to be learned through the experiences this transit brings.

Transiting Sun Conjunct Natal Uranus

An impulse toward personal freedom and independence characterizes this transit. The individual exhibits increased personal magnetism, sparkle, and originality. Unexpected social and romantic involvements often occur. Friendships may develop with unusual people, particularly those involved in science or the occult. The individual may assume a role of personal leadership among friends and in organizations. Sudden opportunities for realization of personal goals and objectives arise as the will power and personal capacity for leadership are energized. Friends can be instrumental in the realization of one's goals and objectives.

There is a desire for exciting new experiences and a boredom with humdrum routines. There can be a desire for freedom without responsibility if this conjunction receives adverse contacts from other transiting planets or is afflicted in the natal chart.

This is a favorable period for involvement in science, engineering, and corporate enterprises. Progressive or unusual educational methods for children may capture the individual's interest.

There is usually an expanded level of consciousness during this transit. Interest in astrology, reincarnation, parapsychology, and occult subjects may emerge or grow. Sometimes, there are unusual occult or intuitive experiences. Intuitive inspiration in art and in other creative expressions becomes evident.

Erratic heart action often occurs, even though it cannot be detected on a cardiogram.

Transiting Uranus conjuncts the natal Sun once in eighty-four years and marks a major epoch in a person's awakening to a higher level of consciousness. This transit can last approximately a year when retrograde motion is taken into consideration. Hence, its effects are far more significant and important than the brief four-day influence of the transiting Sun conjunct natal Uranus. These brief contacts of the Sun to Uranus are merely preparatory stages for major aspects of transiting Uranus to the natal Sun. Often, this transit occurs either very early or very late in life. When this is the case, the individual is deprived of the full range of personal freedom of opportunity for original creative self-expression and for the realization of goals which comes to those who receive this transit during the prime years of their lives. If it occurs in childhood, the child is likely to be treated in an enlightened way by those guiding his or her development. If it occurs late in life, profound spiritual realizations can prepare the individual for the transition called death.

Transiting Sun Conjunct Natal Neptune

Intuitive, creative imagination characterizes this transit. It is excellent for artists, musicians, photographers, and cinematographers. Idealistic romances may develop. However, if the Sun or Neptune is afflicted in the natal chart, this transit may bring on secret love affairs, inappropriate romantic attachments, or psychological aberrations. Afflictions to the Sun, whether natally or by other transiting planets, also introduce the danger of self-deception, especially in the area of romance.

The intuitive faculties and potential clairvoyant abilities are stimulated. These can take the form of telepathy, precognition, memory of past lives, or other unusual psychic occurrences. Many individuals experience vivid dreams which reveal important subconscious messages.

Mystical or artistic activities can be carried on in the home. This is a good transit for meditation and the development of the intuitive faculties. In particular, it brings intuitive psychological understanding of children. One often becomes more aware of oneself as a spiritual being.

The individual can become involved with cultural institutions, hospitals, asylums, and religious retreats, often in a leadership role. However, an inflated sense of spiritual self-importance, often involving some cult or master, can make the individual feel that he or she is a special emissary chosen from on high.

If the Sun or Neptune is afflicted, loss can result from unwise speculation or gambling. Unwanted pregnancies may also occur during this transit if either the Sun or Neptune is afflicted. Unwise pursuit of pleasure, drinking or drug abuse can be used as psychological escape mechanisms.

Individuals with a predisposition to psychological imbalance may seek to escape from practical responsibilities during this period. They may woolgather, daydream, or evade responsibility in general. There is a need to apply intuitive insights in a realistic and practical way. Brooding and negative use of the imagination should be avoided during this transit.

Transiting Neptune conjunct the natal Sun occurs about every 164 years; hence, it may not occur in the lifetime of every individual. When it does, important subtle changes occur in the individual's psychology, inner awareness, and level of spiritual understanding. Many karmic conditions come to fruition, and important psychological transformation is undergone, for better or worse.

Transiting Neptune conjunct the natal Sun has basically the same significance as the transiting Sun conjunct natal Neptune; however, it lasts about two years longer, due to retrograde motion.

Transiting Sun Conjunct Natal Pluto

Intensified will power characterizes this transit. This may take the form of leadership or efforts at self-improvement on some level. Many individuals initiate fundamental changes that have far-reaching consequences for themselves and others. Increased leadership and self-assertion and more dynamic self-expression are characteristic of these changes.

There could be involvement in important corporate business affairs, advanced scientific or technological activities, occult affairs, and matters concerning life and death. There also may be a personal involvement with insurance, taxes, inheritance, and goods of the dead.

For some individuals, this transit will be a strong sexual stimulus which can result in intense romantic involvements and possible sexual jealousy and intrigues. Many individuals have profound occult experiences and the intuitive faculties are frequently heightened. Efforts will be made toward improving methods of child rearing. This is a period when the individual eliminates useless, outworn ideas, possessions, conditions, and attitudes or finds new and resourceful uses for them.

If the Sun or Pluto is afflicted, the individual may attempt to dictate to or coerce others. In some cases, individuals become interested in magic or occult practices.

Transiting Pluto conjunct the natal Sun occurs once in 245 years; therefore, it cannot occur in the lifetime of everyone. This transit has the same effect as the transiting Sun conjunct natal Pluto; however, its effects last over a two-year period and bring major transformations in the individual's life and self-expression.

Transiting Sun Conjunct the Natal North Node and
Opposition the Natal South Node

Personal popularity and self-expression in harmony with prevailing social attitudes characterize this transit. It indicates an ability to personally influence popular fads and attitudes. The individual's creative artistic endeavors can receive popular recognition and acceptance. Good fortune comes through social or romantic activity, speculation, or dealing with children and their education.

Transiting North Node conjunct the natal Sun has the same meaning as the transiting Sun conjunct the natal North Node; however, its influence lasts approximately a month, as opposed to the two or three days of the transiting Sun conjunct the natal North Node.

Transiting Sun Conjunct the Natal South Node and Opposition the Natal North Node

Conservative attitudes toward current popular beliefs and fads and identification with traditional cultural standards characterize this transit. There may be withdrawal from participation in social activity. Many individuals apply a more conservative child-rearing approach during this time.

Transiting South Node conjunct the natal Sun has the same significance as the transiting Sun conjunct the natal South Node; however, it is of longer duration, approximately one month.

Transiting Sun Conjunct the Natal Ascendant and Opposition the Natal Descendant

Increased vitality and positive self-assertion characterize this transit. The individual expresses enthusiasm, self-confidence, and personal leadership. If the transit is afflicted, however, egotistical self-centered attitudes may become evident.

Transiting Sun Conjunct the Natal Midheaven and Opposition the Natal Nadir

Professional and political ambition characterize this transit. It favors politicians and performers and those who depend upon public acclaim for their success. Individuals experiencing this transit often receive public support and recognition for some creative achievement or act of personal leadership. Children may receive recognition and approval for worthwhile accomplishments from their parents or teachers. This is a favorable time to approach those in positions of power and authority. Social or romantic activity may come about through the individual's profession.

Transiting Sun Conjunct the Natal Descendant and Opposition the Natal Ascendant

Interaction with powerful and dynamic partners characterizes this transit. The individual is self-assertive in seeking out social and romantic relationships. There is a strong need to be noticed and appreciated by others.

Transiting Sun Conjunct the Natal Nadir and
Opposition the Natal Midheaven

Dynamic self-expression in the domestic environment characterizes this transit. Personal leadership is exercised in family affairs. Romantic, social, artistic, or child-oriented activities often take place in the home.

Transit Sun Sextiles

Transiting Sun Sextile the Natal Sun

Improved vitality and new ideas for creative self-expression characterize this transit. Individuals with this transit tend to assume a role of personal leadership among their friends and in the groups and organizations with which they are associated. Communications and short trips involving social and romantic activities often result in new opportunities for expression.

This is a favorable period for dealing with children and helping them with their development. Opportunities for financial speculation can prove to be profitable.

Transiting Sun Sextile the Natal Moon

Improved vitality and new ideas for creative self-expression in the home characterize this transit. Social and family gatherings in the home are likely. Individuals come up with ideas for making money, helping the family budget, or improving the domestic environment.

This is a favorable transit for public relations activities, business activities, and financial speculation related to food, farming, real estate, and home and domestic products and services.

There can be much coming and going and communication between brothers, sisters, neighbors, and co-workers regarding everyday affairs. It is a favorable time for enjoying old friends or meeting new friends. Communications with romantic partners or with the opposite sex are favored. Romantic and business opportunities involving the opposite sex can arise.

Individuals with this transit gain insights into their subconscious motivations.

Transiting Moon sextile the natal Sun has much the same effect as transiting Sun sextile the natal Moon; however, it is of much shorter duration, lasting only a few hours as opposed to the four days of the transiting Sun sextile the natal Moon. Inconsequential everyday affairs are likely to be the source of the activities associated with the transiting Moon sextile the natal Sun.

Transiting Sun Sextile Natal Mercury

Authoritative communication of personal ideas and creative intellectual activity characterize this transit. Ideas for literary or artistic self-expression can emerge. This is a good time to present ideas to those in positions of power and authority. Friends will be instrumental in helping individuals with this transit gain acceptance for their ideas. Friendly communication and productive exchange of ideas can take place between these individuals and their brothers, sisters, neighbors, friends, and co-workers. The individual takes an interest in communicating with or educating children and young people.

Short trips related to children, social activity, romance, work, and health will be productive. Games of mental skill are a special source of pleasure during this transit.

Transiting Mercury sextile the natal Sun has the same meaning as the transiting Sun sextile natal Mercury. Usually Mercury is faster in motion than the Sun. If Mercury is retrograde or stationary, however, transiting Mercury sextile the natal Sun can last as long as two weeks, thereby giving the transit a greater significance. The activities associated with transiting Mercury sextile the natal Sun often begin through a communication received by the individual.

Transiting Sun Sextile Natal Venus

Enjoyment of social activities, art, music, and romance characterizes this transit. It is a favorable time for short pleasure trips, social and romantic communications, and businesses related to art, music, entertainment, and luxury items. The individual is happier, more charming, affectionate, considerate and optimistic during this period. A new kindness and consideration toward children grows out of a better understanding of their emotional needs.

Transiting Venus sextile the natal Sun has the same significance as the transiting Sun sextile natal Venus; however, it may last for a lesser or greater period of time than transits of the Sun to natal Venus. When transiting Venus sextiles the natal Sun, the individual is likely to respond to external, aesthetic social or artistic stimulus.

Transiting Sun Sextile Natal Mars

Energetic mental activity and increased self-confidence characterize this transit. Well-thought-out, dynamic, and constructive activities are carried out in one's business and professional affairs. This is a favorable time for businesses related to manufacturing and engineering and for engineering projects. It is a good time to work with machinery and tools and to take on jobs that require strenuous physical exertion.

Sports, romantic encounters, and physical activities can be a source of pleasure. The transit is favorable for children and those who supervise them.

Transiting Mars sextile the natal Sun lasts for seven days or longer, while the transiting Sun sextile natal Mars lasts approximately four days. In other respects, it has basically the same significance as the transiting Sun sextile natal Mars.

Transiting Sun Sextile Natal Jupiter

Enthusiastic pursuit of educational, cultural, religious, philosophic, and charitable goals and objectives characterizes this transit. These activities are shared with friends and group associates. Romantic opportunities can arise through one's religious, educational, or cultural activities. Often, the individual assumes a role of personal leadership in cultural or educational affairs. This is a good period to seek the support of religious, educational, or cultural institutions for one's creative projects. Lecturing, teaching, publishing, artistic, and theatrical presentations are favored.

The transit creates a favorable atmosphere for seeking recognition and support from those in positions of power and authority. It is also favorable for dealings with legal, cultural, religious, and charitable institutions. This is an excellent time for handling important legal matters and for reasonable financial speculation.

It is favorable for long journeys in pursuit of pleasure, knowledge, or spiritual enlightenment. Benefit can come through foreign cultures and through other religious traditions. This is also a favorable period for helping in the education and religious training of children and young people and for seeking admittance to an institution of higher education. Family cultural activities are favored.

Transiting Jupiter sextile the natal Sun has basically the same significance as the transiting Sun sextile natal Jupiter. However, this transit lasts for at least a month and, therefore, produces greater benefits than the transiting Sun sextile natal Jupiter. Opportunities arise from the cultural environment which encourage individuals with this transit to express themselves creatively.

Transiting Sun Sextile Natal Saturn

Constructive ambition, good organization, prudence, and a mature attitude characterize this transit. Individuals can gain practical insights into ways of furthering their business, professional, or political progress. Artists, designers, mathematicians, and architects experiencing this transit have an enhanced sense of structure and form.

This is a favorable time for important communications with those in positions of power and authority. Friendships with mature individuals are likely to develop. The individual can participate in the activities of groups and organizations which have a serious purpose.

This is a favorable time for stabilizing important social and romantic relationships. Romantic opportunities can arise through one's professional or business contacts.

The individual may take on the responsibility of guiding and disciplining children in a way that will help build meaningful structure into their lives.

Generally, individuals make steady progress in the realization of their goals under this transit. There will be an increased sense of personal dignity and authority.

Transiting Saturn sextile the natal Sun has basically the same meaning as the transiting Sun sextile natal Saturn; however, because it lasts much longer, its effects are more significant. The opportunities presented by this sextile can bring about the realization of long-range goals and objectives.

Transiting Sun Sextile Natal Uranus

Increased freedom for original creative self-expression in friendships, groups, and organizations characterizes this transit.

The individual may be inspired with original intuitive ideas. This is especially true for inventors and creative artists. The transit creates a favorable atmosphere for gaining acceptance of one's personal ideas and creative projects. Sudden opportunities arise to realize personal goals and objectives.

Some individuals develop an intellectual interest in science, engineering, electronics, astrology, or occult subjects. This is a good period to introduce children to scientific and metaphysical concepts.

Unusual and stimulating opportunities for social activities tend to arise, and new friendships and group associations are often formed. Romantic opportunities can arise through friendships and through groups and organizations.

Progress can be made in corporate business affairs. Speculative investments related to inventions are favored.

Transiting Uranus sextile the natal Sun has basically the same significance as the transiting Sun sextile natal Uranus; however, it lasts much longer and marks an important period in the fruition of the individual's original creative potential.

Transiting Sun Sextile Natal Neptune

The intuitive, creative, and imaginative faculties are stimulated during this transit. Intuitive inspiration enables the individual to assume a leadership role in cultural affairs.

This is a favorable time for dealing with hospitals, asylums, and religious and cultural institutions. Individuals with this transit express kindness and generosity to those less fortunate than themselves. This is a favorable period for instructing children in religious, spiritual, and psychological concepts. There is also an increased awareness of the moods, feelings, and activities of children.

This transit often brings about an appreciation of art and beauty. It provides a favorable atmosphere for work in the performing arts, photography, and cinematography. Imaginative creativity is often expressed by improving the home environment.

Individuals with this transit gain insights into the workings of their own subconscious minds and experience a creative vision of future possibilities. Intuitive and clairvoyant faculties often influence the thinking processes. Some individuals hear or visualize past experiences or thought projections as though they were happening at the present time. This is a good transit for spiritual meditation and development. Spiritual values are shared with brothers, sisters, neighbors, and group associates.

Romance and social activities during this transit tend to have an exotic aspect.

Transiting Neptune sextile the natal Sun has basically the same significance as the transiting Sun sextile natal Neptune. However, because the individual undergoes this influence for an extended period of time, due to retrograde motion, important, lasting, and beneficial improvements in the individual's spiritual and creative understanding can take place.

Transiting Sun Sextile Natal Pluto

Increased will power, resourcefulness, enterprise, and intuitive awareness characterize this transit. A deeper level of understanding of the fundamental purpose of life can motivate the individual to increased efforts at constructive action and at spiritual, mental, and physical self-improvement.

Some individuals gain penetrating insights into the working of universal laws. This is a good time for spiritual disciplines designed to raise the level of consciousness. The individual takes steps to eliminate useless, outworn ideas, attitudes, and possessions. There may be involvement with occult groups or organizations or an interest in metaphysical studies and pursuits.

Some individuals experience an increased interest in science and technology. Resourcefulness is exhibited in the recycling of discarded items. The individual also tends to be resourceful and courageous in emergency situations.

This is a favorable time for handling corporate business affairs, matters related to joint finances, insurance, taxes, inheritances, or goods of the dead. The transit provides a favorable atmosphere for starting new business enterprises or for making speculative financial investments in scientific corporate enterprises, but only if the natal chart and other transits concur.

Transiting Pluto sextile the natal Sun has basically the same significance as the transiting Sun sextile natal Pluto; however, it lasts for a longer period of time and can thus contribute significantly to improving the individuals' levels of understanding and the conditions surrounding their lives. During this transit, individuals will express constructive, dynamic leadership.

Transiting Sun Sextile the Natal North Node and
Trine the Natal South Node

Modes of self-expression that are in harmony with prevailing cultural trends and attitudes characterize this transit. The individual is likely to engage in the social activities and forms of artistic expression which are in vogue. Adjustment to current cultural values comes easily. The individual's activities during this transit are characterized by intellectual innovation and responsiveness to current fads and attitudes. Some individuals assume a role of personal leadership in influencing current attitudes and fads. They usually enjoy social popularity.

Transiting Sun Sextile the Natal South Node and Trine the Natal North Node

This transit has basically the same significance as the transiting Sun sextile the natal North Node and trine the natal South Node. During this particular transit, however, there is an easy harmonizing with current fads and attitudes, combined with an intellectual awareness of traditional cultural values.

Because the nodes move backward through the Zodiac at the approximate rate of one degree every twenty days, transiting aspects of the nodes generally last for about a month. The transiting sextile aspect or trine aspect to the natal Sun then marks a sustained period of personal involvement with cultural trends and attitudes.

Transiting Sun Sextile the Natal Ascendant and Trine the Natal Descendant

Increased confidence in self-expression and dynamic cooperation in relationships characterize this transit. Social activity and close personal relationships open new avenues of self-expression.

Transiting Sun Sextile the Natal Midheaven and Trine the Natal Nadir

Dynamic creative expression in professional and domestic affairs characterizes this transit. Professional activities often involve art, music, or speculative ventures. This is a favorable time for decorating the home or office. It is a good period for approaching those in positions of power and authority. Professional and domestic responsibilities are balanced in a harmonious manner during this transit.

Transiting Sun Sextile the Natal Descendant and Trine the Natal Ascendant

This transit has basically the same effects as the transiting Sun sextile the natal Ascendant and trine the natal Descendant; however, there is an emphasis on intellectual understanding of relationships and an easy flow in personal creative self-expression.

Transiting Sun Sextile the Natal Nadir and Trine the Natal Midheaven

This transit has basically the same effects as the transiting Sun sextile the natal Midheaven and trine the natal Nadir; in addition, there is intellectual activity in the home and an easy flow in professional affairs.

Transit Sun Squares

Transiting Sun Square the Natal Sun

Problems with autocratic attitudes, false pride, and egotism characterize this transit. In general, one should avoid trying to force one's will on others during this time. There can be difficulties in dealing with children or their education. Some individuals find that their unwise pursuit of pleasure or overindulgence in romantic activities interferes with creative personal self-expression, and this in turn leads to frustration. Gambling and unwise speculation should be especially avoided during this transit.

Problems arise in getting along with those in positions of power and authority. This is not a good time to ask superiors for special favors.

On the positive side, this transit makes the individual more ambitious and, if handled constructively, can lead to worthwhile accomplishments.

Transiting Sun Square the Natal Moon

Emotional difficulties in family and domestic situations or in dealing with the opposite sex characterize this transit. Conflict between the conscious will and subconscious habits can cause difficulties in personal self-expression and in family relationships.

This is not a good period for family gatherings or social activities. Children rebel against parental authority during this transit. Difficulties often arise in romantic relationships.

This is not a good time to ask favors from those in power and authority.

Unconscious emotional problems often interfere with creative self-expression, and some individuals are lazy and self-indulgent during this period. Artistic endeavors are likely to be mediocre.

Unnecessary and ostentatious expenditures on pleasure and social activities during this transit could cause later financial embarrassment. Difficulties can arise over the family budget. This is not a good time for speculation, gambling, or unnecessary financial expenditures. Nor is it a good time to purchase real estate or domestic products or services.

In general, the individual feels emotionally upset and frustrated during this transit. The individual may have digestive problems or feel out of sorts.

Transiting Moon square the natal Sun has much the same meaning as the transiting Sun square the natal Moon; however, it lasts only a few hours.

Transiting Sun Square Natal Mercury

Individuals with this transit often identify their egos with their personal viewpoints to the extent that their ability to impartially perceive reality is distorted. Pride gets in the way of impartial reasoning ability.

Ego conflicts and communication difficulties arise in social contacts, in the work environment, and with romantic partners, family members, neighbors, friends, children, and those in positions of power and authority. There can be conflicts and disagreements during games of mental skill, especially over correct procedures. Breakdown of promises and agreements is often a problem under this transit. Social activities and work responsibilities tend to interfere with each other. Extravagance or poor taste in dress or personal hygiene often gives rise to comment or disapproval.

Transiting Mercury square the natal Sun has much the same meaning as the transiting Sun square natal Mercury. However, it is usually of shorter duration and the events associated with it are often precipitated through communications, either received or initiated by the individual.

Transiting Sun Square Natal Venus

Lack of industry, self-indulgence, and unwise pursuits of pleasure characterize this transit. There may also be financial extravagance.

The tendency to spoil children is a possibility. Some individuals experience a childish need for personal attention and admiration, which can lead to extravagance and ostentation. Self-centered attitudes, misguided sympathy and sentimentality are also pitfalls. The individual tends to avoid disagreeable or unpleasant tasks.

Emotional slights and hurts are possible in social and romantic relationships. Sensuality and sexual overindulgence is also a possibility. This is not a good period to plan a party or social gathering: differences of taste or emotional misunderstandings are likely. The individual who selects art, music, or entertainment during this time is likely to exercise poor taste.

This transit can be helpful, however, to those who are normally shy and retiring, as it helps to overcome social inhibitions.

Transiting Venus square the natal Sun has the same significance as the transiting Sun square natal Venus. However, it may last for a shorter or longer period of time due to either retrograde or rapid forward motion of Venus.

Transiting Sun Square Natal Mars

Problems arising from aggressive, impulsive, competitive, or inconsiderate behavior characterize this transit. Impulsiveness, anger, authoritarian attitudes, and attempts to impose one's will on others can all arouse resentment and lead to angry confrontations. In extreme cases, these confrontations are physical. Accidents or physical injury can result from careless use of fire, tools, guns, machinery, sharp instruments, or dangerous chemicals.

The "might makes right" or egocentric attitudes of some individuals make cooperation with others difficult. This is an unfavorable time for approaching those in positions of power and authority—they are likely to resent the intrusion. Impulsive financial speculation can lead to loss.

Romantic and social relationships are apt to be disturbed by ego conflicts or aggressive sexual behavior. Uncontrolled desires and aggressive sexual behavior can be a source of trouble in general.

The physical overexertion and discordant emotional attitudes experienced during this transit often lead to physical or emotional exhaustion, ill health, or injury. This is not a favorable transit for those with heart conditions, and they should take care to avoid overexertion.

Transiting Mars square the natal Sun has basically the same significance as the transiting Sun square natal Mars. However, it lasts for a longer period of time. Should it be stationary or retrograde, its effects can last for several weeks. Transiting Sun square the natal Mars occurs approximately once a year, whereas the transiting Mars square natal Sun occurs twice a year.

Transiting Sun Square Natal Jupiter

Problems arising from hypocrisy, extravagance, and an inflated sense of self-importance characterize this transit. Overexpansion, foolish optimism, and waste are some extremes associated with this transit. There is a tendency to promise more than one can deliver. Self-indulgence, lack of attention to detail, and lack of industry are common. Gambling and unwise speculation should be avoided.

Impractical attitudes regarding religion, philosophy, and higher education can cause problems. The individual is inclined to narrow-minded or dogmatic religious, cultural, and educational viewpoints. These, in turn, often create problems in romantic, social, political, administrative, or business situations. Generosity and charity are tinged with a desire for personal recognition and praise.

Extravagance and poor taste are frequently displayed in art, music, entertainment, and social activity under this transit square.

Transiting Jupiter square the natal Sun has the same significance as the transiting Sun square natal Jupiter. However, it lasts for a much longer period of time, especially if Jupiter is stationary or retrograde, and consequently the inherent problems can be greater.

Transiting Sun Square Natal Saturn

Frustration of personal ambition and need for self-expression characterize this transit. Burdensome professional responsibilities devitalize the individual and interfere with social and romantic activities. This is an unfavorable transit in general for social and romantic activity.

A period of loneliness can result from the individual's adopting an autocratic and unsympathetic attitude toward others. The tendency to adopt hard, rigid attitudes associated with this transit is usually a result of an ego defense mechanism. This rigidity sometimes takes the form of blind adherence to traditional attitudes and beliefs.

Lowered vitality, fatigue, and depression are associated with this transit, and these cause problems in self-expression. Resentments arise from the individual's tendency to use personal power and authority for selfish ends. There are difficulties with employers, authority figures, and government agencies. This is a poor time to seek favors from those in positions of power and authority—they are likely to be unsympathetic or negative. Hard work, discipline, and organization are necessary to achieve recognition for one's personal creative efforts.

Children with this transit often feel unloved or harshly treated by those in charge of them. Adults with this transit tend to adopt a harsh, unsympathetic attitude toward children.

Transiting Saturn square the natal Sun has the same significance as the transiting Sun square natal Saturn. However, it lasts much longer and indicates a period of test and trial for the individual.

Transiting Sun Square Natal Uranus

Desire for personal freedom at all costs characterizes this transit. If this takes the form of desire for freedom without personal responsibility, serious difficulty will develop sooner or later. Some individuals adopt a double standard, demanding absolute personal freedom but at the same time expecting others to adhere strictly to duty.

Egotistical, headstrong attitudes blind the individual to good advice. In general, the individual's behavior is apt to be erratic, inconsistent, and unreliable.

Inconsistent behavior will be especially evident in one's social affairs or romantic relationships. Sudden romantic attachments can occur; however, they are seldom stable or lasting. In extreme cases, the attachment results in the shattering of the individual's family and social and financial security. Friendships with eccentric or unstable people are not in the individual's best interest at this time. Inconsistent handling of children is also a danger during this transit.

This is an unfavorable transit for occult activities or involvement with groups and organizations: unexpected hardships and problems can arise. Astrological judgments made under this transit can be superficial and faulty.

Joint finances and corporate business affairs are often a source of difficulty. Gambling or unwise speculation can be ruinous during this transit.

The transit can also produce hard-to-diagnose, irregular heart action.

The circumstances of the individual's life can be disrupted by cultural, political, or economic forces beyond his or her control. In some cases, the individual who has worked hard to build up some kind of creative self-expression destroys or abandons it through some foolish act.

Major changes should not be precipitated under this transit; however, if changes are forced, the individual should adjust gracefully, as the changes will be instrumental in opening doors that will eventually lead to fulfillment of personal goals and objectives. The outcome of this transit depends upon the purity of the individual's motivation. Even adverse transits of Uranus can have a liberating, consciousness-expanding effect. Properly used, this transit can provide intuitive insights that awaken the individual to a higher level of consciousness.

Transiting Uranus square the natal Sun has the same significance as the transiting Sun square natal Uranus. However, its influence can extend over a year or more. It marks a period of major readjustment.

Transiting Sun Square Natal Neptune

Problems arising from a tendency toward self-deception and a desire to escape practical responsibility characterize this transit. The individual is subject to daydreaming, woolgathering, drug abuse, overuse of alcohol, preoccupation with romance, gambling, or what masquerades as art or mysticism. Dissipation through excessive sexual indulgence or social activities is possible. Misuse of medication or drugs can confuse and debilitate the individual.

The unconscious mind can distort both the individual's self-concept and reality in general. Lack of clear direction or serious purpose can lead to unpleasant psychic experiences, uncontrolled imagination, and consequent confusion in the individual's life. In general, during this transit, the individual lacks the discipline to implement inspired ideas or understanding even if they do occur.

A secret love affair or some kind of deception in romance is likely under this transit. Unwanted pregnancies can also occur. Mishandling of children and confusion in giving them clear direction can cause serious family problems.

Delusions of grandeur and an inflated sense of self-importance are also likely. Often, this is related to some form of cultism or guru worship. Dabbling in unwise psychic practices can expose the individual to undesirable entities and influences.

Get-rich-quick schemes and unwise speculations can be disastrous. Gas, oil or water leakage can be a problem.

Transiting Neptune square the natal Sun has the same significance as the transiting Sun square natal Neptune. However, its influence can last for two years, during which the individual's grip on reality can be severely tested.

Transiting Sun Square Natal Pluto

A tendency to become involved in power struggles characterizes this transit. Such intrigues are usually related to corporate business dealings or matters related to joint finances, insurance, taxes, alimony, and goods of the dead.

Aggressive sexual behavior and jealousy in sexual relationships are also a source of trouble. There is a tendency to be harsh or unsympathetic toward children or one's own romantic partners.

The individual's life can be disrupted by forces beyond his or her personal control, resulting in a new sense of values and a new direction in life. In extreme cases, the individual can become involved in issues of life and death. Hidden dangers or behind-the-scenes activities that may be detrimental to the individual are also a possibility. Some individuals are exposed to psychic dangers through involvement in occult or magic practices.

Transiting Pluto square the natal Sun has the same significance as the transiting Sun square natal Pluto; however, it can last for two years, thus marking a period of major transformation in the individual's life.

Transiting Sun Square the Natal North Node and Square the Natal South Node

A conflict between the individual's self-expression and prevailing trends and popular beliefs characterizes this transit. Ineptitude in social situations brings about lowered popularity and difficulties in romance. This is not a favorable period for gaining public support for personal creative endeavors. Losses can occur through unwise speculations. Methods of raising children or the behavior of children are often out of harmony with traditional cultural standards.

Transiting Sun Square the Natal South Node and Square the Natal North Node

See "Transiting Sun Square the Natal North Node and Square the Natal South Node."

Transiting Sun Square the Natal Ascendant and Square the Natal Descendant

Power struggles, ego confrontations, and dogmatic attitudes in relationships characterize this transit. Individuals are confused about their self-images and awkward in their social lives. Ego confrontations give rise to romantic and marital problems. Problems with children or difficulties in partnerships cause confusion and self-doubt.

Transiting Sun Square the Natal Midheaven and
Square the Natal Nadir

Conflicts and other problems with authority figures and family members characterize this transit. Increased professional and domestic responsibilities limit the individual's self-expression. Family problems arise over children and their education.

Transiting Sun Square the Natal Descendant and
Square the Natal Ascendant

See "Transiting Sun Square the Natal Ascendant and Square the Natal Descendant."

Transiting Sun Square the Natal Nadir and
Square the Natal Midheaven

See "Transiting Sun Square the Natal Midheaven and Square the Natal Nadir."

Transit Sun Trines

Transiting Sun Trine the Natal Sun

Harmony in social activity, in romance, in artistic endeavors, and in creative self-expression, along with increased vitality and self-confidence, characterize this transit. This is a favorable period for working with children and for their education.

The individual's capacity for personal leadership can be expressed with favorable results. It is a good time to approach those in positions of power and authority to seek support for personal creative endeavors. It is a favorable period for organizing social functions and activities. Personal financial investments and speculations are favored. Pleasure trips and travel related to education can benefit the individual and expand his or her outlook on life.

Transiting Sun Trine the Natal Moon

Harmonious relationships with the family and with the opposite sex, improved vitality, and an easy flow in one's everyday affairs characterize this transit.

This is a favorable period for family gatherings and social activities. The individual enjoys or participates in gourmet cooking. It is a good period for business activities related to entertainment, food, farming, real estate, home, and domestic products or services and children and their education.

Personal financial speculation is also favored. It is a good period for approaching those in power and authority for favors or financial assistance. This transit provides a favorable atmosphere for romantic relationships.

Conscious will and subconscious habit tendencies are in harmony at this time. The individual balances action and receptivity in both social interaction and self-expression.

Transiting Moon trine the natal Sun has basically the same significance as the transiting Sun trine the natal Moon; however, this transit lasts only a few hours, whereas the transit of the Sun lasts four or five days.

Transiting Sun Trine Natal Mercury

Creative intellectual self-expression and intellectual activity characterize this transit. Personal ideas are communicated with clarity and self-confidence.

This is a good period for romantic and social communication and for intelligent communication and work with brothers, sisters, neighbors, and co-workers. Social and romantic opportunities can arise through these communications and activities. Pleasure trips are favored. Games of mental skill, such as chess, can be a source of pleasure. The individual is likely to be humorous and witty during this transit.

The individual takes an interest in attractive and aesthetically pleasing clothes. There is an increased awareness of proper diet and personal hygiene. This is a good period for helping in the education and intellectual training of children.

The individual's confident manner of communication wins the support of others for his or her ideas and projects. This is a favorable time for study, writing, teaching, lecturing, research, and publishing. Some individuals take an interest in literary art forms or plays.

Communication with those in positions of power and authority is likely to be favorably received at this time. It is a good transit for formulating agreements and signing contracts. The individual can assume a role of personal leadership in promoting ideas to improve work efficiency and methodology.

Transiting Mercury trine the natal Sun has the same significance as the transiting Sun trine natal Mercury however, it lasts for a longer or shorter period of time, depending on how fast Mercury is moving and whether Mercury is stationary or retrograde.

Transiting Sun Trine Natal Venus

Artistic self-expression and romantic and social activity characterize this transit. The individual has a happy and optimistic outlook on life. Increased personal charm and attraction usually accompanies this transit. It is a good period for planning social events. The individual is more aware of and considerate of the needs of others, especially where the opposite sex is concerned. The individual is kind and sympathetic toward children and understands their emotional needs. This transit can bring romantic and marriage opportunities if other indications in the chart are favorable.

This is a good time for all kinds of creative artistic expression, for projects involving music and entertainment, and for buying art objects or luxury items. This is also a good period for seeking financial or social favors. Business, marital, and legal partnerships are also favored.

Transiting Venus trine the natal Sun has the same significance as the transiting Sun trine natal Venus; however, it lasts for a longer or shorter period of time, depending on the speed of Venus's motion and whether Venus is stationary or retrograde.

Transiting Sun Trine Natal Mars

Increased energy, courage, self-confidence, and personal authority characterize this transit.

During this period, the individual is likely to bring his or her constructive ideas and goals into effective action. This often takes the form of worthwhile professional and business leadership. Political affairs or matters related to corporate business are also favored during this time.

Physical work and exercise during this period improve one's health and appearance. The individual will probably take an active interest in outdoor activities, sports, or the performing arts. It is a good period for involvement in the physical education of children or young people. The individual is more assertive in his or her social and romantic affairs. Artistic endeavors requiring energy and exertion are favored.

Transiting Mars trine the natal Sun has basically the same significance as the transiting Sun trine natal Mars; however, it lasts for a longer period of time and thus indicates a sustained period of action.

Transiting Sun Trine Natal Jupiter

A benevolent, positive outlook characterizes this transit. The individual gains support and recognition from cultural, religious, and educational institutions and from those in positions of power and authority.

During this period, the individual is very intuitive and often gains insights into future cultural trends and developments. This is a favorable transit for moral or educational self-improvement. It is a good period for seeking admission to schools of higher education. Social and romantic opportunities arise through universities and churches or through cultural or religious institutions. This is a favorable period for the cultural and religious training of children.

In general, the individuals are more generous and considerate toward others, especially those less fortunate than themselves. Long journeys for pleasure and education are favored. Some individuals develop an interest in foreign cultures and their traditions. This is also a favorable time for long-distance commerce and dealing with those in or from distant places. Social or romantic relationships may be established with people of foreign birth or from distant places. Artists and performers enjoy popularity and success during this period. This transit provides protection for those in difficult circumstances. The individual can never be completely down and out. In general, the individual is likely to reap the rewards of previous good deeds.

This is also a favorable period for handling legal affairs.

Transiting Jupiter trine the natal Sun has the same significance as the transiting Sun trine natal Jupiter; however, it lasts for a much longer interval and thus marks an important period of progress in the individual's life.

Transiting Sun Trine Natal Saturn

An increased sense of personal responsibility and constructive professional ambition characterize this transit.

Past social and romantic relationships are often renewed. The individuals become more conscientious about their responsibilities toward children. Constructive guidance and other benefits come through older or established individuals.

During this period, the individual becomes more concerned with long-range goals and objectives. This is a favorable period for executives, politicians, and businessmen. Steady progress can be made in business and professional affairs. This is also a favorable period for handling serious legal affairs. The individual shows qualities of organization, efficiency, and application, which are recognized by those in authority.

There is a greater inclination to put creative ideas into practical manifestation. Creative artists experiencing this transit have an improved sense of form and structure.

Transiting Saturn trine the natal Sun has the same significance as the transiting Sun trine natal Saturn; however, it lasts much longer and indicates a sustained period of steady progress in the individual's life.

Transiting Sun Trine Natal Uranus

Originality, creative self-expression, and unexpected good fortune characterize this transit.

Individuals enjoy increased popularity among their friends, group associates, and social contacts. They are likely to experiment with new life styles and establish interesting new friendships and group associations with exciting people. A desire for greater freedom in personal self-expression leads to a broadening of the individual's experience. Exciting adventures and unusual social and romantic adventures are apt to arise.

This is a favorable transit for corporate business, reasonable speculation, or seeking financial support for creative projects. It is a good time to introduce children to scientific or metaphysical ideas.

Often, this transit presents unusual opportunities for realizing one's goals and objectives. It endows the individual with increased will power to carry out constructive endeavors and efforts at self-improvement.

Intuitive and clairvoyant faculties are stimulated. Creative artistic expression will be intuitively inspired. Some individuals develop an interest in occult, astrological, or scientific studies.

Transiting Uranus trine the natal Sun has the same significance as the transiting Sun trine natal Uranus; however, it lasts up to two years, as opposed to approximately four days when the transiting Sun trines natal Uranus. Transiting Uranus trine the natal Sun marks a major period of unfoldment and self-expression for the individual.

Transiting Sun Trine Natal Neptune

Stimulation of the creative imagination characterizes this transit. The individual gains insights into the workings of his or her unconscious. Intuitive abilities and spiritual awareness are also enhanced at this time, and this can result in an increased interest in religion, philosophy, mysticism, and occult subjects. Telepathy, precognition, and prophetic insights into future cultural trends are possible.

An ideal love enters the lives of some individuals under this transit. Intuitive empathy with children and their emotional needs is often expressed.

This is a favorable time for dealing with hospitals, religious, or cultural institutions. Long journeys or religious pilgrimages are favored. The individual can receive benefit through a spiritual teacher or could become such a teacher.

Transiting Neptune trine the natal Sun has the same significance as the transiting Sun trine natal Neptune; however, it lasts for approximately two years and marks a major period of constructive development for the individual, while the transiting Sun trine natal Neptune lasts only a few days.

Transiting Sun Trine Natal Pluto

Increased will power, resourcefulness, and efforts at spiritual, mental, and physical self-improvement characterize this transit.

The individual can assume a personal role of leadership in business and professional affairs. This is a favorable period to start corporate business enterprises or to become involved in them, as well as in scientific research, advanced technology, and occult studies. Intuitive clairvoyant faculties can be stimulated under this transit. The study of metaphysics or spiritual practices is favored.

Often, the individual benefits through insurance, inheritance, government funding, tax rebates, grants, or joint monies.

Individuals often express their resourcefulness by remaking or improving existing conditions and resources and by finding new uses for discarded objects.

Transiting Pluto trine the natal Sun has the same significance as the transiting Sun trine natal Pluto; however, it lasts for approximately two years, as opposed to approximately four days of the transiting Sun trine natal Pluto, and it marks a major period of inner growth and self-improvement.

Transiting Sun Trine the Natal North Node and
Sextile the Natal South Node

See "Transiting Sun Sextile the Natal South Node and Trine the Natal North Node."

Transiting Sun Trine the Natal South Node and
Sextile the Natal North Node

See "Transiting Sun Sextile the Natal North Node and Trine the Natal South Node."

Transiting Sun Trine the Natal Ascendant and
Sextile the Natal Descendant

See "Transiting Sun Sextile the Natal Descendant and Trine the Natal Ascendant."

Transiting Sun Trine the Natal Midheaven and
Sextile the Natal Nadir

See "Transiting Sun Sextile the Natal Nadir and Trine the Natal Midheaven."

Transiting Sun Trine the Natal Descendant and
Sextile the Natal Ascendant

See "Transiting Sun Sextile the Natal Ascendant and Trine the Natal Descendant."

Transiting Sun Trine the Natal Nadir and
Sextile the Natal Midheaven

See "Transiting Sun Sextile the Natal Midheaven and Trine the Natal Nadir."

Transit Sun Oppositions

Transiting Sun Opposition the Natal Sun

Ego confrontations and power struggles characterize this transit. Conflicts over authority are likely to arise, especially in marital and romantic relationships. A democratic attitude is needed if there is to be harmony in important relationships during this transit. A firm, kind attitude is essential in dealing with children. Partnerships or cooperative endeavors with powerful, energetic individuals are favored at this time.

Transiting Sun Opposition the Natal Sun

Difficulties in dealing with the opposite sex, authority figures, or family members characterize this transit.

Ego confrontations over emotional issues can cause problems. Often, there are upsets in domestic affairs. The individual is likely to experience difficulties in dealing with children. Lack of vitality or digestive problems are likely during this period. This is not a favorable time for social or romantic activities.

Care should be exercised in spending money on social activities and domestic needs. This is not a good period for financial speculation: emotional impulses can interfere with good judgment.

Transiting Moon opposition the natal Sun has basically the same significance as the transiting Sun opposition the natal Moon; however, it lasts for a shorter period of time—only a few hours—while the Sun's transit takes four or five days.

Transiting Sun Opposition Natal Mercury

Identification of the ego with one's personal viewpoints characterizes this transit. Ego confrontations arise over communications or ideas, and these in turn interfere with the impartial perception of facts. The individual is likely to feel restless or ill-disposed toward work or study. Excessive social communications often interfere with work. Difficulties arise in communications with those in positions of power and authority. This is an unfavorable time to ask favors of employers or authority figures or to sign contracts or formulate agreements.

Consideration and diplomacy are needed in communication with brothers, sisters, neighbors, and co-workers. There are communication difficulties with romantic partners or social contacts. Confusion or delays arise in transportation and arrangements to meet with others. Individuals with this transit usually find that they have difficulty in communicating with children or that children make them nervous in some way.

Transiting Mercury opposition the natal Sun has the same significance as the transiting Sun opposition natal Mercury; however, it can last for a longer or shorter period of time, depending on the speed of Mercury's motion and whether Mercury is stationary or retrograde.

Transiting Sun Opposition Natal Venus

During this transit, it is especially important to establish harmony in business, social, romantic, and marital relationships.

Important relationships often suffer from financial problems and from lack of emotional sensitivity. Kindness tempered with wisdom is needed in dealing with children. Children experiencing this transit often demand extra attention and emotional support from parents and teachers.

The individual is likely to become actively involved in art, music, entertainment, and social and romantic activities. However, excessive social activity sometimes interferes with the individual's serious responsibilities. Extravagance, social ostentation and an exaggerated view of one's desirability should be guarded against.

If there is an awareness and proper attitude toward this transit, it can bring much pleasure and enjoyment.

Transiting Venus opposition the natal Sun has the same significance as the transiting Sun opposition natal Venus; however, it may last for a longer or shorter period of time, depending on the rate of motion of Venus and whether Venus is stationary or retrograde.

Transiting Sun Opposition Natal Mars

Ego confrontations and competition in business, professional, and political affairs characterize this transit. A "me first" attitude often causes difficulties in important relationships.

Conflicts arise over power and authority, and rash and impulsive behavior often causes problems. The individual's aggressive, autocratic attitudes are apt to arouse resentment in others. If the natal horoscope shows aggressive or uncooperative tendencies, the individual can get into difficulty with the police or other authority figures.

For some individuals, this transit indicates physical confrontations. Care should be exercised in handling fire, guns, knives, tools, machinery, and automobiles. The individual should be especially careful to avoid injury from games and sports.

Additional conflicts can arise over joint finances, insurance, taxes, inheritance, alimony, and corporate money. Financial speculation should be avoided.

The individual needs to be kind and considerate toward children, while refusing to give in to unreasonable demands or to permit them to get out of control.

Transiting Mars opposition the natal Sun has the same significance as the transiting Sun opposition natal Mars; however, it lasts longer and thus indicates a sustained period of potential conflict.

Transiting Sun Opposition Natal Jupiter

An inflated sense of self-importance, opinionated religious, educational, and cultural viewpoints, and a general tendency toward overexpansion characterize this transit.

Unwise speculation, undue optimism, and financial extravagance can cause loss and later embarrassment. Condescension, moral hypocrisy, and generosity with an ulterior motive are also pitfalls during this transit. The individual tends to be permissive or overindulgent toward children. Social buffoonery or a tendency to take too much for granted in relationships often causes trouble. The individual may try to subtly control others by creating a sense of obligation in them. Such hypocrisy can lead to resentments. Fanatical or narrow-minded religious and cultural viewpoints should be guarded against.

Transiting Jupiter opposition the natal Sun has the same significance as the transiting Sun opposition natal Jupiter; however, it lasts for a longer period of time and presents a more serious test of the individual's judgment and discrimination.

Transiting Sun Opposition Natal Saturn

Rigid egotistical attitudes, ego defense mechanisms, and selfish ambition are all dangers during this transit.

Individuals in positions of power and authority should guard against oppressive, unreasonable attitudes at this time. These attitudes are often accompanied by a tendency to be blindly subservient to those in authority. Usually, these rigid authoritarian attitudes are based on feelings of fear and insecurity. Although they can sometimes be justified in the name of law and order, they are likely to arouse resentment and opposition.

In some cases, a power struggle for status and supremacy in the individual's business or profession is indicated. This is a difficult time to achieve professional advancement. Even modest gains in business and professional affairs require a great deal of work, discipline, and cooperation. Those in positions of power and authority may make heavy demands on the individual. This is not a favorable period for financial speculations.

There is a tendency to resist change and new methods even when they represent a necessary improvement. This is, in fact, an unfavorable period for initiating new endeavors. In general, it is best to perform those routine responsibilities that are necessary and wait for a more favorable time to initiate changes.

Heavy business and professional responsibilities can lower the individual's vitality and restrict social and romantic activities. Lack of social and romantic opportunities often accompanies this transit. Lack of self-confidence and social inhibition often make the individual feel lonely and unloved. Responsibility for children can become burdensome and the individual may become overly severe in his or her treatment of them. Children experiencing this transit tend to feel unloved and harshly treated.

Health problems with back, heart, bones, skin, and teeth can emerge at this time.

Transiting Saturn opposition the natal Sun has the same significance as the transiting Sun opposition natal Saturn; however, it is of longer duration, and thus indicates a sustained period of difficulty.

Transiting Sun Opposition Natal Uranus

A desire for freedom and a rebellion against authority characterize this transit. The individuals tend to insist on complete freedom for themselves, while expecting others to conform to their wishes of discipline and conformity.

Unpredictable social behavior and involvement with friendships and group associations of an unreliable nature are possible. Romantic situations are likely to be unstable and short-lived.

The individual's tastes in art, music, and social activities tend to be peculiar and perhaps eccentric. Instability and experimentation with new life styles are common. There is a tendency to engage in peculiar occult practices or join strange organizations.

Rash, impulsive acts and decisions frequently have undesirable consequences. Gambling and unwise speculation can be especially disastrous. Joint finances, corporate money, insurance, inheritance, alimony, and taxes are often a source of conflict. Corporate financial involvements are not likely to proceed smoothly or according to plan.

In general, it is important to examine one's personal motives and exercise common sense during this transit.

Transiting Uranus opposition the natal Sun has the same significance as the transiting Sun opposition natal Uranus; however, it lasts much longer, and thus indicates a major period of instability in the individual's life.

Transiting Sun Opposition Natal Neptune

Self-deception in relationships and delusions of grandeur characterize this transit. The individual's unrealistic attitudes extend to pleasure, social activity, romantic relationships, children, and financial speculation. Unwanted pregnancies or pregnancies where the fatherhood is in question frequently occur.

Neurotic tendencies can be stimulated; escapism through alcohol, drugs, social activity, sex, gambling, or other unwise pursuits is possible at this time.

Important relationships can stimulate subconscious neurotic tendencies, and these in turn cause confusion in the individual's mind about the relationship. Awareness of subtle psychological factors is necessary if self-deception or deception by others is to be avoided.

Transiting Neptune opposition the natal Sun has the same significance as the transiting Sun opposition natal Neptune; however, it lasts for approximately two years and thus indicates a sustained period of possible self-deception and psychological confusion.

Transiting Sun Opposition Natal Pluto

Individuals with this transit attempt to dominate, coerce, or remake others, or they may be subjected to such treatment by others. Naturally, this causes resentment and, if the individual does not combat these tendencies, there may be problems. Thus, this transit is likely to bring about conflicts over power and authority. Other relationship problems arise in the areas of business, joint finances, corporate money, insurance, taxes, inheritance, alimony, and goods of the dead. Sexual conflicts are likely to arise in romantic or marital relationships, usually because of sexual demands on the part of one of the individuals. Romantic relationships may be terminated.

Correct handling of children is important during this transit. Discipline should be maintained without cruelty or excessive severity. Impulsive, headstrong attitudes should be avoided during this period.

Used positively, this transit can bring constructive accomplishment and self-improvement. The individual can become involved with dynamic, powerful people who will have a profound influence in some way.

Transiting Pluto opposition the natal Sun has the same significance as the transiting Sun opposition natal Pluto; however, it lasts for approximately two years and has a significant effect on transforming the individual's life.

Transiting Sun Opposition the Natal North Node and Conjunct the Natal South Node

See "Transiting Sun Conjunct the Natal South Node and Opposition the Natal North Node."

Transiting Sun Opposition the Natal South Node and Conjunct the Natal North Node

See "Transiting Sun Conjunct the Natal North Node and Opposition the Natal South Node."

Transiting Sun Opposition the Natal Ascendant and Conjunct the Natal Descendant

See "Transiting Sun Conjunct the Natal Descendant and Opposition the Natal Ascendant."

Transiting Sun Opposition the Natal Midheaven and Conjunct the Natal Nadir

See "Transiting Sun Conjunct the Natal Nadir and Opposition the Natal Midheaven."

Transiting Sun Opposition the Natal Descendant and Conjunct the Natal Ascendant

See "Transiting Sun Conjunct the Natal Ascendant and Opposition the Natal Descendant."

Transiting Sun Opposition the Natal Nadir and Conjunct the Natal Midheaven

See "Transiting Sun Conjunct the Natal Midheaven and Opposition the Natal Nadir."

20 Transits
of the Moon

Transit Moon Through the Houses

Transiting Moon Through the Natal First House

Changeable moods, emotional excitability, and emotional self-expression characterize this transit.

The individual is concerned with his or her family and domestic affairs and with finances related to these matters. Increased contacts are also likely at this time. If the Moon is under stress aspects while transiting the natal First House, family strife and ego confrontations within the family are possible.

The appetite is increased and the individual eats more.

There is a tendency toward emotional impulsiveness at this time. In some cases, the individual becomes overly sensitive to the point of overreacting to others' opinions of him or her. Extreme emotional reactions of this type tend to annoy others and make the individual unpopular.

Transiting Moon Through the Natal Second House

Family and domestic finances, purchases for the home, food and domestic shopping, and real estate concerns are all emphasized during this transit. If the Moon is under stress aspects, extravagance or financial difficulties in these matters are possible.

Financial transactions are common at this time and women are likely to play a significant part in the individual's financial or business affairs. Business activities are likely to be related to domestic products and services or real estate. The individual is inclined to purchase art or luxury items for the home.

Individuals with this transit feel a greater need for emotional and domestic security, and material security, or lack of it, will have a greater effect than usual on their emotional well-being. If the transiting Moon is under stress aspects, an excessive concern with material security can lead to a materialistic outlook.

Transiting Moon Through the Natal Third House

An unusual degree of communication with family, friends, neighbors, and co-workers characterizes this transit, as do short trips having to do with household items.

Individuals with this transit are likely to have visitors come into their homes, or they engage in much conversation concerning everyday affairs. If the Moon is under stress aspects while transiting this house, there tends to be excessive talk about trivial inconsequential matters, often in the form of long telephone conversations with neighbors, friends, or co-workers.

During this period, the individuals' thinking is likely to be biased by their emotions. Emotional disturbances can cause nervousness and an inability to concentrate. Often, decisions are made from an instinctual level. However, this transit also stimulates the intellectual interests and motivates the individual to incorporate them into the family and domestic life.

This is a favorable transit for business correspondence or the mail-order business.

Transiting Moon Through the Natal Fourth House

Emotional involvement in family and domestic affairs characterizes this transit. There will be increased interaction with parents, family members, or others in the domestic environment.

Family loyalty and religious, ethnic, racial, or national feelings of identification and patriotism will probably be stimulated. Family activities and finances will be of concern to the individual. Business activities are likely to be conducted in the home.

There is a need for domestic comfort and security. The individual can become concerned with domestic chores, such as cooking, cleaning, or doing the laundry. In women, strong domestic and maternal instincts are aroused.

If the Moon is under stress aspects while transiting this house, the individual can become hypersensitive over family issues.

Transiting Moon Through the Natal Fifth House

An emotional concern with romance, pleasure, children, and social activity characterizes this transit. Women experiencing this transit are particularly vulnerable to pregnancy and to intensified maternal impulses. Romantic and sexual issues can be a source of emotional agitation.

Social and romantic activities take place in the home environment. Families tend to participate together in games and sports. Some individuals engage in artistic expression or financial speculation.

Usually, this transit indicates involvement with entertainment, the pursuit of pleasure and social activities, usually with women or family members. However, if the Moon makes stress aspects while transiting the natal Fifth House, excessive pursuit of pleasure may lead to the dissipation of time, energy and money.

Transiting Moon Through the Natal Sixth House

A concern with health, household chores, and family diet, hygiene, and clothing characterizes this transit. Household order and cleanliness become important to the emotional well-being of the individual. If the Moon is well aspected, this is a good time to buy clothing, health aids, or household items that improve cleanliness and efficiency.

If the Moon makes stress aspects while transiting this house, emotional problems can cause ill health in the individual. Problems with work, especially if they involve women, are likely to arise at this time. Difficult emotional situations at work are likely to make the individual feel nervous and ill at ease.

Transiting Moon Through the Natal Seventh House

A concern with domestic, marital, and partnership issues characterizes this transit. Emotional, domestic, and financial affairs strongly affect the individual's partnerships, marriage, or other close personal relationships.

The individual is likely to have more contact than usual with the public at this time. Interaction with women will play an important part in this.

Individuals with this transit are likely to have strong emotional reactions in regard to their involvement with others and others' attitudes toward them. This transit can enhance a sense of companionship and personal warmth; however, if the Moon makes stress aspects while transiting this house, interaction with others can cause emotional upsets, and marital quarrels can arise over financial, family, and domestic affairs.

Transiting Moon Through the Natal Eighth House

Business activities related to food, farming, and domestic products and services characterize this transit.

Family finances, taxes, insurance, inheritance, alimony, and sex can all become emotional issues. Psychic perceptions, hunches, and intuitions are often stimulated by this transit. The individual often feels a desire to end old conditions and old emotional ties.

If the Moon makes stress aspects while transiting this house, and if other factors in the natal horoscope concur, this transit can coincide with the death of a family member.

Transiting Moon Through the Natal Ninth House

The incorporation of religious, educational, and cultural values into the family life characterizes this transit. The individual's family conditionings and religious, ethnic, racial, national, and economic background have a particular influence on his or her religious, educational, and philosophic values at this time. If the Moon makes stress aspects while transiting the natal Ninth House, the individual's attitudes can be biased or prejudiced by these conditionings.

Contact with women comes about through educational, religious, or cultural institutions. This transit often coincides with foreign travel, long-distance family trips, or visits from family members or from people who have come a long way.

Transiting Moon Through the Natal Tenth House

During this transit, the individual experiences an emotionally oriented concern with his or her public reputation and family status. Business and professional activity is often geared to achieve domestic security. The individual's business or professional affairs are frequently related to real estate, food, and domestic products and services.

This period often coincides with public exposure, personal public appearances, or personal recognition for achievements, even if these are associated with everyday affairs. However, if the Moon makes stress aspects while transiting this house, the individual can receive unfavorable publicity, and domestic problems can interfere with professional performance.

The individual will frequently have dealings with women of social prestige and power. Women may play an important part in the individual's professional affairs.

Transiting Moon Through the Natal Eleventh House

An unusual degree of involvement with friends, groups, and organizations characterizes this transit. These relationships, as well as one's personal goals and objectives, affect the family and domestic life at this time. Business affairs and financial expenditures tend to be related to friends, groups, and organizations and geared to the attainment of personal goals. However, if the Moon makes stress aspects while transiting this house, the individual's friendships or group associations can be disturbed by emotional problems.

Some individuals undergo sudden, unexpected changes in emotional attitude. A greater degree of emotional detachment is often achieved. Friendships with women may be established. Associations with women often arise through groups and organizations.

Transiting Moon Through the Natal Twelfth House

Subconscious forces affect the individual's moods and emotional attitudes more strongly than usual during this transit. Psychic sensitivity, moodiness, loneliness, or shyness occur frequently. This period can be used effectively for meditation and spiritual inner search. Individuals with this transit express greater sympathy toward their family members or toward those less fortunate than themselves.

If the Moon makes stress aspects while transiting this house, and if the rest of the horoscope concurs, the individual can be subjected to emotional hardships and personal confinement or the confinement of a family member, usually in a hospital or an institution.

Transit Moon Conjunctions

Transiting Moon Conjunct the Natal Sun

See "Transiting Sun Conjunct the Natal Moon."

Transiting Moon Conjunct the Natal Moon

Routine domestic and family activities characterize this transit: domestic expenditures, cooking, eating, household chores, family interactions, care of children, business related to the home, domestic products and services, food, farming, and real estate. Interaction with women is probable, and business activities are likely to involve women in some way. The individual is apt to be emotionally sensitive at this time.

Transiting Moon Conjunct Natal Mercury

Communications regarding family and domestic affairs characterize this transit. It is likely to coincide with visitors in the home, receipt of mail and telephone calls, especially from family members, and an emphasis on ordinary household chores. Discussions and activities with friends and groups are likely to take place in the home. The individual's activities and communications are likely to involve women in some way. Communications with brothers, sisters, neighbors, and co-workers are frequent and friendly during this transit.

Business communications and work are apt to relate to food, farming, real estate, the home, and domestic products and services. The individual tends to make many short trips involving food, household shopping, laundry, or health needs.

During this period, the individual often gets practical ideas for improving work efficiency and methodology in everyday tasks. If the conjunction is afflicted, however, idle chatter can interfere with work efficiency. The individual's health affects his or her work productivity, for better or worse. This transit can bring an increased awareness of the need for proper dietary habits, dress, and personal hygiene.

Many individuals gain insights into the influence of family and cultural conditioning on their emotional habit patterns.

Transiting Mercury conjunct the natal Moon has the same significance as the transiting Moon conjunct natal Mercury; however, it lasts for a longer period of time. How long depends on Mercury's speed of motion and whether Mercury is retrograde, stationary, or direct.

Transiting Moon Conjunct Natal Venus

Family, domestic, and social activities characterize this transit. The individual is likely to have an emotionally serene and happy outlook, to be kind and considerate toward women and family members, and sensitive to the emotional needs and feelings of others. This transit stimulates romantic feelings and sexual drives.

This is a good time to beautify the home and improve marital and romantic relationships. The increased sensitivity to beauty and the stimulation of the imagination which this transit provides make this a good period for artistic and musical expression.

Business activities, especially those related to food, real estate, domestic products and services, art, entertainment, and luxury items are favored by this transit. The individual will probably experience increased business and financial opportunities and greater prosperity. This is a favorable time for public relations work and for all dealings with women.

If the conjunction is afflicted by other planets, there can be laziness and maudlin sentimentality, as well as a tendency toward sensuality and overindulgence in eating and drinking.

Transiting Venus conjunct the natal Moon has the same significance as the transiting Moon conjunct natal Venus; however, it lasts for a longer period of time, depending on how fast Venus is moving and whether it is stationary, retrograde, or direct.

Transiting Moon Conjunct Natal Mars

Anger and loss of temper over petty annoyances are common to this transit. Family quarrels and domestic and business aggravation are possible. The individual will initiate energetic activity in the home. This is a good period for home do-it-yourself projects, but it is especially important to observe safety measures.

Family financial needs motivate the individual's business and professional ambitions during this period. Business activities are likely to relate to food, real estate, farming, or domestic products and services.

This is not a favorable time for dealing with women. Salesmen or aggressive people may be a source of annoyance to the individual. In general, it is important to exercise control over the emotions and, at the same time, remain sensitive to the feelings of others. Emotional upsets can cause indigestion during this transit.

If the conjunction is afflicted by other planets, fires or accidents are a possibility.

Transiting Mars conjunct the natal Moon has the same significance as the transiting Moon conjunct natal Mars; however, it lasts for a longer period of time. How long depends on how fast Mars is moving and whether it is retrograde, stationary, or direct.

Transiting Moon Conjunct Natal Jupiter

The home is often the place of educational, religious, and cultural activities during this transit. People from faraway places may visit the home, or the individual may take up residence far away from home. It is a favorable period for changing one's residence.

This transit arouses the patriotic or religious feelings that were instilled during early childhood. Individuals with this transit are more willing than usual to apply spiritual principles to everyday life. Their emotional attitudes are serene and peaceful, and they are likely to express kindness, benevolence, and emotional understanding toward family members and those in need of help.

Increased business and financial prosperity are likely during this period, especially for businesses related to food, farming, real estate, and domestic products and services.

This is a favorable time for dealing with women in connection with educational, cultural, or business affairs.

If the conjunction is afflicted by other planets, the individual is in danger of feeling maudlin sentimentality and overindulging in food and drink.

Transiting Jupiter conjunct the natal Moon has the same significance as the transiting Moon conjunct natal Jupiter; however, it lasts for a longer period of time. This transit, including retrograde and direct motion contacts, occurs once every twelve years and thus indicates a sustained period of opportunity for improved family and financial conditions.

Transiting Moon Conjunct Natal Saturn

Financial difficulties and emotional depression characterize this transit; the former is often caused by business problems or family expenses.

The individuals' responsibilities and the demands made upon them at this time tend to drain their vitality. This, in turn, can lead to a negative emotional outlook. It is important to remember that this condition does not last forever.

The individual may feel or express coldness or lack of sympathy to family members, often because of his or her negative emotional attitude. Caring for an incapacitated or elderly member of the family may become a burdensome responsibility. A tendency to indulge in self-pity at this time may prove to be destructive for the individual. In general, this transit tends to stimulate unpleasant memories based on childhood conditioning.

This is an unfavorable period for dealing with women or for public relations activities. Nor is it favorable for initiating major actions or moves. Necessary tasks should be handled efficiently and practically.

Obstacles can arise in professional and business affairs. Professional problems can isolate one from one's family, and domestic responsibilities can in turn interfere with career advancement and professional responsibilities. However, this transit can indicate practical accomplishment through hard work and discipline.

Old and forgotten associations with women can be renewed under this transit.

The individual's physical problems at this time tend to be water retention and sluggish digestion.

Transiting Saturn conjunct the natal Moon has the same significance as the transiting Moon conjunct natal Saturn. However, because it can last for a month or more, its effects are more serious—the individual is likely to undergo emotional strain for a longer period. It is important to maintain a healthy attitude and to get sufficient rest to avoid lowered vitality and associated emotional depression.

Transiting Moon Conjunct Natal Uranus

Sudden changes of mood and abrupt, unexpected actions both by and toward family and friends are common to this transit. Unexpected events can affect family and domestic affairs. Daily routines can be disrupted in unusual and unexpected ways, adding a note of adventure and excitement.

Friends, groups, and organizations affect the home in some way, often through activities that take place in the home. Friends are likely to drop in unexpectedly during this transit. Relationships with women during this transit are likely to be exciting and unpredictable.

Sudden gains or losses in business often occur during this time. The individual is likely to become involved in corporate finances, other people's money, or matters related to insurance, taxes, alimony, or goods of the dead. These affairs are often related to women or the family in some way.

This is a favorable period for original, innovative home improvements, often involving electronic gadgetry such as electric tools, stereos, and other appliances. If Uranus and the Moon are afflicted natally or by transit, the individual should take care to avoid electrical shocks or accidents.

Some individuals have interesting intuitive experiences and clairvoyant perceptions at this time. Such experiences, or contacts with those who have them, often lead to an interest in astrological or occult subjects.

Transiting Uranus conjunct the natal Moon has the same significance as the transiting Moon conjunct natal Uranus; however, this transit lasts a year or longer, and thus indicates a sustained period of change in the individual's family, domestic, and financial affairs. Often, these changes are brought about by forces beyond the individual's control.

Transiting Moon Conjunct Natal Neptune

Unconscious memories and the intuitive imagination are stimulated during this transit. If these unconscious memories are painful, they can cause psychological difficulties and, in extreme cases, irrational behavior. Sometimes, this takes the form of hallucinations or disturbing psychic experiences, but more often it is simply an unwillingness to cope with the practical affairs of life and psychological withdrawal from interaction with others. Escape into nonproductive daydreaming and woolgathering should be avoided.

On the positive side, precognition, intuitive awareness of the moods and feelings of others, intuitive guidance, and stimulation of the creative artistic imagination can emerge at this time. Some individuals recall their past lives during this transit. Mystical or religious activities may take place in the home, or the individual may use the home as a place of retreat and meditation. Because the effect of this transit is highly emotional, there is a need for a balanced, rational outlook at this time. The individual may seek out ashrams, retreats, or places of seclusion. There is often an increased sensitivity to beauty. Artistic talent may be expressed in decorating the home.

Dealings with hospitals, asylums, religious retreats, and cultural organizations are likely to come about through family needs and activities. Family contacts may be made with people from distant places or foreign countries. This transit can be used constructively for incorporating educational, religious, and cultural values into family life.

Transiting Neptune conjunct the natal Moon has the same significance as the transiting Moon conjunct natal Neptune; however, it can last for a year or longer, indicating an important period in the emotional and spiritual development of the individual. If psychological breakdowns occur during this period, the individual is apt to be institutionalized.

Transiting Moon Conjunct Natal Pluto

Heightened intuitive sensitivity and emotional intensity characterize this transit, as do financial dealings involving corporate business, other people's money, goods of the dead, insurance, taxes, and inheritance. Women tend to play an important role in the individual's business or financial affairs.

There is a strong desire to alter or improve family and domestic conditions. These changes generally involve intense emotional interaction with women or family members. This transit can be used constructively for innovative, resourceful home improvement projects.

There is the probability of dominating or being dominated by family members. A change of residence or the death of a family member is possible under this transit.* The home may be disrupted by large-scale political, economic, cultural, or geological forces, often wars or natural catastrophes, beyond the individual's control.

Individuals tend to be belligerent, coercive, or uncooperative during this transit. This is not a good period for involvement in public relations or being a part of large crowds.

Transiting Pluto conjunct the natal Moon has the same significance as the transiting Moon conjunct natal Pluto; however, it lasts about two years, off and on, as opposed to a few hours of the transiting moon conjunct natal Pluto. It indicates fundamental changes of great importance that affect the individual's emotional outlook, as well as financial, family, and domestic conditions. Important and sometimes irrevocable changes can come about under transiting Pluto conjunct the natal Moon; however, the transiting Moon conjunct natal Pluto can trigger the decisive event, which has been led up to by other long-range influences.

---

* Family deaths are more likely with transiting Pluto conjunct natal Moon than with transiting Moon conjunct natal Pluto. Other confirming influences must be present for a family death to occur.

Transiting Moon Conjunct the Natal North Node and
Opposition the Natal South Node

Favorable relations with the public and the ability to get along in family and domestic relationships characterize this transit. The individuals tend to conform to the cultural expectations of their families. There is an automatic tendency to uphold prevailing cultural attitudes, beliefs, and values. Patriotic feelings are likely to be stimulated by this transit and by one's tendency to identify emotionally with the religious, cultural, or ethnic group to which one belongs.

Transiting North Node conjunct the natal Moon and transiting South Node opposition the natal Moon has the same significance as the transiting Moon conjunct the natal North Node and opposition the natal South Node; however, it lasts for a longer period of time, and marks a sustained period of emotional agreement with prevailing social and cultural attitudes.

Transiting Moon Conjunct the Natal South Node and
Opposition the Natal North Node

Difficulties in accepting the current attitudes and beliefs of one's family and culture characterize this transit. The individual tends to identify with traditional or conservative values, adopt a serious or pessimistic emotional outlook, and avoid public or social contact.

Parental disapproval, slowdown in business activity, and difficulties in public relations tend to occur during this transit.

Transiting South Node conjunct the natal Moon and transiting North Node opposition the natal Moon has the same meaning as the transiting Moon conjunct the natal South Node and opposition the natal North Node; however, it marks a longer period of emotional maladjustment to prevailing social attitudes.

Transiting Moon Conjunct the Natal Ascendant and
Opposition the Natal Descendant

Emotional self-expression and impulsiveness characterize this transit. The individual tends to be concerned with family and domestic affairs. A desire to be noticed, dealings with women and an unusual degree of activity in both personal and domestic affairs are likely at this time.

Transiting Moon Conjunct the Natal Midheaven and Opposition the Natal Nadir

Public relations and family activities that influence the individual's status and career characterize this transit. The individual is likely to attract public notice in some way. Professional activity tends to be related to family affairs, women, food, farming, real estate, or domestic products and services.

Transiting Moon Conjunct the Natal Descendant and Opposition the Natal Ascendant

Contact with the public, domestic and marital issues and dealings with women characterize this transit. Important close personal relationships, especially those involving women, influence the individual's emotional outlook and his or her business, domestic and family affairs, either favorably or unfavorably.

Transiting Moon Conjunct the Natal Nadir and Opposition the Natal Midheaven

Involvement in family and domestic affairs and in emotional issues characterize this transit. The individual's subconscious mind is likely to be stimulated in some way by current domestic issues which bring out past family and cultural conditioning. Business and financial affairs are related to purchases for home, food, farming, or domestic products and services.

Transit Moon Sextiles

Transiting Moon Sextile the Natal Sun

See "Transiting Sun Sextile the Natal Moon."

Transiting Moon Sextile the Natal Moon

Harmonious family and domestic activity and good communication with women and family members characterize this transit. The individual is able to maintain an unusual degree of emotional stability and to be at peace.

Routine letterwriting, telephoning, and short trips for food and household items can be handled satisfactorily at this time. This is a good period for cooking, dietary improvements, domestic improvements, household chores, and business activities concerning food, farming, real estate, and domestic products and services. Business dealings involving women, business communication, and short business trips are favored. This transit is also favorable for family get-togethers and entertaining guests in the home. The individual finds it easier to understand and cooperate with women.

Individuals should be aware of when this transit occurs, so that they can take advantage of the opportunities it offers during its short duration.

Transiting Moon Sextile Natal Mercury

Intellectual activity in the home and insight into the workings of the unconscious mind characterize this transit.

Reading and literary pursuits or occupational activities are likely to take place in the home. The individual will communicate a great deal through conversations, letters, and visits with family members, neighbors, friends, group associates, and co-workers. Individuals with this transit tend to be more practical and rational than usual in their automatic response patterns to outside stimuli.

This is a good time to attend to personal clothing, hygiene, and diet, as well as to household cleanliness and other domestic chores, and to make short shopping trips for clothing, food, and household needs.

This transit favors mail-order businesses, especially those related to women's needs and tastes, health products, household products, and printed matter. It is a good period for advertising, public relations, and dealing with women in the working environment. The individual will have workable ideas for improved business and work effectiveness.

Transiting Mercury sextile the natal Moon has the same significance as the transiting Moon sextile natal Mercury; however, it lasts for a longer period of time, depending on the speed of Mercury and whether Mercury is stationary, retrograde, or direct.

Transiting Moon Sextile Natal Venus

Domestic harmony and consideration for the needs and feelings of others characterize this transit. The individual is likely to have a cheerful and happy emotional outlook and to experience emotional calm.

Social, artistic, and romantic activities are likely to take place in the home. This is a favorable time for decorating the home, gourmet cooking, or entertaining friends in the home. It is a good period for dealings with women, purchasing for the home (especially art and luxury items), and engaging in social activities with family and friends.

This period generally brings business prosperity, especially for businesses dealing with art, entertainment, luxury items, food, real estate, and domestic products and services. Public relations activity or participation in artistic, musical, and cultural events are favored. This can be a period of creative achievement for musicians and artists. In general, this transit enhances the individual's sensitivity and responsiveness to beauty.

Transiting Venus sextile the natal Moon has the same significance as the transiting Moon sextile natal Venus; however, it is of longer duration. How long depends on how fast Venus moves and whether it is stationary, retrograde, or direct. The Moon transiting Venus lasts only a few hours, while Venus sextile to the Moon lasts a day or longer and indicates a sustained period of social and artistic activities.

Transiting Moon Sextile Natal Mars

Energetic emotional expression characterizes this transit. Individuals express their feelings and attitudes directly and honestly. Dynamic communication and interaction with women is likely.

Individuals are apt to promote business and professional affairs by contact with the public. They are energetic and ambitious with regard to both business affairs and domestic tasks. This is a favorable time for home improvement projects that require the use of tools and physical exertion. Actions are likely to be intelligently planned and work efficiency increased.

This transit usually confers greater energy and physical vitality; thus, it is a good time for sports and physical exercise. The individual is likely to work up a healthy appetite which may express itself in enjoyment of hot, spicy foods.

Transiting Mars sextile the natal Moon has the same significance as the transiting Moon sextile natal Mars; however, it lasts for a considerably longer period of time, especially if Mars is stationary or retrograde, and thus marks a sustained period of energetic emotional and physical activity.

Transiting Moon Sextile Natal Jupiter

Ideas for incorporating educational, religious, and cultural values into the family life and home environment characterize this transit.

Cultural, educational, or religious group activities can take place in the home. People from faraway places are likely to visit the home, or individuals of educational, religious, or cultural distinction are entertained in the home. This is a good period for social or business dealings with women and for long journeys or family trips.

This transit can stimulate either conscious or subconscious memories of happy experiences. The individuals have a greater degree of optimism and peace in their emotional outlook and are likely to express greater kindness and consideration toward women, family members, or those less fortunate than themselves.

There is increased prosperity in family finances and businesses, especially those related to food, farming, real estate, and domestic products and services.

Transiting Jupiter sextile the natal Moon has the same significance as the transiting Moon sextile natal Jupiter; however, it lasts longer and thus indicates a sustained period of family and domestic harmony and well-being.

Transiting Moon Sextile Natal Saturn

Attention to domestic chores and the organization of family and domestic affairs characterizes this transit. The individual exercises good judgment in both family finances and outside business affairs.

One is likely to be emotionally controlled and reserved during this transit. This stability is in turn conducive to serious work and study.

There will probably be serious communications concerning business, domestic, and professional affairs. This is a favorable transit for steady progress in businesses related to food, farming, real estate, domestic products and services.

Friendships may be established with older, mature individuals, especially if they are women. This is a good period for dealing with parents or older authority figures. Older women, especially the individual's mother, may give good advice or financial help.

This transit does not produce dramatic effects; however, it does further a conscientious, cautious, conservative, and introspective attitude, which makes it possible to set the practical affairs of life in order.

Transiting Saturn sextile the natal Moon has the same significance as the transiting Moon sextile natal Saturn; however, it lasts for a much longer period of time, a period during which the individual can organize his or her professional, business, and domestic affairs.

Transiting Moon Sextile Natal Uranus

Interesting and unexpected happenings, especially in the family and domestic environment, can interrupt daily routine during this transit. It is an exciting period—humdrum activities and boredom are not present at this time.

The individual tends to have unusual or original ideas for changing the domestic environment. Activities with friends and groups are likely to take place in the home.

The individual can become involved with unusual and intellectually stimulating women.

Unusual and unexpected business opportunities often arise. Some individuals come up with original ideas concerning business and financial affairs, especially those related to inventions, electronics, food, farming, real estate, domestic products and services, joint finances, corporate finances, insurance, taxes, or goods of the dead.

Transiting Uranus sextile the natal Moon has the same significance as the transiting Moon sextile natal Uranus; however, it lasts much longer, and indicates a sustained period of unusual activity and creative intuitive insights. The individual may become involved in exciting new groups or organizations.

Transiting Moon Sextile Natal Neptune

Under this transit, individuals are especially sensitive to the feelings and moods of others. There is a greater sympathy for and psychological understanding of women, family members, and those who are in need.

Stimulation of the intuitive imagination also characterizes this transit. The individual can develop the ability to tap the intuitive wisdom and memory resources of the subconscious mind. Intuitive insights can be gained into ways of handling family finances and business affairs, and sometimes there is telepathic communication with family members. Meditative, mystical, or religious activities are carried on in the home. The creative imagination is enhanced, and artistical and musical endeavors are favored.

Transiting Neptune sextile the natal Moon has the same significance as the transiting Moon sextile natal Neptune; however, it is of longer duration, and indicates a sustained period of inner spiritual growth and awareness.

Transiting Moon Sextile Natal Pluto

Ideas for improving home and family affairs characterize this transit. This is a favorable time for improving relationships with women or family members.

The psychic faculties are stimulated and the individual becomes very aware of everyday occurrences and their long-range significance. The will power to improve efficiency in handling everyday matters becomes available. The individual becomes especially aware of the need to improve his or her eating habits.

Progress can be made in business affairs and matters related to joint moneys, insurance, taxes, inheritance, and corporate business affairs.

This is a favorable time for finding new uses for old or discarded items and for getting rid of those which no longer serve a useful purpose.

Transiting Pluto sextile the natal Moon has the same significance as the transiting Moon sextile natal Pluto; however, it lasts for a much longer interval, and indicates a sustained period of emotional self-regeneration and improvement in business and family affairs.

Transiting Moon Sextile the Natal North Node and Trine the Natal South Node

During this transit, individuals incorporate currently popular cultural values and attitudes into their family affairs. They develop a feeling for the public mood and a rapport with current fads, trends, and attitudes which can be used advantageously in public relations or in business.

Transiting North Node sextile the natal Moon and transiting South Node trine the natal Moon has the same significance as the transiting Moon sextile the natal North Node and trine the natal South Node; however, it lasts longer and, therefore, its influence is more significant.

Transiting Moon Sextile the Natal South Node and Trine the Natal North Node

This transit has basically the same significance as that of the transiting Moon sextile the natal North Node and trine the natal South Node. However, in this case there is a more critical evaluation of current popular attitudes and a greater adherence to traditional cultural values.

Transiting South Node sextile the natal Moon and transiting North

Node trine the natal Moon has the same significance as the transiting Moon sextile the natal South Node and trine the natal North Node; however, it lasts for a longer period of time, and therefore is more significant.

Transiting Moon Sextile the Natal Ascendant and Trine the Natal Descendant

Improved relationships with family members and emotional harmony in the individual's self-expression characterize this transit. This is a period of harmony in partnerships, as well as in marital and domestic affairs. It is also favorable for business dealings with women, public relations, family finances, and money-making endeavors.

Transiting Moon Sextile the Natal Midheaven and Trine the Natal Nadir

Progress in public relations related to one's profession and harmony between one's professional and domestic affairs characterize this transit. The individual perceives intuitively what is needed to make professional affairs run smoothly.

There is enjoyment and harmony in domestic and family activities. This period is favorable for relations with the public, for entertaining business or professional associates in the home, and for business activities related to real estate, farming, food, home, and domestic products and services.

Transiting Moon Sextile the Natal Descendant and Trine the Natal Ascendant

This has basically the same significance as the transiting Moon sextile the natal Ascendant and trine the natal Descendant. However, a more intellectual approach to personal and business relationships and public relations, coupled with increased harmony in emotional self-expression, accompanies this transit.

Transiting Moon Sextile the Natal Nadir and Trine the Natal Midheaven

This transit has basically the same significance as the transiting Moon sextile the natal Midheaven and trine the natal Nadir; however, this transit brings a more intellectual approach to domestic affairs, and harmony in professional affairs.

Transit Moon Squares

Transiting Moon Square the Natal Sun

See "Transiting Sun Square the Natal Moon."

Transiting Moon Square the Natal Moon

Moodiness, inertia, and emotional and domestic problems characterize this transit. Difficulties can arise through women and their emotional problems.

Domestic and professional responsibilities are likely to conflict with each other during this period. This is an unfavorable time for business or for purchasing real estate, food, or household items. Good judgment should be exercised in eating and drinking during this transit.

Transiting Moon Square Natal Mercury

Emotional difficulties tend to interfere with mental concentration during this transit. Environmental distractions can interfere with work and concentration and, in some cases, cause nervousness. Excessive talking about inconsequential matters can also interfere with work efficiency.

Misjudgments or other problems may arise concerning financial expenditures and business affairs. In some cases, delayed shipments or communication breakdowns interfere with business or work. Deficiencies in work methodologies tend to hinder the individual's earning ability or business efficiency. There is a tendency to miss opportunities or overlook important details. This is not a favorable time to formulate contracts or sign agreements. Difficulties of some kind in daily comings and goings and communication breakdowns with women, work associates, or family members are likely.

The individual's dress, personal hygiene, and dietary habits can be the source of problems. There can be temporary ill health or psychosomatic illness.

Subconscious emotional problems stemming from early childhood conditioning tend to interfere with reason and good judgment and with effective organization. Emotional problems can arise in communicating with family members, neighbors, friends, and co-workers.

Normal family routines can be interrupted by unexpected visits or communications. This is an unfavorable time for purchasing clothes or shopping for household items.

Transiting Mercury square the natal Moon has the same significance as the transiting Moon square natal Mercury; however, it lasts for a longer period of time, especially if Mercury is retrograde or stationary. In the latter case, the effects can be much more important than they would be otherwise, and there may be a longer period of difficulty in communication and work and of emotional problems interfering with practical responsibilities.

Transiting Moon Square Natal Venus

Feelings of being unloved, maudlin sentimentality, and ineptitude in social relations are all characteristic of this transit.

Emotional hurts and misunderstandings are apt to arise in marriage, family, or romantic relationships. Imagined hurts and slights where none were intended can make the individual appear emotionally hypersensitive.

There is a tendency to be overprotective of family members, romantic partners, or children. This smothering-love syndrome can thwart the independence and growth of those upon whom it is bestowed, and cause problems for both the individual and his or her associates.

Problems can arise in business and public relations. There is a tendency to avoid work or the unpleasant facts of life. This escapism can take the form of overeating, excessive social activity, sexual overindulgence, or financial extravagance.

The individual's aesthetic taste and good judgment in social situations are at a low point during this period. There is a tendency toward hypocrisy in one's social life in order to avoid unpleasantness.

Transiting Venus square the natal Moon has the same significance as the transiting Moon square natal Venus; however, it lasts for a longer period of time, and thus has a greater effect on the individual.

Transiting Moon Square Natal Mars

Impatience, emotional instability, irritability, and emotional impulsiveness characterize this transit. Family quarrels, problems with women, or loss of temper over petty annoyances are common. Family problems are likely to interfere with business and professional responsibilities.

Emotional upsets and anger under this transit can cause indigestion or stomach upsets.

Accidents and fires in the home are a possibility at this time, usually as a result of impatience, carelessness, or emotional anger that causes the individual to become careless. During this transit, special caution should be exercised in the use of tools and machinery.

This is not a favorable time for public relations. Problems with business or professional affairs can cause irritability, which in turn will be detrimental to harmonious family relationships. This is an unfavorable time for business dealings involving food, farming, real estate, or home products and services.

Transiting Mars square the natal Moon has the same significance as the transiting Moon square natal Mars; however, it lasts for a longer period of time, which varies according to whether Mars is stationary or retrograde. Consequently, this transit can be more than just a passing irritation.

Transiting Moon Square Natal Jupiter

Unrealistic optimism and financial extravagance characterize this transit. Problems often arise over differences in cultural, educational, and religious outlooks within the family. There is a tendency to take too much for granted.

The individual is especially subject at this time to biases based on family, cultural, educational, and religious conditioning. These biases often take the form of family, class, religious, racial, or national prejudice. The excessive need for emotional security engendered by this transit can prove to be debilitating. Maudlin sentimentality and misplaced sympathy often cause these individuals to either become emotionally dependent upon others, especially upon women, or allow others to become emotionally dependent on them. There is a tendency to give in to one's psychological weaknesses, especially escapist tendencies.

Inerita or sentimentality tends to interfere with sound practical judgment. Unrealistic expectations in business or financial matters can cause problems. Domestic projects often turn out to be more costly than anticipated. The individual should guard against a tendency to make promises that cannot be fulfilled.

The individual should be especially careful not to overeat or put on excess weight during this transit.

Transiting Jupiter square the natal Moon has the same significance as the transiting Moon square natal Jupiter; however, it lasts for a much longer period of time and is therefore likely to cause serious mistakes and overindulgences.

Transiting Moon Square Natal Saturn

Emotional depression, sluggish digestion, and oppressive family and business responsibilities characterize this transit.

Difficulties arise in dealings with parents or with older established authority figures or women. Family and professional responsibilities can conflict with each other. Some individuals take on the responsibility of caring for a disabled or older family member.

Problems in everyday affairs force the individual to come to grips with practical reality. Business slowdowns and financial difficulties are likely at this time. Financial, business, professional, and domestic problems are apt to cause worry and anxiety. During this period, it is best to maintain the status quo and leave major changes to a more propitious time.

Painful subconscious memories are often stimulated and cause depression and negative emotional attitudes, which in turn have an adverse effect on practical affairs and family relationships. Some individuals withdraw from others or adopt a cold, unsympathetic attitude. The individual who feels rejected may fail to realize that his or her own negative attitude has brought this about.

Transiting Saturn square the natal Moon has the same significance as the transiting Moon square natal Saturn; however, it is of longer duration, and indicates a sustained period of problems that need attention, plus hardships, lowered vitality, and emotional depression. Transiting Saturn square the natal Moon occurs approximately every fourteen and one-half years.

Transiting Moon Square Natal Uranus

Emotional instability and erratic interactions with women characterize this transit. This is not a good period for important dealings with women.

The individual's unpredictable changes of mood affect family members. Family members may disapprove of the individual's friends or group associates. Problems involving money or emotional issues tend to develop between the individual and his or her friends and associates. Temporary separations from friends, family members, and women associates tend to occur under this transit.

Unexpected deaths of friends or family members is a possibility. Unexpected changes of residence and unanticipated disruptions of daily routines are also likely at this time.

This is not a favorable time to invite friends into the home or carry on organizational activities in the home. Unexpected domestic problems can arise regarding alimony, joint finances, corporate money, insurance, taxes, and inheritance. Household electrical problems with appliances or wiring can come up during this time, and caution should be used in dealing with these problems.

Some individuals behave eccentrically in order to gain attention and arouse an emotional reaction in others. Impulsive spending should be avoided at this time.

Despite all these negative influences, if this transit is used correctly, it can be an important stimulus to the intuitive faculties.

Transiting Uranus square the natal Moon has the same significance as the transiting Moon square natal Uranus; however, it lasts, off and on, for a year or more, thus marking a sustained period of emotional, family, and financial change and readjustment. Large-scale forces beyond one's control may suddenly disrupt one's family, home, and financial affairs. This transit occurs approximately every forty-two years—it is experienced twice in the normal life span.

Transiting Moon Square Natal Neptune

During this transit, the individual is subject to woolgathering, emotional confusion and unwanted psychic impressions.

Subconscious neurotic tendencies may arise, often in the form of difficulties in family relationships and the impractical use of money and possessions. The individual tends to withdraw psychically from family responsibilities. Uncontrolled imagination, daydreaming, and impractical religious and spiritual ideas tend to interfere with the efficient handling of daily responsibilities. Some individuals are attracted to lunatic fringe mystical cults, guru worship, and other unsound mystical practices.

The subconscious mind has a negative influence during this period. The individual's sense of values may be distorted and the stimulation of subconscious memories may evoke inappropriate behavior and emotional reactions. In extreme cases, the individual withdraws into a private world or is institutionalized in some way.

The individual is both prone to deceit and subject to deception by others in financial affairs. Confusion may arise in family activities, and frequently there are emotional problems involving women.

Some specific problems that the individual may have to face during this transit are difficult-to-diagnose digestive disorders and intestinal gas problems, and household difficulties with water, gas, or oil.

Transiting Neptune square the natal Moon has the same significance as the transiting Moon square natal Neptune; however, it lasts, off and on, for a year or longer, and thus indicates a prolonged period of psychic and emotional stress which the individual must learn to handle. This transit occurs only once in the average individual's life.

Transiting Moon Square Natal Pluto

Eruption of deep-seated emotional problems characterizes this transit.

Psychological domination of or by women is a danger. Family conflicts over authority may arise from the individual's attempts to emotionally dominate and remake family members. Joint finances, inheritances, taxes, insurance, alimony, and goods of the dead are often a source of family or business problems. The need to renovate the home can arise, causing a disruption of normal domestic activities. The home and the emotional stability of the individual are often disrupted by large-scale forces. This transit often coincides with the death of a family member. (This is more likely to occur, however, when transiting Pluto is squaring the natal Moon.)

Unpleasant psychic experiences often occur.

Often, the individual feels a desire to sever old emotional and family ties. In general, there is a need to eliminate or regenerate outworn conditions, attitudes, and emotional habits and to regenerate the contents of the subconscious mind. The emotional issues that the individual faces demand such a readjustment.

Transiting Pluto square the natal Moon has the same significance as the transiting Moon square natal Pluto; however, it lasts for a much longer period of time, a year or longer, and indicates a prolonged period of emotional and domestic transformation. This transit occurs only once in an average lifetime.

Transiting Moon Square the Natal North Node and
Square the Natal South Node

Personal emotional attitudes that are out of harmony with prevailing cultural attitudes and expectations characterize this transit.

The individual's difficulty in adjusting to family expectations and cultural requirements can lead to domestic problems. Conflicts with parents are especially likely.

This is an unfavorable time for public relations or business activities involving public contact.

The transiting North and South Nodes square the natal Moon has the same significance as the transiting Moon square the natal North Node and square the natal South Node; however, it lasts longer, and indicates a period of emotional difficulty in adjusting to cultural norms.

Transiting Moon Square the Natal South Node and Square the Natal North Node

See "Transiting Moon Square the Natal North Node and Square the Natal South Node."

Transiting Moon Square the Natal Ascendant and Square the Natal Descendant

Conflict between the conscious will and subconscious conditioning characterize this transit. This conflict often takes the form of emotional difficulties in self-expression and in relating to others, especially to women and to the general public. Emotional difficulties can also arise over marital or domestic problems. This is not a favorable transit for business affairs; emotional problems can cause the individual to spend impulsively.

Transiting Moon Square the Natal Midheaven and Square the Natal Nadir

Emotional problems interfere with professional and domestic responsibilities during this transit. A conflict between domestic and professional responsibilities is likely. This is an unfavorable time for real estate transactions, for domestic or business purchases, and for professional or family dealings that involve women or the public.

Transiting Moon Square the Natal Descendant and Square the Natal Ascendant

See "Transiting Moon Square the Natal Ascendant and Square the Natal Descendant."

Transiting Moon Square the Natal Nadir and Square the Natal Midheaven

See "Transiting Moon Square the Natal Midheaven and Square the Natal Nadir."

Transit Moon Trines

Transiting Moon Trine the Natal Sun

See "Transiting Sun Trine the Natal Moon."

Transiting Moon Trine the Natal Moon

An easy flow in family, domestic, social, cultural, and financial affairs characterizes this transit. It is a favorable time for social activities such as dinner parties and family gatherings and for shopping trips—especially those for food and household items. Business activities related to food, farming, real estate, and domestic products and services are also favored at this time. The individual enjoys cooking and household chores and activities involving women.

Transiting Moon Trine Natal Mercury

A practical and common-sense approach to everyday tasks characterizes this transit. There are likely to be many telephone conversations, comings and goings and visits in the home involving family members, neighbors, friends, and work associates. Harmonious communication with women and enjoyment of intellectual activity also characterize this transit.

There is an interest in improving one's dress, personal and family hygiene, and household order and cleanliness. This is a favorable period for a routine physical checkup. It is also a good time to inform oneself on matters of diet, hygiene, and medicine.

Interest in improving environmental, ecological conditions often develops. The individual is likely to make an effort to bring educational activities into the family life, especially in relation to children.

This is a favorable time for mail-order businesses, especially if they relate to printed matter, clothing, or food or household products and services.

Communication with those in the working environment is improved; ideas for improving work efficiency and methodology will probably be exchanged. This is also a favorable period for public relations work and advertising.

Transiting Mercury trine the natal Moon has the same significance as the transiting Moon trine natal Mercury; however, it lasts for a longer period of time, which varies according to the speed of Mercury's motion and whether Mercury is stationary, retrograde, or direct. Therefore, the improved understanding brought on by this transit may have a long-term significance.

Transiting Moon Trine Natal Venus

Popularity with women, a happy emotional outlook, and enjoyment of social and romantic activities in the home characterize this transit. This is a favorable time for romantic and marital relationships, because of the increased emotional sensitivity and consideration for the needs and feelings of others which this period engenders.

The individual expresses greater emotional understanding and kindness toward family members. This is also a good period for dealing with women or approaching women of wealth and prominence. It is a good time to organize or attend social functions.

This period favors financial prosperity and the enjoyment of the good things of life. It is a favorable time for businesses related to food, the home, domestic products and services, art, music, entertainment, and luxury items. It is a good time to decorate or beautify the home, change residences, or accept new members into the home environment.

Transiting Venus trine the natal Moon has the same significance as the transiting Moon trine natal Venus; however, it lasts for a longer period of time, which varies according to the speed of Venus's motion and whether or not Venus is stationary, retrograde, or direct. It indicates a sustained period of a happy emotional outlook, along with social and financial benefits.

Transiting Moon Trine Natal Mars

Increased energy and vitality and constructive action in the home characterize this transit. The individuals who are experiencing it are likely to be straightforward and honest in expressing their feelings. They can clear the air of their pent-up feelings in a manner that is not destructive. Emotional shyness and timidity can be overcome during this transit. The new adjustments in family relationships that often take place can prove beneficial for both parties. Dynamic and harmonious interaction with women during this time will produce constructive accomplishments.

This is a favorable period for do-it-yourself projects and strenuous physical activity. It is also favorable for the physical work involved in moving or changing residence and for family participation in sports and games.

The individual expresses greater ambition and enterprise in business and professional affairs. This transit is especially favorable for businesses related to engineering, construction, food, farming, real estate, and domestic products and services.

Transiting Mars trine the natal Moon has the same significance as the transiting Moon trine natal Mars; however, it lasts for a longer period of time, which varies according to the speed of the motion of Mars and whether Mars is stationary, retrograde, or direct. It indicates a sustained period of constructive action in domestic and business affairs.

Transiting Moon Trine Natal Jupiter

Kindness, consideration, and cooperation in family relationships and an optimistic emotional outlook characterize this transit. Improved family living conditions and financial prosperity are a good possibility. This is a favorable time for family vacation trips and for entertaining people from distant places. The individual takes an interest in incorporating educational, religious, and cultural values into the family life. This period is favorable for pregnancy and child care, or for expanding the domestic circle in some way.

It is a good time for fundraising for religious, cultural, charitable, or educational institutions, and for visiting relatives in hospitals or institutions. This is a favorable time for dealing with religious institutions, hospitals, schools, or asylums.

It is an excellent time for cooperation with women and with those in positions of cultural prominence.

Business activities related to food, farming, domestic products and services, publishing, real estate, and the financial affairs of religious, cultural, and educational institutions are favored by this transit.

Transiting Jupiter trine the natal Moon has the same significance as the transiting Moon trine natal Jupiter; however, it lasts much longer and indicates important long-range benefits, as opposed to momentary ones. This transit occurs twice in the twelve-year cycle of Jupiter.

Transiting Moon Trine Natal Saturn

This transit is a time to set one's house in order. The emotions are stabilized, and a practical approach prevails in both business and domestic responsibilities. The individual is more cautious and reserved in his or her emotional expressions and responses. There is a greater sense of loyalty both from and toward established friends and a tightening of organizational ties. Marital and family relationships can be put on good footing.

This is a favorable time for dealing with older or established individuals, especially if they are women.

The individual takes a well-organized and responsible approach to business, professional, and domestic affairs. Family and business finances are organized effectively and with greater discipline so that unnecessary expenditures are avoided and the individual's financial position is stabilized. This is a favorable time for businesses involving home and domestic products and services, real estate, farming, and business related to women.

Transiting Saturn trine the natal Moon has the same significance as the transiting Moon trine natal Saturn; however, it lasts for a much longer interval, and indicates a sustained period of stabilization of emotions, domestic affairs, and personal and business finances. This transit occurs twice in Saturn's twenty-nine-year cycle.

Transiting Moon Trine Natal Uranus

Individuals under this transit experience intuitive guidance and inspiration in their family, domestic, and financial affairs. Their intuitive and clairvoyant potential is stimulated, often suddenly and unexpectedly.

These individuals can gain sudden insights into the workings of their subconscious minds and their conditioned habit patterns. Emotional satisfaction can be gained through friendships and through groups and organizations. There are also likely to be exciting interactions with unusual women. Social interaction with friends and groups in the home will be a source of pleasure during this period.

Public relations activities have a unique appeal at this time.

The individual has intuitively inspired original ideas for making money and for improving the domestic environment. Gadgets or modern electrical innovations are often introduced into the home or business.

Ecological concerns and the recycling of waste products become a concern.

Unexpected benefits often arise through insurance, taxes, inheritance, joint money, or corporate business. Unexpected financial and social gains or rewards can come through women or group associates.

A sudden, beneficial change of residence is possible at this time. A friend may either come to live with the individual or be instrumental in providing a new and better home.

Transiting Uranus trine the natal Moon has the same significance as the transiting Moon trine natal Uranus; however, it is of much longer duration, lasting, off and on, for a year or longer and indicating a sustained period of sudden and unusual changes in emotional outlook, intuitive awareness, and domestic affairs.

Transiting Moon Trine Natal Neptune

Intuitive inspiration and stimulation of the imagination characterize this transit. The individuals enjoy the rewards of past good actions in subtle ways, although they may not understand fully how this has come about, and attribute it simply to good fortune.

Individuals under this transit can gain intuitive insights not only into the workings of their own subconscious minds, but into the subconscious processes of their family members. This enables them to be more understanding and compassionate toward the needs and feelings of others, especially those less fortunate than themselves. This is a favorable transit for relating to women and understanding their emotional needs.

The psychological insights gained during this period can help the individual overcome negative habit patterns, and the intuitive guidance it provides can benefit practical affairs such as family finances and business matters.

Artistic and musical expression is enhanced by this transit's stimulation of the imaginative ability. The individuals seek to incorporate artistic, religious, and mystical values and activities into their homes and family lives. This often includes artistic beautification of the home.

This is a favorable time for meditative spiritual practices and for working with astrology or with extrasensory perceptions. It is also a good time for dealing with hospitals and institutions.

Transiting Neptune trine the natal Moon has the same significance as the transiting Moon trine natal Neptune; however, it is of much longer duration, lasting intermittently for a year or longer, and thus marking a sustained period of important psychological evolution in the individual.

Transiting Moon Trine Natal Pluto

During this transit, the individual experiences increased will-power, directed toward improving the status quo of domestic conditions.

This is a favorable time to overcome negative emotional habit patterns. The enhanced intuitive abilities stimulated by this transit make it possible to understand one's past emotional conditions and eliminate that which is detrimental. Increased awareness of the occult side of life which many individuals experience can bring about a better understanding of death and life after death. This transit can also give insights into mass psychology and how to influence it.

The individuals are likely to benefit from joint finances, insurance, taxes, corporate business, and inheritance. They are more resourceful in business and financial affairs and spend money wisely.

A concern with ecological and environmental issues often develops. Old or useless items come to the individual's attention. They are either discarded or put to a creative, and sometimes profitable, use. This is a favorable transit for businesses related to real estate, farming, food, domestic products and services, building, and ecological concerns.

This is a favorable period of dieting, fasting, or other health regimes.

Transiting Pluto trine the natal Moon has the same significance as the transiting Moon trine natal Pluto; however, it lasts for a much longer period of time, intermittently for more than a year, and thus brings about transformations in the everyday conditioning of life which have important and far-reaching consequences.

Transiting Moon Trine the Natal North Node and Sextile the Natal South Node

See "Transiting Moon Sextile the Natal South Node and Trine the Natal North Node."

Transiting Moon Trine the Natal South Node and Sextile the Natal North Node

See "Transiting Moon Sextile the Natal North Node and Trine the Natal South Node."

Transiting Moon Trine the Natal Ascendant and Sextile the Natal Descendant

See "Transiting Moon Sextile the Natal Descendant and Trine the Natal Ascendant."

Transiting Moon Trine the Natal Midheaven and Sextile the Natal Nadir

See "Transiting Moon Sextile the Natal Nadir and Trine the Natal Midheaven."

Transiting Moon Trine the Natal Descendant and Sextile the Natal Ascendant

See "Transiting Moon Sextile the Natal Ascendant and Trine the Natal Descendant."

Transiting Moon Trine the Natal Nadir and Sextile the Natal Midheaven

See "Transiting Moon Sextile the Natal Midheaven and Trine the Natal Nadir."

Transit Moon Oppositions

Transiting Moon Opposition the Natal Sun

See "Transiting Sun Opposition the Natal Moon."

Transiting Moon Opposition the Natal Moon

The need for domestic and family cooperation characterizes this transit. The individual must develop more sensitivity toward everyday household tasks and interpersonal interactions. Failure to do this can cause friction with those in the immediate environment. The individual will probably be subject to periods of moodiness, which will make emotional interaction with others difficult. This is not a favorable time for dealing with women, especially if sensitive emotional issues are involved.

Difficulties may arise in everyday business transactions, or in the handling of family finances. Financial mismanagement may disrupt family relationships.

Emotional disturbances or poor dietary habits often cause indigestion during this period. There is a tendency to overindulge in food and drink. This transit only lasts a few hours and, therefore, the disturbances associated with it are of short duration.

Transiting Moon Opposition Natal Mercury

A tendency to inconsequential talk, disagreement over household duties, and emotionally caused communication difficulties often accompany this transit. Communications about everyday affairs are apt to be confused, or lacking altogether. Disagreements often arise in communications with family members, neighbors, and co-workers, especially women, usually as a result of emotional disturbances of one type or another. Necessary chores in the household or work environment tend to be neglected, and this in turn brings about problems and disagreements with others in the environment.

Individuals under this transit tend to suffer from colds or digestive upsets, usually caused by emotional upsets or improper diet. They often show poor judgment in personal hygiene, dress, speech, and work habits.

Emotional biases and prejudices may interfere with impartial, rational processes, making it difficult for the individuals or those with whom they are dealing to take all pertinent facts into consideration. Gossip can also be a problem, and unnecessary conversation can interfere with work efficiency.

This is not a favorable time for formulating agreements, signing contracts, or making important decisions or communications.

Petty environmental disturbances are likely to interfere with concentration and make the individual nervous and irritable. Annoyances can also arise from unwanted visits by family members, neighbors, or work associates. In some cases, the individuals daydream or let their minds wander. They tend to miss appointments or get lost on the road.

This is not a favorable time for advertising or public relations because the individual's thinking tends to be out of harmony with the public mood.

Transiting Mercury opposition the natal Moon has the same significance as the transiting Moon opposition natal Mercury; however, it lasts for a longer period of time, depending on how fast Mercury is moving and whether it is stationary, retrograde, or direct. Consequently, it marks a sustained period of emotional and mental confusion and need for cooperation.

Transiting Moon Opposition Natal Venus

Emotional upsets in marital, romantic, social, business, and family relationships characterize this transit. There is a special need for cooperation in these areas.

The individuals or those with whom they are associated are prone to hypersensitivity and hurt feelings. Kindness and emotional sensitivity is needed in family relationships if disharmony or separations are to be avoided. Unnecessary expenditures are a common source of family disagreements during this transit.

Social, romantic, and business dealings with women demand special cooperation from the individual or they will give rise to disharmony and emotional upsets.

Financial extravagances on unnecessary luxury items and excessive pursuit of pleasure can be the source of later embarrassment. Art or luxury items purchased at this time are often more expensive than anticipated or lack aesthetic refinement. Excessive eating, drinking, socializing, and sexual activity can result in dissipation, lack of accomplishment, and problems in relationships.

The individual is prone to misplaced sympathy and maudlin sentimentality.

This is not a favorable transit for business related to art, music, luxury items, food, or domestic products and services. Much activity may take place regarding these matters, but there is likely to be a general lack of awareness and cooperation.

Transiting Venus opposition the natal Moon has the same significance as the transiting Moon opposition natal Venus; however, it lasts for a longer period of time. How long depends on whether Venus is stationary, retrograde, or direct. Consequently, it indicates a longer period of susceptibility to emotional, financial, and sexual problems.

Transiting Moon Opposition Natal Mars

Emotional impulsiveness, lack of consideration for the feelings of others, and emotional family conflicts are all typical of this transit. Emotional sensitivity toward others and consideration for their feelings are needed if conflicts and separations are to be avoided at this time. This is especially true in family and business situations, marriages, and dealings with women. There is a tendency to be impatient and annoyed with what the individual considers to be the moodiness and emotional neuroses of others. Sexual aggressiveness can cause anger and resentment in romantic and marital relationships. The individual's domestic and professional responsibilities are likely to conflict. The individual should exercise special diplomacy in business dealings with women so as to avoid unfavorable publicity and injury to status. Impulsive spending is likely to bring about financial difficulties at this time.

The individual may suffer from indigestion brought on by emotional upsets, feelings of anger, or hot, spicy foods.

There is a need to guard against fire, injury, or accidents in the home or place of business. Care should be exercised in handling tools, firearms, and dangerous chemicals.

Transiting Mars opposition the natal Moon has the same significance as the transiting Moon opposition natal Mars; however, it lasts for a longer period, which varies according to how fast Mars is moving and whether it is stationary, retrograde, or direct. Consequently, it marks a sustained period of emotional agitation and petty annoyances.

Transiting Moon Opposition Natal Jupiter

Maudlin sentimentality and misdirected sympathy characterize this transit. There is a tendency to be overly optimistic and financially extravagant.

Religious, ethnic, racial, national, and cultural prejudices instilled by family conditioning are likely to cause problems at this time. Family problems or problems with women tend to arise over differences in cultural, religious, and educational beliefs and attitudes. Individuals with this transit are often hypocritical in these areas—they tend to espouse, but not act upon, noble sentiments and ideologies. In general, they tend to promise more than they can deliver.

There is a tendency toward inertia and procrastination where work and study are concerned and overindulgence in eating and drinking. There is also a tendency to take too much for granted in family and domestic relationships.

Changes in residence, travel, and financial expenditures may not turn out as well as one anticipates. There is a need for caution and conservatism in business and financial dealings, especially if they concern food, farming, real estate, and domestic products and services. Individuals who deal with hospitals and religious, educational, or cultural institutions are likely to experience difficulties.

Transiting Jupiter opposition the natal Moon has the same significance as the transiting Moon opposition natal Jupiter; however, this transit lasts for a longer period of time. How long depends on the speed of Jupiter's motion and whether Jupiter is stationary, retrograde, or direct. This transit occurs once in twelve years and marks a sustained period of emotional self-indulgence and financial extravagance.

Transiting Moon Opposition Natal Saturn

Lowered vitality, sluggish digestion, loneliness, and emotional depression all characterize this transit. Coldness is likely to develop in family relationships and painful subconscious memories can be stimulated. There is often a lack of sympathy and understanding toward or from women and family members.

This is not a favorable transit for dealing with women, older individuals, or those in established positions of power and authority. There can be particular difficulties in relating to parents and older women. Difficulty in family relationships at this time is often the result of a conflict between professional and domestic responsibilities or of financial limitations.

Often, emotional depression and lack of self-confidence have a paralyzing effect on the individual.

This is not a favorable time for business, especially business related to real estate, building, farming, food, and domestic products and services. Public relations and politics are not favored. Difficulties may be imposed by government agencies or public officials.

The difficulties associated with this transit can be offset if the individual cultivates a happy, optimistic outlook and cooperates in a reasonable manner with those in positions of power and authority.

Transiting Saturn opposition the natal Moon has the same significance as the transiting Moon opposition natal Saturn; however, it lasts for a much longer period of time, and indicates a sustained period of emotional frustration and heavy responsibility. This transit occurs once in every twenty-nine years, and lasts from about a month to several months, depending on the speed of Saturn's motion and whether Saturn is stationary, retrograde, or direct during the transit.

Transiting Moon Opposition Natal Uranus

Emotional instability and erratic, sudden disruptions of daily routines often accompany this transit. Sudden changes of mood, an unwillingness to cooperate, and a desire for unrestricted personal freedom can cause difficulties in family relationships.

Sudden, unexpected visits from the individual's friends or group associates often disrupt the domestic scene and cause annoyance for other members of the household. Family members tend to disapprove of the individual's friends during this period. Group and organizational ties can interfere with family business and domestic responsibilities. Relationships with women are likely to be unstable and subject to unexpected erratic changes.

Financial fluctuations and malfunctioning of household or business electrical systems or appliances often occur during this transit. Difficulties can arise over alimony, taxes, insurance, joint moneys, inheritance, corporate money, or goods of the dead. It is important to avoid unnecessary impulsive spending at this time. Unexpected, sudden expenses can arise which make heavy demands on financial reserves.

Transiting Uranus opposition the natal Moon has the same significance as the transiting Moon opposition natal Uranus; however, it lasts intermittently for at least a year, and marks a major period of emotional, financial, and domestic instability and change. This transit occurs once in eighty-four years.

Transiting Moon Opposition Natal Neptune

Sentimentality, misplaced sympathy, and confusing, unwanted psychic impressions characterize this transit. Stimulation of painful subconscious memories can interfere with normal family relationships. In some cases, the individual withdraws into a private dream world, thereby evading practical domestic or business responsibilities. Overindulgence in the wrong foods, alcohol, and drugs is also a danger.

Confusing, deceptive or psychologically distorted relationships with women are also a possibility at this time.

Confusion, indecisiveness, and muddle in everyday affairs can result from an unrealistic attitude toward the necessity for cooperation in family and business affairs and toward the handling of practical responsibilities.

The individual tends to entertain impractical ideas in the areas of education, culture, or religion. These can take the form of negative and undesirable psychic practices, such as involvement in cults, guru worship, or entertaining undesirable psychic influences.

Mismanagement of financial resources can result in the dissipation of money with little understanding of how or why this has occurred. Problems can arise with gas, oil, or water in the home or place of business. Lack of proper hygiene in handling food or in the domestic environment can result in the individual's illness.

Transiting Neptune opposition the natal Moon has the same significance as the transiting Moon opposition natal Neptune; however, it lasts, off and on, for at least a year, indicating a sustained period of emotional and psychic confusion. This transit occurs only once in a normal life span.

Transiting Moon Opposition Natal Pluto

During this transit, the individual lacks consideration for the moods and emotional needs of others. Emotional confrontations and separations can occur in family relationships as a result of family members trying to emotionally dominate or remake each other.

Emotional confrontations with women are likely to occur at this time.

Drastic changes or domestic upheavals can occur in the individual's life, sometimes as a result of ecological, geological, political, economic, or cultural forces beyond the individual's control. This transit can coincide with the death of a family member or with forced changes of residence or business.

In some cases, there is a need to improve the efficiency and the safety of the home environment and expenditure on such improvements may be a necessity.

Financial difficulties can arise through joint finances, corporate money, insurance, taxes, and alimony.

Subconscious forces surface and demand regeneration at this time. The individual may receive disturbing or unwanted psychic impressions. This is not a favorable time for indiscriminate dabbling in occult or psychic practices.

This period can be used constructively, if the individual discards old, inappropriate, and useless habits and attitudes.

Transiting Pluto opposition the natal Moon has the same significance as the transiting Moon opposition natal Pluto; however, it lasts for a longer period of time—at least a year—and demands a sustained effort at regenerating old emotional, domestic, and financial conditions.

Transiting Moon Opposition the Natal North Node and Conjunct the Natal South Node

See "Transiting Moon Conjunct the Natal South Node and Opposition the North Node."

Transiting Moon Opposition the Natal South Node and Conjunct the Natal North Node

See "Transiting Moon Conjunct the Natal North Node and Opposition the Natal South Node."

Transiting Moon Opposition the Natal Ascendant and Conjunct the Natal Descendant

See "Transiting Moon Conjunct the Natal Descendant and Opposition the Natal Ascendant."

Transiting Moon Opposition the Natal Midheaven and Conjunct the Natal Nadir

See "Transiting Moon Conjunct the Natal Nadir and Opposition the Natal Midheaven."

Transiting Moon Opposition the Natal Descendant and Conjunct the Natal Ascendant

See "Transiting Moon Conjunct the Natal Ascendant and Opposition the Natal Descendant."

Transiting Moon Opposition the Natal Nadir and Conjunct the Natal Midheaven

See "Transiting Moon Conjunct the Natal Midheaven and Opposition the Natal Nadir."

21 Transits of Mercury

Transit Mercury Through the Houses

Transiting Mercury Through the Natal First House

Curiosity, intellectual self-confidence and self-expression, and communication of ideas all characterize this transit. One's personal responses are speeded up, and one seems more intelligent and alert.

People become more intellectually competitive during this transit. They initiate communications with their brothers, sisters, neighbors, friends, and co-workers, and tend to take many short trips related to work or matters of personal intellectual interest. This is a favorable transit for lecturing, writing, teaching, study, and correspondence. There will be communication about improving work methods.

Individuals under this transit become more self-conscious and devote more thought to personal goals and self-projection. They become more concerned with their personal dress, diet, and hygiene.

If Mercury makes stress aspects while transiting the natal First House, the individuals tend to become nervous and agitated or adopt a know-it-all attitude. They are easily distracted by environmental disturbances and likely to engage in idle chit-chat that disturbs work efficiency.

Transiting Mercury Through the Natal Second House

During this transit, the individuals are preoccupied with financial matters and with business activities related to intellectual pursuits. They become interested in doing more reading or in undergoing specialized training to improve their earning potentials. Their primary concern is with ideas that have practical application and value.

This is a favorable time for financial planning and for thinking through ways of increasing business efficiency and productivity. Business agreements are often formulated and contracts signed.

Short trips for business reasons or for shopping are likely to be frequent during this transit. Money is often spent on intellectual pursuits. Trips or financial expenditures are often made for health reasons.

If Mercury makes stress aspects while transiting the natal Second House, the individual may have financial worries or be forced to revise business plans and methodologies. Caution should be exercised in formulating business agreements or signing contracts under such stress aspects.

Transiting Mercury Through the Natal Third House

Increased curiosity, communication, and intellectual activity characterize this transit.

The individual is likely to become involved with study, writing, reading, lecturing, correspondence, teaching, telephoning, short trips, or involvement with the news media in some manner. Intellectual activities are likely to involve one's brothers, sisters, neighbors, friends, co-workers, and group associates.

The mental processes are accelerated. This transit often corresponds with important decisions or formulation of plans for the future.

If Mercury makes stress aspects while transiting the natal Third House, communication breakdowns, transportation difficulties, nervousness, mental vacillation, and misunderstandings can arise. Care should be exercised in making important decisions or signing contracts.

Transiting Mercury Through the Natal Fourth House

Communication with family members, intellectual activities in the home, and concern with family intellectual activity are stimulated by this transit.

The individual will have ideas for solving family and domestic problems or for increasing the efficiency of household work methodologies. There will be concern with family health, diet, and hygiene and with household order and cleanliness. Short trips involving family activities or household needs are likely at this time. Friends, co-workers, family members, group associates, neighbors, and people with whom the individual shares intellectual interests are likely to visit in the home.

If Mercury makes stress aspects while transiting the natal Fourth House, emotional problems can interfere with clear thinking. The individual may have difficulty in communicating with family members or about how family concerns should be handled.

Transiting Mercury Through the Natal Fifth House

Enjoyment of literary art forms, intellectual pleasures, and concern with the education of children all are characteristic of this transit.

The individual tends to develop an intellectual interest in sex, games of skill, theater, art, and child psychology.

Romantic opportunities arise in connection with intellectual activities and short trips, or through association with one's neighbors, co-workers, brothers and sisters, or the groups and organizations to which one belongs.

There is likely to be an unusual amount of social activity and communication and comings and goings involving children, romantic partners, co-workers, brothers and sisters, neighbors, friends, or intellectually inclined people.

The individual approaches investments by studying the stock market or other financial areas very carefully.

If Mercury makes stress aspects while transiting this house, pleasurable pursuits may distract the individual from study or work, or lead to ill health.

Transiting Mercury Through the Natal Sixth House

A concern with health, diet, and hygiene, with dress and with work methodologies accompanies this transit. Many individuals take up the study of diet, health, and hygiene.

Often, individuals under this transit learn new work skills or seek education as a means of improving their job status. They tend to come up with new ideas for improving work efficiency. There is increased communication with employers and co-workers and a greater awareness of the need for neatness and order in the work environment.

Short trips may be taken for health reasons or to purchase clothing, tools, or work-related items.

If Mercury makes stress aspects while in this house, there can be worry and concern over the work and health of brothers and sisters, neighbors, friends, or group associates. The individual can become nervous or ill. Idle conversation tends to interfere with work efficiency. Late shipments or technical problems might also interfere with the individual's work, and problems can arise in understanding or communicating with those in the work environment. The individual's health may be endangered by overwork or by occupational hazards.

Transiting Mercury Through the Natal Seventh House

Increased communications with marriage partners, business partners, and the public, along with an intellectual interest in the psychology of others, characterize this transit.

Social interactions with brothers and sisters, neighbors, friends, coworkers, and group associates have an intellectual bent. Some individuals establish close relationships with intellectual or scholarly people.

This transit often coincides with personal involvement in advertising or in public relations activities. Often, the individual is involved with negotiations, bargaining, or the formulation of legal contracts.

There tends to be a concern with the health, dress, hygiene, ideas, and intellectual activities of one's partners, close friends, and spouse.

If Mercury makes stress aspects while transiting this house, the individual may suffer from communication problems with important relationships, or experience legal difficulties or disagreements in marriage and partnerships. Problems might arise in relation to the health or work situation of the individual's partner.

Transiting Mercury Through the Natal Eighth House

Communications concerning joint finances, corporate business, wills, insurance, taxes, alimony, and goods of the dead often accompany this transit.

The individual tends to develop a curiosity about life after death, reincarnation, occult philosophy, and all types of mysterious phenomena. Communication with discarnate entities is a possibility.

Short trips for research or investigation or simply for business reasons are likely at this time.

Involvements with secret communications, with scientific research, or with business, political, or military strategy are also possible. The individuals gain intuitive insights into business, scientific, mystical, political, or military affairs. They are apt to be intrigued by unsolved mysteries or by the secret political and economic machinations of others.

Sex can be the object of scientific curiosity or intellectual interest, especially if Mercury is linked to Uranus, Neptune, or Pluto while transiting this house.

If Mercury is making stress aspects while transiting the natal Eighth House, financial plans may need to be revised. The individual's secret investigations might subject him or her to personal danger. The individual may also be the subject of investigation by others.

Transiting Mercury Through the Natal Ninth House

An intellectual interest in philosophy, education, religion, and law or in foreign cultures and their histories is characteristic of this transit.

If Mercury makes favorable aspects while transiting this house, it is a favorable period for applying for admittance to or work in a university or institution for higher education.

The individual is inclined toward philosophic study and thought. Prophetic insight can be gained into future cultural trends and developments. At any rate, there will be a greater intellectual awareness of what is happening in the larger cultural context.

This is a favorable time for writing, publishing, lecturing, and for long or short-distance traveling or communicating with people of cultural distinction or people associated with universities. Communication with people from distant places is likely.

If Mercury makes stress aspects while transiting this house, the individual's ideas and knowledge may be too general to allow for practical application. Disagreements can arise over religious, philosophic, educational, and cultural concepts.

Transiting Mercury Through the Natal Tenth House

Thought, study, and communications concerning professional and business affairs characterize this transit. During this period, people tend to evaluate ideas in terms of their practical value.

There will be correspondence, telephoning, and short-distance traveling for business and professional reasons. Increased communication is likely with employers and supervisors and with government agencies and those in positions of power and authority. This will probably be a time of professional and business decision-making and, in some cases, the formation of agreements and the signing of contracts.

Some individuals develop an intellectual interest in politics and political organizations. Professional activities are likely to be related to news and the communications media in some way, and public notice and attention from the news media in connection with political and professional activity is a possibility. The individuals' professional affairs are likely to be influenced by their brothers and sisters, neighbors, friends, co-workers, and their more intellectual associates. They may seek specialized training as a means to professional advancement.

If Mercury makes stress aspects while transiting the natal Tenth House, difficulties can arise through disagreements with superiors or through confusion in professional communication or work methodologies. There is also a danger of unfavorable publicity or damage to personal reputation.

Transiting Mercury Through the Natal Eleventh House

Increased communication with friends and with groups and organizations frequently accompanies this transit.

Some individuals develop an interest in scientific subjects or in matters of humanitarian or occult interest. They learn much through discussions with people from all walks of life. Lively discussions can take place with brothers and sisters, neighbors, friends, and group or organizational contacts. Short trips related to friends, groups, and organizations are likely at this time. In general, this transit brings greater universality and impartiality in the individual's point of view.

The individual may experience sudden intuitive ideas and insights, and these may find expression in unique, original achievements. This is a favorable transit for inventors or technological innovators. Involvement in labor union organizations or other professional organizations is also a strong possibility at this time.

If Mercury makes stress aspects while transiting this house, the individual may give or receive erroneous advice or may entertain impractical or eccentric ideas.

Transiting Mercury Through the Natal Twelfth House

Secret communications, psychological insights into the subconscious, and private studies or secret investigations are all common during this transit.

Some individuals develop an intellectual interest in meditation, psychic practices, or intuitive perceptions. If other indications are favorable, the individual may act as an intuitive channel of information from a higher source. Because the intuitive imagination is stimulated, this is a favorable time for creative artists of all types.

The individual tends to communicate with or visit hospitals, asylums, or institutions.

If Mercury makes stress aspects while transiting this house, the individual is subject to woolgathering, daydreaming, subconscious mental distortions, escapist tendencies, secret schemes, misinformation, and distorted communication. All of these factors may contribute to ill health and, in extreme cases, institutionalization.

Transit Mercury Conjunctions

Transiting Mercury Conjunct the Natal Sun

See "Transiting Sun Conjunct Natal Mercury."

Transiting Mercury Conjunct the Natal Moon

See "Transiting Moon Conjunct Natal Mercury."

Transiting Mercury Conjunct Natal Mercury

This is a time of intensified intellectual activity, the beginnings of intellectual projects, curiosity, original ideas, and the expression of one's personal ideas.

This is a favorable time for study, writing, lecturing, teaching, and for all other mental activities. It is especially favorable for scientific studies and pursuits.

It is a time of rational analysis. Individuals under this transit are likely to mentally formulate their goals and objectives and to make important decisions. Some people develop ideas for improving work efficiency and methodologies. Some decide to change their diets, dress and work habits, or their health regimes.

Intensified communication and intellectual activity will take place among brothers, sisters, friends, and co-workers. Some individuals become involved with news or the communications media. Much correspondence, telephoning, and short-distance traveling can take place.

There will be an increase in nervous energy, and this will make the individual seem more alert and aware.

Transiting Mercury Conjunct Natal Venus

Business, social, and romantic communications characterize this transit. The individual is likely to receive welcome news.

Business transactions, invitations or other social communications will be carried on through the mails, especially if these relate to art, music, entertainment, or luxury items. The individual is likely to take an intellectual interest in art, music, and entertainment. There can be an interest in beautifying the work environment and in communicating socially with co-workers. However, if the latter is carried too far, idle chit-chat can interfere with work efficiency. If this conjunction of transiting Mercury to natal Venus receives stress aspects, there can be a tendency to superficiality in social communications.

The individual's mental outlook is cheerful and friendly. There is a curiosity about the psychology of others. This is a favorable period for advertising and public relations.

Individuals under this transit express greater wit, charm, and humor than usual, along with a more diplomatic and charming manner of speech that enhances their personal attractiveness. There is a greater interest in clothing and personal adornment to increase personal attractiveness.

Transiting Venus conjunct natal Mercury has the same significance as transiting Mercury conjunct natal Venus. However, it may last for a slightly longer period of time, depending on how fast Venus is moving and whether Venus is stationary, retrograde, or direct, and it may be accompanied by a slightly greater emphasis on the social aspects of communication.

Transiting Mercury Conjunct Natal Mars

Intellectual debate, contest, and competition characterize this transit.

Individuals are likely to be more aggressive than usual in expressing their ideas and defending their points of view.

This is a good period for business, professional, political, and military strategy. The determination to get the job done and solve problems and the desire to ferret out mysteries are increased. The mental energy and enterprise the individuals apply to their work and study can improve their work efficiency and help them find solutions to their problems.

Heated arguments can be a problem under this transit. If this conjunction receives stress aspects, irritation, argumentativeness, and sarcastic speech may become a serious problem. Political debates or arguments over economic affairs are common.

There is a tendency to nervous irritation, impulsive decisions, and sarcastic speech. Impatience in work can increase the danger of occupational hazards and ruin a job or cause personal injury. Infections, inflammations, injuries, or the need for surgery might occur during this transit.

Secret investigations may involve the individual in some way.

Transiting Mars conjunct natal Mercury has the same significance as transiting Mercury conjunct natal Mars. It occurs about once every two years, is of longer duration, and marks a sustained period of mental excitement and impulsive speech and decision-making. This period varies, however, depending upon how fast Mars is moving and whether Mars is direct, stationary, or retrograde.

Transiting Mercury Conjunct Natal Jupiter

Long-range planning, educational activity, travel, expansion in work, and mental optimism all characterize this transit. The positive thinking which this transit encourages can direct the individual's energy into channels that lead to worthwhile achievements and to greater success and prosperity.

The individual may develop an intellectual interest in religion, philosophy, foreign cultures, or higher education. This is a favorable time to apply for admission to a college or university.

This is also a good period for writing, teaching, lecturing, submitting manuscripts for publication, or dealing with news and communications media. It is favorable for advertising and publicity, and for formulating contracts and agreements.

This is also a favorable time for both short and long journeys. These may be undertaken for work, education, health, or religious reasons or they might be visits to friends or family members.

Transiting Jupiter conjunct natal Mercury has the same significance as transiting Mercury conjunct natal Jupiter; however, it lasts much longer, and indicates a sustained period of mental growth, harmonious communication, and intellectual cultural enrichment. It is characterized by an intensification of religious, philosophic, and educational interests, and it is especially favorable for teachers, lecturers, writers, students, commentators, lawyers, ministers, and reporters. This transit occurs once in twelve years.

Transiting Mercury Conjunct Natal Saturn

Individuals with this transit exercise increased discipline in improving their work efficiency, study habits, scientific methodology, health, diet, personal hygiene, and business and professional affairs.

They are apt to be unusually precise, mathematical, scientific, organized, and systematic at this time. Communications and important decisions concerning professional affairs are likely to arise. The individuals may be subject to heavy work loads and serious responsibilities which can weigh on their minds and possibly sap their vitality. The serious responsibilities may arise through friends, groups, or organizations, or in connection with the individuals' long-range personal goals.

Individuals who are not mature enough to respond to this transit constructively may become worried, mentally depressed, and fearful and consequently develop a negative mental attitude which temporarily closes the door to happiness, growth, and development.

Serious communications are likely to take place with older people and people in established positions and with the individuals' brothers, sisters, neighbors, friends, and co-workers.

This transit often coincides with the signing of contracts and the formulation of serious professional or business agreements. The individual may become involved in writing papers or important reports relating to business or professional affairs.

This is a favorable transit for mathematicians, engineers, scientists, designers, researchers, and efficiency experts.

If this conjunction receives stress aspects, overwork or worry can lead to ill health or unemployment.

Transiting Saturn conjunct natal Mercury has the same significance as transiting Mercury conjunct natal Saturn; however, it lasts for a much longer period of time during which sustained discipline in work and study is required. It occurs once in twenty-nine years, and can last for several months.

Transiting Mercury Conjunct Natal Uranus

Original ideas, sudden intuitive insights, and communication with unusual, interesting people are all common to this transit.

The individual may develop an intellectual interest in scientific or occult subjects, such as electronics, physics, astrology, reincarnation, life after death, and psychology. Some individuals experience an increased interest in using modern technological innovations to speed up work and improve work methodologies. This transit also stimulates original ideas about business and corporate affairs. Sudden decisions or communications may arise concerning corporate business, insurance, taxes, inheritance, alimony, or joint finances.

Work will be more interesting and intellectually stimulating. Unexpected and exciting communications and short trips come about through the individual's friends, groups, associations, and through work, study, research, or scientific activities. These can lead to new friends and new group associations.

The original intellectual inspiration associated with this transit is especially favorable for writers, lecturers, teachers, inventors, reporters, commentators, and scientific researchers. It is an excellent transit for those in the communications media.

However, if Mercury's conjunction to natal Uranus receives stress aspects, the individual's ideas may lack practicality and common sense.

Transiting Uranus conjunct natal Mercury has the same significance as transiting Mercury conjunct natal Uranus; however, it lasts much longer, and indicates a sustained period of creative, intuitive, intellectual insight. This transit occurs only once in the average lifetime.

Transiting Mercury Conjunct Natal Neptune

The individual's intuitive creative imagination is stimulated during this transit. This transit is especially helpful to those engaged in artistic or literary fields.

Insights can be gained into the workings of one's subconscious mind; however, if transiting Mercury conjunct natal Neptune has other natal or transiting stress aspects, conscious reasoning can be distorted by subconscious biases and prejudices. Woolgathering, daydreaming, and uncontrolled imagination can accompany this condition.

Telepathic and clairvoyant abilities may also be stimulated by this transit. The ability to see things projected on one's internal screen of vision is also enhanced. This visualizing ability can be a tremendous help to designers, mathematicians, scientists, and artists.

The individual may gain prophetic insight into future events and cultural trends. Even when dramatic psychic occurrences are not in evidence, the individual is often influenced by an unconscious telepathic interplay that operates on a subliminal level and influences attitudes without the individual's understanding why. An interest in the occult, parapsychology, or mysticism, or in spiritual forms of healing may develop at this time. There is an increased susceptibility to dietary changes, drugs, alcohol, or medications. Any of these can have an undesirable influence if the individual is not cautious. There may also be a susceptibility to serious or hard-to-diagnose illness.

The individual's communications and short trips during this period may involve universities, cultural institutions, hospitals, or asylums.

If the conjunction of transiting Mercury to natal Neptune has stress aspects from other transiting or natal planets, the individual is subject to deception or confusion in communications. This is not a favorable time for formulating or signing contracts because of the possibility of hidden factors.

Transiting Neptune conjunct natal Mercury has the same significance as transiting Mercury conjunct natal Neptune; however, it lasts, off and on, for a year or longer and indicates a sustained period of either intuitive, intellectual inspiration or mental, psychological confusion. This transit occurs only once in an average lifetime.

Transiting Mercury Conjunct Natal Pluto

During this transit, the individual may experience penetrating scientific or occult insights, make irrevocable decisions, or undertake secret communications and investigations related to joint finances, corporate money, insurance, taxes, alimony, or goods of the dead.

This is a favorable time for the study of advanced scientific subjects, parapsychology, and paranormal phenomena. In some cases, intuitive, clairvoyant, and telepathic faculties are stimulated and sometimes result in communication with discarnate entities.

For some individuals, this is a period of uncompromising adherence to personal ideas and viewpoints. It is a favorable time for bettering one's health and diet and for improving work methodologies.

Individuals with this transit may receive critical news concerning their brothers, sisters, neighbors, friends, or co-workers.

If the conjunction of transiting Mercury to natal Pluto has stress aspects from other transiting or natal planets, the individual either experiences or subjects others to mental domination and coercion.

Transiting Pluto conjunct natal Mercury has the same significance as transiting Mercury conjunct natal Pluto; however, it lasts for a year or longer and indicates a sustained period of intellectual, intuitive sensitivity, and critical communications and decisions. This transit can occur only once in a lifetime, because of the long period of Pluto's orbit.

Transiting Mercury Conjunct the Natal North Node and Opposition the Natal South Node

Curiosity about popular cultural trends and attitudes is typical of this transit. The individuals' own particular ideas and communications meet with social approval. Publicity or public notice in some form may come their way. This is a favorable transit for dealing with the fields of advertising and communications. Individuals are likely to adhere intellectually to current cultural attitudes and viewpoints. They are popular with their friends, neighbors, brothers, sisters, and work associates.

Transiting North Node conjunct natal Mercury and transiting South Node opposition natal Mercury has the same significance as transiting Mercury conjunct the natal North Node and opposition the natal South Node; however, it lasts for a longer period of time and indicates a sustained period of intellectual agreement with the social norm.

Transiting Mercury Conjunct the Natal South Node and Opposition the Natal North Node

During this transit, one's intellectual viewpoints are out of sympathy with the current social norm. The individual is likely to identify with traditional rather than currently popular cultural values and ideas and is inclined to be reserved in expressing personal ideas and viewpoints. This transit is unfavorable for dealing with the public or the communications media.

Transiting South Node conjunct natal Mercury and transiting North Node opposition natal Mercury has the same significance as transiting Mercury conjunct the natal South Node and opposition the natal North Node; however, it lasts for a longer period of time and indicates a sustained period when personal intellectual viewpoints are out of sympathy with currently popular social norms.

Transiting Mercury Conjunct the Natal Ascendant and Opposition the Natal Descendant

The dynamic expression of one's personal ideas and increased personal involvement in intellectual activities characterize this transit.

Individuals with this transit are likely to initiate communications and to engage in study, reading, logical thinking, or literary and educational activities. They are also likely to take many short trips.

This is a good period to inaugurate ideas for improving work efficiency or to take steps to improve health through diet and hygiene. There is often a concern with clothing as a means of improving personal appearance.

Transiting Mercury Conjunct the Natal Midheaven and Opposition the Natal Nadir

Intellectual ambition, professional communications, thinking and study related to career activities, and education for the purpose of professional advancement characterize this transit.

The individuals' career activities are likely to involve them in dealing with the communications media, in taking short trips or in making important decisions. Communication and paperwork, often in the form of writing reports or proposals, is likely at this time, usually in connection with one's supervisors, employers, government agencies, or those in established positions of power and authority.

Publicity can affect the individual, whether favorably or unfavorably depends on how Mercury is aspected in the natal chart.

Transiting Mercury Conjunct the Natal Descendant and Opposition the Natal Ascendant

Increased communication with marriage and business partners and partnerships with intellectual people characterize this transit. Discussions and debates are common.

The individual may become involved in legal matters. This is a favorable time for the formulation of contracts and agreements, unless Mercury is under stress aspects natally or by transit.

Dealings with the public and with communications media are likely. The individual may develop an interest in the psychology of human relationships.

Transiting Mercury Conjunct the Natal Nadir and Opposition the Natal Midheaven

Communication with family members and intellectual activities in the home are increased during this transit. Brothers, sisters, neighbors, friends, co-workers, or group associates are likely to visit. Much reading, writing, telephoning, and discussion is likely to take place in the home. The individual may come up with ideas for doing household chores more efficiently or for solving other household problems. Family health, hygiene, order, and cleanliness take on more importance. The individual tends to make short trips for family reasons or household shopping.

If transiting Mercury is under stress aspects, confusion can arise in family communications.

Transit Mercury Sextiles

Transiting Mercury Sextile the Natal Sun

See "Transiting Sun Sextile Natal Mercury."

Transiting Mercury Sextile the Natal Moon

See "Transiting Moon Sextile Natal Mercury."

Transiting Mercury Sextile Natal Mercury

Intellectual activity, original ideas, and increased study, reading, and communications characterize this transit.

This is a favorable period for dealing with the communications media, or engaging in advertising or public relations work. This is also a favorable time for writing, teaching, studying, and attending classes.

Much short-distance traveling related to work, health, friends, intellectual interest, and group and organization activities can be expected.

Transiting Mercury Sextile Natal Venus

Harmonious communication with social contacts and with business, romantic, and marital partners characterizes this transit.

It is a favorable transit for public relations work, advertising, and business communications. It also favors work or businesses related to art, music, entertainment, or luxury items. A harmonious atmosphere in the working environment becomes especially important.

Individuals with this transit tend to express an appreciation for literary art forms. They exhibit an unusual degree of grace, diplomacy, and tact in their speech and communication and become more interested in pleasing others in their dress and personal adornments.

This is a favorable transit for short trips related to business or romance or to the individual's social and artistic activities.

Some individuals develop an interest in human relationships and psychology. Harmonious communications and harmonious relationships with brothers, sisters, neighbors, co-workers, group and organizational associates can be brought into being at this time.

Transiting Venus sextile natal Mercury has the same significance as transiting Mercury sextile natal Venus; however, it usually lasts for a longer period of time, depending on how fast Venus is moving and whether or not it is stationary, retrograde, or direct, thus indicating a longer period of harmonious social and intellectual interchange.

Transiting Mercury Sextile Natal Mars

A positive and dynamic assertion of one's personal ideas characterizes this transit.

This is a favorable period for debates and intellectual contests. Communications and short trips related to work, corporate affairs, business, engineering, scientific pursuits, or physical activity such as sports are likely.

The individual tends to develop ideas for improving professional, business, and work efficiency. In general, this transit provides the opportunity to put one's ideas into practical application.

It is a good period for formulating business contracts and agreements and for professional and business strategy and planning. Matters relating to joint finances, corporate business, insurance, taxes, and alimony can be efficiently handled at this time.

The individual displays greater energy and initiative in study, especially in fields related to science, engineering, economics, and military affairs.

This is a favorable time for investigative work of all types. It is also a good period for skilled artisans and craftsmen who work with their hands.

The individual is able to communicate honestly and directly about sexual and emotional issues.

Transiting Mars sextile natal Mercury has the same significance as transiting Mercury sextile natal Mars; however, it usually lasts for a longer interval, depending on the speed of Mars and whether it is stationary, retrograde, or direct in motion, thus indicating a sustained period of mental initiative.

Transiting Mercury Sextile Natal Jupiter

Positive thinking, intellectual optimism, and curiosity about philosophy, religion, and higher education characterize this transit.

It is a favorable transit for both short and long journeys and for communication with those in faraway places. The individual experiences a heightened curiosity concerning foreign cultures, religions, histories, languages, and traditions. This is a good time to apply for admission to a college or university or to submit a manuscript for publication. This transit is favorable for writers, teachers, lecturers, and those engaged in literary pursuits, and for those involved with news and communications media. The individual's work tends to proceed harmoniously during this transit.

There is likely to be involvement in cultural, religious, philosophic, or educational studies, groups, or organizations. Prophetic insights into future trends and developments are sometimes gained.

This is a favorable time for formulating and signing contracts and agreements. Mail-order and shipping business are favored.

This is a favorable transit for seeking accurate medical diagnosis and treatment.

Transiting Jupiter sextile natal Mercury has the same significance as transiting Mercury sextile natal Jupiter; however, it lasts for a much longer period of time, and indicates a sustained interval of intellectual and cultural enrichment. This transit occurs twice in twelve years and marks important periods of intellectual, religious, and cultural growth and expansion.

Transiting Mercury Sextile Natal Saturn

Realistic thinking, mental organization, serious study, work organization, and long-range planning characterize this transit.

This is an excellent transit for serious study and work in such fields as mathematics, science, business, and engineering. It is also a good period for serious scientific or professional research or writing. The individual is able to muster up the discipline to write term papers, articles, and reports. Education may be sought as a means to career advancement. Some people become involved with serious educational, scientific, or professional groups and organizations, and new professional and educational opportunities can arise through such involvements. Short trips and communications related to business and professional affairs may also bring new opportunities to the individual during this transit. Serious contractual or partnership agreements are favored.

The individual becomes more serious concerning proper diet, health regimes, and hygiene.

Serious communication with brothers, sisters, friends, co-workers, and group associates is likely. Contacts with old friends or group associates tend to be re-established. The individual can benefit from the advice of older, mature, or experienced individuals.

Transiting Saturn sextile natal Mercury has the same significance as transiting Mercury sextile natal Saturn; however, it is of longer duration and marks a sustained period of serious mental concentration and discipline. This transit can last for several months, depending on whether Saturn is retrograde, stationary, or direct. It occurs twice in a twenty-nine-year period.

Transiting Mercury Sextile Natal Uranus

During this transit, the individual engages in unexpected, unusual, or interesting communications and gains intuitive ideas and insights.

This is a favorable transit for work with scientific technology, electronics, or new techniques for improving work efficiency and productivity. The individual may get involved with electronic communications media, astrology, occult subjects, or scientific study or research. Latent intuitive or clairvoyant faculties are sometimes stimulated at this time. The individual may develop an interest in unusual healing methods.

Unexpected communications frequently take place with one's brothers, sisters, neighbors, friends, group associates, and co-workers.

Short trips are likely in connection with scientific interests, friends, or groups and organizations. Intellectually stimulating group and organizational ties often bring sudden opportunities for the realization of personal goals and objectives.

Transiting Uranus sextile natal Mercury has the same significance as transiting Mercury sextile natal Uranus; however, it lasts, intermittently, for a year or longer, indicating a sustained period of intellectual development. This transit occurs twice in eighty-four years.

Transiting Mercury Sextile Natal Neptune

An improved ability to visualize ideas, telepathic communication, heightened intuitive awareness, and insights into the subconscious mind characterize this transit.

This is a favorable period for the study of mystical and occult subjects. The individual may become a channel for information from a spiritual source.

Short trips are likely. Opportunities for work or education that involve hospitals, churches, asylums, or other institutions often open up during this transit.

Creative literary expression and other art forms are favored, especially photography, drawing, and painting.

The individual may become party to secret information that can be worked to advantage in some way.

Transiting Neptune sextile natal Mercury has the same significance as transiting Mercury sextile natal Neptune; however, it lasts, off and on, for a year or longer, indicating a sustained period of intuitive mental awakening. This transit occurs once or twice in the average lifetime.

Transiting Mercury Sextile Natal Pluto

Breakthroughs in scientific understanding and insights into the occult laws of nature and the fundamental causes behind all manifestation characterize this transit.

Clairvoyant perceptions, telepathic communications, and intuitive guidance are often experienced during this transit. This is a favorable period for the study of parapsychological or mystical subjects. The individual may become a party to secret privileged information which can be used for his or her benefit.

The individual tends to be motivated toward educational or intellectual self-improvement. Some individuals develop an interest in subjects such as physics, mathematics, economics, genetics, and sex.

The need to regenerate health, diet, and personal hygiene becomes apparent to the individual.

Ideas, decisions, and communications and work related to joint finances, corporate money, taxes, insurance, inheritance, and goods of the dead are favored at this time. These business and financial activities are likely to bring about the need for short trips.

Transiting Pluto sextile natal Mercury has the same significance as transiting Mercury sextile natal Pluto; however, it is of much longer duration and indicates a sustained period of profound thought, study, and opportunities for improvement of the mind, perceptive abilities, work, health, and communications. This transit occurs only once, at most twice, in a lifetime.

Transiting Mercury Sextile the Natal North Node and Trine the Natal South Node

Increased personal communication and ideas that are in harmony with currently popular trends, customs, and cultural attitudes characterize this transit.

At this time, the individual may be able to influence cultural attitudes and opinions in his or her immediate circle and, perhaps, outside it. This is a favorable period for public relations, advertising, or short trips involving contact with the public.

The apparel and eating habits of the individual are likely to reflect current vogues.

Transiting North Node sextile natal Mercury and transiting South Node trine natal Mercury has the same significance as transiting Mercury sextile the natal North Node and trine the Natal South Node; however, it lasts longer and indicates a sustained period of harmonious intellectual interaction with the prevailing cultural milieu.

Transiting Mercury Sextile the Natal South Node and Trine the Natal North Node

This transit has basically the same significance as transiting Mercury sextile the natal North Node and trine the natal South Node—the difference is a greater intellectual interest in traditional cultural thought, and an easy flow in relation to currently popular ideas.

Transiting South Node sextile natal Mercury and transiting North Node trine natal Mercury has the same significance as transiting Mercury sextile the natal South Node and trine the natal North Node; however, it is of longer duration, indicating a prolonged period of constructive communication with the public and understanding of mass psychology.

Transiting Mercury Sextile the Natal Ascendant and Trine the Natal Descendant

An easy flow in communication and harmony in the expression of ideas characterize this transit. It is favorable for communication with the public, close friends, and marital and business partners. It is also favorable for intellectual endeavors, short trips, communications in general, and dealings with the communications media. This is a good period for improving work efficiency and for bettering one's health, diet, and dress.

Writing and study are also favored. The individual is likely to experience increased intellectual self-expression, intellectual creativity, and harmony with others.

Transiting Mercury Sextile the Natal Midheaven and Trine the Natal Nadir

Communication that furthers professional and domestic progress is characteristic of this transit. The individual has ideas for improving professional and domestic efficiency. This is a good period for approaching those in power and authority with ideas and communications. Public relations work and intellectual activities in the home environment are favored.

Transiting Mercury Sextile the Natal Descendant and Trine the Natal Ascendant

This has basically the same significance as transiting Mercury sextile the natal Ascendant and trine the natal Descendant. Here, however, there is a greater ease in intellectual expression and a more analytical approach in communicating with others.

Transiting Mercury Sextile the Natal Nadir and Trine the Natal Midheaven

This has basically the same significance as transiting Mercury sextile the natal Midheaven and trine the natal Nadir. This transit brings about an easy flow of professional ideas and communications and an analytical approach to understanding family and domestic affairs.

Transit Mercury Squares

Transiting Mercury Square the Natal Sun

See "Transiting Sun Square Natal Mercury."

Transiting Mercury Square the Natal Moon

See "Transiting Moon Square Natal Mercury."

Transiting Mercury Square Natal Mercury

Mental frustration, nervousness, problems with health and work, and difficulties in communication and transportation as well as difficulties with brothers, sisters, and neighbors all characterize this transit.

The individual is likely to exercise poor judgment and experience difficulty in getting his or her ideas and viewpoints recognized. Problems may arise in dealing with news and communications media. Delays in mail and shipments or transportation difficulties may interfere with the individual's work efficiency. Problems may arise in connection with clothing, diet, or personal hygiene. The individual tends to feel impatient with his or her work, study, or intellectual endeavors.

Transiting Mercury Square Natal Venus

Difficulties in social or romantic communication are common during this transit.

The individual tends to be reticent in expressing honest feelings and opinions in order to avoid possible unpleasantness. Some people become emotionally hypersensitive to the attitudes of others or find that they must deal with people who are.

This is not a favorable period for social calls or telephone conversations or for public relations, business communications, communications with women, or literary expressions. It is also an unfavorable time to ask for a raise or to seek social or financial favors.

The individual's mental discipline tends to weaken. Favoritism or emotional likes and dislikes can interfere with logical and practical decisions. Gossip or trivial social talk may interfere with the individual's work.

Unnecessary financial expenditures or poor taste in the selection of clothes or personal adornment often accompany this transit. There is a tendency to overindulge in sweets or rich foods.

Transiting Venus square natal Mercury has the same significance as transiting Mercury square natal Venus; however, it lasts for a longer period, depending on how fast Venus is moving and whether or not it is stationary, retrograde, or direct. This transit indicates a longer time of difficulty and problems with social communication and interaction.

Transiting Mercury Square Natal Mars

A tendency to mental irritation, heated arguments, back-biting, sarcasm, and verbal expression of anger characterizes this transit.

Difficulties in business communications and disagreements over joint finances, corporate money, taxes, insurance, inheritance, alimony, and professional activities are likely under this transit.

This is not a good period for approaching authority figures with one's personal ideas and projects.

Disagreements may arise over work methodologies. Occupational hazards or work-related accidents are a danger at this time, and special care should be exercised in the use of tools, sharp instruments, firearms, and fire. Impulsiveness and irritation are likely to cause automobile accidents during this time. Environmental noise, pollution, and confusion have an especially irritating effect on the individual.

Indigestion and infectious diseases are also a danger at this time.

Transiting Mars square natal Mercury has the same significance as transiting Mercury square natal Mars; however, it usually lasts for a longer period of time—how long depends on how fast Mars is moving and whether Mars is stationary, retrograde, or direct. It indicates a longer period of work and health problems, including mental irritations.

Transiting Mercury Square Natal Jupiter

Unrealistic thinking, impractical studies and intellectual pursuits, mental laziness, and lack of attention to detail characterize this transit.

The individual may lack the discipline to put ideas into practical application. Confusion in keeping appointments, transportation problems, and lack of clear focus in intellectual endeavors can also make the individual less effective at this time. The proper use of factual information tends to be a problem.

Misplaced sympathy and hypocrisy in one's educational, philosophic, religious, and cultural ideas are typical of this transit.

This is not a favorable period for travel, change of occupation, seeking admittance to a school or university, or dealings with religious, educational, or cultural institutions.

During this transit, family upbringing and educational, religious, philosophic, and cultural views tend to interfere with a practical and objective view of reality. The individual's ideas during this period may be too grandiose for the time, money, energy, and resources available. Nor is this a favorable period for dealing with those who are far away or with matters relating to long-distance communication and commerce. In particular, problems may arise in communicating with foreigners or in dealings with matters relating to foreign cultures.

Transiting Jupiter square natal Mercury has the same significance as transiting Mercury square natal Jupiter; however, it is of longer duration, and indicates a sustained period of lack of clear mental focus. It occurs twice during Jupiter's twelve-year cycle.

Transiting Mercury Square Natal Saturn

A pessimistic mental outlook, worry and anxiety, inhibitions in communications, and a heavy work load characterize this transit.

This can be a difficult time for students or those whose work requires intellectual discipline. There can be a lack of mental inspiration, as well as difficulties in dealing with bosses and superiors. This is not a good time to apply for a job or to seek communication with those in positions of power and authority.

Disagreements and problems can arise with friends, groups, and organizational associates. One can experience unsympathetic attitudes from one's brothers and sisters, neighbors, friends, or co-workers, or from elderly people or those in established positions of power and authority.

Work and productivity can be slowed by delayed communications and shipments. Legal difficulties, red tape, trouble with government agencies, and responsibility connected with older people may present problems at this time.

Ill health due to overwork, environmental hazards, lowered vitality, or worry and mental strain is typical of this transit. Health problems are likely to involve the nerves, lungs, teeth, skin, bones, knees, or intestines.

Transiting Saturn square natal Mercury has the same significance as transiting Mercury square natal Saturn; however, it lasts for a much longer interval, and indicates a sustained period of worry and responsibility. This transit occurs twice in the twenty-nine-year cycle of Saturn.

Transiting Mercury Square Natal Uranus

Impractical ideas, lack of mental continuity, impulsive decisions, and inability or unwillingness to apply ideas in a practical way characterize this transit.

Unexpected problems can also interfere with the work of well-organized and disciplined individuals at this time.

Nervousness, impulsiveness, intellectual conceit, and association with eccentric or unreliable people can make one ineffectual in both one's ideas and one's endeavors. The individual should beware of a tendency to jump to conclusions without sufficient information. Good advice is likely to be ignored, due to fixed opinions and attitudes. Mental vacillations in response to the opinions of one's friends, neighbors, brothers, sisters, and co-workers may become a problem.

Unexpected events can disrupt plans; the individual may lose his or her job unexpectedly. This is not a good period to seek employment or change positions. Caution should be exercised in formulating contracts and agreements or in making plans involving friends, groups, and organizations; unforeseen difficulties will probably arise.

Unexpected difficulties may also arise concerning corporate money, joint finances, insurance, taxes, alimony, and goods of the dead. Electronic equipment, such as computers, telephones, radios, and televisions, is likely to malfunction at this time. The individual should drive very cautiously during this transit.

Uneven or spasmodic blood circulation may affect the health at this time.

Transiting Uranus square natal Mercury has the same significance as transiting Mercury square natal Uranus; however, it is a much longer interval, indicating a sustained period of mental confusion and difficulty. This transit usually occurs twice during the eighty-four-year cycle of Uranus.

Transiting Mercury Square Natal Neptune

Woolgathering and subconscious distortion of the reasoning process characterize this transit.

The individual is likely to experience mental confusion, vagueness, psychological withdrawal, fantasizing, and evasion of work. There is often a tendency to notice some facts and ignore others, as dictated by subconscious emotional prejudices. The individual's thinking can become so vague or general that practical application of his or her ideas becomes difficult or impossible. Confusion, deception, or misunderstanding in communication often brings on undesirable consequences, and unintentional divulging of secrets can be troublesome for the individual.

Misuse of drugs or medication during this transit is more likely than usual to bring about disorientation. The individual may also be troubled by disturbing psychic experiences.

This is an unfavorable period for formulating contracts or signing agreements: hidden factors can cause difficulties that could undermine the situation.

Transiting Neptune square natal Mercury has the same significance as transiting Mercury square natal Neptune; however, it is of longer duration, and indicates a prolonged period of psychological confusion and problems. This transit occurs only once in an average life span, as Neptune takes 164 years for its orbital cycle.

Transiting Mercury Square Natal Pluto

Prying curiosity, suspicion, mistrust, secret investigations, power struggles, mental coercion, and sarcastic speech all characterize this transit.

Difficult business decisions and the discomfort of possessing secret information are often associated with this transit. Unpleasant or disturbing psychic or telepathic experiences may be a problem.

Problems involving joint finances, taxes, insurance, alimony, and goods of the dead may arise. This is not a good time to sign contracts and agreements.

Personal diet, dress, and hygiene may need revision or reform. Often there are disagreements over sex. Social diseases are often contracted during this transit. Occupational hazards and ecological problems may also endanger the individual's life and health. Traveling often presents a danger. Short trips through dangerous neighborhoods or places where mobs and gangs are present should be avoided at this time.

The necessity for new methodologies in the working environment will affect the individual in some way.

Individuals with this transit may be forced to discard old ideas and concepts and radically change their viewpoints. Their mental concerns are with large-scale problems that affect civilization as a whole.

Transiting Pluto square natal Mercury has the same significance as transiting Mercury square natal Pluto; however, it lasts for a much longer period of time and occurs only once in an average life span, thus marking an interval of intense mental stress and pressure. The cycle of Pluto lasts for about 245 years.

Transiting Mercury Square the Natal North Node and Square the Natal South Node

The individual's ideas and communications tend to be out of harmony with the prevailing cultural norm during this transit. A critical attitude toward popular trends and social beliefs is frequently adopted. Social communications are often limited in some way, or even cut off. This is an unfavorable time for engaging in public relations activity or dealing with the communications media.

Transiting North and South Nodes square natal Mercury has the same significance as transiting Mercury square the natal North Node and square the natal South Node; however, it brings about a sustained period of intellectual and social maladjustment that creates problems for the individual.

Transiting Mercury Square the Natal South Node and Square the Natal North Node

See "Transiting Mercury Square the Natal North Node and Square the Natal South Node."

Transiting Mercury Square the Natal Ascendant and Square the Natal Descendant

Problems in personal communications and disagreements in one's marriage, partnerships, and public relations characterize this transit.

Disagreements, problems or misunderstandings involving brothers, sisters, neighbors, friends, co-workers, or group associates are likely to arise at this time. Transportation difficulties may be an additional source of annoyance.

Nervousness and work and health difficulties often emerge. This is an unfavorable period for writing, teaching, lecturing, or other intellectual activities.

Transiting Mercury Square the Natal Midheaven and Square the Natal Nadir

Difficulties in public relations and in professional and domestic communications characterize this transit.

Problems are likely to arise in the individual's professional and domestic work responsibilities. Overwork or unfavorable communications of some kind may give rise to ill health.

The individual's reputation or family relationships may be damaged by unfavorable talk, news, or gossip. The meddling of brothers, sisters, neighbors, friends, or co-workers in the individual's professional, family or domestic affairs are another frequent source of problems.

Transiting Mercury Square the Natal Descendant and
Square the Natal Ascendant

See "Transiting Mercury Square the Natal Ascendant and Square the Natal Descendant."

Transiting Mercury Square the Natal Nadir and
Square the Natal Midheaven

See "Transiting Mercury Square the Natal Midheaven and Square the Natal Nadir."

Transit Mercury Trines

Transiting Mercury Trine the Natal Sun

See "Transiting Sun Trine Natal Mercury."

Transiting Mercury Trine the Natal Moon

See "Transiting Moon Trine Natal Mercury."

Transiting Mercury Trine Natal Mercury

An easy flow in communications and creative thinking, especially where creative ideas for improving work efficiency are concerned, characterize this transit.

It is a good period to apply for a job or to formulate contracts or sign agreements. This is a favorable transit for all intellectual or educational endeavors, especially writing, reading, teaching, lecturing, and mathematical and scientific work. Communications with brothers and sisters, neighbors, friends, group and work associates are also favored.

Transiting Mercury Trine Natal Venus

Grace in speech, improved personal appearance, harmonious social communications, and a greater awareness of and communication regarding the needs and feelings of others characterize this transit.

This is an excellent transit for communications and correspondence that require tact and diplomacy. It is favorable for businesses related to clothing, food, restaurants, art, music, entertainment, health, beauty products, and luxury items.

The individual will intellectually appreciate and enjoy art, music, theater, and other cultural and artistic activities. Both short and long trips may be taken for work, pleasure, or social reasons; travel during this period often combines work and pleasure. Social and romantic opportunities arise through work, through one's brothers and sisters, or through neighbors and friends.

Transiting Venus trine natal Mercury has the same significance as transiting Mercury trine natal Venus; however, it usually lasts for a longer period of time, depending on how fast Venus is moving and whether Venus is stationary, retrograde, or direct.

Transiting Mercury Trine Natal Mars

Intelligently directed energy, decisiveness, and the ability to plan effective actions characterize this transit.

Individuals with this transit are able to coordinate their thoughts and their physical actions. They are enterprising and efficient in their work. They express initiative in study, writing, and research or in the fields of communications, business strategy, science, or engineering. This is an excellent time for work requiring skilled craftsmanship in the use of tools. It is also an excellent period for formulating and signing contractual agreements.

This is a favorable transit for political discussions and debates and for planning military strategy. Police and military activities are favored.

The individual's health is likely to improve through exercise and physical fitness programs.

Transiting Mars trine natal Mercury has the same significance as transiting Mercury trine natal Mars; however, it usually lasts for a longer period of time, depending on the speed of the motion of Mars and whether Mars is retrograde, stationary, or direct. It marks a sustained period of creative and constructive mental initiative.

Transiting Mercury Trine Natal Jupiter

An expansive, optimistic mental outlook characterizes this transit.

Because of this optimism, the individuals relax and, consequently, their health is improved through the relaxation of the nervous and glandular systems.

This is an excellent time for study, writing, teaching, lecturing, dealing with communications media, applying for admission to a university, or for long- or short-distance traveling related to philosophy, religion, and higher education. Trade and long-distance commerce are favored, as are dealings with foreigners, foreign countries, or foreign cultures.

Job opportunities or promotions arise if the individual's past efforts warrant such expansion.

This is a favorable time for cultural public relations and for advertising and promotional efforts. Communication in family and domestic relationships improves. Individuals with this transit can benefit both themselves and others through participation in cultural, religious, and educational groups and organizations.

There is a good balance between attention to practical details and a comprehensive view of things. The ethical use of information is of particular concern to the individual.

Transiting Jupiter trine natal Mercury has the same significance as transiting Mercury trine natal Jupiter; however, it lasts for a longer period of time. How long depends on how fast Jupiter is moving and whether Jupiter is retrograde, stationary, or direct. It indicates a sustained period of intellectual growth and mental optimism.

Transiting Mercury Trine Natal Saturn

Accuracy in communication, practical thinking, and good business and professional planning characterize this transit.

The individual may be motivated to seek specialized training or education for purposes of career advancement. Many people are inclined to implement their ideas in a practical way, and this too aids them in careers as well as improving their work efficiency.

Helpful guidance and counsel may be obtained from older or more experienced people or, if the individual is qualified, he or she may act as a guide and counselor to others. It is a favorable period for communicating with those in positions of established power and authority.

It is an excellent time for writing and lecturing and for teaching serious subjects. Serious study of mathematics, engineering, science, and economics or other mental disciplines that require an organized approach is also favored. One tends to be more serious concerning the organization and efficiency of one's work in general.

This is a good period for architects, designers, and skilled technicians.

The individual is inclined to exercise greater discipline in matters of personal diet, health, and hygiene.

Transiting Saturn trine natal Mercury has the same significance as transiting Mercury trine natal Saturn; however, it lasts much longer—how long depends on the speed of Saturn's motion and on whether Saturn is retrograde, stationary, or direct. It marks a sustained period of mental discipline and organization.

Transiting Mercury Trine Natal Uranus

Creative original thinking, sudden intuitive insights, and heightened telepathic faculties characterize this transit. It is often accompanied by intellectual excitement and a quickening of the mental processes.

The individual may become involved in work related to electronic technology and communications. This is a favorable transit for engineers. The individual may have ideas for using scientific technology in improving work efficiency or for realizing personal goals and objectives. Frequently, there is unexpected good news relating to personal goals and objectives.

This is also a favorable transit for those interested in the study of parapsychology, astrology, or other occult subjects.

It is a favorable time to make decisions or handle communications regarding insurance, corporate money, joint finances, taxes, and business activities.

Teachers, writers, students, lecturers, researchers, and scholars receive original creative inspiration in their work at this time. The individual tends to engage in intellectually stimulating activities with friends or to begin new friendships. There are unusual communications with or news concerning brothers and sisters, friends, neighbors, group associates, and co-workers.

Unexpected short trips usually prove to be interesting and profitable during this transit.

Transiting Uranus trine natal Mercury has the same significance as transiting Mercury trine natal Uranus; however, it lasts much longer, off and on for a year or so, and indicates a sustained period of creative intellectual and intuitive inspiration.

Transiting Mercury Trine Natal Neptune

Stimulation of the imaginative faculties and an increase in telepathic abilities and creative intuitive mental processes characterize this transit.

The individual may be able to uncover valuable information from the subconscious mind. Often, it becomes easier to visualize intuitive ideas. This is an excellent period for study of psychology and for gaining insights into subconscious motivations.

The increased imagination and intuitive ability associated with the transit can be utilized to solve work-related problems.

This is an especially good transit for writers, actors, artists, poets, musicians, or those engaged in religious or mystical and occult fields. The individual may become involved in religious or mystical group activities.

The individual may become involved in work related to hospitals, institutions, or religious retreats or develop an interest in spiritual healing of some type. This is a favorable transit for visiting those in hospitals or institutions.

It is a good period for communication with foreigners.

Transiting Neptune trine natal Mercury has the same significance as transiting Mercury trine natal Neptune; however, it lasts, off and on, for a year or longer, and indicates a sustained period of telepathic potential and intuitive mental awareness.

Transiting Mercury Trine Natal Pluto

Sharpened clairvoyant perceptions and intensified scientific and occult insights characterize this transit. The stimulation of the clairvoyant or intuitive faculties brought about by this transit can bring insights into the fundamental laws and processes of nature. The extent of this insight, however, depends on the promise of the natal horoscope.

The individual may develop an intellectual interest in scientific studies, economics, sex, parapsychology, and in hidden mysteries of all types.

This is a favorable time for planning business, political, financial, and military strategy, for handling matters related to joint finances, corporate money, business activities, insurance, taxes, and alimony and for formulating and signing important contracts and agreements.

The individual makes efforts at self-improvement through health regimes, diet, personal hygiene, and apparel. Often an interest in improved methods of handling and recycling waste products arises.

Transiting Pluto trine natal Mercury has the same significance as transiting Mercury trine natal Pluto; however, it lasts, off and on, for a year or longer and indicates a sustained period of intellectual insight.

Transiting Mercury Trine the Natal North Node and Sextile the Natal South Node

See "Transiting Mercury Sextile the Natal South Node and Trine the Natal North Node."

Transiting Mercury Trine the Natal South Node and Sextile the Natal North Node

See "Transiting Mercury Sextile the Natal North Node and Trine the Natal South Node."

Transiting Mercury Trine the Natal Ascendant and Sextile the Natal Descendant

See "Transiting Mercury Sextile the Natal Descendant and Trine the Natal Ascendant."

Transiting Mercury Trine the Natal Midheaven and Sextile the Natal Nadir

See "Transiting Mercury Sextile the Natal Nadir and Trine the Natal Midheaven."

Transiting Mercury Trine the Natal Descendant and Sextile the Natal Ascendant

See "Transiting Mercury Sextile the Natal Ascendant and Trine the Natal Descendant."

Transiting Mercury Trine the Natal Nadir and Sextile the Natal Midheaven

See "Transiting Mercury Sextile the Natal Midheaven and Trine the Natal Nadir."

Transit Mercury Oppositions

Transiting Mercury Opposition the Natal Sun

See "Transiting Sun Opposition Natal Mercury."

Transiting Mercury Opposition the Natal Moon

See "Transiting Moon Opposition Natal Mercury."

Transiting Mercury Opposition Natal Mercury

Intellectual disagreements, nervousness, and restlessness and the need to see another's point of view characterize this transit.

Communication difficulties or breakdowns tend to occur in the working environment. Confusion can arise in attempts to coordinate schedules or arrange meetings.

Schedules or appointments tend to be upset by transportation difficulties. Delays in mail or shipments can also interfere with business or work efficiency. The individual may make wrong decisions based on incorrect or incomplete information.

The individual may have a difficult time making decisions related to work, health, dress, brothers and sisters, neighbors, friends, or co-workers. Confusion and misunderstanding can arise in relations with brothers and sisters, neighbors, friends, and co-workers.

Transiting Mercury Opposition Natal Venus

Breakdowns in business, social, romantic, and marital communications characterize this transit.

In particular, difficulties tend to arise in businesses related to food, clothing, art, literature, communications, and luxury items. Meaningless chit-chat and gossip can interfere with work efficiency.

The individual tends to display a lack of judgment in matters of personal mannerism, dress, hygiene, work habits, speech, and diet.

The individual may either become emotionally hypersensitive to the remarks and attitudes of others or be forced to deal with others of this temperament. In some cases, hypocrisy is resorted to in order to avoid social unpleasantness.

The effects of this transit can be harmonious, however, if the individual is aware of the needs, feelings, and attitudes of others and acts accordingly. There is a special need for honesty and diplomacy in business, social, and personal relationships.

The individual may become involved in business or financial negotiations. Some people participate in cultural, literary, or artistic endeavors.

Transiting Venus opposition natal Mercury has the same significance as transiting Mercury opposition natal Venus; however, it generally lasts for a slightly longer period of time, which can vary according to how fast Venus is moving and whether Venus is stationary, retrograde, or direct. It marks a longer period of need for social awareness.

Transiting Mercury Opposition Natal Mars

Arguments and disagreements, caustic speech and mental aggravation characterize this transit.

This is not a favorable time for professional or business negotiations: it would be difficult for the parties to reach an agreement. Matters related to joint finances, corporate money, insurance, taxes, inheritance, and alimony can be a source of difficulty at this time.

The individual may be subject to frustrations at work and to irritability arising from these frustrations. Delayed shipments and transportation breakdowns can interfere with work or business. There is a special need to exercise caution, consideration, and diplomacy in all communications, and especially with those in the working environment.

An ego identification with one's own point of view can lead to a lack of objectivity and result in frequent heated arguments and debates. Arguments and disagreements tend to arise with brothers and sisters, neighbors, friends, co-workers, and organizational associates.

Any attempts at mental coercion, either by the individual or directed toward him or her, are likely to cause difficulties.

The individual is particularly susceptible to infectious diseases during this transit.

Transiting Mars opposition natal Mercury has the same significance as transiting Mercury opposition natal Mars; however, it lasts for a longer period of time—how long depends on the speed of motion of Mars and whether Mars is stationary, retrograde, or direct—thus marking a longer period of mentally irritating difficulties at work and a need for cooperation. This transit occurs once in two years.

Transiting Mercury Opposition Natal Jupiter

Overoptimism, verbal rambling, absentmindedness, and unrealistic goals and promises characterize this transit.

Ideas for work and communications concerning work may be so general as to lack specific application. As with Mercury's stressful transits to natal Neptune, there can be a tendency to daydreaming and woolgathering.

Intellectual disagreements can arise over educational, religious, or cultural beliefs, and difficulties may be experienced in dealing with religious, educational, or cultural institutions.

Long-distance traveling or communications or dealings with foreigners or people from faraway places may lead to disappointment. Hypocrisy is sometimes present in communications with brothers and sisters, neighbors, friends, or group associates.

The individual may suffer ill health due to improper diet.

Transiting Jupiter opposition natal Mercury has the same significance as transiting Mercury opposition natal Jupiter; however, it lasts longer and indicates a sustained period of intellectual overgeneralization. This transit occurs once in the twelve-year cycle of Jupiter and requires realism, if serious errors in judgment are to be avoided.

Transiting Mercury Opposition Natal Saturn

Worry, a negative mental outlook, and unwillingness to accept the ideas of others characterize this transit.

Other people, especially those in positions of power and authority, are likely to react negatively to the individual's ideas. They may criticize the individual, behave uncooperatively, or impose a heavy work load. All this can make the individual feel devitalized and depressed. The individual may suffer ill health due to this overwork or occupational hazards. Specific health problems are likely to involve the skin, bones, teeth, knees, ankles, nerves, intestines, and digestive system.

Delays in mail and shipments can also interfere with work and business. Red tape or court appearances may also interfere with work and normal routines. Lawsuits, legal difficulties, or the need to fill out legal forms can lead to mental depression. This is an unfavorable period for signing legal contracts and agreements. Important decisions should be postponed to a more favorable time.

Adverse publicity is likely to affect the individual's status and reputation. There may be temporary estrangements from brothers and sisters, neighbors, friends, group associates, or co-workers.

Lack of inspiration can make the individual feel dull and in a rut. A negative mental outlook may make things appear worse than they really are.

Transiting Saturn opposition natal Mercury has the same significance as transiting Mercury opposition natal Saturn; however, it is of longer duration and marks a period of sustained worry and heavy work responsibility. This is an especially difficult time for students or those engaged in professions that require mental work. This transit occurs only once in the twenty-nine-year cycle of Saturn.

Transiting Mercury Opposition Natal Uranus

Impractical ideas, nervousness, irritability, unexpected disruptions of work routines, and communications with eccentric or unreliable individuals all characterize this transit.

This is an unfavorable transit for making decisions regarding joint finances, corporate money, inheritance, insurance, taxes, or alimony.

Transportation problems may arise unexpectedly. Erratic, unpredictable driving behavior on the part of the individual or others can be a source of danger.

Spasmodic and impractical communications with brothers and sisters, neighbors, friends, group associates, and co-workers may be a source of confusion. The individual may also receive sudden unfavorable news regarding them.

Sensible and realistic cooperation with others is needed under this transit, and a sensible and practical approach is especially necessary in scientific, occult, and astrological studies and endeavors.

Poor circulation problems with the ankles and debility due to nervousness are possibilities with this transit.

Transiting Uranus opposition natal Mercury has the same significance as transiting Mercury opposition natal Uranus; however, it lasts for a much longer period of time, off and on for a year or so, thus marking a sustained period of intellectual confusion and radical change in mental outlook. This transit occurs once in eighty-four years.

Transiting Mercury Opposition Natal Neptune

Daydreaming, woolgathering, unwanted or disturbing psychic experiences, and unrealistic thinking characterize this transit.

During this period, some individuals become so absorbed in their private dream worlds that they are oblivious to their environment and unable to respond to the moods and ideas of others. The individual tends to lack awareness or to use evasive or deceptive tactics in communications with brothers and sisters, neighbors, friends, group associates, or co-workers.

Subconscious psychological problems can interfere with truthful communication and an accurate perception of reality. In some cases, the individual is either the initiator or the victim of deliberate deception in communication.

The individual may subconsciously resort to hypochondria as a means of avoiding responsibilities. Absentmindedness and forgetfulness can interfere with work efficiency and fulfilling agreements.

There can be confusion or delays in the handling of mail or shipments.

This is an unfavorable time to sign contracts or formulate agreements —they may contain hidden flaws. There is a tendency to forget appointments, be confused about communications, or get lost while traveling. Absentmindedness while driving can be especially dangerous during this transit.

The individual tends to entertain impractical educational, philosophic, or religious ideas at this time.

Any tendency to mental illness is aggravated. Ill health during this transit often results from the misuse of drugs, medication, or alcohol. Illnesses can be psychosomatic or hard to diagnose.

Transiting Neptune opposition natal Mercury has the same significance as transiting Mercury opposition natal Neptune; however, it lasts, off and on, for a year or longer and indicates a sustained period of mental and psychological confusion and a need for realistic thinking. This transit occurs only once in the average life span.

Transiting Mercury Opposition Natal Pluto

Sarcasm in speech, suspicion, secret investigations, fanatical viewpoints, and mental coercion of some sort are all characteristic of this transit. Circumstances may force drastic changes in the individual's mental outlook.

Individuals with this transit should be careful not to attempt to remake the ideas and opinions of others, nor should they allow themselves to be subjected to such treatment. Cooperation in communication and work is required during this transit, and if this is impossible, it is best to seek a new situation. The need for cooperation is important for the regeneration of one's work and health.

Some individuals become suspicious of the motives of others or others become suspicious of theirs. This may result in spying, intrigues, and secret communications.

This is not a good time for formulating or signing agreements or contracts related to corporate business, joint finances, insurance, taxes, inheritance, and alimony.

The individual's life or health might be endangered by occupational hazards, especially those related to environmental pollution or ecological issues. Health problems can also result from improper elimination at this time. Some individuals are subject to unpleasant psychic disturb-ances. They become mentally preoccupied with death, life after death, reincarnation, or with other occult subjects.

News of the death of a brother, sister, neighbor, friend, co-worker, or group associate may come under this transit.

Observance of safe driving rules is a must at this time.

Transiting Pluto opposition natal Mercury has the same significance as transiting Mercury opposition natal Pluto; however, it lasts, off and on, for a year or longer and marks a sustained period of mental tension and suspense. This transit occurs only once in an average lifetime.

Transiting Mercury Opposition the Natal North Node and Conjunct the Natal South Node

See "Transiting Mercury Conjunct the Natal South Node and Opposi-tion the Natal North Node."

Transiting Mercury Opposition the Natal South Node and Conjunct the Natal North Node

See "Transiting Mercury Conjunct the Natal North Node and Oppo-sition the Natal South Node."

Transiting Mercury Opposition the Natal Ascendant and Conjunct the Natal Descendant

See "Transiting Mercury Conjunct the Natal Descendant and Oppo-sition the Natal Ascendant."

Transiting Mercury Opposition the Natal Midheaven and Conjunct the Natal Nadir

See "Transiting Mercury Conjunct the Natal Nadir and Opposition the Natal Midheaven."

Transiting Mercury Opposition the Natal Descendant and Conjunct the Natal Ascendant

See "Transiting Mercury Conjunct the Natal Ascendant and Opposi-tion the Natal Descendant."

Transiting Mercury Opposition the Natal Nadir and
Conjunct the Natal Midheaven

See "Transiting Mercury Conjunct the Natal Midheaven and Opposition the Natal Nadir."

22 Transits
of Venus

Transit Venus Through the Houses

Transiting Venus Through the Natal First House

Individuals with this transit experience a desire to please others, make efforts to increase their personal attractiveness and charm, and take the initiative in romantic and social activity.

They take a greater interest than usual in artistic, romantic, social, business, and personal creative self-expression. It is a favorable time for personal involvement in businesses related to art, music, entertainment, psychology, and luxury items. Because the individual is conscious of what is needed to make a favorable impression on others, this is a good period for public relations activity.

If transiting Venus makes stress aspects while in the natal First House, the individual can become narcissistic, extravagant, self-indulgent, or emotionally hypersensitive.

Transiting Venus Through the Natal Second House

Business transactions related to art, music, entertainment, and luxury items characterize this transit.

Individuals with this transit can profit through painting, art, music, and other artistic expressions. They are motivated to acquire possessions of beauty, quality, and refinement as a means of achieving emotional satisfaction and status. There is an interest in the enjoyment of physical comforts of all kinds. However, if Venus makes stress aspects while transiting the natal Second House, sensuality, sexual overindulgence, and a desire for material luxury and comfort for its own sake can stand in the way of one's growth and progress.

This is a favorable time for dealing with banks or seeking financial support from wealthy people. The individual is likely to become involved in business partnerships of various kinds.

Transiting Venus Through the Natal Third House

Harmonious social, romantic, marital, and business communications characterize this transit.

The individual is likely to be graceful, tactful, and diplomatic in speech and communication. Hence, this is a favorable time for public relations, advertising, and promotional activities. Dealings with news and communications media are also likely to be pleasant and productive.

This is a good time for short trips connected with social activity, pleasure, romance, or business or artistic endeavors. The individual is able to communicate harmoniously with brothers, sisters, neighbors, friends, group associates, and co-workers.

If Venus makes stress aspects while transiting the natal Third House, the individual may say insincere or hypocritical things to avoid unpleasantness. There may also be a tendency to waste time talking about inconsequential and trivial matters.

Transiting Venus Through the Natal Fourth House

Family social gatherings and social, artistic, and romantic activities in the home characterize this transit.

The individual expresses greater kindness and consideration toward family members, and relationships with parents are harmonious.

The individual takes an interest in beautifying the home and is sensitive to the beauties of nature. This can take the form of purchasing art or luxury items for the home, gardening, or landscaping. The individual may become involved in business activities related to real estate, home furnishings, or art and luxury items for the home.

If Venus makes stress aspects while transiting the natal Fourth House, the individual may overindulge in rich foods and domestic comforts and luxuries.

Transiting Venus Through the Natal Fifth House

Romantic and social activities, especially social activities involving children, characterize this transit.

The individual expresses greater understanding, kindness, and generosity toward children. Women seeking pregnancy are likely to be successful at this time.

This period often brings romantic and sexual involvements. However, if Venus makes stress aspects while transiting the natal Fifth House, overindulgence in sex and other sensual pleasures can lead to dissipation.

It is a favorable time for businesses related to art, music, entertainment, and financial speculation. The enjoyment of art, music, and entertainment is indicated, and creative artists of all types are favored.

Transiting Venus Through the Natal Sixth House

Harmonious relationships in the working environment, increased personal attractiveness through improved health, personal adornment, especially the purchase of beautiful clothing, characterize this transit.

Individuals with this transit may become involved in work related to art, music, entertainment, and luxury items. They seek to beautify or improve their working environments. This is a favorable time to make improvements in working conditions or apply for a salary increase. There are likely to be social activities connected with work.

The individual seeks to improve his or her health, dress, and personal hygiene in order to be more attractive to the opposite sex. Women can play a significant part in the individual's work, hygiene, and dress.

If Venus makes stress aspects while transiting the natal Sixth House, the individual may be prone to overindulgence in rich foods and lack of motivation to work.

Transiting Venus Through the Natal Seventh House

Harmonious public relations, social activities, and relationships with marriage and business partners characterize this transit.

The individual enjoys the companionship of other people and displays outgoing, sociable tendencies. The individual is personally attractive to others during this transit. It is a favorable time for marrying or establishing partnerships, and for dealing with women.

Businesses related to art, music, entertainment, and luxury items are also favored.

If Venus makes stress aspects while transiting the natal Seventh House, the individuals are apt to take too much for granted in relationships or allow others to lead them into social dissipations.

Transiting Venus Through the Natal Eighth House

Harmonious handling of joint finances and gains through gifts, grants, corporate funds, financial partnerships, and inheritances characterize this transit.

Business opportunities may arise through social interactions. The increased sexual drive and social–business involvement indicated by this transit may lead to sexual encounters. However, if Venus makes stress aspects while transiting the natal Eighth House, excessive or promiscuous sexual involvement can affect the individual adversely.

The individual's artistic interests or social and romantic involvements may be linked in some way to scientific, occult, or business activities.

Transiting Venus Through the Natal Ninth House

Social activities related to educational, cultural, or religious institutions and enjoyment of religious art and music characterize this transit.

Individuals with this transit tend to develop an interest in foreign cultures and art forms. Social, romantic, and business opportunities may arise through their participation in cultural, educational, or religious activities. The individuals' personal philosophies will be evident in their handling of social, romantic, and business relationships. However, if Venus makes stress aspects while transiting the natal Ninth House, they may by hypocritical in handling these affairs.

Transiting Venus Through the Natal Tenth House

An enhanced social reputation and an increased desire for social prestige and status characterize this transit.

On the one hand, social, romantic, marital, and business opportunities tend to come through career and political activities, and, on the other, romantic, marital, and business partners, along with social acquaintances and women, all tend to play an important part in the individual's career.

The individual's social activities tend to be related in some manner to business and professional affairs, and professional activities are often related in some way to art, music, or entertainment.

Professional partnerships are often formed during this transit, and professional dealings with women often take place.

The individual tends to feel ambitious for material wealth and status. This is a favorable time to seek favors from women or those in positions of power and authority.

If Venus makes stress aspects while transiting the natal Tenth House, the individual may be tempted to use his or her professional status and position for gaining personal, material, sexual, and social advantage.

Transiting Venus Through the Natal Eleventh House

Kindness and consideration toward and from friends, along with humanitarian feelings, characterize this transit.

The individual tends to become involved in artistically or socially oriented friendships, groups, and organizations. These friendships and group activities are often related to art, music, entertainment, and luxury items, or business connected with them. Friendships and organizational activities can lead to business or romantic opportunities. However, if Venus makes stress aspects while transiting the natal Eleventh House, the individual may seek out friendships or group activities for purposes of sexual encounters or material gratification.

Transiting Venus Through the Natal Twelfth House

Emotional sympathy and understanding, kindness toward those in need, and appreciation of beauty characterize this transit.

One's understanding of others can reach a more spiritual and compassionate level. The imagination, the sense of beauty, and the intuitive awareness of the harmonies of nature are intensified.

Social activities are likely to involve places of retreat and privacy. Private and secret romantic involvements often occur. However, if Venus makes stress aspects while in the natal Twelfth House, secret romances or other self-indulgences may have an undermining effect on the individual's reputation and social status.

Behind-the-scenes business activities related to art, music, entertainment, hospitals, and institutions are favored. This transit can help individuals who are shy to overcome their social inhibitions.

Transit Venus Conjunctions

Transiting Venus Conjunct the Natal Sun

See "Transiting Sun Conjunct Natal Venus."

Transiting Venus Conjunct the Natal Moon

See "Transiting Moon Conjunct Natal Venus."

Transiting Venus Conjunct Natal Mercury

See "Transiting Mercury Conjunct Natal Venus."

Transiting Venus Conjunct Natal Venus

Harmony and grace in social and artistic expression characterize this transit.

The individual is more inclined than usual to be cooperative and sympathetic. It is a favorable time for artistic and musical endeavors, and for romantic fulfillment. It is also a favorable transit for business activities related to art, music, and entertainment and for business, social, and romantic dealings with women.

If the conjunction is affected by stress aspects, extravagance, ostentation, and excessive sensuality should be avoided.

Transiting Venus Conjunct Natal Mars

Dynamic artistic energy and the desire for romantic fulfillment characterize this transit.

It is often associated with sexual stimulation and involvement in sexual relationships. However, sexual attractions that develop during this period do not necessarily indicate mental, emotional, or cultural compatibility.

If the conjunction receives stress aspects from other transiting planets, there can be an excess sensuality and a lack of sensitivity to the feelings of others, or the individual may be subjected to such treatment.

Some individuals are motivated to musical or artistic expression of some sort. It is a good transit for artistic expressions in general and for social activities involving physical expression, such as dancing.

Business activities and partnerships related to art, music, and luxury items are frequently formed under this transit. Businesses related to entertainment, social activity, romance, or sex are favored. Financial gain can come through partnerships, marriage, corporate business, gifts, endowments, insurance, or inheritance.

Transiting Mars conjunct natal Venus has the same significance as transiting Venus conjunct natal Mars; however, it usually lasts for a longer period of time; how long depends on how fast Mars is moving and whether Mars is stationary, retrograde, or direct. Thus, it indicates a longer period of aggressive business, social, and sexual self-expression.

Transiting Venus Conjunct Natal Jupiter

A happy, optimistic emotional outlook, generosity toward others, and social popularity characterize this transit. The individual is likely to show increased kindness and consideration for and a new emotional awareness of the needs of others. This is an excellent time for expanding one's musical, artistic, social, and romantic activities.

Social activities during this transit are likely to relate to religion, philosophy, higher education, and cultural activities related to these. Business, romantic, and social opportunities may come through association with universities, churches, and other cultural institutions. Social activities are also frequently related to fundraising for cultural institutions, and both business and social activities are often related to foreigners, people from faraway places, or people associated with educational, religious, or cultural institutions. The individual is likely to travel for pleasure and to develop an interest in foreign art forms. It is a good period for businesses related to art, music, entertainment, luxury items, and cultural activities.

Transiting Jupiter conjunct natal Venus has the same significance as transiting Venus conjunct natal Jupiter; however, it lasts longer and indicates a sustained period of cultural, social, and business expansion, as well as good fortune in the romance department. This transit occurs once every twelve years.

Transiting Venus Conjunct Natal Saturn

A reserved emotional outlook and social, romantic, or business involvement with older or mature individuals characterize this transit. Most people develop a formal, cautious, and reserved social manner.

A greater desire for both emotional and financial security develops.

Serious business or professional partnerships are often initiated. This period often coincides with critical junctures in romantic relationships: either the relationship grows cold or it is cemented into a permanent mutual commitment. Old romantic, business, or partnership associations may be renewed during this transit.

The individual may take on increased practical responsibilities in handling the emotional problems of others. Loneliness or lack of romantic opportunity may be a problem.

Those engaged in artistic endeavors will discover that their sense of structure is enhanced. However, serious business, professional, or financial responsibilities may interfere with artistic, social, or romantic fulfillment. Business or professional activities during this transit are often related in some way to art, music, entertainment, or luxury items. Financial hardships and limitations often occur, though such difficulties can be a constructive stimulus.

If the conjunction receives stress aspects from other transiting planets, loneliness and emotional depression can be the result.

Transiting Saturn conjunct natal Venus has the same significance as transiting Venus conjunct natal Saturn; however, it is of much longer duration, and indicates a sustained period of emotional restriction. This transit occurs once in twenty-nine years.

Transiting Venus Conjunct Natal Uranus

Exciting new friendships, social relationships, and romantic infatuations characterize this transit.

Social, business, and romantic opportunities arise through friends, groups, and organizations. The individual is likely to be the recipient of unexpected gifts, and unexpected financial and social opportunities often present themselves.

There is a greater feeling of emotional freedom and self-expression. This usually takes the form of adventuresomeness and willingness to experiment in business, social, artistic, and romantic activities. There is a tendency to depart from or disregard traditional social, sexual, and financial values.

The individual often develops an interest in electronic or modernistic art forms. This transit intensifies intuitive inspiration in artistic and musical endeavors. One may also gain intuitive insights into the emotional feelings and reactions of others and, at the same time, one's own personality is enhanced by an emotional, effervescent, or sparkling quality. This is a good time for public relations and for dealing with women.

If transiting stress aspects are made to this conjunction, unexpected financial expenditures or inappropriate sexual adventures may occur. As with Venus-Mars and Venus-Pluto transits, this transit acts as a powerful sexual stimulus.

Transiting Uranus conjunct natal Venus has the same significance as transiting Venus conjunct natal Uranus; however, it lasts, off and on, for a year or longer, and indicates a sustained period of artistic, emotional, social, and romantic liberation. It provides the individual with the opportunity to realize long-cherished personal, social, financial, artistic, and romantic goals and objectives. This transit occurs once in eighty-four years; therefore, it is, literally, a once-in-a-lifetime opportunity.

Transiting Venus Conjunct Natal Neptune

Stimulation of the intuitive, aesthetic, clairvoyant, and imaginative faculties characterizes this transit. The individual experiences an increased telepathic rapport with others.

This transit is a powerful stimulus to the artistic, creative imagination, which makes this a highly creative period for artists, musicians, photographers, and those in the entertainment industry. The individual experiences an increased sensitivity to beauty.

Travel for pleasure is likely, and interest in the cultures and art forms of foreign countries is stimulated.

The individual may become involved with secret business activities or secret romantic and sexual involvements.

This is a favorable transit for dealing with religious, educational, and cultural institutions, and with hospitals, retreats, and asylums.

If the conjunction receives stress aspects from other transiting planets, deception and lack of practicality in social, romantic, and financial activities can endanger the individual's well-being. Idleness and laziness should be avoided.

Transiting Neptune conjunct natal Venus has the same significance as transiting Venus conjunct natal Neptune; however, it lasts, off and on, for a year or longer, and can occur only once in a lifetime.

Transiting Venus Conjunct Natal Pluto

Intense emotional, romantic, sexual, and aesthetic experiences characterize this transit.

Social or romantic relationships have a transforming effect on the individual, for better or worse.

During this period, there is a need to regenerate attitudes regarding close personal relationships. If the conjunction receives stress aspects from other transiting planets, sexual jealousy and unfair manipulations are especially to be avoided.

This transit provides intuitive inspiration for artists and musicians.

The individual is likely to have financial dealings related to joint finances, corporate money, insurance, taxes, alimony, and goods of the dead. These often are connected with businesses related to public relations, entertainment, luxury items, music, and art. Many individuals exhibit an interest in finding new uses for old, discarded art objects and in renovation in general.

Transiting Pluto conjunct natal Venus has the same significance as transiting Venus conjunct natal Pluto; however, it lasts, off and on, for a year or longer, and can occur only once in an average life span. Thus, it marks a period of important, transforming emotional involvements.

Transiting Venus Conjunct the Natal North Node and Opposition the Natal South Node

The ability to conform to accepted standards of social behavior and popularity characterize this transit. Most individuals with this transit accept popular social attitudes and find themselves in agreement with prevailing trends. They enjoy and participate in currently popular artistic, musical, and social expressions.

Transiting North Node conjunct natal Venus and transiting South Node opposition natal Venus has the same significance as transiting Venus conjunct the natal North Node and opposition the natal South Node; however, it lasts longer, and indicates a sustained period of harmonious social interaction.

Transiting Venus Conjunct the Natal South Node and Opposition the Natal North Node

A reserved social manner and indifference to currently popular artistic, social, and sexual attitudes characterize this transit. The individual is likely to identify emotionally with traditional musical, artistic, social, or sexual attitudes.

A slowdown in business and financial affairs may occur at this time.

Transiting South Node conjunct natal Venus and transiting North Node opposition natal Venus has the same significance as transiting Venus conjunct the natal South Node and opposition the natal North Node; however, it lasts longer, and indicates a sustained period of social indifference or restrictions.

Transiting Venus Conjunct the Natal Ascendant and Opposition the Natal Descendant

Charming personal mannerisms and socially outgoing tendencies characterize this transit. The individuals have a happy, optimistic outlook and their personal attractiveness is enhanced.

It is a favorable time for artistic, musical, social, and romantic self-expression. The individual may benefit through a business partnership or through moneymaking endeavors. There is a tendency to purchase luxury items and personal adornments.

Transiting Venus Conjunct the Natal Midheaven and Opposition the Natal Nadir

During this transit, the individual's social activities are likely to be related to his or her professional affairs. It is favorable for public relations work and for dealing with important and prominent women.

Recognition or support for artistic, musical or business achievements often comes during this transit. Raises in pay or favors from employers or superiors are likely. This is a favorable period for professional activities related to art, music, and entertainment. There is apt to be a greater sense of harmony in business and professional partnerships and in marriages.

Transiting Venus Conjunct the Natal Descendant and Opposition the Natal Ascendant

Harmonious social relationships and a desire to please others characterize this transit. There is a cooperative attitude both toward and from others. This transit is conducive to harmony in marriage, in business partnerships, in close friendships, and in dealings with women and the public. Business partnerships related to art, music, and luxury items may be formed.

Transiting Venus Conjunct the Natal Nadir and
Opposition the Natal Midheaven

Social and romantic activity in the home characterizes this transit. It is a favorable time for family social gatherings and cooperation with family members. Artistic and musical activities often take place in the home. This is a good time to purchase art objects and luxury items for the home and family and to garden or work with the soil.

Transit Venus Sextiles

Transiting Venus Sextile the Natal Sun

See "Transiting Sun Sextile Natal Venus."

Transiting Venus Sextile the Natal Moon

See "Transiting Moon Sextile Natal Venus."

Transiting Venus Sextile Natal Mercury

See "Transiting Mercury Sextile Natal Venus."

Transiting Venus Sextile Natal Venus

Refined intellectual insight in artistic, musical, and social endeavors characterizes this transit.

Friendliness and grace are frequently exhibited in one's speech and communications. The individual will probably be involved in an unusual degree of communications involving his or her business, social, or romantic relationships. This is a favorable period for public relations or for dealing with women. The transit is also characterized by communications regarding art, music, entertainment, and luxury items.

Transiting Venus Sextile Natal Mars

A tendency to take the initiative in business, social, romantic, and artistic expressions characterizes this transit.

This is a favorable period for sexual harmony in marriage and romantic relationships. Women who wish to become pregnant are often successful during this transit.

The individual's business, social, artistic, and romantic activities often bring about short trips and communications.

The individual may have ideas for creative expression in art, music, entertainment, and social activity. Social activities are likely to involve dancing or other physical forms of expression.

This is a favorable period for activity involving business, joint finances, corporate money, taxes, insurance, alimony, art, music, entertainment, and luxury items. It is also a good period for business and professional public relations.

Transiting Mars sextile natal Venus has the same significance as transiting Venus sextile natal Mars; however, it lasts longer and indicates a sustained period of personal assertion, initiative, and planning in one's business, social, romantic, and artistic expressions.

Transiting Venus Sextile Natal Jupiter

A happy, optimistic, outgoing attitude and consideration for the moods, feelings, and needs of others characterize this transit.

The individuals can benefit both themselves and others through ideas for and participation in social activities, particularly those involving religion, philosophy, and higher education.

Often, there is social, business, artistic, or romantic involvement with foreigners or with people who are associated with religious, educational, or cultural institutions. Some individuals become involved in fundraising activities for social, cultural, educational, or religious organizations.

Travel for reasons of business, education, religious pilgrimage, pleasure, or social or romantic activity can be undertaken successfully.

Romantic and marital opportunities may present themselves at this time, providing the natal chart holds this promise.

The individual experiences a new appreciation of art, music, and natural beauty during this transit. Writers or musicians may receive financial support or public recognition. This is a favorable period for businesses related to art, music, entertainment, education, publishing, and cultural activities.

Transiting Jupiter sextile natal Venus has the same significance as transiting Venus sextile natal Jupiter; however, it lasts for a longer period of time, and indicates harmony in close personal relationships, financial prosperity, and kindness both toward and from others. This transit occurs twice in the twelve-year cycle of Jupiter.

Transiting Venus Sextile Natal Saturn

A reserved formal manner characterizes this transit.

The individual has ideas for organizing and stabilizing business and financial affairs. This is a favorable transit for seeking financial support for personal projects from those in positions of power and authority. An opportunity for a business partnership may arise at this time, if the individual's natal chart concurs.

Some individuals become socially or romantically involved with older or well-established persons, or even marry an older person, if the natal chart concurs.

This is a favorable period for public relations work and for dealing with legal, political, or important business matters.

The individual tends to develop a serious, intellectual appreciation of traditional art forms. This is also a good period for creating serious art forms, especially those that require a sense of form and structure.

Transiting Saturn sextile natal Venus has the same significance as transiting Venus sextile natal Saturn; however, it is of longer duration, and indicates a sustained period of opportunity to stabilize important close relationships and business affairs. This transit occurs only twice in the twenty-nine-year cycle of Saturn.

Transiting Venus Sextile Natal Uranus

Unusual, exciting, and unexpected business, social, and romantic opportunities tend to occur at this time.

The individual is apt to be vivacious, sparkling, and fun-loving in his or her social life. Unexpected opportunities often arise for marriage or business partnerships, providing this is promised in the natal chart.

Exciting and unexpected opportunities for short trips involving friendships, social activities, group activities, and scientific, artistic, or business interests also tend to arise at this time.

The individual may have original ideas for making money, especially in the fields of entertainment, art, music, electronics, luxury items, science, or the occult.

Artists and musicians may receive original intuitive inspiration in their work under this transit.

Transiting Uranus sextile natal Venus has the same significance as transiting Venus sextile natal Uranus; however, it lasts for a much longer period of time, and indicates a sustained interval of happiness and social freedom. This transit occurs twice in an average life-span.

Transiting Venus Sextile Natal Neptune

The creative imagination is stimulated during this transit.

Religious and artistic inspiration are often closely linked at this time. The increased sensitivity to and appreciation of beauty which many individuals experience during this period may lead to artistic inspiration. An increased ability to visualize will enhance the individual's creative artistic talent. Moneymaking activities or financial expenditures often involve art, music, entertainment, photography, and cinematography.

There is greater sympathy for others and an intuitive awareness of their moods, feelings, and thoughts. Some individuals adopt an idealistic attitude toward romantic and social friendships. This is a favorable time for visiting relatives or friends in hospitals, asylums, or other institutions.

Transiting Neptune sextile natal Venus has the same basic significance as transiting Venus sextile natal Neptune; however, it lasts much longer, and indicates a sustained period of emotional and aesthetic refinement. This transit can occur as often as twice in an average lifetime.

Transiting Venus Sextile Natal Pluto

New insights into ways of regenerating emotional habits and relationships characterize this transit.

The individuals may receive inspiration in their artistic, musical, and creative endeavors. Art or natural beauty has a spiritually uplifting effect during this transit.

The individuals often have good ideas for business ventures and corporate financial enterprises, especially if they relate to art, entertainment, or luxury items.

Sexual stimulation is also a characteristic of this transit, and if the natal chart concurs, this transit can bring marriage or romantic opportunities.

Transiting Pluto sextile natal Venus has the same significance as transiting Venus sextile natal Pluto; however, it lasts, off and on, for a year or longer, thus marking an extended period of constructive energizing of the emotions and the intuitive artistic abilities.

Transiting Venus Sextile the Natal North Node and Trine the Natal South Node

Harmonious social cooperation with prevailing social standards and trends characterizes this transit.

The individuals have an intellectual appreciation of current social customs and fads, and enjoy engaging in discussions of them. They will find themselves more popular socially under this transit.

Transiting North Node sextile natal Venus and transiting South Node trine natal Venus has the same significance as transiting Venus sextile the natal North Node and trine the natal South Node; however, it lasts longer, and indicates a longer period of being in the social swim.

Transiting Venus Sextile the Natal South Node and Trine the Natal North Node

This transit has basically the same significance as transiting Venus sextile the natal North Node and trine the natal South Node; however, the individual is likely to identify emotionally with traditional social and intellectual values.

Transiting South Node sextile natal Venus and transiting North Node trine natal Venus has the same significance as transiting Venus sextile the natal South Node and trine the natal North Node; however, it is of longer duration, and indicates a sustained period of evaluation of currently popular trends in light of traditional experience.

Transiting Venus Sextile the Natal Ascendant and Trine the Natal Descendant

Harmony in marital, social, and business relationships characterizes this transit. The individual enjoys harmonious self-expression, especially in the fields of art and music. There is an ease in social relationships, and greater personal charm and attractiveness.

Cooperation in social, business, and romantic endeavors comes easily at this time.

Transiting Venus Sextile the Natal Midheaven and Trine the Natal Nadir

Harmony and cooperation in professional and family relationships characterize this transit.

Social activities related to professional and family affairs are favored. Social, artistic, and romantic activities often take place in the home during this transit. It is a good time to purchase art and luxury items for the home or family.

This is also a good period for professional public relations and for seeking favors from those in positions of power and authority.

Transiting Venus Sextile the Natal Descendant and Trine the Natal Ascendant

This transit has basically the same significance as transiting Venus sextile the natal Ascendant and trine the natal Descendant; however, there is a more intellectual focus on the psychology of relationships.

Transiting Venus Sextile the Natal Nadir and Trine the Natal Midheaven

This transit has basically the same significance as transiting Venus sextile the natal Midheaven and trine the natal Nadir; however, there is a more intellectual focus on domestic relationships and an easy flow in professional relationships.

Transit Venus Squares

Transiting Venus Square the Natal Sun

See "Transiting Sun Square Natal Venus."

Transiting Venus Square the Natal Moon

See "Transiting Moon Square Natal Venus."

Transiting Venus Square Natal Mercury

See "Transiting Mercury Square Natal Venus."

Transiting Venus Square Natal Venus

Misplaced sympathy, laziness, self-indulgence, and emotional hypersensitivity characterize this transit. Poor aesthetic taste is often expressed during this period. This is not a favorable time for social and artistic endeavors. The individual may experience difficulties in relating to women. Financial extravagance during this period is likely to cause embarrassments later.

Transiting Venus Square Natal Mars

Problems in romantic and sexual relationships characterize this transit.

Jealousy is often expressed in business, marital, or romantic relationships by either the individuals or their associates. Sexual overindulgence and lack of consideration for the feelings and moods of others are among the dangers of this transit.

Both social and financial difficulties frequently arise. Joint finances, insurance, taxes, alimony, and goods of the dead are often the source of difficulties. The individual should avoid financial extravagance, especially where luxury items and pleasures are concerned.

The artistic and musical tastes of the individual often lack refinement during this time.

Transiting Mars square natal Venus has the same significance as transiting Venus square natal Mars; however, it lasts for a slightly longer period of time, and indicates a more serious problem with emotional passions and desires. The length of this transit depends on how fast Mars is moving and whether Mars is stationary, retrograde, or direct.

Transiting Venus Square Natal Jupiter

Self-indulgence, laziness, misplaced sympathy, and maudlin sentimentality, especially in religious and cultural matters, characterize this transit. Its effects are similar to those of transiting Venus square natal Venus.

The individual tends to lack social grace and to make insincere gestures of friendliness to avoid unpleasantness.

Procrastination and financial extravagance are frequently associated with this transit. The individual tends to engage in nonproductive fantasies and lack of moderation in the pursuit of pleasure and luxurious living.

Social or financial difficulties tend to arise in the individual's dealings with churches, hospitals, universities, and other cultural institutions. Problems may also arise from dealings with foreigners or with people from distant places.

Vacations, pleasure trips, stays in hospitals, or institutions may prove more costly than anticipated. Overindulgence in social activities may take the individual's attention from more important responsibilities.

Despite all of these possible difficulties, this transit does not, of itself, produce serious problems.

Transiting Jupiter square natal Venus has the same significance as transiting Venus square natal Jupiter; however, it is of longer duration and indicates a sustained period of extravagance and self-indulgence. This transit occurs twice in twelve years.

Transiting Venus Square Natal Saturn

Social, financial, and romantic problems and disappointments characterize this transit.

There is sometimes a coldness and lack of sympathy toward the emotional needs of others. Coldness and estrangements often occur in romantic and marital relationships.

Professional responsibilities may interfere with one's social, romantic, and marital affairs. Selfishness and lack of consideration in business and professional relationships can lead to difficulties and financial loss. This is not a favorable time to seek favors from those in positions of wealth, power, and authority. Difficulties may arise in respect to public relations, legal matters, and partnerships.

Transiting Saturn square natal Venus has the same significance as transiting Venus square natal Saturn; however, it is of longer duration, and indicates a sustained period of loneliness, feelings of being unloved, and lack of warmth in personal relationships. This transit occurs twice in the twenty-nine-year cycle of Saturn.

Transiting Venus Square Natal Uranus

Unstable romantic infatuations and impractical or irresponsible attitudes toward marital responsibilities or sexual conduct characterize this transit.

Excessive pursuit of pleasure or difficult-to-control sexual impulses may become a problem. Impulsive spending on friends or social activities may lead to financial embarrassment, especially since unexpected expenses may arise.

There is often a lack of consideration toward others in social relationships. Romantic or marital partners tend to disapprove of the individual's friends or group associations during this period. The individual's behavior, social and aesthetic tastes may be so bizarre that they amuse or annoy others. All these factors tend to make it difficult for the individual to cooperate with friends or groups. In general, this is not a favorable period for public relations.

Transiting Uranus square natal Venus has the same significance as transiting Venus square natal Uranus; however, the transit is of longer duration and indicates a sustained period of eccentric financial, social, and sexual behavior affecting close personal relationships. This transit occurs only twice in an average life span.

Transiting Venus Square Natal Neptune

Deception and confusion in marital and romantic relationships characterize this transit.

Emotional hypersensitivity and unrealistic romantic fantasizing can also become a problem. Secret love affairs, misplaced sympathy, or psychological withdrawal from social contacts are all possible. The individual is susceptible to "sob" stories or plays for sympathy on the part of others, or may demand sympathy from them. Excessive drinking or drug abuse for psychological escape can contribute to the individual's self-undoing.

Unconscious emotional difficulties based on subconscious memories of past experiences may manifest themselves at this time and cause difficulty in relating to others or even the inability to do so.

Unrealistic "get-rich-quick" schemes can boomerang disastrously. Deception and dishonesty in financial dealing should be avoided.

The individuals may be deluded in their estimation of their own artistic abilities.

This transit can be a constructive influence for those who are naturally reserved or unsympathetic.

Transiting Neptune square natal Venus has the same significance as transiting Venus square natal Neptune; however, it is of longer duration, and indicates a sustained period of emotional, financial, and romantic confusion and sometimes self-deception. This transit can occur only twice in an average life span.

Transiting Venus Square Natal Pluto

Lack of consideration for the emotional needs and feelings of others, as well as difficulty in controlling sexual urges, characterizes this transit.

Emotional attempts to reform or remake others are apt to cause resentment and breakdown of harmony in close personal relationships.

Past emotional attachments and attitudes can be shattered during this transit. Circumstances beyond one's control may force one to adopt an attitude of detachment.

Sexual incompatibility or jealousy can occur in romantic or marital relationships. In extreme cases, the individual may be raped or sexually molested, but only if the natal horoscope concurs.

Problems and disagreements over the handling of joint finances, insurance, taxes, inheritance, alimony, or goods of the dead can arise at this time. Valuable personal possessions or property should be carefully guarded. Criminal elements of society or underworld figures should be avoided at all costs. There is danger of extortion or coercion in financial affairs.

Transiting Pluto square natal Venus has the same significance as transiting Venus square natal Pluto; however, it lasts, off and on, for a year or longer and indicates a sustained period of emotional, sexual, and financial tension and difficulty.

Transiting Venus Square the Natal North Node and Square the Natal South Node

Lack of emotional harmony with prevailing modes of social conduct, aesthetic taste, and sexual morality characterize this transit. There is often a lack of public acceptance of the individual's personal artistic or business endeavors.

Transiting North and South Nodes square natal Venus has the same significance as transiting Venus square the natal North Node and square the natal South Node; however, it lasts longer and indicates a sustained period of inharmony with prevailing cultural and social expectations.

Transiting Venus Square the Natal South Node and Square the Natal North Node

See "Transiting Venus square the Natal North Node and Square the Natal South Node."

Transiting Venus Square the Natal Ascendant and Square the Natal Descendant

During this transit, the individual's moods and feelings tend to be out of sympathy with those of others. Disharmony is frequent in marital, romantic, or business relationships. This is an unfavorable period for public relations and dealings with women.

The individual tends to experience difficulties in the expression of his or her personal, romantic, emotional, or artistic feelings and ideas.

Financial extravagance, laziness, hedonistic tendencies, and self-indulgence can also cause problems for the individual.

Transiting Venus Square the Natal Midheaven and
Square the Natal Nadir

Difficulties in family, professional, social, and financial affairs characterize this transit.

Unnecessary social activities can interfere with domestic and professional responsibilities, and professional and domestic responsibilities can interfere with social, artistic, and romantic gratification. Financial difficulties can interfere in the enjoyment of family and professional activities. In some cases, the individuals feel they must attend or participate in professional, family, or social activities which they do not enjoy. Poor taste is often exercised in decorating either the domestic or the business environment.

Transiting Venus Square the Natal Descendant and
Square the Natal Ascendant

See "Transiting Venus Square the Natal Ascendant and Square the Natal Descendant."

Transiting Venus Square the Natal Nadir and
Square the Natal Midheaven

See "Transiting Venus Square the Natal Midheaven and Square the Natal Nadir."

Transit Venus Trines

Transiting Venus Trine the Natal Sun

See "Transiting Sun Trine Natal Venus."

Transiting Venus Trine the Natal Moon

See "Transiting Moon Trine Natal Venus."

Transiting Venus Trine Natal Mercury

See "Transiting Mercury Trine Natal Venus."

Transiting Venus Trine Natal Venus

The enjoyment of art, music, entertainment, and social activities characterizes this transit.

This period holds the promise for marital happiness and romantic fulfillment. There is a reciprocal exchange of kindness and consideration in close personal relationships. Both business and romantic opportunities are likely to arise through social activities. It is a good time to plan social gatherings and entertainments.

This is also a favorable time for public relations and for business activities related to art, music, entertainment, and luxury items. Artists, musicians, and entertainers are likely to receive support and recognition for their work at this time.

This is a favorable period for dealings with women.

Transiting Venus Trine Natal Mars

Romantic activity and sexual attraction characterize this transit.

Women who seek to become pregnant are able to do so at this time, unless their physical conditions make it impossible for some reason.

Creative action in artistic self-expression is associated with this transit. Hence, this is an excellent period for actors, musicians, and performing artists. The individual can also express greater creativity in enterprise and business. It is easier to make money through personal creative endeavors at this time, especially if they relate to art, music, and entertainment.

The individual enjoys participation in social activity and may gain financially through social contacts. Gifts, funding, and favors from others are all possibilities. This is a favorable period for financial investment in corporate business affairs.

Transiting Mars trine natal Venus has the same significance as transiting Venus trine natal Mars; however, it lasts for a much longer period of time, depending upon how fast Mars is moving and whether it is stationary, retrograde, or direct. Consequently, it indicates a longer period of personal creative initiative in business, artistic, and social affairs.

Transiting Venus Trine Natal Jupiter

A happy, generous outlook on life and kindness and consideration for others characterize this transit.

Harmony in business, social, and romantic relationships comes easily at this time. This can be an inspiring transit for artists and musicians: they are likely to receive greater cultural support and recognition.

Social activities related to educational, religious, and cultural institutions are favored during this period. Social gatherings and fundraising activities for social, educational, cultural, religious, or charitable institutions may be successfully pursued. The individual is able to achieve a harmonious understanding in close personal relationships regarding the cultural, religious, and educational beliefs and values of others. Interaction with foreigners or those associated with educational, cultural, or religious institutions is likely to be harmonious. The individuals will be kindly disposed toward children, young people, and those less fortunate than themselves.

This is a favorable time for study or professional work related to education and law and for taking vacations and long journeys.

Transiting Jupiter trine natal Venus has the same significance as transiting Venus trine natal Jupiter; however, it lasts for a much longer period of time—how long depends on the speed of Jupiter's motion and whether Jupiter is retrograde, stationary, or direct. It indicates a sustained period of religious, educational, social, artistic, cultural, and romantic progress and expansion.

Transiting Venus Trine Natal Saturn

A mature appreciation of beauty and a serious pursuit of art and music characterize this transit.

Individuals often develop an interest in classical music and art forms at this time. The transit is especially good for business related to antiques and classical art forms, especially those that require a sense of structure and composition to be appreciated. Architects and designers are favored.

Close personal relationships are often cemented. Old friendships, partnerships, or romantic relationships are often renewed.

This transit is conducive to a calm, peaceful emotional attitude. The individual's social manner is mature and reserved.

The individual has an increased sense of responsibility in partnerships, business, friendships, and close personal relationships.

Progress can be made in business, financial, and professional endeavors. This is a good period for public relations of a serious business or political nature, or for establishing business and professional partnerships. It is a good time to approach those in positions of power and authority for favors or financial support, asking for a raise in pay, for example.

Transiting Saturn trine natal Venus has the same significance as transiting Venus trine natal Saturn; however, it lasts for a much longer period of time, and occurs twice every twenty-nine years, thus marking a sustained period of steady progress in business, social, artistic, romantic, and marital affairs.

Transiting Venus Trine Natal Uranus

This is a period of unusual creative inspiration for artists, musicians, and performers. The individual tends to enjoy unusual and interesting music and art.

A joyous, happy, sparkling emotional outlook is characteristic. Much social activity involving friends, groups, and organizations is likely to take place. This is a favorable time for business activities related to groups, friends, organizations, entertainment, art, music, luxury items, electronics, and corporate business.

Unusual and exciting friendships, social contacts, and romantic opportunities often come about under this transit. New partnerships or marriage opportunities are possible, providing the natal horoscope promises such unions. In any case, this transit indicates a pleasant interlude.

In general, one enjoys greater emotional, financial, and social freedom to pursue happiness in one's own way.

Transiting Uranus trine natal Venus has the same significance as transiting Venus trine natal Uranus; however, it lasts much longer, and indicates a sustained period of exciting new business, social, friendship, group, artistic, and romantic opportunities. This transit occurs only twice in an average lifetime.

Transiting Venus Trine Natal Neptune

Psychic sensitivity and an enhanced awareness of beauty, creative artistic imagination and intuitive emotional sensitivity to the needs and feelings of others all characterize this transit.

Greater harmony and understanding in romantic, marital, and family relationships may result from this increased emotional sensitivity and kindness.

This transit may bring about an ideal love or romance, or someone who epitomizes this ideal may enter the individual's life.

This is a favorable period for quiet contemplation and meditation and for visiting people in hospitals, asylums, or other institutions. Travel for pleasure or religious pilgrimages is possible.

Financial dealings related to art, music, entertainment, and luxury items are favored. At this time, the individual may either receive gifts or inheritances or bestow them upon others.

Transiting Neptune trine natal Venus has the same significance as transiting Venus trine natal Neptune; however, it lasts much longer and indicates a sustained period of creative imagination and sensitivity and kindness in close personal relationships. This transit occurs only once in an average life span.

Transiting Venus Trine Natal Pluto

Intuitive inspiration in artistic, musical, and creative endeavors characterizes this transit.

The individual may decide to speculate in businesses related to art, music, and entertainment. There is often an interest in restoring old art objects or finding new uses for discarded items. Intuitive inspiration in creative artistic fields sometimes takes the form of ideas for improving on old methods of doing things. This also applies to business and financial affairs. The individual may gain insights into how to use financial resources (and those of a partner, if one exists) more effectively and constructively. Business affairs related to insurance, taxes, corporate affairs, joint money, inheritance, alimony, and recycling are favored. Involvement in joint financial business ventures related to art, music, entertainment, and luxury items is also possible.

The individual may receive uplifting insights into the nature of love. In some cases, a meaningful relationship has a highly regenerative effect on the individual's life. This is a period of strong attractions to the opposite sex. Strong romantic, sexual and, in some cases, marital relationships can have their inception.

Transiting Pluto trine natal Venus has the same significance as transiting Venus trine natal Pluto; however, it lasts for a longer period of time and indicates the possibility of original, creative, sustained effort. The individual gains a new understanding of what is required in close personal relationships. This transit occurs only once in an average life span.

Transiting Venus Trine the Natal North Node and Sextile the Natal South Node

See "Transiting Venus Sextile the Natal South Node and Trine the Natal North Node."

Transiting Venus Trine the Natal South Node and Sextile the Natal North Node

See "Transiting Venus Sextile the Natal North Node and Trine the Natal South Node."

Transiting Venus Trine the Natal Ascendant and Sextile the Natal Descendant

See "Transiting Venus Sextile the Natal Descendant and Trine the Natal Ascendant."

Transiting Venus Trine the Natal Midheaven and Sextile the Natal Nadir

See "Transiting Venus Sextile the Natal Nadir and Trine the Natal Midheaven."

Transiting Venus Trine the Natal Descendant and Sextile the Natal Ascendant

See "Transiting Venus Sextile the Natal Ascendant and Trine the Natal Descendant."

Transiting Venus Trine the Natal Nadir and Sextile the Natal Midheaven

See "Transiting Venus Sextile the Natal Midheaven and Trine the Natal Nadir."

Transit Venus Oppositions

Transiting Venus Opposition the Natal Sun

See "Transiting Sun Opposition Natal Venus."

Transiting Venus Opposition the Natal Moon

See "Transiting Moon Opposition Natal Venus."

Transiting Venus Opposition Natal Mercury

See "Transiting Mercury Opposition Natal Venus."

Transiting Venus Opposition Natal Venus

Excessive social activity or difficulty in expressing or accepting love characterizes this transit.

Diplomacy and sensitivity must be exercised in important relationships. The overactive social life associated with this transit may lead to sensuality and financial extravagance. Unwise expenditures on art objects or entertainment are especially likely.

Transiting Venus Opposition Natal Mars

Jealousy and extreme emotional reactions in close relationships characterize this transit.

The individual's romantic relationships during this period are likely to be based on sexual need rather than a mutual sharing of goals and life direction. Sexual incompatibility or sexual aggressiveness can be a problem.

The individual tends to lack emotional awareness of the needs and feelings of others and this may lead to emotional resentment and antagonisms. There is a tendency to be selfish, and the probability of having to deal with selfish people in romantic, marital, sexual, and financial relationships. Financial extravagance can have an adverse effect on these relationships. Conflicts may arise over joint finances; this is not a favorable transit for important business dealings.

Transiting Mars opposition natal Venus has the same significance as transiting Venus opposition natal Mars; however, it lasts for a longer period of time; how long depends on how fast Mars is moving and whether Mars is stationary, retrograde, or direct. It indicates a somewhat longer period of difficulty in emotional, sexual, and business relationships. This transit occurs once every two years.

Transiting Venus Opposition Natal Jupiter

Emotional and financial extravagance, insincere gestures of friendliness, and maudlin sentimentality characterize this transit.

There is a tendency to overindulge in food, drink, and sex and to display poor aesthetic taste in art and music. Vacations and pleasure trips may prove more costly than anticipated. There is a tendency to laziness, procrastination, and self-indulgence, and this is often encouraged by others.

There is often an element of hypocrisy in the individual's involvement with religious, educational, or cultural activities and the possibility that such involvements may not produce useful results.

There is a special need for cooperation in relationships pertaining to education, philosophy, religion, and cultural activities.

The main danger of this transit is the evasion of important work and responsibilities through the pursuit of nonproductive pleasure-oriented activities.

Transiting Jupiter opposition natal Venus has the same significance as transiting Venus opposition natal Jupiter; however, it lasts longer and indicates a sustained period of extravagance and overexpansion. This transit occurs once in twelve years.

Transiting Venus Opposition Natal Saturn

Emotional depressions and feelings of being unloved characterize this transit.

Loneliness and lack of romantic fulfillment are often the cause of an unhappy emotional state. There may be romantic disappointments and unrequited love. The individual may be separated from loved ones. Professional and work responsibilities may interfere with romantic and marital relationships. Either the individuals are cold and lacking in sympathy or others behave this way toward them.

Shyness, stiff formal manners, and lack of social confidence are also problems. The individual's reserved social manner may be interpreted as snobbishness. This is an unfavorable time for public relations activity or for dealing with those in positions of power and authority.

Frustration and delays can occur in business and financial affairs. The individual tends to be uncomfortably aware of his or her personal financial limitations. Past poor management of finances calls for an accounting at this point. The individual may be forced to economize on pleasures and luxury items.

Transiting Saturn opposition natal Venus has the same significance as transiting Venus opposition natal Saturn; however, because it lasts for a longer period of time, it seems far more oppressive, restrictive, and burdensome. This transit occurs once in twenty-nine years.

Transiting Venus Opposition Natal Uranus

Unstable romantic infatuations and sexual promiscuity and irresponsibility characterize this transit. Such attitudes and actions may cause conflicts in close personal relationships.

The individual is subject to unpredictable emotional responses, likes, and dislikes. Eccentric tastes in art, music, and social activity are often exhibited. Foolishly eccentric friends and social contacts are likely to be a liability.

Disruptions can occur in friendships, group associations, marriages, and other close relationships. Old relationships are often severed and new ones created. Unsuitable sexual and romantic associations often occur under this transit. Such activities bring about the breakdown of established relationships of more lasting value. There is a need for sensible cooperation with friends, group associates, partners, and organizations.

Hedonistic tendencies can cause indifference to practical responsibility and long-range security.

The individual may be subject to unexpected difficulties with joint finances. Losses can come about through unwise, impulsive financial decisions. Conflicts can arise over joint finances, insurance, taxes, inheritance, and alimony. Caution should be exercised in businesses dealing with electronics, advanced technology, art, music, entertainment, and any "get-rich-quick" schemes.

Transiting Uranus opposition natal Venus has the same significance as transiting Venus opposition natal Uranus; however, it lasts longer and indicates a sustained period of eccentric financial, social, and sexual behavior. This transit occurs only once in an average life span.

Transiting Venus Opposition Natal Neptune

Misplaced sympathy, maudlin sentimentality, emotional self-deception, romantic fantasizing, secret love affairs, inappropriate romantic/sexual ties, deception in romantic and marital relationships, and one-sided romantic attractions all characterize this transit.

There can also be poor taste and lack of practicality in social, artistic, and business activities. The individual is vulnerable to confidence artists, "get-rich-quick" schemes, and spurious business deals. This vulnerability stems from an unrealistic attitude toward business and finances. Realism is needed to avoid financial deception. Sentimentality is also likely to interfere with sound business judgment.

Laziness and financial extravagance can stand in the way of success and worthwhile accomplishment.

Art and mysticism can be used as an escape from practical responsibility, as can drugs and alcohol. There may be an attraction to questionable cults and mystical practices.

Transiting Neptune opposition natal Venus has the same significance as transiting Venus opposition natal Neptune; however, it lasts for a year or longer and indicates the danger of a sustained period of emotional escapism. This transit occurs only once in an average life span.

Transiting Venus Opposition Natal Pluto

Selfishness and lack of consideration for the emotions of others characterize this transit.

There is a tendency to use others merely for sexual gratification. The individual is susceptible to sexual seduction. Extramarital love affairs often occur under this transit. Sexual jealousy and difficulty in handling sexual desires are often problems. There is danger of trying to dominate others or being dominated by them for motives of sexual gratification. In some cases, however, this transit can bring about a spiritually meaningful love relationship.

The individual may either attempt to remake or reform others in close personal relationships, or be the subject of such attempts on the part of others. There is a special need for cooperation and fair play in all relationships during this transit.

Conflicts can arise over joint finances, insurance, taxes, goods of the dead, and alimony. Problems can arise in corporate financial relationships. Caution is needed in business dealings, and unethical business practices are particularly to be avoided.

The individual may lack social refinement.

This transit can be channeled into creative artistic expression through the use of the intuition.

Transiting Pluto opposition natal Venus has the same significance as transiting Venus opposition natal Pluto; however, it lasts, off and on, for a year or longer and indicates a sustained period of the need for spiritual regeneration of relationships.

Transiting Venus Opposition the Natal North Node and Conjunct the Natal South Node

See "Transiting Venus Conjunct the Natal South Node and Opposition the Natal North Node."

Transiting Venus Opposition the Natal South Node and Conjunct the Natal North Node

See "Transiting Venus Conjunct the Natal North Node and Opposition the Natal South Node."

Transiting Venus Opposition the Natal Ascendant and Conjunct the Natal Descendant

See "Transiting Venus Conjunct the Natal Descendant and Opposition the Natal Ascendant."

Transiting Venus Opposition the Natal Midheaven and Conjunct the Natal Nadir

See "Transiting Venus Conjunct the Natal Nadir and Opposition the Natal Midheaven."

Transiting Venus Opposition the Natal Descendant and Conjunct the Natal Ascendant

See "Transiting Venus Conjunct the Natal Ascendant and Opposition the Natal Descendant."

Transiting Venus Opposition the Natal Nadir and Conjunct the Natal Midheaven

See "Transiting Venus Conjunct the Natal Midheaven and Opposition the Natal Nadir."

23 Transits of Mars

Transit Mars Through the Houses

Transiting Mars Through the Natal First House

Increased physical energy and competitive drive characterize this transit. The individual's ambition and professional drive are stimulated, and there is a new degree of initiative and self-confidence in action.

The individual is likely to be impulsive and feel a desire for adventure and physical activity. This transit increases the body heat and leads to improved health through exercise. This is a favorable time for physical work, providing safety rules are observed.

If Mars makes stress aspects while transiting this house, the individual is prone to aggressive, self-assertive, headstrong, egocentric, and selfish attitudes.

Transiting Mars Through the Natal Second House

During this transit, the individual feels an increased ambition to acquire money and possessions and take action to obtain them.

The individual is likely to express greater enterprise than usual in business and professional affairs as a means of acquiring the material things that are so important to him or her at this time. This desire for wealth and status, if carried too far, can lead to greed, impulsive spending, or materialistic attitudes. If Mars makes stress aspects while transiting the natal

Second House, there can be danger of theft.

There is often involvement in corporate business enterprises and professional and business activities; these can be related to machinery, steel construction, the manufacture of sharp implements, arms manufacture, or military and police work.

Transiting Mars Through the Natal Third House

Energetic pursuit of knowledge, intellectual competition, debates, and arguments characterize this transit.

The individual is primarily interested in ideas and information that have practical application and can be carried out in action. The individual may engage in scientific research or other types of information seeking.

This transit often involves professional and corporate communications of some sort. The individual may become concerned with professional contracts and agreements. There is likely to be much short-distance traveling connected with business and professional affairs.

There is often an interest in news related to military affairs, politics, business, and sports. The individual may be concerned with such things as automobile repair, road construction, or communication technologies.

Conflicts may arise with brothers, sisters, neighbors, and others in the immediate environment. On the other hand, the individual is likely to take constructive action to improve environmental conditions and neighborhood affairs.

If Mars makes stress aspects while transiting the natal Third House, there is danger of automobile accidents, transportation problems, and a tendency toward sarcastic, caustic speech and mental irritation.

Transiting Mars Through the Natal Fourth House

Physical activity in the home characterizes this transit.

This is a favorable time for do-it-yourself projects and home-construction or improvement efforts. If Mars makes stress aspects while transiting this house, safety precautions to avoid accidents, injury, and fires in the home should be carefully observed.

Emotional upsets can be triggered by subconscious reminders of past painful experiences. Family emotional problems can cause quarrels and emotional outbursts. It is especially necessary to consider the needs and feelings of other family members. Indigestion can be caused by emotional upsets or bad eating habits.

Transiting Mars Through the Natal Fifth House

Intensified sexual desires and need for sensitivity and consideration in romantic relationships and dealings with children characterize this transit.

Sexual jealousy and frustration can stand in the way of the individual's happiness. Aggressive, crude sexual behavior can be a problem if Mars is under stress aspects while transiting this house. Women should avoid dangerous situations during this transit—there is a possibility that they will be molested sexually.

The individual enjoys physical activity, such as sports and physical work. Physical activities for pleasure may involve dancing, sports, sex, or artistic expressions such as sculpture or performing arts. This is a good time for artists and musicians to give form to their ideas and inspirations.

The individual is likely to be aggressive in his or her pursuit of creative self-expression, romance, and other pleasures. If Mars makes stress aspects while transiting this house, there is a tendency to loud, boisterous behavior during social gatherings.

If Mars is afflicted while making this transit, there is a tendency to seek out entertainment of a violent nature, whether via television, movies, sports, or reckless activities.

The individual may have to contend with children who are active and hard to control during this transit. This is a favorable time for engaging in physical games and sports with children, providing safety rules are observed and Mars does not make stress aspects.

Transiting Mars Through the Natal Sixth House

Physical work and energetic accomplishment characterize this transit. The individual's work during this period often involves the use of tools or machinery. The individual may become involved in engineering, medicine, manufacturing, or police or military affairs. If Mars makes stress aspects while transiting this house, occupational hazards can be a danger to the individual; therefore, all necessary safety precautions should be observed.

The individual may become involved in physical-fitness programs to improve health. There is often an interest in clothes or changing the personal appearance in some way.

Conflicts may arise with others in the working environment.

Health problems caused by inflammations or fevers, injury, nervous strain, and surgery can trouble the individual if Mars makes stress aspects while transiting this house. Poor dietary habits may also affect the individual's health.

Transiting Mars Through the Natal Seventh House

Aggressive behavior either toward or from others and a need for cooperation in important relationships characterize this transit.

If Mars makes stress aspects while transiting the natal Seventh House, the individual is likely to become involved in conflicts which, in extreme cases, can be of a physical nature. These often take the form of disagreements in marriage or partnerships that can lead to lawsuits and, possibly, divorce.

However, this transit can bring about energetic cooperation that will achieve practical results. It is favorable for partnerships involving business, engineering, technology, police, and military affairs.

Transiting Mars Through the Natal Eighth House

Business activity, involvement in matters pertaining to joint finances, and the elimination of old conditions and creation of new ones characterize this transit.

Some individuals become actively involved in matters related to corporate business, insurance, taxes, inheritance, or alimony. There can also be activity regarding police and military affairs and demolition. The individual may become involved with heavy industry.

If Mars makes stress aspects while transiting the natal Eighth House, the individual can become involved in conflicts, battles, or other dangerous situations.

There may be an interest in occult or secret affairs. This transit usually increases the sex drive. It can coincide with the death of someone who is important to the individual, if other factors in the horoscope concur.

Transiting Mars Through the Natal Ninth House

Aggressive promotion of one's personal religious, educational, philosophic, political, and cultural values and opinions characterizes this transit. If this is carried to excess, it can lead to fanaticism and cause conflicts and arguments.

Business involvements with foreigners or foreign countries or long-distance commerce may occur at this time. There may be involvement with foreign wars in some way. The individual may be motivated to travel for action and adventure. If Mars makes stress aspects while transiting this house, however, the individual may be exposed to physical danger while traveling or visiting foreign countries.

In some cases, there is active participation in the affairs of cultural, educational, and political institutions. Students attending universities may become involved in political activism or aggressively seek to bring about cultural change. The individuals may find themselves annoyed by those who aggressively promote their own religious or cultural beliefs.

Transiting Mars Through the Natal Tenth House

Professional and business ambition and the exercise of personal authority characterize this transit.

The individual may become involved in political affairs or activities in some manner. This transit often arouses a desire for fame, status, and prominence, especially if the individual is involved in politics or in managerial or executive activities. The individual is inclined to assume a role of leadership in political or professional affairs.

This transit stimulates professional ambition and can lead to dynamic professional actions. Professional activities are likely to be related in some way to police and military affairs, insurance, taxes, heavy industry, steel industries, manufacturing, engineering, politics, or government agencies. In any event, there will be a more energetic and ambitious approach to professional activities. The sign through which Mars is transiting has a lot to do with how this energy is expressed. There is likely to be much physical exertion connected with one's professional work.

New career activities can be initiated at this time. The individual may reorganize his or her business or start a new business.

Authoritarian attitudes may be expressed, either by or toward the individual. Conflicts may arise with employers or government authorities.

If Mars makes stress aspects while transiting this house, the individual can assume an autocratic, dictatorial attitude or cause conflict in business or professional affairs.

Transiting Mars Through the Natal Eleventh House

Energetic action involving friends, groups, and organizations characterizes this transit.

The individual is likely to engage in some kind of physical activity or to work with friends, groups, and associations. Friends or group associates may motivate the individual into action, or the reverse may happen. In some cases, conflicts or competition with friends arise.

If Mars makes stress aspects while transiting this house, the individual and his or her friends may goad each other into reckless, even dangerous, actions. The individual may entertain revolutionary sentiments and seek to overthrow the established power structure.

There is a desire to play a leadership role in groups and organizations.

The individual is likely to take action to support humanitarian and reformist causes, or to achieve his or her personal goals and objectives.

Transiting Mars Through the Natal Twelfth House

Secretive, undercover, or behind-the-scenes activity characterizes this transit, usually for the purpose of avoiding confrontations or opposition. These activities may involve business, corporate affairs, sexual encounters, or matters related to hospitals, asylums, or religious institutions.

This transit is apt to arouse subconscious motivations and psychological drives. The individual may develop an interest in investigating the unconscious, or exploring the occult or parapsychological fields.

If Mars makes stress aspects while transiting this house, the individual may become involved in secret intrigues or be subject to the actions of secret enemies.

In extreme cases, the individual is his or her own worst enemy, and this transit can bring about hospitalization, institutionalization, or imprisonment. Mars rules the principle of desire and action, and misdirected action caused by uncontrolled unconscious desires may cause the individual's self-undoing.

Transit Mars Conjunctions

Transiting Mars Conjunct the Natal Sun

See "Transiting Sun Conjunct Natal Mars."

Transiting Mars Conjunct the Natal Moon

See "Transiting Moon Conjunct Natal Mars."

Transiting Mars Conjunct Natal Mercury

See "Transiting Mercury Conjunct Natal Mars."

Transiting Mars Conjunct Natal Venus

See "Transiting Venus Conjunct Natal Mars."

Transiting Mars Conjunct Natal Mars

Increased initiative, competitiveness, and new beginnings characterize this transit.

Personal restlessness, intensified action, and speeded-up activity, increased energy, aggressive behavior, muscular exertion, and intensified material and sexual desires are associated with this transit.

The business and professional ambitions of the individual are intensified, leading to increased action to achieve status and success. Business activities can involve corporate business, insurance, taxes, inheritance, joint finances, manufacturing, heavy equipment, building, or construction. Some individuals become involved with tools, machinery, or weapons.

Transiting Mars Conjunct Natal Jupiter

Increased enthusiasm, ambition, and self-confidence characterize this transit.

This is a favorable time for seeking employment and career training and advancement.

The individual displays more enterprise than usual in business affairs. Business activities may be related to foreign trade, business trips, or long-distance commerce. It is a good period for handling legal affairs or matters related to joint finances, corporate business, insurance, taxes, alimony, and goods of the dead.

The individual is more inclined than usual to put his or her religious beliefs into action in a practical way.

The individual may also take action in matters related to educational, philosophical, legal, or cultural affairs. The ambition for cultural, religious, or educational authority and distinction is increased. A "might-makes-right" attitude should be avoided in attempting to force one's cultural values on others. If this tendency is carried too far, it can result in fanaticism.

Involvement in sports is likely, especially if the individual is attending a college or university.

This is a favorable period for travel, vacations, or adventure.

Transiting Jupiter conjunct natal Mars has the same significance as transiting Mars conjunct natal Jupiter; however, it is of longer duration and marks a sustained period of enthusiastic and expansive activity. This transit occurs once in the twelve-year cycle of Jupiter.

Transiting Mars Conjunct Natal Saturn

Hard physical work, frustrated impulses to action, and suppressed anger and resentment characterize this transit.

This transit increases the individual's caution, determination, precision, and resourcefulness, especially if the conjunction is in a fixed sign.

This is usually a time of heavy work and responsibility, which require organized action. If the transit is properly handled, the individual carries out his or her work and responsibilities in a deliberate, efficient, and organized way. Because of this organization and discipline, the individual's actions produce concrete practical results.

Some individuals are so hard-driving in their ambitions as to be inconsiderate of others. A hard, unsympathetic attitude can develop. Trouble or conflicts can arise with employers, authority figures, or government agencies. In extreme cases, the individual may be arrested.

The individual may become involved with heavy industry, engineering, corporate business, and legal affairs or government administration and military affairs.

Transiting Saturn conjunct natal Mars has the same significance as transiting Mars conjunct natal Saturn; however, it lasts much longer and indicates a sustained period of hard work and heavy professional responsibility. This transit occurs once in twenty-nine years.

Transiting Mars Conjunct Natal Uranus

A desire for independence in action and impulsive action characterize this transit.

The individual is likely to express greater initiative in business, including corporate business enterprises.

There is also likely to be increased activity in relation to friends, groups, and organizations: the individual may assume a role of personal leadership. If the individual's behavior is aggressive or inconsistent, however, friends or group associates may become alienated.

There is a desire to change the status quo which, in some cases, can lead to revolutionary attitudes. Unexpected, disruptive events may occur in the individual's life. This transit sometimes coincides with the death of a friend or acquaintance.

The individual may become actively involved with occult subjects, astrology, economics, politics, machinery, engineering, or electronics.

If the conjunction receives stress aspects from other natal or transiting planets, there is danger of accidents, outbursts of temper, or possible violence. These dangers are especially probable if the individual is involved with guns, fire, electricity, or automobiles.

Transiting Uranus conjunct natal Mars has the same significance as transiting Mars conjunct natal Uranus; however, it lasts, off and on, for a year or longer and indicates a sustained period of sudden disruptions.

Transiting Mars Conjunct Natal Neptune

Secretive or covert action characterizes this transit. Activity is often carried on secretly to avoid the opposition and disapproval of others.

The individual's subconscious desires and feelings may be stimulated at this time with the result that subconscious forces may bring uncontrolled impulses into the open.

The individual's psychic and intuitive faculties, as well as his or her potential for giving or receiving spiritual healing, are activated. The individual may become involved in activities related to mystical religions, cults, or organizations.

Creative artists and performers will find this transit helpful in expressing their creative imagination in a dynamic way. There is often a desire for travel and adventure.

The individual should exercise caution in business and financial dealings and in all business propositions. Business dealings may be carried on in secret. There is often some kind of involvement with hospitals or institutions. The individual may be exposed to danger through drugs, alcohol, or medication. The wrong anaesthetic might be administered, for example, during an operation.

Transiting Neptune conjunct natal Mars has the same significance as transiting Mars conjunct natal Neptune; however, it can last, off and on, for a year or longer, and it indicates a sustained period of dynamic expression of emotional psychic energy.

Transiting Mars Conjunct Natal Pluto

Aggressive self-assertive action and intensified will power characterize this transit.

The transit can lead to a desire for spiritual, mental, or physical self-improvement.

There may be dynamic activity involving scientific interests or the occult. The individual may become involved in secret research and investigations or in police or military affairs, engineering, or atomic energy.

The individual often engages in energetic physical work. It is a favorable transit for athletes. However, there is need to avoid situations of physical danger, such as mobs or dangerous environments. In extreme situations, the individual is forced to fight for his or her survival.

If this conjunction receives stress aspects from natal or other transiting planets, there is danger of death or physical injury, especially in situations of war, revolution, or social unrest.

This is a favorable time for dealing with corporate business, joint finances, taxes, insurance, and goods of the dead. Individuals with this transit display constructive leadership and resourcefulness in business and scientific enterprises. They are able to eliminate old conditions that have outgrown their usefulness and create new ones in their place.

Transiting Pluto conjunct natal Mars has the same significance as transiting Mars conjunct natal Pluto; however, it lasts, off and on, for a year or longer and indicates a period of drastic change. This transit occurs only once in an average life span.

Transiting Mars Conjunct the Natal North Node and Opposition the Natal South Node

Activities that are in harmony with prevailing cultural trends and attitudes characterize this transit.

The individual may compete for popular recognition in professional, business, or political affairs, or in sports or physical activities.

The individual may receive social or business support for his or her personal business, professional, political or physical activities.

Transiting North Node conjunct natal Mars and transiting South Node opposition natal Mars has the same significance as transiting Mars conjunct the natal North Node and opposition the natal South Node; however, it lasts longer and indicates a sustained period of dynamic cultural involvement.

Transiting Mars Conjunct the Natal South Node and Opposition the Natal North Node

Action in support of traditional social values characterizes this transit.

The individual's professional, business, or political actions may lack public support because of their traditional or unpopular nature. However, they may be supported by traditional institutions.

Transiting South Node conjunct natal Mars and transiting North Node opposition natal Mars has the same significance as transiting Mars conjunct the natal South Node and opposition the natal North Node; however, it lasts longer and indicates a sustained period of unpopular social, business, and political actions on the part of the individual.

Transiting Mars Conjunct the Natal Ascendant and Opposition the Natal Descendant

Impulsiveness and intensified physical activity characterize this transit.

The individual feels a competitive drive and the need for dynamic physical action. Personal initiative is displayed in business and professional affairs. However, there is a tendency toward a "me-first," self-centered attitude if this conjunction receives stress aspects from other transiting planets.

Transiting Mars Conjunct the Natal Midheaven and Opposition the Natal Nadir

Dynamic business, professional, and political action and ambition characterize this transit.

The individual may become involved professionally with corporate business, engineering, heavy industry, or with police or military affairs.

If Mars receives stress aspects from other planets, conflicts may arise with parents, authority figures, or government officials.

Transiting Mars Conjunct the Natal Descendant and Opposition the Natal Ascendant

Relationships with dynamic and energetic people characterize this transit.

The individual may take the initiative in public relations and in business affairs.

Competition and, possibly, conflict often arise in close personal relationships. There is a special need to consider the rights and feelings of others, especially in important relationships.

If Mars receives stress aspects from other transiting or natal planets, the individual may be subject to conflicts and confrontations which, in extreme cases, can be physical.

Transiting Mars Conjunct the Natal Nadir and Opposition the Natal Midheaven

Dynamic activity in the domestic environment characterizes this transit. The individual takes action to achieve domestic security. This is a favorable time for home-improvement projects, but it is especially necessary to observe safety measures. Strong subconscious emotional reactions can be aroused by the stimulation of memories of family upbringing and early conditioning. In some cases, this transit brings a conflict between domestic and professional responsibilities.

Transit Mars Sextiles

Transiting Mars Sextile the Natal Sun

See "Transiting Sun Sextile Natal Mars."

Transiting Mars Sextile the Natal Moon

See "Transiting Moon Sextile Natal Mars."

Transiting Mars Sextile Natal Mercury

See "Transiting Mercury Sextile Natal Mars."

Transiting Mars Sextile Natal Venus

See "Transiting Venus Sextile Natal Mars."

Transiting Mars Sextile Natal Mars

Intelligent action, increased energy, and new opportunities to accomplish one's goals characterize this transit.

Individuals with this transit are motivated to put their ideas into action, and they may gain insights into how to do this. Sometimes, these insights take the form of ideas for furthering their business and professional ambitions. This is a favorable transit for physical programs of self-improvement.

There may be considerable activity involving short trips, automobile mechanics, engineering, machinery, scientific interests, energy-producing technologies, and military, industrial, or political organizations. The individual's activities during this transit often involve friends, groups, and associations. If Mars is stationary, this aspect can last for a month.

Transiting Mars Sextile Natal Jupiter

Steady progress in business and professional affairs characterizes this transit.

Individuals with this transit are very conscious of the need for honesty and forthrightness, and thus they inspire confidence in others.

This is a favorable period for the individuals' educational, cultural, and political advancement. They are enthusiastic about putting their religious, educational, and political ideas into action and gaining greater cultural acceptance for them. They tend to take action to support religious, educational, or cultural projects.

This is a good period for handling legal affairs that concern business or professional matters and matters involving religious, charitable, cultural, and educational institutions. It is a good period for handling long-distance commerce and matters pertaining to shipping and transportation. This is an excellent time for sports and outdoor activities.

Transiting Jupiter sextile natal Mars has the same significance as transiting Mars sextile natal Jupiter; however, it lasts longer and indicates a sustained period of constructive action. This transit occurs twice in the twelve-year cycle of Jupiter.

Transiting Mars Sextile Natal Saturn

Increased professional discipline and organization, as well as efficiency and resourcefulness in work, characterize this transit.

A desire to protest the status quo may lead to a more conservative political attitude. The individual tends to become involved in business transactions with those in established positions of power and authority.

The individual often enters into business, professional, or political contracts or agreements during this transit.

It is a favorable transit for those involved in construction, engineering, or fields requiring skilled physical labor, and especially for craftsmen, technicians, engineers, and scientists who do precise mechanical or scientific work, such as drafting, mathematics, precision machining, and optical work. This is an excellent time for working with tools, machinery, and construction projects.

Transiting Saturn sextile natal Mars has the same significance as transiting Mars sextile natal Saturn; however it is of longer duration and indicates a sustained period of well-organized, purposeful action and professional endeavor. This transit occurs twice in the twenty-nine-year cycle of Saturn.

Transiting Mars Sextile Natal Uranus

Original creative activity and a desire for independence characterize this transit.

The individual expresses resourcefulness and initiative in business activities and in achieving his or her goals and objectives. Effective action can be undertaken with friends, groups, and organizations.

This is a favorable time for dealing with joint finances, corporate business, insurance, taxes, and inheritances. It is a good period for those involved in electronics, science, engineering, and technological fields.

It is a good transit for occult and astrological work or study.

Transiting Uranus sextile natal Mars has the same significance as transiting Mars sextile Uranus; however, it lasts much longer and indicates a sustained period of dynamic original action. This transit occurs only twice in an average life span.

Transiting Mars Sextile Natal Neptune

Individuals with this transit are guided by their intuitions in their business and professional affairs. Their imaginations will give them insights into how to carry out their actions more skillfully and effectively.

Activities are often carried on behind the scenes during this period. This is a good period for understanding and overcoming negative, subconscious emotional habit patterns and desires. It is favorable for dealing with psychological and occult subjects and activities, and for receiving or administering spiritual healing.

The individual can do constructive work in connection with charitable institutions, hospitals, schools, churches, or other cultural institutions. There can also be constructive action in artistic fields, especially in the field of music.

Transiting Neptune sextile natal Mars has the same significance as transiting Mars sextile natal Neptune; however, it is of longer duration and indicates a sustained period of intuitively inspired constructive action. This transit occurs only once or twice in the average life span.

Transiting Mars Sextile Natal Pluto

Intensified will-power in action and the desire for adventure characterize this transit.

The individual may develop an interest in investigating scientific or occult subjects. The transit favors involvement in police and military affairs. The individual may take constructive action in corporate business affairs, professional matters, and things related to joint finances, taxes, insurance, and goods of the dead.

This is a favorable transit for physical self-improvement and for projects that require strenuous physical exertion.

Transiting Pluto sextile natal Mars has the same significance as transiting Mars sextile natal Pluto; however, it lasts much longer and indicates a sustained period of dynamic, constructive, well-thought-out action, and self-improvement. This transit occurs only once in an average life span.

Transiting Mars Sextile the Natal North Node and Trine the Natal South Node

A desire for social acceptance and cultural approval of one's personal actions characterizes this transit.

Individuals with this transit may initiate action to improve social conditions, as well as action that will help them benefit from currently popular trends in business. Often, they take an interest in popular sports and physical activities.

Transiting North Node sextile natal Mars and transiting South Node trine natal Mars has the same significance as transiting Mars sextile the natal North Node and trine the natal South Node; however, it lasts longer and indicates a sustained period of dynamic involvement in currently popular trends.

Transiting Mars Sextile the Natal South Node and Trine the Natal North Node

This transit has basically the same significance as transiting Mars sextile the natal North Node and trine the natal South Node; however, the individual is more intellectually aware of cultural traditions and finds it easy to adapt to the current development of these traditions.

Transiting South Node sextile natal Mars and transiting North Node trine natal Mars has the same significance as transiting Mars sextile the natal South Node and trine the natal North Node; however, it lasts longer and indicates a sustained period of adaptation in action to culturally acceptable modes of activity.

Transiting Mars Sextile the Natal Ascendant and Trine the Natal Descendant

Increased physical energy and initiative characterize this transit. This is a favorable transit for physical-fitness programs, sports, mechanical work, engineering, and other endeavors requiring resourcefulness. There is active cooperation in important relationships and business affairs.

Transiting Mars Sextile the Natal Midheaven and Trine the Natal Nadir

Dynamic professional ambition and constructive action in domestic and professional affairs characterize this transit. Physical activity involving the home and family can be handled with good results. It is a good period for do-it-yourself home-improvement projects. This is also a favorable transit for professional involvement with corporate business, manufacturing, engineering, and politics.

Transiting Mars Sextile the Natal Descendant and Trine the Natal Ascendant

This transit has basically the same significance as transiting Mars sextile the natal Ascendant and trine the natal Descendant; however, there is a more intellectual focus on action as it concerns relationships, and an easy flow in self-expression through action.

Transiting Mars Sextile the Natal Nadir and Trine the Natal Midheaven

This transit has basically the same significance as transiting Mars sextile the natal Midheaven and trine the natal Nadir; however, there is a greater intellectual awareness of family and domestic activity and an easy, harmonious flow in professional activities.

Transit Mars Squares

Transiting Mars Square the Natal Sun

See "Transiting Sun Square Natal Mars."

Transiting Mars Square the Natal Moon

See "Transiting Moon Square Natal Mars."

Transiting Mars Square Natal Mercury

See "Transiting Mercury Square Natal Mars."

Transiting Mars Square Natal Venus

See "Transiting Venus Square Natal Mars."

Transiting Mars Square Natal Mars

Impulsive, aggressive behavior characterizes this transit. Conflicts over authority and leadership may result from selfish ambition and a desire for supremacy. Anger, fights, battles, outbursts of temper, rash, inconsiderate actions, and, in extreme cases, physical confrontations are also characteristic of this transit. Unrestrained sexual desires and impulses may give rise to difficulties.

The danger of conflicts and disagreements makes this a poor time to initiate new business or professional endeavors. A rash, "me-first" attitude can cause resentment.

Accidents or injuries may result from rash, ill-considered actions or physical overexertion. There is a tendency toward fevers and infections.

The individual should exercise caution in handling fire, guns, explosives, and dangerous tools and chemicals.

Transiting Mars Square Natal Jupiter

An inflated sense of one's own importance and a tendency to take too much for granted characterize this transit. Frequently, the individual lacks moderation in his or her actions.

Strong ambitions for religious, educational, political, business, or cultural authority and leadership are likely to be present, but improper preparation for such roles can cause trouble. It is not a favorable time for initiating new endeavors involving religious, educational, or cultural institutions.

The individual is prone to narrow-minded, fanatical religious and philosophical viewpoints, and subject to proselytization by fanatically aggressive religious organizations.

Often, the temptation to engage in unethical business profiteering arises. There is a tendency to extravagance in business and financial affairs. Unnecessary financial and physical risks should be avoided. Problems involving joint finances, corporate business, legal affairs, insurance, taxes, alimony, or goods of the dead may arise. This is not a good time to become involved in legal battles. Caution should be exercised in business dealings with foreigners or those in far-away places or in long-distance commerce.

Impatience, recklessness, and carelessness are also dangers during this transit. The individual may be exposed to danger while traveling, while visiting in foreign countries, or during an involvement in a foreign war.

Transiting Jupiter square natal Mars has the same significance as transiting Mars square natal Jupiter; however, it lasts longer and indicates a period of extravagance and misdirected energy. This transit occurs twice in the twelve-year cycle of Jupiter.

Transiting Mars Square Natal Saturn

Frustrated ambitions, a hard, unsympathetic emotional outlook, smoldering anger, and ruthless ambition for power characterize this transit.

The individual may be subject to a heavy work load and responsibilities. It appears to take twice the effort to accomplish the same amount of work during this period. There is a tendency to work in spurts, rather than at a steady pace, and there is danger of physical injury or physical exhaustion from overwork.

Skin inflammations, rashes, falls, bruises, broken bones, and dental problems are the ailments commonly associated with this transit.

Professional problems, frustrations, and aggravations are likely to arise at this time, as are legal battles, and conflicts with authorities, older people, and government agencies. The individual may be subject to hardships, physical danger, and even arrest.

Transiting Saturn square natal Mars has the same significance as transiting Mars square natal Saturn; however, it is of longer duration and indicates a sustained period of hardship and frustration. This transit occurs twice in the twenty-nine-year cycle of Saturn.

Transiting Mars Square Natal Uranus

Impulsive action, explosive outbursts of temper, the desire for freedom at any cost, and egotistical, self-centered attitudes which can alienate the individual's friends characterize this transit.

Disagreements or quarrels with groups and organizations, as well as with friends, are likely to arise.

Joint finances, corporate money, administrative affairs, taxes, insurance, inheritance, or alimony may all be sources of conflict. This is not a good time to initiate professional or business projects: many unexpected factors can emerge.

Large-scale forces beyond the individual's control may suddenly disrupt the affairs of his or her life. The individual may hear of the sudden death of a friend or group associate. Danger can arise through explosives, electricity, automobile accidents, or mishandling of machinery or firearms.

Transiting Uranus square natal Mars has the same significance as transiting Mars square natal Uranus; however, it is of longer duration and indicates a sustained period of disruptive events in the individual's life. This transit can occur twice in an average life span.

Transiting Mars Square Natal Neptune

Suppressed anger, secret intrigues, secretive actions, and difficulty in controlling one's subconscious desires characterize this transit.

There may be secret sexual involvements or abnormal sexual behavior. Sexual excesses present a danger.

Secretiveness or subconsciously motivated self-destructive tendencies also present a danger. Excessive drinking and drug abuse can be a source of trouble.

Dangers can also arise through unwise occult or psychic experimentation. The individual may be upset by disturbing dreams or psychic experiments.

Hard-to-diagnose illnesses and infections which have a debilitating effect on the individual are another potential source of trouble. The individual is subject to danger through poisons or wrong anaesthetic applications or cruel or abusive treatment while confined in hospitals or institutions.

Deception may arise in business and professional affairs. Individuals with this transit or those with whom they associate may be tempted to use devious means to achieve their business, professional, or political ambitions. There is danger of fraud involving insurance, taxes, joint finances, corporate business, or alimony.

Woolgathering can cause inefficiency in work.

Transiting Neptune square natal Mars has the same significance as transiting Mars square natal Neptune; however, it lasts, off and on, for a year or longer and indicates a sustained period of danger through secret intrigues, power struggles, and self-deception. This transit usually occurs twice in the average human life span, although it may occur only once.

Transiting Mars Square Natal Pluto

Impulsive action, power struggles, the need for self-regeneration, and attempts to forcibly remake, coerce, or remold others characterize this transit.

The individual may be aggressive and angry during this period. It is important to exercise caution, diplomacy, and good judgment.

The individual may express or be subjected to dominating, dictatorial attitudes in his or her relationships. Conflict may arise over joint finances, corporate money, insurance, taxes, or goods of the dead. There is also danger of sexual violence or jealousy during this period.

Power struggles involving political, professional, or military affairs are likely at this time. The individual should be especially careful to avoid situations of potential violence or danger, especially mobs and crowds or association with underworld or criminal activities. In situations of war, revolution, or natural disaster, the individual may also be in danger of injury or death. Caution is also needed in handling tools, machinery, guns, dangerous chemicals, or radioactive substances, especially if Pluto is square Mars in the natal horoscope.

Transiting Pluto square natal Mars has the same significance as transiting Mars square natal Pluto; however, it is of much longer duration and indicates a sustained period of anger, conflict, and struggle. This transit occurs only once in an average life span, and it often involves life-and-death issues.

Transiting Mars Square the Natal North Node and
Square the Natal South Node

During this transit, the individual's personal actions tend to be out of harmony with prevailing cultural attitudes and traditions.

There may be poor timing in business and professional affairs. The individual's behavior may express anti-social attitudes and disrespect for social traditions and mores.

Transiting North and South Nodes square natal Mars has the same significance as transiting Mars square the natal North Node and square the natal South Node; however, it lasts longer and indicates a sustained period of anger directed toward accepted social customs.

Transiting Mars Square the Natal South Node and Square the Natal North Node

See "Transiting Mars Square the Natal North Node and Square the Natal South Node."

Transiting Mars Square the Natal Ascendant and Square the Natal Descendant

Impulsive action and lack of consideration and cooperation in relationships characterize this transit. The individual may be either unable or unwilling to cooperate.

Intensified sexual desires may lead to overly aggressive behavior. Arguments, disagreements, conflicts, and confrontations often arise. The behavior of either the individuals or their associates tends to be aggressive and self-centered.

Physical overexertion or being present at dangerous situations may lead to physical injury.

Transiting Mars Square the Natal Midheaven and Square the Natal Nadir

Conflict and crisis situations in professional and domestic affairs characterize this transit. The individual may be subject to intense professional competition. Conflicts may arise with parents, bosses, or other authority figures. This is not a good time to initiate new professional or domestic projects. Caution should be exercised to avoid occupational and domestic hazards.

Transiting Mars Square the Natal Descendant and Square the Natal Ascendant

See "Transiting Mars Square the Natal Ascendant and Square the Natal Descendant."

Transiting Mars Square the Natal Nadir and Square the Natal Midheaven

See "Transiting Mars Square the Natal Midheaven and Square the Natal Nadir."

Transit Mars Trines

Transiting Mars Trine the Natal Sun

See "Transiting Sun Trine Natal Mars."

Transiting Mars Trine the Natal Moon

See "Transiting Moon Trine Natal Mars."

Transiting Mars Trine Natal Mercury

See "Transiting Mercury Trine Natal Mars."

Transiting Mars Trine Natal Venus

See "Transiting Venus Trine Natal Mars."

Transiting Mars Trine Natal Mars

Creative action, constructive ambition, physical vitality, and increased self-confidence all characterize this transit.

Individuals with this transit display a greater capacity for initiative and leadership. They are likely to enjoy sports, construction work, and other physical activities. This is a good period for work requiring physical exertion or the use of tools and machinery.

It is a good time to travel or initiate new projects in connection with one's business and professional affairs. Police work and military affairs are especially favored.

Transiting Mars Trine Natal Jupiter

Constructive, expansive action, enthusiasm, self-confidence, and love of adventure characterize this transit.

The individual can achieve significant progress and expansion in business and professional affairs. This is a favorable period for handling legal affairs and for home-improvement projects. The individual is more likely than usual to put his or her religious and philosophic beliefs and ideals into action. The transit favors religious, educational, and cultural organizations and their projects.

The individual can benefit from foreign travel and from contact with foreigners and foreign cultures.

This is a good transit for sports and outdoor activities. The individual will be concerned with honor and fair play.

Transiting Jupiter trine natal Mars has the same significance as transiting Mars trine natal Jupiter; however, it lasts much longer and indicates a sustained period of expansion through constructive action. This transit occurs twice in the twelve-year cycle of Jupiter.

Transiting Mars Trine Natal Saturn

Efficient expenditure of energy, intensified ambition, and a practical determination to succeed characterize this transit.

This is a favorable period for practical accomplishment through discipline and hard work. The individual expresses initiative and good organization in business and professional affairs. This transit favors managerial and administrative efforts. Industrial, police, or military affairs can be handled especially efficiently. This is also a favorable transit for those in the engineering, building, architectural, or manufacturing professions and for work involving tools, machinery, and precision craftsmanship.

Practical accomplishments may be brought about through association with friends, groups, and organizations.

This is a favorable period for dealing with authority figures and government agencies.

Transiting Saturn trine natal Mars has the same significance as transiting Mars trine natal Saturn; however, it lasts much longer and indicates a sustained period of practical accomplishment through discipline, hard work, and good organization. This transit occurs twice in the twenty-nine-year cycle of Saturn.

Transiting Mars Trine Natal Uranus

Constructive dynamic action, exciting adventure and the desire for freedom of expression characterize this transit.

The individual expresses increased self-confidence in trying new things in professional and business affairs, in the fields of engineering, science, the occult, and physical activities.

There is an increased interest in programs of physical, mental, and spiritual self-improvement. The individual is likely to engage in dynamic, constructive action with friends, groups, and organizations.

This is an excellent time for work related to electronics, scientific technology, and for business related to these fields. Occult and astrological work and experimentation are also favored.

Transiting Uranus trine natal Mars has the same significance as transiting Mars trine natal Uranus; however, it is of longer duration and indicates a sustained period of creative, dynamic, and unusual actions. This transit occurs twice in an average life span.

Transiting Mars Trine Natal Neptune

Stimulation of the intuitive and imaginative faculties, as well as energetic expression of artistic creativity, characterizes this transit.

This is a favorable transit for dancers and performing artists.

The individual experiences harmony while giving expression to his or her deeper desires. Latent abilities for spiritual healing are stimulated. An interest in pursuing religious, mystical, educational, or spiritual activities in the home environment often develops. These may involve meditation or other spiritual practices.

This is an excellent transit for secret research and investigations. Progress can be made in secret, behind-the-scenes work or activity.

Individuals with this transit actively promote their personal religious, educational, and philosophic beliefs. Often, they are instrumental in bringing about constructive changes in hospitals or institutions.

They may benefit through corporate finances, business, insurance, tax rebates, or inheritance.

Transiting Neptune trine natal Mars has the same significance as transiting Mars trine natal Neptune; however, it lasts, off and on, for a year or longer and indicates a sustained period of increased energy in the expression of the creative, imaginative faculties.

Transiting Mars Trine Natal Pluto

Intensified energy and will power and the exercise of personal leadership in business and professional affairs characterize this transit.

There is a greater willingness to defend one's principles whenever this is necessary.

The individual has an energetic, constructive impetus toward accomplishment. This is an excellent time to find ways to improve professional efficiency.

Joint finances and corporate money are used effectively at this time and progress can be made in corporate business affairs, scientific research, and technological endeavors.

The individual expresses greater will power in efforts at physical and spiritual self-improvement. This is a favorable time for self-development and constructive occult work and for athletes or those whose work requires strenuous physical exertion.

Transiting Pluto trine natal Mars has the same significance as transiting Mars trine natal Pluto; however, it is of longer duration and indicates a sustained period of dynamic, purposeful action and improvement of the status quo. This transit occurs once in the average life span.

Transiting Mars Trine the Natal North Node and Sextile the Natal South Node

See "Transiting Mars Sextile the Natal South Node and Trine the Natal North Node."

Transiting Mars Trine the Natal South Node and Sextile the Natal North Node

See "Transiting Mars Sextile the Natal North Node and Trine the Natal South Node."

Transiting Mars Trine the Natal Ascendant and Sextile the Natal Descendant

See "Transiting Mars Sextile the Natal Descendant and Trine the Natal Ascendant."

Transiting Mars Trine the Natal Midheaven and Sextile the Natal Nadir

See "Transiting Mars Sextile the Natal Nadir and Trine the Natal Midheaven."

Transiting Mars Trine the Natal Descendant and
Sextile the Natal Ascendant

See "Transiting Mars Sextile the Natal Ascendant and Trine the Natal Descendant."

Transiting Mars Trine the Natal Nadir and
Sextile the Natal Midheaven

See "Transiting Mars Sextile the Natal Midheaven and Trine the Natal Nadir."

Transit Mars Oppositions

Transiting Mars Opposition the Natal Sun

See "Transiting Sun Opposition Natal Mars."

Transiting Mars Opposition the Natal Moon

See "Transiting Moon Opposition Natal Mars."

Transiting Mars Opposition Natal Mercury

See "Transiting Mercury Opposition Natal Mars."

Transiting Mars Opposition Natal Venus

See "Transiting Venus Opposition Natal Mars."

Transiting Mars Opposition Natal Mars

Inconsiderate and aggressive behavior either toward or from others characterizes this transit. This behavior usually stems from an egotistical need for personal authority and power. Battles and confrontations may arise over emotional issues, and disagreements over joint finances, corporate money, insurance, taxes, inheritance, alimony, and business and professional affairs are common.

This is not a good time to seek favors from those in positions of power and authority.

Physical danger or injury can result from careless use of fire, guns, tools, machinery, automobiles, and dangerous chemicals.

Impulsive, aggressive behavior may get the individual in trouble. In extreme cases, the individual can become involved in physical confrontations or even be subject to arrest.

Transiting Mars Opposition Natal Jupiter

Extravagance and waste of resources and overexpansion in business characterize this transit.

There is danger of a "might-makes-right" attitude, overconfidence, and a tendency to make empty promises. The individual tends to suffer from an inflated sense of self-importance.

The individual may be exposed to danger while traveling or encounter difficulties in foreign countries.

Conflicts, particularly within the family, are likely to arise over educational, religious, and cultural beliefs and attitudes. Difficulties may come up in the individual's dealings with universities, hospitals, asylums, and other cultural institutions. Lawsuits or legal difficulties may arise.

Transiting Jupiter opposition natal Mars has the same significance as transiting Mars opposition natal Jupiter; however, it lasts longer and indicates a sustained period of extremism in the individual's religious, educational, and cultural attitudes. This transit occurs once in the twelve-year cycle of Jupiter.

Transiting Mars Opposition Natal Saturn

Excessive physical strain and exertion characterize this transit. The individual is subject to broken bones, problems with teeth, skin irritations, "hot-and-cold flashes," and occupational hazards. Caution should be exercised in handling tools, automobiles, machinery, guns, and knives.

The individual's desire for action may be frustrated by conflict with authority figures or older people. The individual may either express authoritarian, dictatorial attitudes or be subjected to them by others. This is not a good time to seek favors from those in positions of power and authority. The individual may experience problems with parents, employers, or government agencies. In extreme cases, the individual is arrested or apprehended by the police. The individual may have the unwanted burden of taking care of older people.

Frustrations and problems are likely to arise in business and professional affairs. Important changes in business or profession should not be made during this transit.

Legal difficulties and lawsuits may occur at this time.

Transiting Saturn opposition natal Mars has the same significance as transiting Mars opposition natal Saturn; however, it is of longer duration and indicates a sustained period of hardship and frustration. This transit occurs only once in the twenty-nine-year cycle of Saturn.

Transiting Mars Opposition Natal Uranus

Conflicts with friends, rash, impulsive actions, and outbursts of temper characterize this transit.

The individual should exercise caution in the use of tools, electricity, explosives, firearms, and automobiles. Danger may also arise through police or military affairs. This transit often arouses revolutionary sentiments and a desire to overthrow the existing power structure.

Impatience and impulsiveness can cause difficulties in the realization of goals and objectives. This is an unfavorable time for initiating new projects or group activities.

Conflicts may also arise over the financial affairs of groups and organizations and over joint finances, corporate business affairs, insurance, alimony, taxes, or goods of the dead.

Those engaged in technological or engineering fields may experience opposition or difficulties in their work. Dangers may arise through the wrong kind of occult experimentation, such as contacting astral entities or communicating with the dead.

Transiting Uranus opposition natal Mars has the same significance as transiting Mars opposition natal Uranus; however, it lasts much longer and indicates a sustained period of sudden, drastic changes and emotional, physical, and nervous stress. This transit occurs once in an average life span.

Transiting Mars Opposition Natal Neptune

Secret intrigues and self-undoing through secret plots and undercover activity characterize this transit.

Suppressed anger and difficult-to-control subconscious desires tend to trouble the individual at this time. Subconscious anger may be expressed in subtle ways. Psychosomatic or hard-to-diagnose illnesses and infectious diseases are also associated with this transit. Drugs and alcohol are likely to have an adverse effect at this time. Dangers can arise through dubious occult practices, such as spirit communications, seances, and sexual magic. The individual may be subjected to ill treatment or neglect while confined to hospitals or institutions. Problems involving gas, oil, or water leakage or bacterial contamination may arise.

This is an unfavorable period for marital, business, and professional relationships. Important business affairs should not be handled during this transit, as deception and hidden influences may be at work. Fraud and deception may arise through joint finances, corporate financial affairs, taxes, insurance, inheritance, alimony, and professional activities. They are likely to be present in business dealings with hospitals, institutions, and religious organizations. The individual or those with whom he or she must deal may try to evade their financial obligations.

The individual needs to exercise a realistic and practical outlook on life at this time.

Transiting Neptune opposition natal Mars has the same significance as transiting Mars opposition natal Neptune; however, it is of longer duration and indicates a sustained period of psychological and emotional confusion in relationships. Unpleasant psychic experiences may also occur at this time. This transit occurs only once in an average life span.

Transiting Mars Opposition Natal Pluto

Aggressive, autocratic attitudes, conflicts, and power struggles characterize this transit.

It is important not to attempt to coerce others or allow oneself to be coerced by them. Dangerous occult practices, such as attempts to control others mentally, should be avoided.

Conflicts may arise over professional affairs, corporate money, insurance, taxes, inheritance, alimony, goods of the dead, and joint finances.

The individual is in danger of injury or death in cases of war, riots, revolutions, or involvement in criminal or underworld activities. Danger can also come through radioactivity, weapons, dangerous chemicals, machinery, mobs, and other sources of physical danger.

Sexual jealousy and uncontrolled sex impulses may cause problems. Regeneration is called for in sexual, personal, and business relationships.

On the positive side, this transit can be used for energetic, constructive accomplishment through cooperation with others.

Transiting Pluto opposition natal Mars has the same significance as transiting Mars opposition natal Pluto; however, it lasts much longer and indicates a sustained period of danger, stress, and conflict. This transit occurs only once in an average life span.

Transiting Mars Opposition the Natal North Node and Conjunct the Natal South Node

See "Transiting Mars Conjunct the Natal South Node and Opposition the Natal North Node."

Transiting Mars Opposition the Natal South Node and Conjunct the Natal North Node

See "Transiting Mars Conjunct the Natal North Node and Opposition the Natal South Node."

Transiting Mars Opposition the Natal Ascendant and Conjunct the Natal Descendant

See "Transiting Mars Conjunct the Natal Descendant and Opposition the Natal Ascendant."

Transiting Mars Opposition the Natal Midheaven and Conjunct the Natal Nadir

See "Transiting Mars Conjunct the Natal Nadir and Opposition the Natal Midheaven."

Transiting Mars Opposition the Natal Descendant and Conjunct the Natal Ascendant

See "Transiting Mars Conjunct the Natal Ascendant and Opposition the Natal Descendant."

Transiting Mars Opposition the Natal Nadir and Conjunct the Natal Midheaven

See "Transiting Mars Conjunct the Natal Midheaven and Opposition the Natal Nadir."

24 Transits of Jupiter

Transit Jupiter Through the Houses

Transiting Jupiter Through the Natal First House

An optimistic outlook and an increased self-confidence, which inspires confidence in others, characterize this transit.

Individuals with this transit are likely to become interested in spiritual self-improvement and a more constructive way of life. They often develop a personal interest in higher education, religion, and philosophy, and they may assume a personal role of religious, educational, or cultural leadership.

Often, there is a strong desire for travel at this time. The transit is sometimes accompanied by a tendency to put on weight.

If Jupiter makes stress aspects while transiting the natal First House, the individual can have an inflated sense of self-importance.

Transiting Jupiter Through the Natal Second House

A constructive sense of values and an optimistic outlook toward business affairs characterize this transit.

Individuals with this transit enjoy improved financial fortunes. This is a good time to ask for a raise in pay or apply for a loan. They may also become more generous with money and material resources, often in the form of contributions to educational, religious, and charitable causes. It is important, however, to avoid unnecessary extravagances, especially if Jupiter makes stress aspects while transiting this house.

The individual may benefit financially through higher education and travel and through understanding and capitalizing on sociological trends by anticipating public buying habits.

Transiting Jupiter Through the Natal Third House

A positive mental attitude, intellectual inspiration, and a philosophical approach characterize this transit. However, a tendency to think in generalities may indicate a lack of practicality in applying ideas.

The individual enjoys harmonious communication and visits with brothers, sisters, neighbors, and friends and does more traveling than usual, both long- and short-distance.

This is a favorable period for study, teaching, lecturing, writing, travel, and publishing. There is an increased interest in finding constructive uses for factual knowledge. The individual takes an interest in educational, philosophical, religious, and cultural subjects.

If Jupiter makes stress aspects while transiting the natal Third House, there can be intellectual pride and prejudiced religious, educational, and cultural views.

Transiting Jupiter Through the Natal Fourth House

The incorporation of religious, philosophical, educational, and cultural values into family affairs characterizes this transit.

Harmonious family relationships are enjoyed, and there is a mutual sharing and caring in the home at this time. The home environment may be expanded to include more members of the family circle, and the home may be used as a place of spiritual retreat and meditation. Both living conditions and family prosperity are likely to improve. This is an auspicious time for a change of residence or taking up residence in a distant place. The home is generally safe and protected while Jupiter transits the natal Fourth House.

The individual can benefit financially through real estate, food farming, building, and domestic products and services.

If Jupiter makes stress aspects while transiting the natal Fourth House, there may be a tendency to inertia, which can interfere with the effective handling of domestic responsibilities.

Transiting Jupiter Through the Natal Fifth House

Expanded social activity and fulfillment in artistic expression and romance characterize this transit.

It is a favorable time for social activities related to religious, educational, and cultural organizations. The individual may develop an interest in religious art forms or the art forms of foreign cultures. There is often an interest in travel for pleasure at this time. Creative artists, musicians, and performers are likely to receive both inspiration and cultural recognition.

This transit is favorable for happiness in romance. Women who seek pregnancy are likely to be successful at this time. The individual takes a greater interest in the well-being of children and their proper educational, moral, and religious development. This is a favorable period for teachers and those who work with young people.

If Jupiter does not make stress aspects while transiting this house, the individual can benefit through financial speculation. If Jupiter does make stress aspects, the individual can become overindulgent in the pursuit of pleasure.

Transiting Jupiter Through the Natal Sixth House

Opportunities for employment, improved working conditions, and benefit through work associations characterize this transit.

The individual is likely to be kind and considerate toward employees or fellow workers. The individual's work during this transit is likely to be related in some way to publishing, teaching, travel, educational institutions, hospitals, churches, or other cultural institutions. If Jupiter receives stress aspects while transiting this house, there is a tendency toward laziness and taking too much for granted where one's work is concerned.

A greater concern often develops for the practical implementation of one's religious, philosophic, and educational convictions—this might take the form of an interest in spiritual healing or better health care.

The individual can enjoy good health and obtain good medical care during this period. There is, however, a need to develop sensible dietary habits. Many individuals take an interest in expanding their wardrobes and improving their personal appearances.

Transiting Jupiter Through the Natal Seventh House

Kindness and consideration both toward and from others characterize this transit.

This is a favorable period for harmony in marriage and in partnerships of all kinds. The individual may have some good marriage or partnership opportunities at this time. If Jupiter receives stress aspects while transiting the natal Seventh House, however, the individual can take too much for granted in relationships.

This is a favorable period for handling public relations activities.

It is a favorable transit for artists, lecturers, teachers, ministers, psychologists, politicians, public relations men, employers, judges, and arbiters. This is a good time to handle legal affairs.

Transiting Jupiter Through the Natal Eighth House

Religious and philosophic interest in life after death or in the occult characterize this transit.

This transit can stimulate the psychic faculties, and the individual may use them in business or to help others. A philosophic interest in life after death and reincarnation may come about through an intuitive experience of a religious nature.

The individual may benefit or take an interest in matters related to joint finances, insurance, taxes, inheritance, corporate business, and goods of the dead. Activities during this transit are likely to be related in some way to law, publishing, higher education, hospitals, institutions, or cultural affairs. There may also be involvement in foreign commerce, travel for business, and business activity related to real estate. If Jupiter receives stress aspects while transiting this house, litigation or difficulties can arise over business and financial affairs.

Transiting Jupiter Through the Natal Ninth House

An interest in religion, philosophy, higher education, and travel and activities related to them characterize this transit. The individual has a greater sense of spiritual, ethical, and moral responsibility.

This is a favorable transit for association with universities and cultural institutions. It is also a good period for teaching, lecturing, travel, and dealing with foreigners.

This is a favorable transit for developing increased cultural and spiritual awareness. Individuals with this transit tend to become interested in finding a religious or philosophical system by which to guide their lives. When they have settled on a personal set of beliefs, they are likely to actively promote them. However, if Jupiter makes stress aspects while transiting this house, there is a danger of narrow-minded, fanatical, sectarian viewpoints.

Transiting Jupiter Through the Natal Tenth House

Professional advancement and expansion along with public honor and recognition characterize this transit.

This is a good period for seeking favors from those in positions of established power and authority.

The individual is ambitious to receive cultural distinction and recognition. If Jupiter makes stress aspects while transiting this house, however, the individual can abuse power and prestige for selfish reasons and suffer later disgrace and downfall.

This is a favorable transit for lawyers, politicians, educators, lecturers, and for professions dealing with foreign trade, philosophy, laws, publishing, teaching, and institutions of higher education. This is a good time for professional association with universities, churches, and cultural institutions. The individual can benefit from travel for professional and business reasons and from professional association with foreigners.

Transiting Jupiter Through the Natal Eleventh House

During this transit, the individual can benefit from friendships and from groups and organizations.

Activities involving friends, groups, and organizations are expanded—often they take place in the home. However, if Jupiter makes stress aspects to other planets while transiting this house, there can be hypocrisy and self-serving motives in friendships and group and organizational associations.

The individual expresses an open-minded interest in cultural, intellectual, and scientific ideas. Friendships are established with people who are associated with universities, churches, and other cultural institutions, and often with foreigners.

There are unusual opportunities to realize personal goals and objectives. These may include expanding one's circle of friends and becoming involved in humanitarian, occult, scientific, religious, philosophical, or educational groups and organizations.

Individuals with this transit express kindness toward their friends and receive it in return. They have an increased sense of social and cultural participation or belonging, an increased sense of universal brotherhood, and humanitarian concern for the happiness and well-being of others.

Transiting Jupiter Through the Natal Twelfth House

A new understanding of subconscious motivations and a compassionate understanding of those in need characterize this transit.

The individual's past experience can provide him or her with important insights into past and future trends. This transit confers an appreciation of the beauty and evolutionary purpose of life and enables the individual to compassionately understand people in all situations of life.

Constructive work can be done for or contributions made to worthwhile cultural institutions. This is a good time for associations with hospitals, churches, and other cultural institutions.

The individual can benefit from introspection and meditation at this time and is likely to seek a spiritual retreat and seclusion. The individual's appreciation of art, religion, music, philosophy, and natural beauty is deepened.

One is usually protected from harm during this transit, providing one's past actions and motivations have been constructive.

If Jupiter makes stress aspects while transiting this house, self-pity, misplaced sympathy, sentimentality, self-indulgence, and escapist tendencies can emerge. In extreme cases, the individual is subject to institutionalization.

Transit Jupiter Conjunctions

Transiting Jupiter Conjunct the Natal Sun

See "Transiting Sun Conjunct Natal Jupiter."

Transiting Jupiter Conjunct the Natal Moon

See "Transiting Moon Conjunct Natal Jupiter."

Transiting Jupiter Conjunct Natal Mercury

See "Transiting Mercury Conjunct Natal Jupiter."

Transiting Jupiter Conjunct Natal Venus

See "Transiting Venus Conjunct Natal Jupiter."

Transiting Jupiter Conjunct Natal Mars

See "Transiting Mars Conjunct Natal Jupiter."

Transiting Jupiter Conjunct Natal Jupiter

An optimistic, confident, moral outlook and efforts at self-improvement characterize this transit. There may be improvements in family and domestic conditions.

The individual is likely to develop an interest in understanding cultural trends and their future potential development. Often, there is an intensified interest in religion, philosophy, law, education, travel, cultural pursuits, foreign countries, and foreigners.

This is a favorable time for dealing with churches, hospitals, and institutions and for publishing, lecturing, teaching, or handling legal affairs.

Should this conjunction receive stress aspects from planets, there is danger of overextension in commitments and financial expenditures. This transit occurs once in the twelve-year cycle of Jupiter.

Transiting Jupiter Conjunct Natal Saturn

A serious-minded and industrious attitude, along with a concern for long-range goals and purposes, characterizes this transit.

There is a need to combine growth and expansion with prudence and good management. At the same time, the individual should seek to make practical affairs conform to philosophic ideals wherever possible. In other words, there is a necessity for high-level ethical performance during this period, especially in handling practical business, professional, organizational, and political affairs. Sound financial management and judgment is essential in all personal and professional dealings.

Past actions can bear fruit at this time, and critical events often arise which can influence the individual's status and reputation for a long time to come, for better or worse, depending on his or her motivation and method of handling the situation.

This is a favorable transit for systematic handling of business and professional affairs. It is often a time of new beginnings in educational, legal, business, and professional affairs. The individual may become involved in activities related to law and government in some way. There may also be involvement in serious, educational, philosophical, business, professional, and political pursuits.

The individual's activities during this transit often are concerned with administrative responsibilities, public relations, and responsibilities related to schools, churches, and organizations. The individual may travel for professional or business reasons.

Transiting Saturn conjunct natal Jupiter has the same significance as transiting Jupiter conjunct natal Saturn; however, it usually lasts longer and indicates a sustained period of important professional, business, cultural, and political activity. This transit occurs only once in twenty-nine years.

Transiting Jupiter Conjunct Natal Uranus

Increased tolerance for all points of view and ways of life characterizes this transit.

Latent intuitive or clairvoyant faculties are often stimulated at this time. Intuitive prophetic insights may be gained into future trends and developments. The individual may become interested in the occult and develop an occult approach to religion and astrology. Some individuals develop a scientific view of religious or mystical subjects during this transit. An interest in life after death, reincarnation, and out-of-the-body experiences may arise.

Sudden good fortune in financial affairs and unexpected financial gain through gifts, joint finances, inheritance, tax benefits, insurance, corporate business, or government appropriations and grants often accompany this transit.

The individual has greater freedom to travel and pursue higher studies, and unexpected opportunities for travel and higher education often arise. Unusual friendships with foreigners or people from distant places may be established during this transit.

The individual's friendships and group associations are often both culturally stimulating and intuitively enlightening during this transit, and the individual can benefit through new friendships and organizational associations.

A humanitarian desire to help those in need is frequently expressed. This transit can stimulate humanitarian or reformist tendencies in the individual, often through his or her associations with religious, educational, cultural, scientific, occult, or mystical groups or organizations.

Transiting Uranus conjunct natal Jupiter has the same significance as transiting Jupiter conjunct natal Uranus; however, it lasts longer and indicates a sustained period of personal growth and enlightenment through expanded cultural, scientific, humanitarian, and occult under-standing. This transit occurs only once in an average life span.

Transiting Jupiter Conjunct Natal Neptune

Increased intuitive spiritual awareness, manifested in expressions of joy and generosity of spirit, characterizes this transit.

The individual tends to become associated with churches, religious cults, gurus, or ashrams. Mystical tendencies are stimulated, and the individual may develop an interest in meditation and other mystical practices. This transit can inspire awe and reverence for God and the universe, and religious conversions frequently occur.

The idealism and emotional fervor of this transit may cause the individual to lack mental objectivity and practicality in the implementation of his or her ideals. However, the individual does express understanding and compassion toward those in need, even if only on an emotional level. The individual may benefit through associations with hospitals, asylums, ashrams, universities, or other religious or cultural institutions. There is a tendency to generosity and kindness toward family members.

There is a strong urge to go on long journeys, especially for the purpose of religious pilgrimages and exploring foreign cultures. Many individuals feel the desire to escape dull, humdrum daily routines.

This is a favorable time for artistic and musical inspiration and expression, especially the expression of religious or mystical ideas.

If the conjunction receives stress aspects from other planets, escapist tendencies are sometimes manifested, often in the form of excessive drinking or drug abuse.

Transiting Neptune conjunct natal Jupiter has the same significance as transiting Jupiter conjunct natal Neptune; however, it is of longer duration and indicates a sustained period of search for higher mystical truths. This transit occurs once in an average life span.

Transiting Jupiter Conjunct Natal Pluto

Constructive efforts at spiritual self-improvement characterize this transit.

This transit can bring about important and permanent changes in religious and philosophic outlook. There is a greater reliance on internal spiritual guidance. Individuals with this transit can gain spiritual insights based on direct personal experiences of higher occult reality. There is a deeper understanding of life's mysteries, and often a special interest in life after death, reincarnation, and karma. This is a favorable transit for occult and religious practices.

These individuals feel the need to put their religious and philosophic ideals into action. This is a favorable period for work designed to regenerate and reform existing cultural, educational, and religious institutions, and the individual often takes a role of personal leadership in these efforts.

Financial benefits may come through corporate business, tax rebates, insurance, grants, inheritance, or joint finances. This is a favorable time to handle business or legal affairs concerning these matters.

If the conjunction makes stress aspects to other transiting or natal planets, there is a tendency to exploit others financially or to harbor fanatical religious or cultural viewpoints.

Transiting Pluto conjunct natal Jupiter has the same significance as transiting Jupiter conjunct natal Pluto; however, it lasts much longer and indicates a sustained period of constructive, regenerative action in cultural affairs.

Transiting Jupiter Conjunct the Natal North Node and Opposition the Natal South Node

Increased social prestige and public recognition and support for one's personal beliefs and ideals characterize this transit. The individual experiences an increased awareness of prevailing cultural attitudes, beliefs, and standards and can benefit from them in some way. There may be active participation in currently popular religious, philosophic, educational, and cultural trends.

Transiting North Node conjunct natal Jupiter and transiting South Node opposition natal Jupiter has the same significance as transiting Jupiter conjunct the natal North Node and opposition the natal South Node; however, it usually lasts longer and indicates a sustained period of personal involvement in current cultural trends.

Transiting Jupiter Conjunct the Natal South Node and Opposition the Natal North Node

Belief in traditional moral standards, combined with an individualistic approach to currently popular cultural standards of ethical and social conduct, characterizes this transit.

The individual tends to be critical of currently popular attitudes and beliefs, and, as a result, may lack popular support for his or her own personal educational, religious, and cultural goals.

Transiting South Node conjunct natal Jupiter and transiting North Node opposition natal Jupiter has the same significance as transiting Jupiter conjunct the natal South Node and opposition the natal North Node; however, it is of longer duration and indicates a sustained period of individual differences with prevailing cultural trends.

Transiting Jupiter Conjunct the Natal Ascendant and Opposition the Natal Descendant

The individual is self-confident and optimistic in his or her creative self-expression during this transit.

The individual will have greater self-confidence in his or her cultural expression. There is a sense of spiritual renewal, and the individual makes efforts at religious, educational, philosophic, and cultural self-improvement. However, a self-righteous attitude should be avoided at this time.

Individuals with this transit try to put their religious and philosophic ideals into action. Often, they take on a role of personal leadership in religious, educational, philosophic, and cultural affairs.

There can be a tendency to put on excess weight during this transit.

Transiting Jupiter Conjunct the Natal Midheaven and Opposition the Natal Nadir

Progress in business and professional affairs characterizes this transit.

The individual may become more ambitious for cultural prestige and recognition. This recognition and increased status may be forthcoming as a result of the individual's cultural achievements and contributions. The individual may develop an increased awareness of ethical responsibilities in public duties. However, if the conjunction receives stress aspects from other transiting or natal planets, the individual may be tempted to misuse power and prestige for personal ends.

Opportunities may arise for professional advancement. This is a favorable transit for professions related to law, politics, religion, philosophy, higher education, teaching, publishing, lecturing, foreign trade, shipping, and commerce. The individual may receive help and recognition from those in established positions of power and authority.

Transiting Jupiter Conjunct the Natal Descendant and
Opposition the Natal Ascendant

Harmony and good will in important relationships characterize this transit.

It is a favorable time for marriage (there is a new willingness to cooperate), partnerships, public relations, and association with those connected with religious, educational, and cultural institutions. This is a good time to handle legal affairs and arbitration. Disputes can be settled amicably.

It is a good period for dealing with foreigners or those in or from distant places.

If Jupiter receives stress aspects from transiting or natal planets to this conjunction, there can be a tendency to take too much for granted in relationships.

Transiting Jupiter Conjunct the Natal Nadir and
Opposition the Natal Midheaven

Expansion in family and domestic affairs characterizes this transit.

There is increased good will and cooperation in family relationships. The individual seeks to incorporate religious, ethical, cultural, and educational activities and values into family life. It is a favorable period for spiritual retreat and meditation in the home.

There may also be an improvement in family finances. However, if Jupiter receives stress aspects to this conjunction from transiting or natal planets, there is a tendency to financial extravagance in domestic affairs.

The individual may benefit through real estate and activities related to farming, building, food, and domestic products and services.

Transit Jupiter Sextiles

Transiting Jupiter Sextile the Natal Sun

See "Transiting Sun Sextile Natal Jupiter."

Transiting Jupiter Sextile the Natal Moon

See "Transiting Moon Sextile Natal Jupiter."

Transiting Jupiter Sextile Natal Mercury

See "Transiting Mercury Sextile Natal Jupiter."

Transiting Jupiter Sextile Natal Venus

See "Transiting Venus Sextile Natal Jupiter."

Transiting Jupiter Sextile Natal Mars

See "Transiting Mars Sextile Natal Jupiter."

Transiting Jupiter Sextile Natal Jupiter

Ideas for cultural, religious, and educational expansion characterize this transit.

Opportunities arise for philosophic, educational, or cultural activities. Expanded cultural awareness can bring new opportunities for spiritual and cultural development.

It is a favorable transit for involvement with educational, cultural, religious, philosophic, and philanthropic organizations and for the pursuit of higher education. It benefits teachers, writers, publishers, and lecturers.

The individual can interact harmoniously with neighbors, brothers, sisters, and other family members during this transit. It is also favorable for travel and communication with foreigners or those in distant places.

This transit occurs twice in the twelve-year cycle of Jupiter.

Transiting Jupiter Sextile Natal Saturn

Progress toward the achievement of long-range goals characterizes this transit.

Important educational or career opportunities can arise at this time.

The individual may receive help and recognition from those in established positions of power and authority and from the institutions they represent. Steady progress can be made in achieving business and professional goals and in furthering career, educational, and cultural advancement.

There is greater awareness of the need for honesty in business and professional dealings, and this increases the individual's sense of responsibility and integrity. The individual exhibits a serious-minded philosophic attitude and exercises mature judgment in important affairs.

A good balance between optimism and caution can be achieved in business and professional dealings, in organizational associations, in partnerships, and in other important relationships and areas of responsibility.

Opportunities can arise through friendships with mature individuals. There is also greater harmony in the handling of both domestic and professional responsibilities.

This is a favorable transit for lawyers, politicians, administrators, and businessmen.

Transiting Saturn sextile natal Jupiter has the same significance as transiting Jupiter sextile natal Saturn; however, it generally lasts for a somewhat longer period of time and provides the individual an extended period in which to organize and stabilize the important responsibilities of life. This transit occurs twice in the twenty-nine-year cycle of Saturn.

Transiting Jupiter Sextile Natal Uranus

Increased intuitive awareness and a broadminded, humanitarian outlook characterize this transit.

The individual expresses an optimistic attitude toward life and an eagerness for exciting new adventures. Exciting and unusual friendships can enter into the life at this time.

The individual may benefit through association with religious, educational, cultural, scientific, or occult groups and organizations.

Many people develop an expanded awareness of scientific, educational, religious, philosophic, and spiritual concepts. This transit can awaken an interest in parapsychology, astrology, or occult and mystical pursuits. It is especially favorable for the practice and study of Astrology.

Interest in the religions and cultural traditions of foreign countries is stimulated. Unexpected opportunities may arise for travel and higher education.

Financial assistance for the realization of worthwhile objectives may come from foundations, colleges, universities, and religious and cultural institutions.

The individual may also benefit through corporate business enterprises, insurance, tax rebates, and inheritance.

Help will be given to and received from friends.

Transiting Uranus sextile natal Jupiter has the same significance as transiting Jupiter sextile natal Uranus; however, it lasts for a longer period of time and indicates a sustained opportunity for unusual cultural and spiritual advancement. This transit occurs only twice in an average life span.

Transiting Jupiter Sextile Natal Neptune

Increased spiritual awareness and faith characterize this transit. Individuals often become associated with mystical groups and cults during this period. Many individuals have expansive mystical experiences. An interest in meditation may develop. The individual can benefit from tapping the wisdom and resources of the subconscious mind at this time. Some individuals travel in connection with a spiritual search or pilgrimage.

This is a favorable time for service or association with hospitals, institutions, ashrams, or spiritual retreats.

An increased religious and humanitarian idealism will probably be expressed. Although this transit increases idealism, it does not, by itself, guarantee the ability to express these ideals in a practical way.

The individual tends to express an unusual degree of kindness and consideration toward others, especially toward family members.

The rewards of past good actions can be reaped during this transit.

Transiting Neptune sextile natal Jupiter has the same significance as transiting Jupiter sextile natal Neptune; however, it lasts for a longer period of time and indicates a sustained opportunity for mystical awakening.

Transiting Jupiter Sextile Natal Pluto

Interest in spiritual self-improvement and regeneration characterizes this transit.

The individual expresses a more positive mental outlook.

This transit stimulates latent intuitive, clairvoyant faculties. There may be a religious interest in reincarnation, life after death, and other occult phenomena. This is a favorable time for the study of metaphysics, parapsychology, the occult, and advanced scientific subjects.

Opportunities can arise for advancement and growth along educational, philosophic, and religious lines. Pursuit of higher education, religion, law, and travel are favored by this transit. There may also be an interest in the regeneration and reform of existing social, religious, educational, legal, and cultural institutions.

The individual may benefit through corporate interests and large-scale scientific and business projects.

Transiting Pluto sextile natal Jupiter has the same significance as transiting Jupiter sextile natal Pluto; however, it lasts much longer and indicates a sustained period of opportunity for spiritual growth and improvement. This transit can occur twice, although usually it occurs only once, in an average life span.

Transiting Jupiter Sextile the Natal North Node and Trine the Natal South Node

Harmony with traditional and currently popular educational, philosophic, religious and cultural beliefs characterizes this transit.

The individual can receive social approval and support for his or her personal social and cultural contributions, and there is an increased consciousness of the need to contribute to the existing social order.

Transiting North Node sextile natal Jupiter and transiting South Node trine natal Jupiter has the same significance as transiting Jupiter sextile the natal North Node and trine the natal South Node; however, it lasts longer and indicates a sustained period of harmonious cultural interaction.

Transiting Jupiter Sextile the Natal South Node and Trine the Natal North Node

This transit has basically the same significance as transiting Jupiter sextile the natal North Node and trine the natal South Node; however, there is a greater intellectual awareness of cultural traditions, combined with the ability to adjust easily to currently popular trends and attitudes.

Transiting South Node sextile natal Jupiter and transiting North Node trine natal Jupiter has the same significance as transiting Jupiter sextile the natal South Node and trine the natal North Node; however, it lasts longer and indicates a sustained period of harmonious adjustment to cultural traditions.

Transiting Jupiter Sextile the Natal Ascendant and Trine the Natal Descendant

Harmony in self-expression and in relationships characterizes this transit.

The individual seeks to incorporate religious and educational values into his or her self-expression and into the handling of important relationships. This is a favorable transit for public relations and for marriages and other partnerships.

Foreigners or those of foreign extraction may enter the life of the individual, often presenting opportunities for the individual to expand his or her personal contacts and means of self-expression.

Lawyers, politicians, teachers, lecturers, clergy, and others associated with religious, educational, or medical institutions are especially benefited at this time. This transit occurs twice in the twelve-year cycle of Jupiter.

Transiting Jupiter Sextile the Natal Midheaven and Trine the Natal Nadir

Advancement in professional and domestic affairs characterizes this transit. It is especially favorable for politicians and those in businesses and professions related to publishing, teaching, lecturing, higher education, religion, and law.

Constructive expansion can take place in business and professional affairs. It is a favorable time to seek support from people in positions of power and authority in government agencies or large business enterprises or educational institutions.

There is increased harmony and constructive activity in family and domestic affairs. The individual seeks to incorporate religious and philosophic values into his or her family and professional affairs. This transit occurs twice in the twelve-year cycle of Jupiter.

Transiting Jupiter Sextile the Natal Descendant and Trine the Natal Ascendant

This transit has basically the same significance as transiting Jupiter sextile the natal Ascendant and trine the natal Descendant; however, there is increased intellectual expression in one's relationships and ease in self-expression through cultural activities. This transit occurs twice in the twelve-year cycle of Jupiter.

Transiting Jupiter Sextile the Natal Nadir and Trine the Natal Midheaven

This transit has basically the same significance as transiting Jupiter sextile the natal Midheaven and trine the natal Nadir; however, there is increased intellectual expression in domestic activity and an easy flow in professional affairs. This transit occurs twice in the twelve-year cycle of Jupiter.

Transit Jupiter Squares

Transiting Jupiter Square the Natal Sun

See "Transiting Sun Square Natal Jupiter."

Transiting Jupiter Square the Natal Moon

See "Transiting Moon Square Natal Jupiter."

Transiting Jupiter Square Natal Mercury

See "Transiting Mercury Square Natal Jupiter."

Transiting Jupiter Square Natal Venus

See "Transiting Venus Square Natal Jupiter."

Transiting Jupiter Square Natal Mars

See "Transiting Mars Square Natal Jupiter."

Transiting Jupiter Square Natal Jupiter

Confusion and conflicts over educational, religious, and cultural beliefs and attitudes characterize this transit.

The individual tends toward inertia and possibly hypocrisy in the application of moral and religious principles.

There is a tendency to overindulge in food and drink.

Useless, nonproductive traveling can dissipate time and money. Difficulties may arise with commerce, shipping, or dealings with foreigners or foreign countries.

Deception in business practices should be avoided and the individual should guard against being deceived in financial affairs. "Get-rich-quick" schemes should be especially suspect at this time.

The individual should not neglect family or domestic responsibilities, since there is a tendency to take too much for granted under this transit.

Transiting Jupiter Square Natal Saturn

Legal, business, and professional problems characterize this transit.

The individual's timing in handling business and professional affairs tends to be poor. This is not a favorable period for initiating changes in business and professional affairs. Caution should be exercised in business expansion, so as to avoid indebtedness. There can be unemployment or a slow-down in business activity.

Conflicts may develop between professional and family responsibilities, and family and domestic problems tend to arise.

Often, the individual is faced with a moral crisis concerning ethical, religious, and cultural decisions. There is a tendency to vacillate between extremes of optimism and pessimism, and a tendency to neglect important responsibilities or compromise principles for the sake of expediency.

The individual will probably experience difficulty in receiving support from official institutions and from those in positions of established power and authority.

The individual's reputation may suffer at this time due to past mistakes and inadequacies.

Transiting Saturn square natal Jupiter has the same significance as transiting Jupiter square natal Saturn; however, it is of longer duration and indicates a sustained period of business, professional, and domestic difficulties. This transit occurs twice in the twenty-nine-year cycle of Saturn.

Transiting Jupiter Square Natal Uranus

Overoptimism, impractical idealism, impatience, and a lack of common sense, good organization, and discipline characterize this transit.

The tendency to jump to conclusions and take too much for granted should be avoided. The desire for freedom without responsibility which often accompanies this transit can bring about an unrealistic attitude toward life. Often, the individual feels a desire for travel and adventure which do not serve any useful purpose. Unexpected difficulties may arise while on long journeys or in dealings with foreigners. Individuals with this transit may have to deal with those who have eccentric, unpredictable habits, or they may display such tendencies themselves.

The individual can come into contact with disturbing religious and cultural concepts, or become associated with cults and organizations of a dubious nature. This is not a good period to indulge in strange religious and psychic practices. This is an unfavorable time for psychic and occult experimentation. The individual can make wrong judgments in astrological work during this transit.

Unexpected problems may arise through lawsuits or unstable "get-rich-quick" schemes and improperly considered financial investments. Losses can occur in corporate business enterprises—through heavy taxes, business failures, and unwise financial partnerships.

Transiting Uranus square natal Jupiter has the same significance as transiting Jupiter square natal Uranus; however, it lasts longer and indicates a sustained period of impractical and unrealistic attitudes. This transit occurs only twice in the average life span.

Transiting Jupiter Square Natal Neptune

Daydreaming, woolgathering, impractical emotional idealism, unrealistic expectations, and misplaced sympathy characterize this transit. These are often a means of psychological escape, as are drinking, drugs, travel, and meaningless, impractical educational pursuits.

The individual is subject to misguided religious and mystical devotion. Often, this takes the form of adherence to mystical cults and guru worship of dubious value. The individual may be drawn to these as a means of achieving status and importance or as a means of avoiding the practical responsibilities of life. Generally, there is impracticality in the application of religious and spiritual beliefs.

The individual may bring about his or her self-undoing through unwise expansion and dubious "get-rich-quick" schemes.

Transiting Neptune square natal Jupiter has the same significance as transiting Jupiter square natal Neptune; however, it lasts much longer and indicates a sustained period of emotional escapism and self-deception. This transit occurs only twice in the average life span.

Transiting Jupiter Square Natal Pluto

Coercive tactics in the promotion of one's religious, cultural, educational, and philosophic beliefs characterize this transit. The individual may either perpetrate or be subject to religious, moral, or educational power plays. The desire to reform others can be accompanied by neglect of personal self-improvement.

There is also the possibility that the individual will undergo radical changes in his or her religious and philosophic attitudes.

Temptation can arise to use dishonest means to achieve power and status. There is a need for strict honesty and integrity in all business dealings.

Conflict and litigation may arise over joint finances, corporate funds, insurance, taxes, inheritance, alimony, and goods of the dead.

The individual tends to take on undertakings without laying the proper groundwork. He may display pride and arrogance and neglect small, but important, details.

Dubious occult practices or confused attitudes regarding sexual morality present a danger to the individual during this transit.

Transiting Pluto square natal Jupiter has the same significance as transiting Jupiter square natal Pluto; however, it lasts for a much longer period of time and indicates a sustained interval of struggle with corruption and existing power structures. This transit occurs only once in an average life span.

Transiting Jupiter Square the Natal North Node and Square the Natal South Node

During this transit, either the individual's personal religious, cultural, moral, and educational viewpoints are out of harmony with prevailing cultural standards or the individual adheres blindly to prevailing social and cultural norms.

Transiting North and South Nodes square natal Jupiter has the same significance as transiting Jupiter square the natal North Node and square the natal South Node; however, it lasts longer and indicates a sustained period of maladjustment to prevailing cultural and social expectations.

Transiting Jupiter Square the Natal South Node and Square the Natal North Node

See "Transiting Jupiter Square the Natal North Node and Square the Natal South Node."

Transiting Jupiter Square the Natal Ascendant and Square the Natal Descendant

Indifference to responsibility, lack of realism, unreliability, and a tendency to take too much for granted in relationships characterize this transit.

The individual can make promises that are impossible to fulfill. Religious, philosophical, educational, and cultural differences tend to make themselves felt in relationships. There is often a lack of cultural grace and refinement in the individual's personal expression during this period.

Transiting Jupiter Square the Natal Midheaven and Square the Natal Nadir

There is a tendency to overexpansion in professional and domestic affairs.

The individual may be subjected to professional, religious, or cultural discrimination during this transit. Religious, cultural, educational, or moral controversies tend to arise in professional or family dealings.

There is a tendency to take too much for granted.

The individual should be especially careful to avoid unnecessary expenditures and debts during this transit.

Transiting Jupiter Square the Natal Descendant and Square the Natal Ascendant

See "Transiting Jupiter Square the Natal Ascendant and Square the Natal Descendant."

Transiting Jupiter Square the Natal Nadir and Square the Natal Midheaven

See "Transiting Jupiter Square the Natal Midheaven and Square the Natal Nadir."

Transit Jupiter Trines

Transiting Jupiter Trine the Natal Sun

See "Transiting Sun Trine Natal Jupiter."

Transiting Jupiter Trine the Natal Moon

See "Transiting Moon Trine Natal Jupiter."

Transiting Jupiter Trine Natal Mercury

See "Transiting Mercury Trine Natal Jupiter."

Transiting Jupiter Trine Natal Venus

See "Transiting Venus Trine Natal Jupiter."

Transiting Jupiter Trine Natal Mars

See "Transiting Mars Trine Natal Jupiter."

Transiting Jupiter Trine Natal Jupiter

The individual can benefit through higher education, religion, philosophy, travel, or religious, educational, and cultural institutions during this transit.

The individual may temporarily expound upon or teach cultural, ethical, and religious values. The individual can benefit through the law or through cultural institutions. This transit can bring an improvement in family and domestic affairs.

Pleasure can be gained from education, travel, religion, philosophy, or a religious pilgrimage, and the individual can benefit through contact with foreigners or foreign countries.

Increased financial resources make this a favorable time for business and commerce.

Transiting Jupiter Trine Natal Saturn

Progress in business and professional affairs characterizes this transit.

It is especially favorable for professions related to law, politics, administration, business, education, religion, and travel. This is a good time to seek employment or initiate important business and professional activities, and to consolidate and stabilize one's professional and financial position. This is also a favorable time for handling legal affairs and dealing with the government.

The individual is likely to attempt to apply his or her philosophic, religious, and ethical standards in a practical way.

There can be involvement in constructive activity associated with religious, charitable, scientific, and professional groups and organizations.

The individual can receive effective cooperation from those in positions of power and authority during this period.

Individuals with this transit take a serious-minded, responsible attitude toward achieving their long-range goals and objectives. There can be a good balance between optimism and caution and concern with honesty and integrity.

The individual will display a more responsible attitude toward his or her family and domestic affairs.

Transiting Saturn trine natal Jupiter has the same significance as transiting Jupiter trine natal Saturn; however, it usually lasts longer and indicates a sustained period of growth and stability in professional, business, and domestic affairs. This is a favorable period for seeking education for purposes of professional advancement. This transit occurs twice in the twenty-nine-year cycle of Saturn.

Transiting Jupiter Trine Natal Uranus

Unexpected benefits from grants, insurance, joint finances, corporate money, government funding, and inheritance, along with unusual opportunities for expansion of one's affairs, characterize this transit.

Unexpected opportunities can arise for travel or higher education. New discoveries concerning ancient history or artifacts may intrigue the individual. The individual will express generosity and broadmindedness toward people in all walks of life.

The individual can establish interesting new friendships through his or her travels or through associating with educational, religious, cultural, scientific, or occult organizations. These new friendships and group and organizational associations can have a spiritually uplifting effect on the individual.

This transit often brings out latent intuitive, clairvoyant faculties, and it may result in some startling spiritual revelations and insights. It is an excellent transit for the study and practice of astrology. The individual may gain prophetic insight into future cultural trends and developments and come to an occult or scientific understanding of spiritual laws. Spiritual or occult practices, such as meditation, astrology, or study of parapsychology or new metaphysical concepts can be of benefit to the individual during this transit.

The individual is openminded and receptive to new ideas. This transit can bring a long-awaited opportunity to express unique individual genius or talent. There is a good possibility of a breakthrough that enables the individual to achieve something worthwhile. This is a good period for business related to advanced technology and electronics and for initiating new corporate enterprises or joint financial ventures.

Transiting Uranus trine natal Jupiter has the same significance as transiting Jupiter trine Natal Uranus; however, it lasts for a much longer period of time and indicates a sustained opportunity for spiritual growth and advancement. This transit occurs only twice in the average life span.

Transiting Jupiter Trine Natal Neptune

Religious, spiritual, and intuitive inspiration characterize this transit.

Feelings of mystical contact with the Infinite can occur. It is a favorable transit for meditation and inner, spiritual search, particularly when these take place in the home. The individual may benefit from a spiritual teacher, a religious pilgrimage, or some other long journey. The individual is able to tap the subconscious mind during this transit for valuable knowledge and inspiration.

Greater understanding, generosity, and empathy toward others are exhibited. This is a favorable time for dealings with hospitals, universities, religious retreats, and educational and cultural institutions.

There is an interest in cultural and educational improvement. The creative imagination of people engaged in artistic pursuits is often stimulated, and the individual experiences an increased sensitivity to beauty.

During this transit, the individual frequently reaps the rewards of past good actions.

Transiting Neptune trine natal Jupiter has the same significance as transiting Jupiter trine natal Neptune; however, it lasts for a longer period of time and indicates a sustained interval of intuitive inspiration. This transit occurs only once or twice in the average life span.

Transiting Jupiter Trine Natal Pluto

Interest in spiritual regeneration and self-improvement characterizes this transit.

Benefit may come to the individual through religion, higher education, and occult or esoteric doctrines and studies. Constructive guidance can come from spiritual teachers.

This transit often brings an increased understanding of spiritual laws, and direct intuitive experiences of spiritual realities. Some individuals develop an interest in life after death, karma, and reincarnation. This is a favorable period for constructive metaphysical or occult practices, such as meditation, astrology, or spiritual philosophy.

There is often an interest in social, religious, educational, and cultural reforms. The individual may develop an interest in helping others to help themselves.

This is a favorable time for the elimination of outmoded concepts, beliefs, and attitudes. There will be increased will power to put philosophic and religious ideals into practice. This can be a time of inspiration for educators, artists, and those involved in innovative business enterprises. The individual can express resourcefulness and receive intuitive guidance in business affairs.

Travel related to corporate business, education, and scientific and spiritual quests often occurs at this time.

Important benefits may come through joint finances, corporate business, inheritance, tax rebates, goods of the dead, grants, or government and business funding.

It is also good for home improvements and regeneration of family situations.

Transiting Pluto trine natal Jupiter has the same significance as transiting Jupiter trine natal Pluto; however, it is of longer duration and indicates a sustained period of increased will power directed toward constructive self-improvement. This transit occurs once in an average life span.

Transiting Jupiter Trine the Natal North Node and Sextile the Natal South Node

See "Transiting Jupiter Sextile the Natal South Node and Trine the Natal North Node."

Transiting Jupiter Trine the Natal South Node and Sextile the Natal North Node

See "Transiting Jupiter Sextile the Natal North Node and Trine the Natal South Node."

Transiting Jupiter Trine the Natal Ascendant and Sextile the Natal Descendant

See "Transiting Jupiter Sextile the Natal Descendant and Trine the Natal Ascendant."

Transiting Jupiter Trine the Natal Midheaven and Sextile the Natal Nadir

See "Transiting Jupiter Sextile the Natal Nadir and Trine the Natal Midheaven."

Transiting Jupiter Trine the Natal Descendant and
Sextile the Natal Ascendant

See "Transiting Jupiter Sextile the Natal Ascendant and Trine the Natal Descendant."

Transiting Jupiter Trine the Natal Nadir and
Sextile the Natal Midheaven

See "Transiting Jupiter Sextile the Natal Midheaven and Trine the Natal Nadir."

Transit Jupiter Oppositions

Transiting Jupiter Opposition the Natal Sun

See "Transiting Sun Opposition Natal Jupiter."

Transiting Jupiter Opposition the Natal Moon

See "Transiting Moon Opposition Natal Jupiter."

Transiting Jupiter Opposition Natal Mercury

See "Transiting Mercury Opposition Natal Jupiter."

Transiting Jupiter Opposition Natal Venus

See "Transiting Venus Opposition Natal Jupiter."

Transiting Jupiter Opposition Natal Mars

See "Transiting Mars Opposition Natal Jupiter."

Transiting Jupiter Opposition Natal Jupiter

False optimism, gullibility, deception, and insincerity characterize this transit. The individual is susceptible to overexpansion and extravagance. There is a tendency to take too much for granted in relationships, and the individual sometimes resorts to insincerity and hypocrisy to avoid unpleasantness in important relationships. Disagreements tend to arise over philosophical, religious, educational, moral, and cultural attitudes and beliefs.

Difficulties often arise in affairs related to education, law, publishing, or cultural activities.

Traveling may prove more expensive than anticipated, and difficulties often arise in connection with shipping, commerce, or dealing with those in distant places.

Transiting Jupiter Opposition Natal Saturn

Poor timing in business, professional, and domestic affairs characterizes this transit.

The individual may use questionable tactics to advance his or her business and professional interests. There can be stiff business or professional competition, and lack of support from official institutions or those in positions of power and authority.

The individual may encounter legal difficulties, red tape, or lawsuits during this period. In extreme cases, bankruptcy or a severe financial crisis can occur.

This is a poor time to expand affairs related to education, law, publishing, travel, long-distance commerce, or cultural activities.

Conflict can arise between professional and family responsibilities, and ulterior motives concerning money and status may adversely affect friendships, partnerships, or professional and organizational relationships. Hypocrisy or confusion regarding ethical and moral issues can also cause a breakdown of relationships.

There may be a lack of balance between conservative and optimistic attitudes. Obstacles can be created by conservative or uncompromising attitudes on the part of the individual or those with whom he or she must deal.

Transiting Saturn opposition natal Jupiter has the same significance as transiting Jupiter opposition natal Saturn; however, it usually lasts longer and indicates a sustained period of moral conflict and professional and business adjustments. This transit occurs once in the twenty-nine-year cycle of Saturn.

Transiting Jupiter Opposition Natal Uranus

Impractical idealism and relationships with unreliable and eccentric people characterize this transit.

The individual is likely to lack balance and practicality. This can take the form of foolish extravagance, empty promises, restlessness, or the inability to maintain a sustained and disciplined effort. There is a tendency to attempt unrealistic projects and tasks.

Often, individuals make promises and commitments to friends, groups, and organizations which they will find difficult to fulfill.

Some individuals find that they are unable to apply themselves steadily and consistently to a spiritual path. They go from one spiritual teacher or organization to another, not staying long enough with any one to achieve worthwhile gains. Sometimes, they participate in cults and religious activities of dubious value.

Difficulties may arise in dealings with hospitals and universities, churches and cultural institutions.

Conflicts may arise over insurance, taxes, alimony, corporate money, joint finances, inheritance, lawsuits, and unstable business ventures. Financial affairs are likely to be unpredictable and unstable during this period. "Get-rich-quick" schemes should be especially avoided during this transit, as unsuspected and unforeseen factors are likely to upset plans and normal procedures. The individuals are apt to set themselves up for major losses through unwise expansion, especially if it involves borrowing money.

Unnecessary travel can dissipate the individual's time and money. Unforeseen difficulties can occur while traveling. One's friends during this transit are likely to be well-meaning, but unreliable and eccentric.

Transiting Uranus opposition natal Jupiter has the same significance as transiting Jupiter opposition natal Uranus; however, it lasts longer and indicates a sustained period of unrealistic social, cultural, and financial expectations. This transit occurs once in the average life span.

Transiting Jupiter Opposition Natal Neptune

Impractical religious idealism and possible involvement in mystical cults characterize this transit.

The individual is likely to lack practicality in the application of religious and spiritual ideals.

In some cases, there is an inflated sense of one's cultural and spiritual importance. This can take the form of false humility or vicarious status achieved through following some spiritual teacher or involvement in a religious sect.

Some individuals express maudlin sentimentality and misplaced sympathy. They tend to succumb to "sob" stories and unworthy appeals for help. Confidence artists and promoters of "get-rich-quick" schemes should be avoided at this time, as they could be the factors that cause the individual's self-undoing.

Practical discipline is needed during this transit to maintain a grip on reality. Subconscious distortions and neurotic escapist tendencies may surface at this time. These can take the form of drinking, drug abuse, daydreaming, woolgathering, delusions of grandeur, and emotional dependency on the family. Bizarre dreams, visions, and psychic experiences often occur under this transit. Uncontrolled imagination can lead the individual astray.

Transiting Neptune opposition natal Jupiter has the same significance as transiting Jupiter opposition natal Neptune; however, it is of longer duration and indicates a period during which the individual is susceptible to self-deception. This transit occurs only once in the average life span.

Transiting Jupiter Opposition Natal Pluto

Autocratic promotion of educational, religious, philosophic, and cultural beliefs characterizes this transit. The individual may be either the perpetrator or the victim. Unwise or dangerous occult experimentation, such as attempts to dominate or control others, can have undesirable consequences at this time.

The individual should avoid attempts to reform others while neglecting his or her own personal development. Coercion in the name of religion can cause breakdowns in relationships during this period. Separations and breakdowns in family relations often occur.

There is a tendency to overreach oneself and attempt grandiose, unrealistic projects.

The individual should guard against fraud and deception in financial dealings. Conflicts or difficulties may arise over corporate money, joint finances, taxes, insurance, inheritance, or alimony. Lawsuits or other legal difficulties are a danger.

This is not a favorable time for dealing with hospitals, universities, or other cultural institutions.

Transiting Pluto opposition natal Jupiter has the same significance as transiting Jupiter opposition natal Pluto; however, it lasts much longer and indicates a sustained period during which the individual may be involved in cultural and business power struggles. This transit occurs only once in a lifetime.

Transiting Jupiter Opposition the Natal North Node and Conjunct the Natal South Node

See "Transiting Jupiter Conjunct the Natal South Node and Opposition the Natal North Node."

Transiting Jupiter Opposition the Natal South Node and Conjunct the Natal North Node

See "Transiting Jupiter Conjunct the Natal North Node and Opposition the Natal South Node."

Transiting Jupiter Opposition the Natal Ascendant and Conjunct the Natal Descendant

See "Transiting Jupiter Conjunct the Natal Descendant and Opposition the Natal Ascendant."

Transiting Jupiter Opposition the Natal Midheaven and Conjunct the Natal Nadir

See "Transiting Jupiter Conjunct the Natal Nadir and Opposition the Natal Midheaven."

Transiting Jupiter Opposition the Natal Descendant and Conjunct the Natal Ascendant

See "Transiting Jupiter Conjunct the Natal Ascendant and Opposition the Natal Descendant."

Transiting Jupiter Opposition the Natal Nadir and Conjunct the Natal Midheaven

See "Transiting Jupiter Conjunct the Natal Midheaven and Opposition the Natal Nadir."

25 Transits of Saturn

Transit Saturn Through the Houses

Transiting Saturn Through the Natal First House

Increased sense of personal responsibility and increased self-reliance characterize this transit. The individual tends to exercise a greater degree of constructive self-discipline and to be more reserved and conservative in personal manner and attitude.

This is the beginning of an obscure period for individuals with this transit. Having ended old cycles, they find new directions in their life-work. The individual may experience difficulty in gaining the cooperation of others, in some cases, because of a self-centered attitude.

There is likely to be greater personal responsibility and a heavier work load, accompanied by a tendency to fatigue and the need for regular periods of rest, and, in some cases, slowed digestion and loss of appetite.

If Saturn makes stress aspects while transiting the natal First House, the individual can lack self-confidence and be subject to ill health.

Transiting Saturn Through the Natal Second House

Increased financial and business responsibilities characterize this transit. The individual becomes more frugal and resourceful in business and financial affairs and may develop greater organizational skill, increased efficiency, and insights into the workings of business. A more practical sense of values often develops.

There is a greater need for economy and prudence in one's financial affairs, and greater motivation to set these affairs in order. The individual can acquire wealth through hard work and good organization.

Delays may occur in business affairs and in legal matters affecting finances, often as a result of problems with business partners or government agencies. The individual is subject to worry and anxiety concerning money and material possessions during this transit.

If Saturn makes stress aspects to other natal or transiting planets while transiting the natal Second House, the individual may experience financial loss and limitation.

Transiting Saturn Through the Natal Third House

Serious study, and an interest in the sciences, mathematics, philosophy, economics, and other serious mental disciplines, characterize this transit.

This is a good time to pursue formal programs of education. Many individuals experience an improved mental focus and ability to concentrate. In general, one is capable of a systematic, methodical, sustained application to studies and intellectual disciplines.

The individual's work during this transit is likely to relate to writing, teaching, communications, or scientific research. There tends to be a great deal of writing and communication related to professional affairs.

The individual is likely to be more cautious, reserved, systematic, and conservative in his or her speech and communications.

Caution is needed in signing contracts and formulating agreements: agreements made at this time are likely to be binding for some time into the future.

The individual will feel more responsibility for his or her brothers and sisters, neighbors and friends.

If Saturn makes stress aspects to other planets while transiting the natal Third House, the individual may be prone to negative thinking, worry, and pessimism. There may be transportation difficulties and delays in communications and shipments. Responsibilities and difficulties are likely to arise in connection with one's brothers, sisters, or neighbors.

Transiting Saturn Through the Natal Fourth House

Increased domestic and family responsibility and work characterize this transit. It often corresponds to a period of loneliness and obscurity.

The individual feels an increased need for family and domestic security, and this transit can bring about increased stability in family and domestic affairs. However, the individual may have the burden of caring for an elderly or disabled family member.

This can be a good time for home-improvement projects. Activities related to the individual's business and professional affairs or partnerships are likely to take place in the home. In some cases, domestic and professional responsibilities are in conflict.

The individual may become involved in businesses related to real estate, farming, mining, ecological concerns, and food or domestic products and services.

If Saturn makes stress aspects while transiting the natal Fourth House, the individual may be subject to emotional depression, despondency, or oppressive family responsibilities.

Transiting Saturn Through the Natal Fifth House

Lack of romantic opportunities and stabilization of current romantic relationships characterize this transit. Romantic involvements or children can bring on increased responsibilities. The individual may become involved with the education, guidance, or disciplining of children in some way. In some cases, there is romantic involvement with an older, mature or well-established individual. Old romantic ties may be reactivated.

This can be a period of constructive work, discipline, and giving form to creative ideas for artists, musicians, and performers. There may be business or professional involvement with theater, entertainment industries, the stock market, education, or teaching.

If Saturn makes stress aspects while transiting the natal Fifth House, the individual is subject to loss through financial speculations. There can also be unwanted pregnancies or increased responsibility involving children.

Transiting Saturn Through the Natal Sixth House

Increased work responsibility characterizes this transit. The individual exhibits greater patience, skill, efficiency, and organization in his or her work. This is a good transit for those whose work requires great skill and efficiency. There is often involvement in work related in some way to medicine.

The individual tends to express better judgment and increased discipline in health regimes and dietary habits during this transit. Many individuals become more conservative in their personal appearance and dress.

If Saturn makes stress aspects while transiting the natal Sixth House, the individual may suffer from occupational hazards, unpleasant working conditions, and fatigue or ill health due to overwork. Chronic ill health, restricted digestion, or bone, skin, knee, or kidney disorders and slow recovery from illness can also occur if Saturn is afflicted. The individual may be unemployed, or forced to do uncongenial or unpleasant work.

Transiting Saturn Through the Natal Seventh House

Increased responsibility toward others characterizes this transit. The individual tends to be more aware of the need to consider the rights and well-being of others. There is an intensified sense of justice.

This can be a good period for professional partnerships and professional or organizational public relations, if Saturn does not make stress aspects.

The individual may assume increased responsibility through marriage or other partnerships, and marriage and other important relationships can be stabilized. The individual may marry or enter into partnership with an older, mature, or well-established individual. Such relationships are often karmic in nature.

Saturn transiting the natal Seventh House can also mean a lack of marriage or relationship opportunities.

If Saturn makes stress aspects while transiting the natal Seventh House, the individual may experience lawsuits and legal difficulties or suffer from unpopularity and unfavorable public relations.

Transiting Saturn Through the Natal Eighth House

Increased responsibility regarding joint finances, business, corporate financial affairs, insurance, or goods of the dead characterizes this transit. The individual may become professionally involved in such fields as corporate finance, cooperative business ventures, insurance, tax accounting, or mortuaries. The individual may be given the responsibility of handling the affairs of those who have died. A serious interest in profound scientific or occult subjects often develops.

If Saturn makes stress aspects while transiting the natal Eighth House, the individual may develop a fear of death, be subjected to heavy taxes, or lose important people in his or her life through death. Problems or financial losses can also occur through joint finances and business involvements.

Transiting Saturn Through the Natal Ninth House

A serious interest in history, higher education, religion, law, philosophy, or other cultural affairs characterizes this transit. The individual is likely to seek out higher education as a means to professional advancement. This can result in a practical approach to education—the individual is primarily interested in learning things which can be of practical use. This transit can mean a heavy, difficult academic work load.

The individual is likely to become involved in professional activities related to travel, law, religion, higher education, publishing, and religious, educational, or cultural institutions. This transit is also likely to bring about travel or contact with foreigners for business or professional reasons.

If Saturn makes stress aspects while transiting the natal Ninth House, the individual may develop narrowminded or fanatical religious, educational, or cultural attitudes. There may be difficulties while traveling and difficulties or delays in getting writings published. If Saturn is afflicted, this can also be a difficult time to gain admittance to a university or institution of higher education.

Transiting Saturn Through the Natal Tenth House

Increased professional responsibility and ambition for career position and status characterize this transit. The individual may receive promotion or public recognition for professional achievements and be given increased responsibility in relationships with superiors, government agencies, or established business institutions. The individual can achieve a peak of professional achievement during this transit if Saturn makes favorable aspects.

In any event, this transit usually corresponds to a period of increased worldly responsibility. The individual can become actively involved in political affairs in some way, or assume a position of administrative responsibility and leadership. As a means of furthering his or her ambitions, the individual is likely to become associated with older, established individuals or with those in positions of power and authority. A conservative professional or political attitude may also be adopted as a means of achieving professional or political security and status.

If Saturn makes stress aspects while transiting the natal Tenth House, the individual can suffer public disgrace and fall from power or undergo social disgrace or unemployment. Difficulties can arise with government agencies, authority figures, employers, or parents if Saturn is afflicted. An afflicted transiting Saturn in the natal Tenth House can also mean an oppressive work load.

Transiting Saturn Through the Natal Eleventh House

Involvement in serious or professional friendships, groups, and organizations characterizes this transit. This is a favorable time for pursuit of serious intellectual and scientific interests. The individual is concerned with understanding and applying universal laws and principles of life and often becomes involved with organized efforts to achieve serious long-range scientific, humanitarian, occult, or professional goals and objectives. The individual may assume a role of leadership or administrative responsibility in a group or organization.

There is a greater sense of loyalty toward friends and toward group and organizational affiliations. This is a favorable time for friendships with older, mature, or established individuals, or for renewing old friendships.

However, ulterior motives of money and status may enter into one's friendships and group or organizational associations if Saturn makes stress aspects while transiting the natal Eleventh House.

Transiting Saturn Through the Natal Twelfth House

Professional responsibilities involving hospitals, asylums, and institutions characterize this transit. The individual can become professionally involved with psychology, secret government work, secret organizations, or other work that goes on in secret or behind the scenes.

A serious interest in meditation, the study of mysticism, and parapsychology often develops. The individual may become involved with ashrams and spiritual retreats in some way. Some individuals under the influence of this transit become involved with psychological therapy or some form of systematic probing of the unconscious mind.

This is a time of culmination of karma in preparation for a new cycle of self-expression.

If Saturn makes stress aspects while transiting the natal Twelfth House, one can become one's own worst enemy through neurotic fears, subconscious hangups, reclusiveness, moodiness, emotional depression, or attempts to use devious, underhanded means to achieve one's ambitions. In some cases, the individual is vulnerable to danger from secret enemies, but this is usually more imagined than real. If Saturn is afflicted, in extreme cases the individual can be institutionalized, incarcerated, or imprisoned.

Transit Saturn Conjunctions

Transiting Saturn Conjunct the Natal Sun

See "Transiting Sun Conjunct Natal Saturn."

Transiting Saturn Conjunct the Natal Moon

See "Transiting Moon Conjunct Natal Saturn."

Transiting Saturn Conjunct Natal Mercury

See "Transiting Mercury Conjunct Natal Saturn."

Transiting Saturn Conjunct Natal Venus

See "Transiting Venus Conjunct Natal Saturn."

Transiting Saturn Conjunct Natal Mars

See "Transiting Mars Conjunct Natal Saturn."

Transiting Saturn Conjunct Natal Jupiter

See "Transiting Jupiter Conjunct Natal Saturn."

Transiting Saturn Conjunct Natal Saturn

The ending of crystallized professional conditions and the beginning of new ones characterizes this transit. Serious responsibilities arise which require caution and maturity.

The individual feels a greater need for material security and a meaningful place in his or her world. There is a desire to work toward long-range goals and objectives, usually associated with some kind of career ambition. The increased ambition and staying power associated with this transit make the initiation of long-range projects possible. The need to settle into a definite, established life routine upon which one can build one's future security results in a more conservative outlook on life, especially in regard to business and professional affairs and politics. This transit can bring an involvement with serious mathematical, scientific, business, or political activities.

The results of past actions come up for evaluation and correction at this time. Whether these consequences advance or hinder the individual depends upon the merits of these past actions. If the individual deals with these affairs in a responsible and realistic manner, he or she will be free to make a new start in the important affairs of life.

When this transit occurs in individuals between the ages of twenty-seven and twenty-nine, it indicates the individual's full-fledged assumption of adult responsibilities. When it occurs in individuals between the ages of fifty-seven and fifty-nine, it marks the high point of the individual's career.

This conjunction of Saturn to its own place occurs approximately every twenty-nine years.

Transiting Saturn Conjunct Natal Uranus

Increased responsibility toward friends, groups, and organizations characterizes this transit. The individual often becomes involved with professional groups and organizations and develops an interest in incorporating new methods and modern technologies into professional affairs.

Professional activities during this transit often are related in some way to engineering, manufacturing, or research and development, especially in electronic industries. The individual may become concerned with organizational management of business and professional activities related to these fields.

There is often an increased motivation to realize one's personal goals and objectives. The individual experiences either personal success or a reversal of fortune, in accordance with past actions and motivations. These consequences often come about through sudden and unexpected karmic circumstances.

This is a favorable time for serious scientific or mathematical work and for the practical application of original ideas and intuitive inspirations.

Transiting Uranus conjunct natal Saturn has the same significance as transiting Saturn conjunct natal Uranus; however, it usually lasts longer and indicates a sustained period of purposeful group activity and a radical change in professional affairs. This transit occurs once in eighty-four years.

Transiting Saturn Conjunct Natal Neptune

Steady concentration and a psychological focus characterize this transit. Business activities related to art, music, entertainment, photography, chemicals, drugs, hospitals, asylums, universities, and cultural institutions are often associated with this transit. Some individuals develop an interest in cultural history and in the religious, artistic, and cultural traditions of foreign countries.

This is a favorable period for meditation and serious disciplines. There is often an increased capacity for practical visualization of how to achieve one's important purposes and goals.

Emotional depression can arise as a result of the stimulation of painful or unpleasant subconscious memories of past experiences. The individual should face these honestly and understand them for what they are—otherwise, they can be the cause of irrational or inappropriate behavior. Irrational fears and anxieties can bring about the individual's undoing. Institutionalization is a possibility if this conjunction is afflicted. Brooding and self-pity should be avoided at all costs: they will prevent the individual from finding honest solutions to his or her challenges and psychological problems. Dangerous psychic practices, such as seances, are especially to be avoided during this transit.

Uncertainties can arise in business, in partnerships, and in family affairs. Afflictions to this conjunction can indicate deception in business, legal, and professional affairs, as well as the possibility of public disgrace and scandal.

Some individuals become involved with professional or governmental secrecy or business or political intrigues. Although secret enemies can stand in the way of the individual's success, should this conjunction be afflicted, they are usually more imagined than real, and the individual may end up as his or her own worst enemy.

Transiting Neptune conjunct natal Saturn has the same significance as transiting Saturn conjunct natal Neptune; however, it is of longer duration and indicates a sustained period of secret professional activity and the need to take a conscious look at the subconscious mind. This transit occurs once in an average life span.

Transiting Saturn Conjunct Natal Pluto

Professional responsibilities of far-reaching consequence characterize this transit.

It can intensify the individual's will power and focus. At the same time, however, the individual usually undergoes severe discipline in some way.

This transit can bring about the end of old experiences, especially in one's professional, business, and political affairs, and the beginnings of new ones. The personal reputation of the individual during this transit is dependent upon his or her past performance and motivations.

This is a favorable period for self-improvement projects, the improvement of business and professional affairs, and the improvement of work efficiency and professional methodologies. It is a good time for spiritual self-development and meditation. This is a favorable time for scientific, mathematical, or occult study and research. Latent clairvoyant faculties are often stimulated, and there may be serious activities involving advanced scientific studies and the occult.

Some individuals become involved with governmental, political, or professional secrecy, and some with political and corporate intrigues and power struggles.

The individual may be hindered or helped by vested interests and corporate monopolies in some manner. There are likely to be professional or business involvements with taxes, insurance, inheritance, corporate finances, or goods of the dead. Business, professional, and ecological issues tend to be in the forefront during this transit. Binding commitments and business responsibilities can weigh heavily on the individual.

The individual may experience paranoia and feelings of danger if the conjunction is afflicted. In extreme cases, life-and-death issues may have to be dealt with. The death of someone of consequence to the individual may occur during this period.

Transiting Pluto conjunct natal Saturn has the same significance as transiting Saturn conjunct natal Pluto; however, it is usually of longer duration and indicates a period of sustained involvement in serious scientific, business, professional, and political matters. This transit occurs once in an average life span.

Transiting Saturn Conjunct the Natal North Node and
Opposition the Natal South Node

Conservative attitudes toward currently popular beliefs and trends characterize this transit. The individual may feel a need for social conformity as a means of protecting personal security. However, professional activities may involve the individual with these popular trends in some way.

Transiting North Node conjunct natal Saturn and transiting South Node opposition natal Saturn has the same significance as transiting Saturn conjunct the natal North Node and opposition the natal South Node; however, it is usually of slightly longer duration and indicates a period of sustained involvement in popular trends and customs on a professional, and usually conservative, level.

Transiting Saturn Conjunct the Natal South Node and
Opposition the Natal North Node

Critical attitudes toward popular beliefs and attitudes characterize this transit. The individual may appear anti-social or reclusive. Professional responsibilities are likely to limit one's social and cultural activities during this period.

There is a tendency to overidentify with one's personal viewpoints and with conservative attitudes.

Transiting South Node conjunct natal Saturn and transiting North Node opposition natal Saturn has the same significance as transiting Saturn conjunct the natal South Node and opposition the natal North Node; however, it is usually of slightly longer duration and indicates a period of sustained involvement in either the critical review of popular social customs and trends or temporary withdrawal from direct interaction on this level. Such lack of interplay may be due to professional responsibilities that must be handled.

Transiting Saturn Conjunct the Natal Ascendant and
Opposition the Natal Descendant

Increased responsibility and a need for personal security characterize this transit. It marks the start of an obscure period of life, during which one must learn new skills and work with the resources one has accumulated up to this period.

This is a favorable period for efforts at self-discipline and at organizing one's future goals and objectives. This is the time to lay the groundwork for future success. The long-range projects begun at this time will reach their peak twenty-one years later.

There is increased personal responsibility toward partners and others with whom the individual deals in a public-relations capacity. The individual adopts a more cautious, conservative manner and appearance.

In some cases, the digestion is slowed down. If Saturn makes stress aspects to this conjunction, the individual can lack energy and self-confidence.

Transiting Saturn Conjunct the Natal Midheaven and Opposition the Natal Nadir

The culmination of one's career and professional ambitions characterizes this transit. The individual can enjoy fame and recognition for past good works. However, if this conjunction receives stress aspects from natal or transiting planets, disclosure of past misdeeds may lead to reversals of fortune and falls from high position.

In any event, the individual experiences a new start in his or her career and profession, which reaches its conclusion approximately seven years later when transiting Saturn conjuncts the natal Ascendant.

Increased professional responsibilities also characterize this transit. Conservative political and professional attitudes are often adopted. The individual expresses greater ambition for worldly status and security, and this can bring about involvement with corporate business, partnerships, government, and politics.

Transiting Saturn Conjunct the Natal Descendant and Opposition the Natal Ascendant

Increased responsibility in marriage and partnerships characterizes this transit. This is a favorable period for involvement in professional partnerships and political or business public relations. In any event, there is increased responsibility toward others. The individual establishes ties with older, serious-minded individuals. This transit can indicate marriage to an older, established individual.

If the conjunction receives stress aspects, the individual may become entangled in legal problems and lawsuits.

Transiting Saturn Conjunct the Natal Nadir and
Opposition the Natal Midheaven

An increased need for domestic and family security characterizes this transit.

This is a favorable period for home-improvement projects and physical activity in the home. Some individuals carry on professional activities in the home. There can be conflicts, however, between professional and family responsibilities.

Business or professional involvements during this transit are often related to real estate, building, farming, the home, food, or domestic products and services.

The individual may have the responsibility of having elderly people or family members in the home. Children experiencing this transit are subject to more discipline from parents or older authority figures.

This can be the beginning of the end of an obscure, lonely period, and the individual should guard against emotional depression and despondency.

Transit Saturn Sextiles

Transiting Saturn Sextile the Natal Sun

See "Transiting Sun Sextile Natal Saturn."

Transiting Saturn Sextile the Natal Moon

See "Transiting Moon Sextile Natal Saturn."

Transiting Saturn Sextile Natal Mercury

See "Transiting Mercury Sextile Natal Saturn."

Transiting Saturn Sextile Natal Venus

See "Transiting Venus Sextile Natal Saturn."

Transiting Saturn Sextile Natal Mars

See "Transiting Mars Sextile Natal Saturn."

Transiting Saturn Sextile Natal Jupiter

See "Transiting Jupiter Sextile Natal Saturn."

Transiting Saturn Sextile Natal Saturn

Good organization and planning in professional, business, and political activities characterize this transit. This is a favorable time to consolidate business and professional gains and to sign business and professional contracts and agreements.

The individual's worldly status and reputation can be enhanced through professional activities, group and organizational affiliations, friends, or through entering into a marriage or partnership. Business and professional opportunities often come through friends, groups, and organizations. The individual finds it easy to gain the friendship and cooperation of older people or those in established positions of power and authority. Purposeful, serious activities may involve the individual with his or her brothers, sisters, neighbors, and friends.

Transiting Saturn Sextile Natal Uranus

During this transit, the individual becomes involved with serious friendships, groups, and organizations and takes on responsibilities associated with them.

This is a favorable time for establishing friendships with mature, educated, serious-minded individuals and for initiating professional and business endeavors.

Opportunities for progress can arise in business and professions related to politics, administrative work, corporate business, government funding, engineering, and scientific research.

A more practical approach to humanitarian goals and projects may be exhibited. During this transit, one is able to combine elements of the old and the new harmoniously.

This transit may give rise to intuitive knowledge through an improved ability to concentrate. The individual may have original and, in some cases, intuitive insights for advancing his or her career, organizational, and business goals. Inspired ideas can be given practical expression at this time. This is an excellent period for scientific or astrological work. The individual may become interested in a serious study of technological, scientific, or occult subjects.

Transiting Uranus sextile natal Saturn has the same significance as transiting Saturn sextile natal Uranus; however, it usually lasts for a longer period of time and indicates a sustained opportunity to employ effective new methods in handling the serious responsibilities of life. This transit occurs twice in an average life span.

Transiting Saturn Sextile Natal Neptune

Insight into the subconscious mind characterizes this transit. One is able to tap deep resources of the memory, which might even go back to previous embodiments, and these provide the individual with profound insights that are useful in the present.

This transit helps steady the mind making deeper levels of concentration or meditation possible. The faculty of creative imagination can be put to effective use under this transit.

The individual can gain intuitive insights into how to conduct his or her business and professional affairs. Past acquaintances and associations often provide opportunities for the individual at this time. This is a favorable period for work in psychology, work related to hospitals, universities, churches, or other cultural institutions or serious work in art and music. The individual's work may involve professional or governmental secrecy in some way.

Transiting Neptune sextile natal Saturn has the same significance as transiting Saturn sextile natal Neptune; however, it lasts for a longer period of time and indicates a sustained opportunity for the practical application of intuitive knowledge. This transit occurs only twice in the average life span.

Transiting Saturn Sextile Natal Pluto

The intuitive mental faculties are stimulated during this transit. It can provide the individual with significant insight into scientific, mathematical, and occult laws. This transit also has the effect of increasing mental concentration and discipline. It is a favorable period for serious study of science, mathematics, and metaphysics.

Professional advancement is gained through resourcefulness and worthwhile accomplishments, and new opportunities open up for the individual during this transit. Professional activities often involve secrecy in some way.

Financial benefits may come through inheritance, taxes, corporate money, funding, or investments.

Transiting Pluto sextile natal Saturn has the same significance as transiting Saturn sextile natal Pluto; however, it lasts for a longer period of time and indicates a prolonged opportunity for professional advancement through a resourceful and sustained application of the will. This transit occurs only once or twice in an average life span.

Transiting Saturn Sextile the Natal North Node and Trine the Natal South Node

Professional or business activity geared for public acceptance characterizes this transit. The individual identifies with prevailing cultural attitudes and viewpoints as a means of gaining personal security and professional advancement. The individual exercises caution in dealing with the public and seeks support and approval from the conservative elements of society.

Transiting North Node sextile natal Saturn and transiting South Node trine natal Saturn has the same significance as transiting Saturn sextile the natal North Node and trine the natal South Node; however, it is usually of slightly longer duration and indicates a sustained period of public acceptance of the individual's professional and business activities, and often advancement through appeal to society's conservative elements.

Transiting Saturn Sextile the Natal South Node and Trine the Natal North Node

This transit has basically the same significance as transiting Saturn sextile the natal North Node and trine the natal South Node; however, there is a greater tendency to identify with cultural tradition. The individual is likely to be more critical of currently popular attitudes and beliefs.

Transiting South Node sextile natal Saturn and transiting North Node trine natal Saturn has the same significance as transiting Saturn sextile the natal South Node and trine the natal North Node; however, it is usually of slightly longer duration and indicates a sustained period of identification with traditional cultural beliefs, and often a focused intellectual awareness of ways for shaping current popular attitudes and beliefs.

Transiting Saturn Sextile the Natal Ascendant and
Trine the Natal Descendant

Caution and propriety in self-expression and in personal relationships characterize this transit. The individual works for security and stability in personal relationships.

Benefits can come through relationships with older, established individuals. This is a favorable time to communicate with one's superiors or with those in positions of power and authority.

The individual expresses increased self-discipline in the important affairs of his or her life. Ideas for business and professional advancement can be implemented in a practical way. This is a favorable time for handling legal affairs or dealing with government agencies. It is also a good period for establishing professional partnerships.

Transiting Saturn Sextile the Natal Micheaven and
Trine the Natal Nadir

Ideas for professional advancement and stabilization of professional and domestic affairs characterize this transit. The individual achieves steady progress in both professional and family affairs. This is a favorable transit for business and political activity.

Professional benefits can come to the individual through older, established and mature individuals.

Transiting Saturn Sextile the Natal Descendant and
Trine the Natal Ascendant

This transit has basically the same significance as transiting Saturn sextile the natal Ascendant and trine the natal Descendant; however, there is a more intellectual approach to relationships and a more conservative self-expression.

Transiting Saturn Sextile the Natal Nadir and
Trine the Natal Midheaven

This transit has basically the same significance as transiting Saturn sextile the natal Midheaven and trine the natal Nadir; however, there is a more intellectual approach to domestic responsibilities and an easy flow in professional affairs.

Transit Saturn Squares

Transiting Saturn Square the Natal Sun

See "Transiting Sun Square Natal Saturn."

Transiting Saturn Square the Natal Moon

See "Transiting Moon Square Natal Saturn."

Transiting Saturn Square Natal Mercury

See "Transiting Mercury Square Natal Saturn."

Transiting Saturn Square Natal Venus

See "Transiting Venus Square Natal Saturn."

Transiting Saturn Square Natal Mars

See "Transiting Mars Square Natal Saturn."

Transiting Saturn Square Natal Jupiter

See "Transiting Jupiter Square Natal Saturn."

Transiting Saturn Square Natal Saturn

Worry, anxiety, and negative, pessimistic attitudes characterize this transit. Frustrations and obstacles usually arise at this time, blocking the individual's professional and political ambitions.

Increased and burdensome business and professional responsibilities are likely. The individual may be subject to unemployment and financial difficulty. There may be conflicts with the government or with authority figures. The individual may be subject to legal problems. This is not a favorable period for dealing with property or real estate.

The individual may have to care for or take on the responsibility of older people in some way. Parents or other authority figures may establish restraints on the individual.

Unpopularity with friends, groups, and associates can also be a problem at this time. Difficulties involving bones, teeth, and skin may surface at this time.

Transiting Saturn Square Natal Uranus

The individual encounters obstacles in the practical application of creative ideas during this transit. Unexpected difficulties and reversals of fortune can occur in the individual's business or career, especially if past motivations have been selfish. Selfish motivations can also bring about sudden and unexpected damage to one's personal reputation and status. The individual is likely to feel frustrated in efforts to realize his or her goals and objectives.

Some individuals take inconsistent and fanatical attitudes toward professional and political affairs.

This is not a favorable period for joining or working with groups and organizations—unexpected factors are likely to arise. The individual or his or her friends may prove to be unreliable, inconsistent, or selfishly motivated. The individual is likely to either mistrust others or be mistrusted.

Lawsuits and legal difficulties related to partnerships, joint monies, corporate business, insurance, professional matters, contracts, taxes, alimony, or inheritance are possible.

Health problems such as broken bones, circulation difficulties, dental problems, skin irritations, and nervous disorders often accompany this transit.

There is a tendency toward inconsistency and spasmodic work habits during this transit. A tendency to demand freedom without responsibility can also cause problems.

Transiting Uranus square natal Saturn has the same significance as transiting Saturn square natal Uranus; however, it lasts longer and indicates a sustained period of instability and frustration in one's personal business and professional affairs. This transit occurs only twice in an average life span.

Transiting Saturn Square Natal Neptune

Irrational fears, phobias, and anxieties characterize this transit. There is often a desire to avoid practical responsibilities and work. The psychological problems of one's family members or others with whom one must deal are likely to interfere with one's professional work performance and success.

This planetary combination is often associated with mental illness. Some individuals, or those with whom they must deal, manifest irrational tendencies. Depression or paranoia based on subconscious memories may become evident at this time.

Negative emotional states and, in some cases, unwise psychic practices such as seances, drug abuse, and so on may subject the individual to undesirable psychic influences, such as astral entities and destructive thought forms. This can, in turn, aggravate tendencies to mental illness and, in extreme cases, lead to hospitalization, institutionalization, or imprisonment. Misuse of drugs and alcohol is likely to have an especially damaging effect at this time.

The individual may become the target of secret slander, or secret misdeeds from the past may be publicly revealed, leading to a reversal of fortune and damage to personal reputation and status. Hidden enemies can undermine the individual's reputation and professional standing, but because the individual is prone to paranoia during this period, these dangers may be more imagined than real. As is usually the case with such afflictions to Neptune, the individual tends to be his or her own worst enemy.

Transiting Neptune square natal Saturn has the same significance as transiting Saturn square natal Neptune; however, it is of longer duration and indicates a sustained period of professional confusion, misconceptions, neuroses, and danger from the improper use of drugs and alcohol. Dangerous psychic practices should be carefully and firmly avoided at this time. This transit occurs only twice in an average life span.

Transiting Saturn Square Natal Pluto

Hard, unsympathetic, and austere attitudes characterize this transit. The individual may be forced to deal with circumstances of a sinister nature, perhaps involving economic, political, or professional power struggles and plots.

The individual may be subject to coercion, blackmail, or threats in his or her professional, business, or political affairs. Taxes, joint finances, corporate interests, insurance, alimony, and goods of the dead can all be sources of conflict. The individual may have to struggle against corruption and dishonesty, and his or her career and reputation may suffer as a result of these problems. Any attempts to use dishonorable means to obtain personal advantage can result in damage to both career and reputation.

The individual may be uninterested in sex and have sexual problems. Paranoia and the fear of death are associated with this transit, but reincarnation or life after death often interest the individual at this time.

This transit can be used constructively to increase will power and the determination to succeed.

Transiting Pluto square natal Saturn has the same significance as transiting Saturn square natal Pluto; however, it is of longer duration and indicates a sustained period of increased will power accompanied by problems, and often by coercion and power struggles—even public scandal—in one's professional, business, and political affairs. This transit occurs only once in an average life span.

Transiting Saturn Square the Natal North Node and Square the Natal South Node

Conservative disapproval of prevailing trends and popular beliefs characterizes this transit. The individual often adopts an anti-social attitude, which can lead to unpopularity and obstacles in business expansion and public relations.

Transiting North and South Nodes square natal Saturn has the same significance as transiting Saturn square the natal North Node and square the natal South Node; however, it is usually of slightly longer duration and indicates a sustained period of unpopularity and difficulty in business and professional affairs, particularly where these relate to cultural trends and popular beliefs.

Transiting Saturn Square the Natal South Node and Square the Natal North Node

See "Transiting Saturn Square the Natal North Node and Square the Natal South Node."

Transiting Saturn Square the Natal Ascendant and Square the Natal Descendant

Inhibited self-expression and cold, unsympathetic attitudes both toward and from others characterize this transit. The individual and those with whom he or she is closely associated are likely to suffer from pessimism, a negative outlook, and lowered vitality. Serious difficulties can arise in relationships and partnerships The individual may be saddled with responsibility for others. Lawsuits and other legal difficulties and obstacles to professional progress can arise at this time.

Transiting Saturn Square the Natal Midheaven and Square the Natal Nadir

A depressed emotional outlook and burdensome domestic and professional responsibilities characterize this transit. Difficulties with parents or responsibility for the care of older persons may be a burden for the individual at this time. Conflict may arise between one's professional and domestic responsibilities. There is an increased need for organization and timing in professional and domestic affairs.

Problems may arise in dealings with government agencies or authority figures, and obstacles tend to arise in one's business affairs.

Transiting Saturn Square the Natal Descendant and Square the Natal Ascendant

See "Transiting Saturn Square the Natal Ascendant and Square the Natal Descendant."

Transiting Saturn Square the Natal Nadir and Square the Natal Midheaven

See "Transiting Saturn Square the Natal Midheaven and Square the Natal Nadir."

Transit Saturn Trines

Transiting Saturn Trine the Natal Sun

See "Transiting Sun Trine Natal Saturn."

Transiting Saturn Trine the Natal Moon

See "Transiting Moon Trine Natal Saturn."

Transiting Saturn Trine Natal Mercury

See "Transiting Mercury Trine Natal Saturn."

Transiting Saturn Trine Natal Venus

See "Transiting Venus Trine Natal Saturn."

Transiting Saturn Trine Natal Mars

See "Transiting Mars Trine Natal Saturn."

Transiting Saturn Trine Natal Jupiter

See "Transiting Jupiter Trine Natal Saturn."

Transiting Saturn Trine Natal Saturn

An increased sense of honesty and integrity characterizes this transit. The individual enjoys serious, meaningful pursuits during this period.

Steady progress can be made in achieving long-range goals and objectives. This is also a favorable period for recognition of one's past performance. The individual is hard-working, well organized, and conscientious in the performance of his or her duties. Greater stability and loyalty will be in evidence in business partnerships and other relationships.

Transiting Saturn Trine Natal Uranus

Practical application of creative inspirational ideas characterizes this transit. It is a favorable time for mental pursuits, especially in the fields of science and philosophy. Significant progress can be made in the realization of one's goals and objectives. Friends, groups, and organizational associates can play an important part in the realization of these goals and objectives.

The focused concentration and greater intuitive awareness that result from this transit may help the individual gain a deeper understanding of universal scientific and occult laws. This is a good period for the study of astrology, parapsychology, and similar disciplines.

Benefits can come through friendship with mature, older, or established people. This is a favorable time for involvement with groups and organizations with serious goals and purposes. The individual may assume a role of personal leadership and responsibility in managing groups and organizational affairs.

The individual's business and professional affairs can benefit through the use of new methods and technological innovations.

Some individuals develop an interest in reforming or regenerating existing political, legal, or business institutions. This is a favorable time for involvement in corporate business and for dealing with insurance, taxes, and goods of the dead. It is especially favorable for those involved in engineering and scientific work.

Worthwhile achievements can lead to unexpected honors and advancement. This is a good period to seek employment or make important professional changes.

Transiting Uranus trine natal Saturn has the same significance as transiting Saturn trine natal Uranus; however, it lasts longer and indicates a sustained period of practical implementation of creative ideas and methodologies. This transit occurs only twice in an average life span.

Transiting Saturn Trine Natal Neptune

The ability to find a practical application for one's imaginative and intuitive inspirations characterizes this transit. The ability to be calm and focus the attention, which this transit confers, is favorable for spiritual and psychological disciplines, such as meditation. Through this process, the individual can gain profound insights. Some individuals are able to tap the deeper levels of memory, even dating back to previous embodiments. The individual can gain deep insights into political, economic, and cultural forces operating now and in the past. These insights may be a part of a sequential pattern of unfoldment, whereby the secret machinations of those in positions of power and authority can be understood. The individual may also develop an interest in history as a means of understanding cultural evolution. During this transit, the individual can benefit through the instruction of a spiritual teacher.

This is a favorable time for those engaged in professions related to psychology or those whose activities put them into contact with hospitals, asylums, prisons, or religious or educational institutions.

Professional, government, or corporate secrecy may involve the individual in some way.

This is a good period for the psychological stabilization of family and domestic affairs.

In general, the individual can reap the benefits of past discipline, organization, and hard work.

Transiting Neptune trine natal Saturn has the same significance as transiting Saturn trine natal Neptune; however, it is of much longer duration and indicates a prolonged period of in-depth insight into economic, business, and political affairs. This transit occurs only twice in an average life span.

Transiting Saturn Trine Natal Pluto

Increased concentration and will power characterize this transit.

This is a favorable time for the pursuit of long-range goals and ambitions because of the sustained will power and stern, severe, purposeful attitude engendered by this transit.

The individual can develop an awareness of intrigues and power struggles within large-scale governmental or corporate organizations, or within his or her own business and professional structure.

This is a favorable transit for spiritual discipline and meditation. The individual can gain insight into profound scientific and spiritual laws, along with an awareness of the need to adhere strictly to universal principles of justice. This is a good time to handle legal matters and conduct secret investigations.

The individual often expresses increased professional ambition and resourcefulness in promoting his or her professional and political ambitions. A desire to reform existing political, economic, and business institutions and power structures may develop. This is a favorable transit for those who are involved in advanced scientific, mathematical, and technical endeavors and for doctors, lawyers, scientists, and engineers.

The individual expresses greater efficiency in work performance and sometimes finds new ways to increase efficiency.

Transiting Pluto trine natal Saturn has the same significance as transiting Saturn trine natal Pluto; however, it lasts for a much longer period of time and indicates a sustained interval of resourcefulness and good organization in one's business, economic, professional, political, scientific or occult endeavors. This transit occurs only twice in an average life span.

Transiting Saturn Trine the Natal North Node and
Sextile the Natal South Node

See "Transiting Saturn Sextile the Natal South Node and Trine the Natal North Node."

Transiting Saturn Trine the Natal South Node and
Sextile the Natal North Node

See "Transiting Saturn Sextile the Natal North Node and Trine the Natal South Node."

Transiting Saturn Trine the Natal Ascendant and Sextile the Natal Descendant

See "Transiting Saturn Sextile the Natal Descendant and Trine the Natal Ascendant."

Transiting Saturn Trine the Natal Midheaven and Sextile the Natal Nadir

See "Transiting Saturn Sextile the Natal Nadir and Trine the Natal Midheaven."

Transiting Saturn Trine the Natal Descendant and Sextile the Natal Ascendant

See "Transiting Saturn Sextile the Natal Ascendant and Trine the Natal Descendant."

Transiting Saturn Trine the Natal Nadir and Sextile the Natal Midheaven

See "Transiting Saturn Sextile the Natal Midheaven and Trine the Natal Nadir."

Transit Saturn Oppositions

Transiting Saturn Opposition the Natal Sun

See "Transiting Sun Opposition Natal Saturn."

Transiting Saturn Opposition the Natal Moon

See "Transiting Moon Opposition Natal Saturn."

Transiting Saturn Opposition Natal Mercury

See "Transiting Mercury Opposition Natal Saturn."

Transiting Saturn Opposition Natal Venus

See "Transiting Venus Opposition Natal Saturn."

Transiting Saturn Opposition Natal Mars

See "Transiting Mars Opposition Natal Saturn."

Transiting Saturn Opposition Natal Jupiter

See "Transiting Jupiter Opposition Natal Saturn."

Transiting Saturn Opposition Natal Saturn

A conservative social and business outlook and a conformity to traditional social norms characterize this transit. This period usually brings about increased responsibility in marriage and partnerships, as well as in one's professional, political, and business relationships.

Important changes can take place in one's awareness of the need for cooperation in important long-range goals and ambitions.

This period brings about increased awareness of the demands of business, economic, political, and professional affairs.

Lawsuits and legal difficulties are a possibility at this time.

There can be increased responsibility through professional, political, and business relationships.

Transiting Saturn Opposition Natal Uranus

Inconsistent attitudes toward personal freedom and responsibility toward others characterize this transit. The individual may rebel against authority while, at the same time, expecting obedience and adherence to his or her own wishes. Relationships necessary to the individual's security may be disrupted by his or her inconsistent actions and attitudes. There is likely to be conflict and disagreement with those in positions of power and authority and frustrations in one's attempts to change existing conditions. Among the conflicts between old and new that characterize this transit is a conflict between established authority figures and the individual's own revolutionary attitudes; a conflict between the old and new methods of doing things in the individual's business or professional affairs; and an extension of these conflicts into friendships and group or organizational associations.

Responsibility in marriage partnerships or other important relationships can limit the individual's freedom. There can also be an increased sense of responsibility toward friends and toward the groups and organizations to which one belongs and a need to cooperate with them.

The individual's ideas concerning business, political, and professional affairs may be eccentric and impractical. Unexpected difficulties may arise in professional or business affairs.

Individuals with this transit, or their associates, may have ulterior motives, such as gain in status or professional advancement, hoping to accomplish through their friends, groups, or associates what they cannot achieve on their own. This can naturally lead to estrangement. If the individuals' motivations are selfish, they can undergo sudden reversals of fortune, such as loss of job or professional standing.

This is an unfavorable period for dealing with corporate money, joint monies, insurance, taxes, or goods of the dead. Lawsuits and financial difficulties related to these matters can arise at this time. Rebellion against or dissociation from conservative institutions may leave the individual without financial support. Problems may also arise with open enemies or competitors.

Transiting Uranus opposition natal Saturn has the same significance as transiting Saturn opposition natal Uranus; however, it lasts longer and indicates a sustained period in which awareness and cooperation are needed with others in business, professional, group, and organizational affairs and partnerships. This transit occurs only once or twice in an average life span.

Transiting Saturn Opposition Natal Neptune

Emotional depression due to relationship problems characterizes this transit. Painful unconscious memories and fear, mistrust, or neurotic attitudes toward others may be stimulated at this time.

The individual is likely to feel lonely and insecure during this transit. He or she may appear to cooperate in important relationships, while secretly undermining or evading the reality and responsibility entailed in the relationships.

One should avoid brooding, self-pity, and blaming others for one's own problems at this time. The relationship difficulties encountered during this period are usually based on anxieties and subconscious fears, although there is a definite possibility of secret enemies undermining the individual's status.

The individual is likely to lack discipline and self-confidence during this period and often becomes a burden to others because of this. Others can become burdensome to the individual for the same reasons.

Latent tendencies toward mental illness, often in the form of evasion of work and responsibility, are often stimulated by this transit. It calls for realistic cooperation and awareness. Paranoia or avoidance of responsibilities may also be due to personal inadequacies and fear of failure. Strict honesty and a practical approach to responsibility, combined with an attempt at an optimistic outlook, are necessary if the individual is to maintain psychological balance.

The misuse of drugs or alcohol or indulgence in psychic practices can also unbalance the individual psychologically and may create the danger of control by undesirable psychic influences.

This is an unfavorable period for dealing with hospitals, asylums, and similar institutions, as well as religious or cultural institutions.

In some cases, there can be underhanded tactics and dishonesty in business and professional dealings. Public disclosures of past secret misdeeds can lead to loss of position, status, and reputation.

Transiting Neptune opposition natal Saturn has the same significance as transiting Saturn opposition natal Neptune; however, it lasts for a longer period of time and indicates a sustained interval of psychological difficulty in important relationships. This occurs only once in an average life span.

Transiting Saturn Opposition Natal Pluto

Attempts at coercion and enforced conformity in important relationships characterize this transit. The individual may be subject to dishonesty, blackmail, coercion, or power struggles in his or her business, professional, and political affairs. Oppressive authoritarian individuals or business, economic, or political institutions may have to be dealt with. People of evil and sinister character should be avoided at all costs during this period, as they could involve the individual in dangerous underworld activities.

Old business, professional, or marital relationships may be severed under this transit. The individual may become involved in lawsuits pertaining to corporate business, joint monies, taxes, insurance, inheritance, or alimony.

Fear of or danger from occult practices can also be a problem. Misuse of occult power or of economic power and authority for personal self-aggrandizement can have serious destructive, long-range consequences for the individual.

This period can be used for constructive accomplishments, providing the necessity for cooperation and improved methodology in business and professional affairs is observed.

Transiting Pluto opposition natal Saturn has the same significance as transiting Saturn opposition natal Pluto; however, it is of longer duration and indicates a sustained period of involvement in serious economic, business, and professional machinations and power struggles. This transit occurs only once in an average life span.

Transiting Saturn Opposition the Natal North Node and Conjunct the Natal South Node

See "Transiting Saturn Conjunct the Natal South Node and Opposition the Natal North Node."

Transiting Saturn Opposition the Natal South Node and Conjunct the Natal North Node

See "Transiting Saturn Conjunct the Natal North Node and Opposition the Natal South Node."

Transiting Saturn Opposition the Natal Ascendant and Conjunct the Natal Descendant

See "Transiting Saturn Conjunct the Natal Descendant and Opposition the Natal Ascendant."

Transiting Saturn Opposition the Natal Midheaven and Conjunct the Natal Nadir

See "Transiting Saturn Conjunct the Natal Nadir and Opposition the Natal Midheaven."

Transiting Saturn Opposition the Natal Descendant and Conjunct the Natal Ascendant

See "Transiting Saturn Conjunct the Natal Ascendant and Opposition the Natal Descendant."

Transiting Saturn Opposition the Natal Nadir and Conjunct the Natal Midheaven

See "Transiting Saturn Conjunct the Natal Midheaven and Opposition the Natal Nadir."

26 Transits of Uranus

Transit Uranus Through the Houses

Transiting Uranus Through the Natal First House

Radical changes in self-awareness and personal outlook on life characterize this transit. The manifestation of intuitive and clairvoyant faculties, as well as new friendships, group associations, and personal interests, can bring an awakening to a higher level of consciousness.

The individual has a desire for greater personal freedom and is willing to sacrifice his or her security to gain it. This is often accompanied by a major change in life style and a new self-image.

There is interest in new ideas, or in very old, forgotten ideas. New interests can include astrology and other occult subjects or scientific fields, such as electronics, physics, archaeology, and so on. During this period, the individual often drops old friendships and associations and initiates new ones.

Greater personal initiative is usually displayed in business and corporate affairs or in making money in new, unusual ways.

If Uranus makes stress aspects while transiting the natal First House, the individual can be impractical, impatient, erratic, and foolishly rebellious.

Transiting Uranus Through the Natal Second House

Erratic fluctuations in financial affairs characterize this transit. The individual is subject to dramatic and unexpected financial gains and losses. There can also be sudden changes in personal values and attitudes toward money and material goods.

The individual may become more detached regarding money or material possessions, or radically change his or her methods for obtaining these things. There is a tendency to spend money on friends, groups, organizations and the new interests associated with them. However, the individual can also make money through contact with friends, groups, and organizations, or through electronics and technological innovations. Technological innovations are often introduced into business and financial affairs.

Financial activities during this transit tend to be related to corporate money, joint finances, government funding, grants, insurance, taxes, inheritance, or financial partnerships. If Uranus makes stress aspects while transiting the natal Second House, the individual is subject to sudden financial losses and impulsive, erratic spending.

Transiting Uranus Through the Natal Third House

Sudden changes in mental outlook, intuitive ideas, and original thinking characterize this transit. This transit usually stimulates intellectual curiosity in new areas of interest. One can have new ideas and intuitive insights into ways of realizing one's goals and objectives.

New or unusual activities may arise involving one's friends, brothers, sisters, and neighbors, and association with friends, groups, and organizations can significantly change one's ideas about key issues. Sudden, unexpected, and interesting short trips or communications are also likely to take place during this transit. These are likely to involve brothers, sisters, neighbors, business associates, friends, and group associates.

The individual may become involved with electronic communications media in some way or develop an intellectual interest in electronics, scientific subjects, astrology, or the occult. This is likely to involve reading books on these subjects, attending lectures and group meetings, and getting involved with friendships or organizations related to these things. This is also a good period for writing or lecturing on scientific or occult subjects.

If Uranus makes stress aspects to other natal or transiting planets while transiting the natal Third House, the individual is subject to nervousness, mental vacillation, restlessness, impractical ideas, and unexpected communication and transportation breakdowns. There is often an unwillingness to listen to good, practical advice. Safe driving is especially important at this time.

Transiting Uranus Through the Natal Fourth House

Changes in one's basic emotional attitudes and a desire for personal freedom in home and family life characterize this transit. The individual is often affected by unusual behavior on the part of family members.

Sudden changes or new conditions can come about in family and domestic conditions. This is a favorable time for home-improvement projects, providing Uranus does not make stress aspects, and for business and scientific activity in the home.

The individual may become interested in ecology and earth-related sciences during this transit. Organic gardening, mining, architecture, and archaeology are among the fields that are apt to draw the individual's attention. The individual can become involved in new business methods and endeavors related to these fields, or in businesses related to home and domestic products and services.

Transiting Uranus Through the Natal Fifth House

Originality in artistic and social expression characterizes this transit. The individual expresses a desire for greater freedom in the pursuit of whatever he or she considers pleasurable. One's social life is likely to be active and exciting during this transit.

This period may bring about unusual, exciting romances; these can be with friends or group associates, or with people met through group activities. However, if Uranus makes stress aspects to other planets while transiting the natal Fifth House, the individual can become involved in unstable romantic infatuations, or be forced to deal with an unplanned pregnancy. Friendships and group activities involving children may arise. Much social or pleasure-oriented activity takes place with friends or through groups and organizations, and sometimes in connection with business affairs.

Financial speculation during this transit is likely to bring about either sudden gains or sudden losses.

The individual may become involved in theatrical groups or artistic and social organizations. Technological innovations tend to play a role in either artistic endeavors or personal pursuit of pleasure during this period.

Transiting Uranus Through the Natal Sixth House

Eccentric tastes in diet and dress and unusual work conditions characterize this transit. The individual may change jobs, begin a new line of work, or make use of technological innovations in his or her work.

At this time, the individual's work may involve technological industries, such as electronics. This is a favorable transit for engineers, scientists, medical personnel, and technicians. Employment opportunities can come about through friends, groups, and organizations. New friendships or group or organizational affiliations often arise during this transit through contact with others in the working environment. In many cases, this means involvement in labor unions.

The individual may develop an interest in new or occult healing methods. This is also a favorable transit for those whose work involves astrological or occult pursuits. It especially favors the use of astrology in medical diagnosis.

If Uranus makes stress aspects to other planets while transiting the natal Sixth House, there can be a sudden loss of job, instability in employment, accidents, sudden illness, nervousness, or eccentric, irregular, uncooperative, or revolutionary attitudes where work is concerned.

Transiting Uranus Through the Natal Seventh House

The need for freedom in relationships and relationships with unusual and talented people characterize this transit. The individual usually undergoes sudden changes in attitudes and ways of dealing with others.

This is a favorable time for cooperation in friendships, groups, and organizations, providing Uranus does not make stress aspects to other planets. The individual may become engaged in business partnerships, particularly those that relate to corporate affairs.

Old relationships may be severed and new ones developed during this period. If Uranus makes stress aspects while transiting this house, there can be an uncooperative attitude or instability and sudden change in one's marriage or other important relationships. This transit often brings about divorce or sudden, unstable, and short-lived marriages and partnerships. Breakdown in close relationships during this transit usually results from a desire for personal freedom without consideration for the needs of others on the part of either one or both individuals. Rapidly changing personal life styles or goals and objectives may also necessitate a change in relationships.

Transiting Uranus Through the Natal Eighth House

The ending of old conditions and the beginning of new ones characterize this transit. There is a need for detachment, especially where material things are concerned.

The individual, or those with whom he or she is associated, sometimes undergoes drastic changes of values and goals, which can necessitate a complete reworking of old business arrangements and modes of operation. Such major changes can affect joint finances, corporate money, taxes, insurance, alimony, goods of the dead, or other jointly owned or controlled resources, for better or worse.

The individual may become involved in large-scale corporate enterprises of a technical nature, involving electronics, science, or engineering. Many individuals become interested in advanced scientific subjects, the occult, parapsychology, life after death, reincarnation, and other related fields. Profound intuitive, clairvoyant, or mystical experiences may occur during this transit. There may also be the sudden or unexpected death of a friend or group or business associate.

Sex often becomes an issue during this transit, and there is a need for a deeper understanding of sexual energy.

If Uranus makes stress aspects while transiting the natal Eighth House, there can be unexpected problems in business, and the unexpected death of a close friend or business associate.

Transiting Uranus Through the Natal Ninth House

Intuitive religious and philosophic insights and inspiration characterize this transit. The individual tends to seek direct personal intuitive religious experience of spiritual truth. There can be intuitive insights into the evolution of cultural trends.

This transit indicates a greater receptivity to occult ideas and philosophies. There is a tendency to seek out occult or religious friendships, groups, or organizations. This is a favorable time for the study of science or occult subjects, especially astrology. The individual may seek higher education in scientific, occult, or humanitarian fields. Exciting or unusual experiences often occur while the individual is attending universities or schools of higher learning. There is often an interest in new, unusual, or progressive methods of higher education or in new spiritual or occult systems of self-development.

During this transit, there is often a desire to reform existing legal, religious or educational institutions.

Sudden opportunities for travel or unexpected travel, especially by air, often occurs during this transit. The individual's travels usually involve friends, groups, organizations, or business affairs, and often result in unusual or exciting experiences. The individual often establishes friendships with foreigners or people from distant places.

If Uranus makes stress aspects while transiting the natal Ninth House, the individual is subject to eccentric, impractical religious, cultural, educational, or philosophic beliefs.

Transiting Uranus Through the Natal Tenth House

Interesting and original professional work characterizes this transit. The individual is likely to employ new and unusual methods of achieving professional goals and ambitions. Often, there is involvement in corporate business politics or in outside political intrigues.

This is a favorable transit for involvement in professional groups and organizations. Friendships and group or organizational associations can come about through the individual's business or profession, and professional opportunities and benefits, in turn, often arise through groups, organizations, and friendships.

The individual's professional activities are likely to be related to scientific, technological, or corporate endeavors during this transit. Professional activity related to occult or astrological fields is also possible.

The individual may undergo sudden changes in professional or political status during this transit. Many individuals promote or support radical, revolutionary, reformist, or liberal political causes and viewpoints during this period.

If Uranus makes stress aspects while transiting the natal Tenth House, the individual is subject to loss of job or other sudden professional or political reversals of fortune.

Transiting Uranus Through the Natal Eleventh House

Sudden changes in friendships, group and organizational associations, and personal goals and objectives characterize this transit. New friendships are often established with interesting and unusual people. Many individuals develop an interest in scientific or occult subjects, and this is likely to bring about involvement in groups, organizations, or friendships related to these subjects.

During this transit, the individual is likely to have a broad-minded and humanitarian attitude toward people in all walks of life. This sometimes leads to involvement in humanitarian or reformist groups and organizations.

Some individuals are aided by corporate money or government funding in realizing their goals and objectives.

If Uranus makes stress aspects to other planets while transiting the natal Eleventh House, the individual can be misled by eccentric, unreliable friends, or his or her own unorthodox or unbalanced attitudes may result in social unpopularity.

Transiting Uranus Through the Natal Twelfth House

Tapping of intuitive knowledge and sudden stimulation of unconscious memories characterize this transit. This is a favorable period for meditation and for the development of one's intuitive and clairvoyant faculties. The individual may experience a sudden release from and understanding of unconscious hangups.

Radical changes in the individual's secret motivations may also come about. The private affairs of the individual's life may suddenly and drastically change, for better or worse.

The individual may become involved in secret activity related to friends, groups, and organizations, perhaps in the form of occult fraternities or mystical societies. Friends can turn out to be secret enemies if Uranus is afflicted.

This transit often brings about an interest of reincarnation and life after death.

The individual's friends may be confined unexpectedly in prisons, hospitals, asylums, or unexpectedly released from them. If Uranus makes stress aspects to other planets while transiting the natal Twelfth House, the individual may be suddenly confined, institutionalized, hospitalized, or imprisoned.

Transit Uranus Conjunctions

Transiting Uranus Conjunct the Natal Sun

See "Transiting Sun Conjunct Natal Uranus."

Transiting Uranus Conjunct the Natal Moon

See "Transiting Moon Conjunct Natal Uranus."

Transiting Uranus Conjunct Natal Mercury

See "Transiting Mercury Conjunct Natal Uranus."

Transiting Uranus Conjunct Natal Venus

See "Transiting Venus Conjunct Natal Uranus."

Transiting Uranus Conjunct Natal Mars

See "Transiting Mars Conjunct Natal Uranus."

Transiting Uranus Conjunct Natal Jupiter

See "Transiting Jupiter Conjunct Natal Uranus."

Transiting Uranus Conjunct Natal Saturn

See "Transiting Saturn Conjunct Natal Uranus."

Transiting Uranus Conjunct Natal Uranus

Detachment from material things and release from mundane responsibilities characterize this transit. It normally occurs at about age eighty-four, at which point the individual often develops an interest in scientific, occult, or mystical subjects, and sometimes in organizations dealing with scientific, occult, or mystical activities. The individual may gain intuitive perceptions concerning spiritual realities, life after death, and reincarnation.

Transiting Uranus Conjunct Natal Neptune

Intensified intuitive perception and sudden confrontation with the unconscious mind characterize this transit. The individual can imagine or gain intuitive insights into ways of achieving his or her goals and objectives.

Sudden changes can come about in the individual's personal and private affairs, sometimes as a result of large-scale social, economic, or political changes beyond his or her personal control.

Friendships sometimes develop with intuitive, artistically talented, and psychic people. This is an excellent period for those in artistic and scientific fields, because of the stimulation of the intuitive and imaginative faculties.

Involvement in secret groups and organizations is quite possible at this time. The individual may become involved in scientific, mystical, or occult friendships, groups or organizations. An interest in astrology or other parapsychological subjects often develops. Some individuals develop an interest in investigating their previous lives. Often, there are prophetic insights into future cultural trends and attitudes.

Unusual or peculiar circumstances can arise concerning corporate finances, joint monies, taxes, insurance, and goods of the dead. Some individuals receive gifts, funding, or inheritances.

If this transiting conjunction is afflicted by other planets, the individual can become involved in unorthodox cults and groups of dubious value.

Transiting Neptune conjunct natal Uranus has the same significance as transiting Uranus conjunct natal Neptune. Both transits last for a year or longer and mark a sustained period of inner, intuitive change and development.

Transiting Uranus Conjunct Natal Pluto

Increased will power to bring about important changes in one's life characterizes this transit. There can be a strong desire to change or regenerate existing conditions. In extreme cases, this can lead to revolutionary sentiments and actions.

Forces of reality can suddenly shatter the individual's false sense of security and outworn concepts. Some individuals have startling and upsetting clairvoyant experiences at this time. Many people develop an interest in life after death, reincarnation, or parapsychological subjects.

During this transit, the individual is likely to sever old friendships and group associations and initiate new ones that are more in keeping with his or her new interests and values. This transit can indicate the sudden emergence of unusual talents and abilities.

Drastic changes can be brought about through cultural, political, social, or economic forces. In extreme cases, this involves war, revolution, natural disaster, or economic chaos. If this transiting conjunction is afflicted, it is important to avoid situations of potential danger.

Sudden, drastic changes can affect, for better or worse, insurance, taxes, alimony, corporate money, business affairs, or goods of the dead.

Transiting Pluto conjunct natal Uranus has the same significance as transiting Uranus conjunct natal Pluto. Both transits last, off and on, for a year or longer and indicate a sustained period of drastic changes in personal goals and objectives, life style, and surrounding cultural conditions.

Transiting Uranus Conjunct the Natal North Node and Opposition the Natal South Node

Individuals with this transit tend to become involved in the latest forms of social and cultural experimentation. In some cases, they rebel against prevailing cultural norms. They may develop businesses or products designed to exploit currently popular fads.

Transiting North Node conjunct natal Uranus and transiting South Node opposition natal Uranus has the same significance as transiting Uranus conjunct the natal North Node and opposition the natal South Node; however, it is of shorter duration.

Transiting Uranus Conjunct the Natal South Node and Opposition the Natal North Node

Rebellion against traditional cultural values characterizes this transit. One's personal life style is often out of harmony with these values, and for this reason, one may be regarded by one's friends as socially eccentric and unpredictable.

Transiting South Node conjunct natal Uranus and transiting North Node opposition natal Uranus has the same significance as transiting Uranus conjunct the natal South Node and opposition the natal North Node; however, it is of shorter duration.

Transiting Uranus Conjunct the Natal Ascendant and Opposition the Natal Descendant

The desire for freedom of expression and a free life style characterize this transit. The individual is willing to sacrifice security for the sake of personal freedom. Many individuals go through an identity crisis during this period: they develop new self-images and awaken to higher levels of spiritual, personal awareness.

These inner changes may surface as dramatic changes in personal appearance and mannerisms. The individual's interest in unusual ideas can take the form of involvement in humanitarian, scientific, and parapsychological activity. New friendships and group and organizational affiliations related to these activities usually arise.

Many individuals take the initiative in the pursuit of unusual adventures. This transit often stimulates unusual creative talents and clairvoyant or intuitive abilities.

If this conjunction is afflicted by other planets, the individual may become eccentric, unreliable, and uncooperative.

Transiting Uranus Conjunct the Natal Midheaven and Opposition the Natal Nadir

Sudden changes in public reputation and status, often in the form of public notice and recognition, characterize this transit. Some individuals adopt progressive and even radical political viewpoints.

The individual is likely to change professions or jobs in a drastic way during this transit. New employment opportunities may come through friends, groups, or organizations, or these may become involved in the individual's professional work in some way. There can be professional involvement with large-scale corporate enterprises or government agencies. Professional activities are often related to the scientific, humanitarian, astrological, or occult fields. The individual develops an interest in using new methods and scientific technology in business and professional affairs.

Transiting Uranus Conjunct the Natal Descendant and Opposition the Natal Ascendant

New levels of awareness in close personal relationships and relationships with unusual and talented people characterize this transit.

The individual may gain important intuitive insights into the psychology of others. This is a favorable time for cooperating with others to achieve unusual goals and objectives.

The individual and those with whom he or she is relating are likely to need and demand freedom in their relationships. There is an aversion to jealousy and possessiveness during this transit. It often coincides with the breakup of old partnerships and friendships and the formation of new ones. If this transiting conjunction is afflicted by other planets, the individual may enter into a sudden, unstable marriage or romantic infatuation, or a business partnership of dubious value.

Transiting Uranus Conjunct the Natal Nadir and Opposition the Natal Midheaven

The desire for freedom in one's home life characterizes this transit.

Family members may suddenly undergo changes of attitude or life style. If this transiting conjunction receives stress aspects from other planets, the individual's home and physical environment can be disrupted by conditions beyond his or her personal control.

This transit can coincide with separation from one's family, or a move or change of residence. Some individuals rebel against their families under this transit.

Often, the individual's friends or group associates become like family members, and much activity involving them is likely to take place in the home. This activity frequently involves scientific, parapsychological, humanitarian, business, group, or organizational affairs. The individual tends to accumulate and use electronic gadgets in the home.

Some individuals develop an interest in the scientific aspects of ecology and the use of natural resources. This can include an interest in geology and the recycling of waste products.

Transit Uranus Sextiles

Transiting Uranus Sextile the Natal Sun

See "Transiting Sun Sextile Natal Uranus."

Transiting Uranus Sextile the Natal Moon

See "Transiting Moon Sextile Natal Uranus."

Transiting Uranus Sextile Natal Mercury

See "Transiting Mercury Sextile Natal Uranus."

Transiting Uranus Sextile Natal Venus

See "Transiting Venus Sextile Natal Uranus."

Transiting Uranus Sextile Natal Mars

See "Transiting Mars Sextile Natal Uranus."

Transiting Uranus Sextile Natal Jupiter

See "Transiting Jupiter Sextile Natal Uranus."

Transiting Uranus Sextile Natal Saturn

See "Transiting Saturn Sextile Natal Uranus."

Transiting Uranus Sextile Natal Uranus

Stimulating new ideas and exciting new information and communications characterize this transit.

This is an excellent transit for creative and original mental expression. Intuitively inspired ideas can help the individual to realize his or her goals and objectives. Some individuals develop an intellectual interest in humanitarian, scientific, and occult subjects.

The interesting and exciting activities associated with this transit may involve brothers, sisters, neighbors, and friends. Often, there is an element of the unusual in the friends and organizations the individual is involved with during this period.

Transiting Uranus Sextile Natal Neptune

Stimulation of the intuitive faculties and insights into the workings and resources of the subconscious mind characterize this transit.

Latent intuitive, clairvoyant faculties can be stimulated at this time, and the individual often develops an interest in mysticism, astrology, and parapsychology. Opportunities will arise for inner, spiritual growth and development.

This is a favorable transit for work requiring creative imagination and artistic ability. The individual usually puts new ideas to use in his or her business affairs. There is also the possibility of receiving gifts or an inheritance under this transit.

Transiting Neptune sextile natal Uranus has the same significance as transiting Uranus sextile natal Neptune. Both transits last, off and on, for a year or longer and indicate a sustained period of opportunity for developing spiritual and psychological understanding.

Transiting Uranus Sextile Natal Pluto

The individual's self-reliance, resourcefulness, and intuitive inspiration in solving problems are all stimulated during this transit.

The new understanding of life which this transit brings about can result in important, constructive changes in the individual's goals and objectives. The individual gains an increased awareness of how to use his or her potential dynamically and constructively. This often comes about through sudden, intuitive insights. The individual may also gain a greater understanding of profound scientific and occult laws. This is an excellent transit for those involved in scientific research, engineering, advanced technology, or parapsychology. The changes in the individual's life usually result in participation in new group and organizational activities.

Many individuals develop an interest in improving and regenerating existing conditions in social institutions.

This is a favorable period for handling joint finances, corporate money, taxes, insurance, alimony, and goods of the dead. The incorporation of modern technology in business affairs can benefit the individual.

Transiting Pluto sextile natal Uranus has the same significance as transiting Uranus sextile natal Pluto. Both transits last, off and on, for a year or longer and indicate a sustained period of opportunity for the realization of personal goals and objectives through insight and resourcefulness.

Transiting Uranus Sextile the Natal North Node and Trine the Natal South Node

An awareness of how to make use of currently popular cultural values in an original and constructive way characterizes this transit. The individual can benefit through intelligent experimentation with new life styles.

Some individuals have a transforming influence upon the cultural values of the world in which they move. In any event, people with this transit are able to discriminate intelligently regarding currently popular cultural attitudes and values.

Transiting North Node sextile natal Uranus and transiting South Node trine natal Uranus has the same significance as transiting Uranus sextile the natal North Node and trine the natal South Node; however, it is of shorter duration.

Transiting Uranus Sextile the Natal South Node and
Trine the Natal North Node

This transit has basically the same significance as transiting Uranus sextile the natal North Node and trine the natal South Node; however, there is a more critical evaluation of traditional cultural values and greater ease in experimentation with new life styles.

Transiting South Node sextile natal Uranus and transiting North Node trine natal Uranus has the same significance as transiting Uranus sextile the natal South Node and trine the natal North Node; however, it is of shorter duration.

Transiting Uranus Sextile the Natal Ascendant and
Trine the Natal Descendant

Greater freedom both in personal self-expression and in relationships characterizes this transit.

The stimulation of the intuitive faculties can develop new awarenesses in the individual. Usually, there is a greater understanding of others. The possibility of relationships with unique, interesting people is present. New friendships and group associations and unexpected partnerships or marriage opportunities can arise at this time.

Business partnerships or activities involving others tend to relate to electronics, advanced technology, or parapsychological interests.

Transiting Uranus Sextile the Natal Midheaven and
Trine the Natal Nadir

Intuitive guidance and unusual opportunities in business, professional, and domestic affairs characterize this transit.

This is a favorable period for the use of technological innovations in one's professional and domestic activities. It is a good time to change one's residence or to make improvements in the home.

Exciting and enjoyable activity in the home may involve friends, groups, and organizations. The individual can become influential in or benefit through professional groups and organizations.

Transiting Uranus Sextile the Natal Descendant and Trine the Natal Ascendant

This transit has basically the same significance as transiting Uranus sextile the natal Ascendant and trine the natal Descendant; however, there is a greater ease in creative original self-expression and a more intellectual approach to communication and understanding in one's relationships.

Transiting Uranus Sextile the Natal Nadir and Trine the Natal Midheaven

This transit has basically the same significance as transiting Uranus sextile the natal Midheaven and trine the natal Nadir; however, there is a greater ease in original professional activities and a more intellectual approach to communication and understanding in family and domestic affairs.

Transit Uranus Squares

Transiting Uranus Square the Natal Sun

See "Transiting Sun Square Natal Uranus."

Transiting Uranus Square the Natal Moon

See "Transiting Moon Square Natal Uranus."

Transiting Uranus Square Natal Mercury

See "Transiting Mercury Square Natal Uranus."

Transiting Uranus Square Natal Venus

See "Transiting Venus Square Natal Uranus."

Transiting Uranus Square Natal Mars

See "Transiting Mars Square Natal Uranus."

Transiting Uranus Square Natal Jupiter

See "Transiting Jupiter Square Natal Uranus."

Transiting Uranus Square Natal Saturn

See "Transiting Saturn Square Natal Uranus."

Transiting Uranus Square Natal Uranus

The desire to be independent of external authority characterizes this transit. The individual is likely to break away from family ties, professional responsibilities, friendships, and group affiliations. In the process of doing so, untidy, unfinished business is often left behind, which can adversely affect both the individual and others for some time to come.

Some individuals are forced to adjust to unfamiliar new circumstances and challenges which make them feel insecure and ill-at-ease. Usually, the individual is faced with the necessity of adjusting to changing social standards and values, and finding his or her own purpose and meaning in life.

This transit occurs at the approximate ages of twenty-one and sixty-three; during these periods, the individual is forced to assume a new role and position in life.

Transiting Uranus Square Natal Neptune

Confusing psychic impressions and nonproductive fantasies characterize this transit. The individual feels a desire to escape from normal life routines and responsibilities.

Psychological and emotional confusion makes this a poor time to engage in psychic experimentation, such as seances and communication with the discarnate.

This transit can bring about the surfacing of unconscious forces and desires. In extreme cases, psychological hallucinations and delusions occur. The individual is likely to lack a sense of direction and be confused about his or her goals and objectives. Excessive use of drugs and alcohol should be avoided, as their use can aggravate the above problems.

Under this transit some individuals delude themselves about past lives as famous or important people. They also tend to become involved with groups or cults of dubious value, and attract friendships or get involved in groups or organizations that are impractical or psychologically confused or deluded. Some individuals seek out such company as a means of escaping the untidy affairs of their own lives. The individual's friends may deliberately or unknowingly be a liability, drawing the individual into impractical or nonproductive activities.

The individual frequently lacks organization in handling financial affairs. Deception can occur in joint finances, corporate business, and matters related to insurance, taxes, alimony, and goods of the dead.

The individual's family and domestic affairs are often psychologically confused or disrupted in some way. Disruption in the individual's life can also come about through large-scale political, economic, and cultural forces beyond his or her personal control.

Transiting Neptune square natal Uranus has the same significance as transiting Uranus square natal Neptune. Both transits last, off and on, for a year or longer, marking a sustained period of psychological confusion and susceptibility to negative psychic influences.

Transiting Uranus Square Natal Pluto

Revolutionary sentiments and drastic alteration in or disruption of one's basic goals and objectives characterize this transit.

This is not a favorable time to initiate changes; however, if adjustments must be made, the individual should recognize that these changes will be valuable in the future. The individual's life may be changed by large-scale forces beyond his or her control. The people to whom this occurs must learn to adjust gracefully to unavoidable changes and make the most of the opportunities afforded by the new set of circumstances. Some individuals have to deal with perilous or dangerous circumstances, or find themselves subject to disturbing psychic or occult influences. This is not a favorable period for psychic or occult experimentation.

Old friendships and group and organizational ties may be severed at this time. People who are meaningful to the individual may die suddenly or unexpectedly.

Unexpected financial loss can come about through joint finances, corporate business, insurance, or goods of the dead. Danger can arise through corporate interests or power structures.

Transiting Pluto square natal Uranus has the same significance as transiting Uranus square natal Pluto. Both transits last, off and on, for a year or longer, marking a sustained period of change and adjustment.

Transiting Uranus Square the Natal North Node and Square the Natal South Node

Rebellion against the prevailing norms and attitudes characterizes this transit. The individual is likely to become a social nonconformist, and be looked upon as inconsistent or inconsiderate by his or her peers.

Transiting North and South Nodes square natal Uranus has the same significance as transiting Uranus square the natal North Node and square the natal South Node; however, it is of shorter duration.

Transiting Uranus Square the Natal South Node and Square the Natal North Node

See "Transiting Uranus Square the Natal North Node and Square the Natal South Node."

Transiting Uranus Square the Natal Ascendant and Square the Natal Descendant

A desire for personal freedom, regardless of consequences, characterizes this transit. The individual can become bored with normal life routines and seek change in a disruptive and impractical way. This can have a disruptive effect on partnerships and friendships. The individual may become involved with unreliable or eccentric friends and group associates. Unwise speculation or occult experimentation is especially dangerous at this time.

Transiting Uranus Square the Natal Midheaven and Square the Natal Nadir

Rebellion against authority and revolutionary business and political attitudes characterize this transit.

Difficult or unpredictable professional, business, or domestic situations can arise at this time. The individual's friends may become an annoyance to his or her family or professional associates. Some individuals are forced to change jobs or places of residence under difficult and unexpected circumstances.

Unexpected factors often cause conflict between domestic and professional responsibilities. One's professional affairs are sometimes disrupted by economic, political, or ecological forces beyond one's personal control.

Transiting Uranus Square the Natal Descendant and Square the Natal Ascendant

See "Transiting Uranus Square the Natal Ascendant and Square the Natal Descendant."

Transiting Uranus Square the Natal Nadir and Square the Natal Midheaven

See "Transiting Uranus Square the Natal Midheaven and Square the Natal Nadir."

Transit Uranus Trines

Transiting Uranus Trine the Natal Sun

See "Transiting Sun Trine Natal Uranus."

Transiting Uranus Trine the Natal Moon

See "Transiting Moon Trine Natal Uranus."

Transiting Uranus Trine Natal Mercury

See "Transiting Mercury Trine Natal Uranus."

Transiting Uranus Trine Natal Venus

See "Transiting Venus Trine Natal Uranus."

Transiting Uranus Trine Natal Mars

See "Transiting Mars Trine Natal Uranus."

Transiting Uranus Trine Natal Jupiter

See "Transiting Jupiter Trine Natal Uranus."

Transiting Uranus Trine Natal Saturn

See "Transiting Saturn Trine Natal Uranus."

Transiting Uranus Trine Natal Uranus

Original and creative modes of self-expression characterize this transit. The individual's intuitive, clairvoyant faculties can be stimulated by interesting new experiences, interests, and friendships. Many individuals establish new, exciting friendships, group associations, or organizational associations during this period.

This is a favorable transit for all unique and original scientific, technological, humanitarian, occult, and astrological pursuits. New methods or modern use of technology enable the individual to make progress in the business world.

Benefits may come through cooperative business enterprises, joint finances, tax rebates, grants, government funding, insurance, or inheritance.

Transiting Uranus Trine Natal Neptune

The intuitive, imaginative faculties are stimulated during this transit. In some cases, this leads to mystical revelations or clairvoyant experiences.

This is a good period for meditation and the pursuit of spiritual practices. The individual is likely to develop an interest in reincarnation or life after death, mental telepathy, parapsychology, or metaphysics. Many individuals experience intuitive artistic inspiration, precognition of coming events, and prophetic insights into future cultural evolution. Insights can be gained into one's own unconscious mind and memories of previous incarnations can sometimes be recovered. This is an excellent transit for the study and practice of astrology.

The individual may also gain insights into advanced scientific principles. Participation in groups and organizations of a scientific, religious, educational, humanitarian, or occult nature can benefit the individual. There is often an interest in uplifting and regenerating existing social conditions. This is a favorable transit for teaching, lecturing, travel, and the pursuit of higher education.

The reappearance of past friends and acquaintances is possible at this time. Activities pertaining to friends, groups, and organizations often take place in the home.

Financial benefits may be gained through cooperative business enterprises, insurance, inheritance, or joint finances.

Transiting Neptune trine natal Uranus has the same significance as transiting Uranus trine natal Neptune. Both transits last, off and on, for a year or longer and both indicate a sustained period of increased awareness of superphysical realities.

Transiting Uranus Trine Natal Pluto

The exercise of the will to bring about a higher level of awareness and creative self-expression characterizes this transit.

The individual may have startling intuitive revelations and mystical experiences which bring about important changes in his or her personal goals and objectives. Many individuals are motivated to terminate old conditions in their lives in order to bring about a more meaningful and exciting new way of life.

This transit stimulates one's resourceful, enterprising qualities. More specifically, it stimulates the will to bring about needed changes and improvements in existing methods and conditions in oneself and the environment.

Irreversible changes can take place in the individual's awareness which lead to better understanding of spiritual laws that govern humanity's life on earth. The individual gains a more satisfactory understanding of death and life after death. This is an excellent transit for involvement in astrology and other occult pursuits.

An interest in reforming and regenerating existing cultural, economic, political, and educational institutions often develops, as well as interest in religion, philosophy, travel, and foreign cultures.

Benefit may come through corporate business, insurance, tax rebates, government funding, or inheritance.

Transiting Pluto trine natal Uranus has the same significance as transiting Uranus trine natal Pluto. Both transits last, off and on, for a year or more and indicate a sustained period of increased awareness of the large-scale changes that come about in this world and that affect the individual existence of each human being.

Transiting Uranus Trine the Natal North Node and
Sextile the Natal South Node

See "Transiting Uranus Sextile the Natal South Node and Trine the Natal North Node."

Transiting Uranus Trine the Natal South Node and Sextile the Natal North Node

See "Transiting Uranus Sextile the Natal North Node and Trine the Natal South Node."

Transiting Uranus Trine the Natal Ascendant and Sextile the Natal Descendant

See "Transiting Uranus Sextile the Natal Descendant and Trine the Natal Ascendant."

Transiting Uranus Trine the Natal Midheaven and Sextile the Natal Nadir

See "Transiting Uranus Sextile the Natal Nadir and Trine the Natal Midheaven."

Transiting Uranus Trine the Natal Descendant and Sextile the Natal Ascendant

See "Transiting Uranus Sextile the Natal Ascendant and Trine the Natal Descendant."

Transiting Uranus Trine the Natal Nadir and Sextile the Natal Midheaven

See "Transiting Uranus Sextile the Natal Midheaven and Trine the Natal Nadir."

Transit Uranus Oppositions

Transiting Uranus Opposition the Natal Sun

See "Transiting Sun Opposition Natal Uranus."

Transiting Uranus Opposition the Natal Moon

See "Transiting Moon Opposition Natal Uranus."

Transiting Uranus Opposition Natal Mercury

See "Transiting Mercury Opposition Natal Uranus."

Transiting Uranus Opposition Natal Venus

See "Transiting Venus Opposition Natal Uranus."

Transiting Uranus Opposition Natal Mars

See "Transiting Mars Opposition Natal Uranus."

Transiting Uranus Opposition Natal Jupiter

See "Transiting Jupiter Opposition Natal Uranus."

Transiting Uranus Opposition Natal Saturn

See "Transiting Saturn Opposition Natal Uranus."

Transiting Uranus Opposition Natal Uranus

Erratic behavior in relationships characterizes this transit. A desire for freedom at all costs can create problems for both the individual and others. Friendships and group affiliations are often disrupted during this transit. Unexpected problems and difficulties can arise in the pursuit of one's personal goals and objectives.

This transit usually occurs when the individual is around forty-two years of age. It coincides with a period of dissatisfaction with normal life routines (sometimes referred to as the "dangerous forties"), a feeling that one has "missed out on" some of the pleasures and freedoms of life, which must now be experienced before it is too late. This dissatisfaction often results in sexual experimentation or activities that are inappropriate by traditional cultural standards.

This can be a period of instability in business and financial affairs. Difficulties may arise involving taxes, insurance, inheritance, alimony, corporate money, joint finances, and goods of the dead. Actions taken at this time can have adverse effects that last much longer than the momentary satisfaction gained. If the individual considers this, serious mistakes can be avoided.

Transiting Uranus Opposition Natal Neptune

Subconsciously motivated erratic behavior characterizes this transit. The individual is subject to unpleasant dreams and psychic experiences. There is often confusion about one's personal goals and objectives during this time. Their fulfillment can be frustrated by an unwillingness to co-operate on the part of the individual or his or her friends.

The individual needs to develop a broader and more universal outlook on life, and a willingness to accept change.

Unwise psychic practices and misuse of drugs and alcohol should be especially avoided at this time. Peculiar difficulties or frauds may arise around matters related to taxes, insurance, corporate money, or goods of the dead.

The personal life of the individual can be disrupted and confused by large-scale economic, political, cultural, or natural forces beyond his or her control. Some individuals are suddenly thrust into strange circumstances where they must deal with unfamiliar people and conditions. There is danger from or toward friends, groups, or organizations. The individual's associates may turn out to be psychologically confused or disoriented. In extreme cases, friends turn out to be secret enemies, who, whether intentionally or unintentionally, mislead the individual.

Transiting Neptune opposition natal Uranus has the same significance as transiting Uranus opposition natal Neptune. Both transits last, off and on, for a year or longer and indicate a sustained period of psychological confusion and difficulty.

Transiting Uranus Opposition Natal Pluto

Elimination of the outworn and the useless characterizes this transit. The existing conditions of the individual's life are subject to drastic change.

Many individuals are forced to drastically revise their goals and objectives. This transit can force a new awareness of the need for change. If the individual can recognize the constructive potential in entering into new and unfamiliar conditions, even disruptive experiences will be meaningful.

Some individuals develop revolutionary sentiments, along with a desire to overthrow the existing order. Normal life routines can be disrupted by natural disasters, wars, revolutions, or other political, economic, or cultural upheavals. Under extreme circumstances, there can be danger to the individual's life.

Often, old friendships and group associations are severed and new ones initiated. This transit sometimes coincides with the unexpected death of someone who is important to the individual.

The individual may become involved in organizational, business, or marital power struggles at this time. Power struggles may also involve partnerships or business relationships with friends or organizations.

Unexpected difficulties may arise involving taxes, joint finances, corporate money, alimony, inheritance, insurance, or goods of the dead.

Involvement in psychic experimentation, such as seances or trance mediumship is dangerous under this transit.

Transiting Pluto opposition natal Uranus has the same significance as transiting Uranus opposition natal Pluto. Both transits last, off and on, for a year or longer and indicate a sustained period of disruptive events and psychological tension.

Transiting Uranus Opposition the Natal North Node and Conjunct the Natal South Node

See "Transiting Uranus Conjunct the Natal South Node and Opposition the Natal North Node."

Transiting Uranus Opposition the Natal South Node and Conjunct the Natal North Node

See "Transiting Uranus Conjunct the Natal North Node and Opposition the Natal South Node."

Transiting Uranus Opposition the Natal Ascendant and Conjunct the Natal Descendant

See "Transiting Uranus Conjunct the Natal Descendant and Opposition the Natal Ascendant."

Transiting Uranus Opposition the Natal Midheaven and Conjunct the Natal Nadir

See "Transiting Uranus Conjunct the Natal Nadir and Opposition the Natal Midheaven."

Transiting Uranus Opposition the Natal Descendant and Conjunct the Natal Ascendant

See "Transiting Uranus Conjunct the Natal Ascendant and Opposition the Natal Descendant."

Transiting Uranus Opposition the Natal Nadir and Conjunct the Natal Midheaven

See "Transiting Uranus Conjunct the Natal Midheaven and Opposition the Natal Nadir."

27 Transits of Neptune

Transit Neptune Through the Houses

Transiting Neptune Through the Natal First House

The imaginative, artistic, clairvoyant, and intuitive faculties are stimulated by this transit. One's personal behavior is influenced to an unusual extent by the subconscious mind. The individual tends to act on intuitive guidance and psychic awareness. A personal interest often develops in art, mysticism, religion, psychology, and the workings of the subconscious mind. The individual may also become interested in meditation or other spiritual practices.

This is a favorable period for artistic and musical inspiration.

Greater sympathy and understanding toward others is usually expressed. In some cases, one's personal activities are carried out in secret.

The individual's health will probably be influenced, favorably or unfavorably, by psychological factors during this period. Psychosomatic illnesses, neurotic conditions, self-deception, woolgathering, and escapist tendencies can become dominant if Neptune makes stress aspects to other natal or transiting planets while transiting the natal First House.

Transiting Neptune Through the Natal Second House

Subtle changes regarding money and possessions characterize this transit. Financial dealings are often secret during this period.

Many individuals employ their imaginations in finding ways to make money. They may become involved in business activity related to photography, art, music, entertainment, psychology, or matters related to hospitals or institutions. There is often some kind of involvement with the business affairs of hospitals or of religious or educational institutions.

If Neptune makes stress aspects while transiting the natal Second House, the individual is likely to lack realism, practicality, and discipline in financial affairs. Confidence men and "get-rich-quick" schemes should be especially avoided if Neptune is afflicted. A realistic attitude is needed in all business affairs.

Transiting Neptune Through the Natal Third House

Intuitively inspired ideas and an intellectual interest in mysticism, occult subjects, or psychology characterize this transit. Mysterious circumstances may arise regarding one's brothers, sisters, neighbors, or friends. Secret communications or short trips often take place under this transit. This transit can also bring about telepathic communication.

This is a favorable time for the study of religion, mysticism, art, music, or psychology.

If Neptune makes stress aspects while transiting the natal Third House, one is prone to evasiveness and dishonesty in speech, and one's thinking may become confused and impractical. There is also a tendency to confuse communications and forget appointments.

Transiting Neptune Through the Natal Fourth House

Emotional sensitivity and moodiness and the stimulation of subconscious memories characterize this transit. Important spiritual revelations and mystical experiences may profoundly influence the individual's basic consciousness.

The home usually becomes a place of retreat and seclusion during this period. Many individuals feel strong emotional, psychological, or spiritual ties with family members. Meditation and religious activities often take place in the home. Some individuals take up residence in ashrams or religious institutions of some kind.

If Neptune makes stress aspects to natal or to other transiting planets while transiting the natal Fourth House, psychological problems may arise with family members, and the individual may be burdened with the responsibility of a disabled or psychologically confused family member. There are likely to be problems with leakage of water, gas, or oil in the home.

Transiting Neptune Through the Natal Fifth House

Intuitive inspiration in art and music characterizes this transit. There is also the possibility of an ideal romance. There can be much romantic fantasy, too, during this transit. Artistic expressions of the creative imagination are favored at this time.

If Neptune makes stress aspects while transiting the natal Fifth House, the individual is subject to psychological hangups about sex and romance. There can be loneliness, romantic isolation, and disappointments or deception in love. An afflicted transiting Neptune in the natal Fifth House can also bring about unwanted pregnancy. There is danger of overindulgence in drugs, alcohol, sex, or other forms of dissipation. The psychological problems of children can also be a problem for the individual. Losses can come through gambling, financial speculation, or unwise stock market investments.

Transiting Neptune Through the Natal Sixth House

Intuitive insights into work-related matters characterize this transit.

The individual expresses greater creative imagination in his or her work during this period. This is a favorable time for work related to art, music, entertainment, photography, psychology, spiritual healing, religion, hospitals, institutions, or the occult.

There is an interest in imaginative, artistically pleasing dress and personal adornment.

If Neptune makes stress aspects while transiting the natal Sixth House, psychological problems can interfere with work efficiency. There can be problems with unemployment or unsuitable work or working conditions. The individual may, in some way, find himself or herself in a condition of servitude. The individual is prone to psychosomatic illnesses. There can be glandular problems, difficult-to-diagnose ailments, or extreme sensitivity to drugs, medication, or anaesthesia. Drinking or drug abuse during this transit usually has an adverse effect on one's health and ability to work. If Neptune is afflicted, the individual tends to be slovenly and unkempt and attempts to escape work responsibility.

Transiting Neptune Through the Natal Seventh House

Intuitive insights into the psychology of others characterizes this transit. There is greater telepathy and intuitive empathy in close personal relationships during this period.

It is a favorable transit for sharing aesthetic and spiritual values in close personal relationships. Psychological factors involving the subconscious mind strongly influence marriage and other important relationships, for better or worse. Behavior in one's relationships is often influenced strongly by subconscious memories during this transit. Some individuals are shy in their social relationships, or gullible or impressionable in their responses to other people.

If Neptune makes stress aspects while transiting the natal Seventh House, there is a tendency toward psychological withdrawal from others and danger of deception in marriage or other important relationships.

Transiting Neptune Through the Natal Eighth House

An interest in life after death, reincarnation, and other occult subjects characterizes this transit. It can bring about some profound and revealing intuitive insights and mystical experiences. One's imagination and intuitive guidance are usually applied to joint finances, corporate money, taxes, insurance, alimony, inheritance, and goods of the dead.

If Neptune makes stress aspects while transiting the natal Eighth House, the individual is prone to self-deception regarding business and financial affairs. In some cases, death occurs through mysterious circumstances.

Transiting Neptune Through the Natal Ninth House

An interest in mystical forms of religion and philosophy characterizes this transit. Some individuals gain prophetic insights into future cultural trends. An interest in the mystical or religious lore, practices, and teachings of foreign cultures often develops.

This transit can bring about direct personal intuitive experiences of spiritual realities. The individual may take long journeys in pursuit of spiritual teachings and cultural enrichment.

If Neptune makes stress aspects while transiting the natal Ninth House, there can be involvement in bizarre religious cults and practices, often motivated by a desire to achieve vicarious status through being the disciple of some supposed guru or spiritual master.

Transiting Neptune Through the Natal Tenth House

Intuitive guidance in professional and political affairs characterizes this transit. The individual may become involved in professional intrigues or secrecy in some way.

During this period, a glamorous career and the chance for personal, charismatic public appeal are strong attractions. One can be drawn to a career in art, music, entertainment, acting, photography, psychology, religion, or in a field related to asylums, hospitals, religious retreats, or educational and cultural institutions. Career activities can also be related to occult or mystical fields in some way. In any event, individuals with this transit seek to use intuitive guidance and creative imagination in their professions, and the enhancement of their public reputations. Fame or notoriety may come to them through mysterious circumstances of some kind.

If Neptune makes stress aspects while transiting the natal Tenth House, the individual can have an unrealistic attitude toward professional responsibilities and what is required to be successful. There may be fantasies about fame and fortune, with no practical action to achieve them. The individual is also subject to scandal through the public disclosure of private affairs.

Transiting Neptune Through the Natal Eleventh House

Friendship with intuitive or artistically talented individuals characterizes this transit. The individual may receive spiritual guidance from friends or give such guidance to them. There are sometimes telepathic exchanges with one's friends or intuitive precognitions concerning them during this transit.

The individual tends to use his or her imagination and intuitive guidance to achieve worthwhile humanitarian goals and objectives. An intellectual and humanitarian interest in areas such as parapsychology, mysticism, occultism, meditation, and mystical religious practices often develops. Many individuals join or participate in cults, groups, or organizations related to these things.

Peculiar situations or mysterious circumstances sometimes arise regarding friends, groups, or organizations with which the individual is associated.

If Neptune makes stress aspects to other natal or transiting planets while in the natal Eleventh House, the individual can mislead or be misled by friends, groups, or organizations. Friends or group associates may turn out to be deceptive, neurotic, or psychologically confused. Misplaced loyalty or sympathy often is a contributing factor in a willingness to be deceived on the part of either the individual or his or her friends. The wrong friendships or group and organizational affiliations have an especially undermining influence on the individual during this transit, particularly if such associations lead to excessive drinking or drug abuse.

Transiting Neptune Through the Natal Twelfth House

Introspection, meditation, and tapping the subconscious mind characterize this transit. The individual may become preoccupied with his or her subjective imagination.

It is a favorable period for inner, intuitive guidance and the discovery of hidden talents and assets. The individual is likely to have a strong desire for privacy and seclusion. Interest in psychology and the workings of the subconscious mind often develops.

This transit often increases a person's capacity for compassion and understanding toward those in need, particularly toward those in psychological difficulty. This sometimes leads to involvement with hospitals, prisons, asylums, religious retreats, monasteries, and ashrams.

Many individuals develop an interest in unfolding intuitive and clairvoyant faculties through meditation and other spiritual practices. This transit may bring about a psychic awareness of past lives.

If Neptune makes stress aspects to other planets while transiting the natal Twelfth House, various types of nonrational, subconscious distortions often occur. The individual may try to evade practical responsibility through woolgathering, fantasy, alcohol, drugs, or various types of irrational, neurotic behavior. One can discover that one is one's own worst enemy during this period. If Neptune is seriously afflicted while transiting the natal Twelfth House, the individual is subject to institutionalization or hospitalization.

Transit Neptune Conjunctions

Transiting Neptune Conjunct the Natal Sun

See "Transiting Sun Conjunct Natal Neptune."

Transiting Neptune Conjunct the Natal Moon

See "Transiting Moon Conjunct Natal Neptune."

Transiting Neptune Conjunct Natal Mercury

See "Transiting Mercury Conjunct Natal Neptune."

Transiting Neptune Conjunct Natal Venus

See "Transiting Venus Conjunct Natal Neptune."

Transiting Neptune Conjunct Natal Mars

See "Transiting Mars Conjunct Natal Neptune."

Transiting Neptune Conjunct Natal Jupiter

See "Transiting Jupiter Conjunct Natal Neptune."

Transiting Neptune Conjunct Natal Saturn

See "Transiting Saturn Conjunct Natal Neptune."

Transiting Neptune Conjunct Natal Uranus

See "Transiting Uranus Conjunct Natal Neptune."

Transiting Neptune Conjunct Natal Neptune

This transit does not occur in a normal life span, except during infancy under Neptune's retrograde and direct motion. In such cases, forces beyond the personal control of the baby or the baby's family can endanger or alter his or her future course.

In political charts, it indicates the karmic forces affecting the country or municipality.

Transiting Neptune Conjunct Natal Pluto

Exploration of the subconscious mind and, in some cases, seemingly supernatural or miraculous occurrences characterize this transit.

It can stimulate latent occult and intuitive abilities, and bring about intuitive, clairvoyant, or mystical experiences that alter the individual's level of awareness. Some individuals act as channels for spiritual inspiration and wisdom during this transit. In extreme cases, the individual learns about, witnesses, or is subject to out-of-the-body experiences, telepathy, precognition, or memory of past lives. Other out-of-the-ordinary experiences can occur, such as seeing UFO's.

This transit brings a need to regenerate the unconscious mind and let go of old, outworn emotional attitudes and hangups by examining one's personal thoughts and consciously tracing them to their origin. Important changes in the individual's life and private affairs can be brought about by large-scale economic, political, ecological, or cultural forces. Peculiar and mysterious circumstances can affect joint finances, corporate business, insurance, taxes, inheritance, and alimony.

In extreme cases, the individual or someone of consequence to him or her can die in a hospital or under mysterious circumstances.

Transiting Pluto conjunct natal Neptune has the same significance as transiting Neptune conjunct natal Pluto. Both transits last, off and on, for a year or longer and both indicate a sustained period of intensified spiritual awareness.

Transiting Neptune Conjunct the Natal North Node and Opposition the Natal South Node

An intuitive awareness of and prophetic insight into cultural trends and popular beliefs characterize this transit. Often, there is an intuitive awareness of the social attitudes of others. There is a strong possibility that the individual will psychologically withdraw from currently popular social fads.

Transiting North Node conjunct natal Neptune and transiting South Node opposition natal Neptune has the same significance as transiting Neptune conjunct the natal North Node and opposition the natal South Node; however, it is of shorter duration.

Transiting Neptune Conjunct the Natal South Node and Opposition the Natal North Node

During this transit, the individual's subconscious attitudes tend to be at variance with traditional standards and beliefs. Many individuals feel a lack of understanding from those with whom they have daily contact. Their social purpose is not defined; consequently, they feel cut off and are likely to withdraw from social involvement.

Transiting South Node conjunct natal Neptune and transiting North Node opposition natal Neptune has the same significance as transiting Neptune conjunct the natal South Node and opposition the natal North Node; however, it lasts for a shorter period of time.

Transiting Neptune Conjunct the Natal Ascendant and Opposition the Natal Descendant

Stimulation of intuitive faculties and an active engagement in mystical or occult activities characterize this transit. Subtle changes tend to occur in one's self-awareness and self-image. There is likely to be increased emotional sensitivity and greater awareness of the subconscious forces operating within one. The emotional state has a direct influence on health and appearance during this period.

Personal activities tend to go on in secret or behind the scenes. There is often personal involvement with hospitals, asylums, or religious, psychiatric, or charitable institutions.

This is a favorable transit for self-expression through art and music of all kinds.

This period can bring the individual the consequences of past actions, be they good or ill.

If the transiting conjunction of Neptune to the Ascendant receives stress aspects from other planets, the individual can suffer from subtle forms of self-undoing, such as self-destructive habits or a tendency toward personal isolation, confusion, woolgathering, or daydreaming.

Transiting Neptune Conjunct the Natal Midheaven and Opposition the Natal Nadir

Professional secrecy and intrigues characterize this transit. Psychological conflicts tend to arise between professional and domestic responsibilities.

Professional activities related to art, music, entertainment, photography, cinematography, and occult and mystical pursuits are favored at this time.

Some individuals develop an appeal to the masses or public charisma during this transit.

Transiting Neptune Conjunct the Natal Descendant and Opposition the Natal Ascendant

An intuitive awareness of the moods and feelings of others characterizes this transit. The individual is interested in understanding the psychology and subconscious motivations of others. There can be telepathic rapport in close personal relationships. However, if this conjunction of Neptune to the Descendant receives stress aspects from other planets, there is danger of deception in one's marriage or partnerships. Subconscious emotional problems might also interfere with relationships.

There is often an interest during this period in public relations concerned with art, music, and entertainment.

Transiting Neptune Conjunct the Natal Nadir and Opposition the Natal Midheaven

During this transit, subconscious memories are stirred, and the individual feels an intuitive rapport with family members. Some people experience a spiritual communication with the earth itself, which may be expressed as an interest in ecology, geology, or archaeology. This is an excellent transit for dowsing. However, problems can arise with gas, oil, or water leakage or seepage in the home.

This is a favorable transit for meditation and religious studies in the home. If this conjunction receives stress aspects from other planets, psychological problems with family members may arise.

Transit Neptune Sextiles

Transiting Neptune Sextile the Natal Sun

See "Transiting Sun Sextile Natal Neptune."

Transiting Neptune Sextile the Natal Moon

See "Transiting Moon Sextile Natal Neptune."

Transiting Neptune Sextile Natal Mercury

See "Transiting Mercury Sextile Natal Neptune."

Transiting Neptune Sextile Natal Venus

See "Transiting Venus Sextile Natal Neptune."

Transiting Neptune Sextile Natal Mars

See "Transiting Mars Sextile Natal Neptune."

Transiting Neptune Sextile Natal Jupiter

See "Transiting Jupiter Sextile Natal Neptune."

Transiting Neptune Sextile Natal Saturn

See "Transiting Saturn Sextile Natal Neptune."

Transiting Neptune Sextile Natal Uranus

See "Transiting Uranus Sextile Natal Neptune."

Transiting Neptune Sextile Natal Neptune

The intuitive and clairvoyant faculties are stimulated during this transit, as is the intuitive imagination. Insights can be gained into one's subconscious mind. This is a favorable transit for emotional and telepathic rapport with others. The individual's creative imagination can also be activated—in such fields as art, music, and literature. This is a good period for dealing with educational, religious, medical, and psychological institutions.

Transiting Neptune Sextile Natal Pluto

Regeneration of the subconscious mind and its motivations characterizes this transit. Opportunities to both develop and study latent intuitive and clairvoyant faculties can also arise.

This is an excellent period for scientific, occult, meditative, or philosophic pursuits. The individual can benefit in some manner from advancements in science, art, or technology. Profound insight can be gained into scientific and occult principles, and an interest in paranormal phenomena, parapsychology, and past lives may develop.

Insights can also be gained into ways of using old or discarded materials and information. There can be interesting and enlightening exchanges of ideas and communications with one's friends.

Transiting Pluto sextile natal Neptune has the same significance as transiting Neptune sextile natal Pluto. Both transits last, off and on, for a year or longer, and both indicate a sustained period of intellectual enlightenment concerning the superphysical forces of nature.

Transiting Neptune Sextile the Natal North Node and Trine the Natal South Node

Intuitive awareness of cultural trends and forces characterizes this transit. The intuitive ability to act in harmony with current social trends and attitudes is enhanced. The transit favors public relations dealing with art, music, and entertainment.

Transiting North Node sextile natal Neptune and transiting South Node trine natal Neptune has the same significance as transiting Neptune sextile the natal North Node and trine the natal South Node; however, it is of shorter duration.

Transiting Neptune Sextile the Natal South Node and Trine the Natal North Node

This has basically the same significance as transiting Neptune sextile the natal North Node and trine the natal South Node. Here, however, there is a greater intellectual awareness of traditional cultural values and a greater ease of individual expression with regard to currently popular trends and fads.

Transiting South Node sextile natal Neptune and transiting North Node trine natal Neptune has the same significance as transiting Neptune sextile the natal South Node and trine the natal North Node; however, it is of shorter duration.

Transiting Neptune Sextile the Natal Ascendant and Trine the Natal Descendant

Intuitive awareness in self-expression and in the handling of relationships characterizes this transit. In some close relationships, a telepathic rapport develops. There is greater kindness and understanding in close relationships of all kinds during this transit. Mystical and psychological interests are often shared. Benefits may come through past associations, and past acquaintances may be renewed.

The individual often develops an interest in psychology, religion, mysticism, and foreign cultures. This is a favorable transit for artists, musicians, and entertainers.

Transiting Neptune Sextile the Natal Midheaven and Trine the Natal Nadir

Intuitive guidance in one's professional and domestic affairs characterizes this transit. The individual develops an aura of professional mystique, along with greater serenity. This is a favorable period for religious and mystical activity in the home.

The individual can benefit through professional public relations or professional activity related to art, music, photography, and the occult.

Transiting Neptune Sextile the Natal Descendant and Trine the Natal Ascendant

This transit has basically the same significance as transiting Neptune sextile the natal Ascendant and trine the natal Descendant; however, it confers greater ease in one's intuitive, emotional, and artistic self-expression. Also, there is a subtle awareness and communication in relationships, which makes for greater psychological understanding.

Transiting Neptune Sextile the Natal Nadir and Trine the Natal Midheaven

This transit has basically the same significance as transiting Neptune sextile the natal Midheaven and trine the natal Nadir; however, there is a greater intuitive awareness of how to promote one's professional affairs, and greater awareness and telepathic communication in family and domestic affairs.

Transit Neptune Squares

Transiting Neptune Square the Natal Sun

See "Transiting Sun Square Natal Neptune."

Transiting Neptune Square the Natal Moon

See "Transiting Moon Square Natal Neptune."

Transiting Neptune Square Natal Mercury

See "Transiting Mercury Square Natal Neptune."

Transiting Neptune Square Natal Venus

See "Transiting Venus Square Natal Neptune."

Transiting Neptune Square Natal Mars

See "Transiting Mars Square Natal Neptune."

Transiting Neptune Square Natal Jupiter

See "Transiting Jupiter Square Natal Neptune."

Transiting Neptune Square Natal Saturn

See "Transiting Saturn Square Natal Neptune."

Transiting Neptune Square Natal Uranus

See "Transiting Uranus Square Natal Neptune."

Transiting Neptune Square Natal Neptune

Subconscious emotional problems and disturbing psychic experiences characterize this transit.

During this period, the individual often attempts to withdraw psychologically from others and seek isolation. Domestic and professional responsibilities are sometimes avoided. Emotional objectivity tends to be lacking because of the emotional confusion which the individual often undergoes during this period.

The stimulation of unpleasant subconscious memories can be a source of emotional difficulties. Psychic stress can have an undermining influence on the individual's health and lead to a hard-to-diagnose illness. In extreme cases, the individual is subject to hallucinations and undesirable astral influences, such as voices or unpleasant visions.

Overindulgence in food, drugs, and alcohol should be avoided during this period.

If other stress aspects compound this transiting square, the individual may be confined or institutionalized in some way. Some people develop confused religious notions, which are actually a means of psychological escape.

Difficulties may arise while traveling or dealing with foreign countries or foreigners.

Transiting Neptune Square Natal Pluto

Psychological coercion, either by or directed at the individual, characterizes this transit. There is a need to understand, work with, and regenerate the subconscious by observing one's personal thoughts and reactions, and examining their origins.

There can be an eruption of subconscious forces, and the temptation to use psychic abilities for selfish purposes. The individual can bring about his or her own undoing through subconscious, uncontrolled selfish impulses. The individual can be subject to undesirable influences and to hallucinations.

Unwise use of drugs and alcohol and unwise psychic practices, such as psychological manipulation either of or by others, are especially dangerous during this transit.

Difficult spiritual problems or conflicts over religious beliefs may arise.

There is danger of deception in matters of joint finances, corporate money, insurance, taxes, or alimony.

The individual tends to be concerned about large-scale problems that affect all of humanity. Personal affairs can be disrupted during this transit by economic, political, cultural, and ecological changes beyond one's personal control. The death of someone of consequence to the individual may occur.

Transiting Pluto square natal Neptune has the same significance as transiting Neptune square natal Pluto. Both transits last, off and on, for a year or longer and indicate a sustained period of psychological stress and involvement in serious cultural problems.

Transiting Neptune Square the Natal North Node and
Square the Natal South Node

Confusion concerning cultural trends and popular beliefs characterizes this transit. The individual can bring about his or her own undoing through blind adherence to useless, destructive cultural fads and popular beliefs. On the other hand, there can be psychological withdrawal from surrounding cultural activities and subconscious rebellion against prevailing cultural norms and popular beliefs.

Social drinking presents dangers to the individual during this transit, as do drug-taking and other self-destructive habits.

Transiting North and South Nodes square natal Neptune has the same significance as transiting Neptune square the natal North Node and square the natal South Node; however, it is of shorter duration.

Transiting Neptune Square the Natal South Node and Square the Natal North Node

See "Transiting Neptune Square the Natal North Node and Square the Natal South Node."

Transiting Neptune Square the Natal Ascendant and Square the Natal Descendant

Confusion both in one's self-expression and in relating to others characterizes this transit.

There is often a psychological withdrawal from others or an unrealistic appraisal of one's personal desirability. One's personal behavior is likely to be misdirected because of distortions in the subconscious mind and an unrealistic outlook on life. The individual is subject to deception or self-deception in marriage or other close personal relationships.

There can be preoccupation with a private fantasy world. The individual daydreams, woolgathers, or is subjected to disturbing psychic experiences.

Transiting Neptune Square the Natal Midheaven and Square the Natal Nadir

Deception or self-deception in professional or domestic affairs characterizes this transit. Psychological conflicts can arise between professional and domestic responsibilities. Often, the profession is used as an excuse to evade family responsibilities, or vice versa.

Subconscious psychological experiences based on childhood and family upbringing can be aggravated at this time. This stimulation of unpleasant subconscious memories can interfere with both professional performance and objectivity in family affairs. Psychological problems involving family members often arise. Household problems during this transit are often related to gas, oil, or water leakage or seepage.

The individual may be subjected to unfavorable publicity, often in the form of public exposure of private wrongdoing, and to confusion and treachery in political and professional affairs. This is not a favorable time for professional activities related to art, music, or psychic abilities.

Transiting Neptune Square the Natal Descendant and Square the Natal Ascendant

See "Transiting Neptune Square the Natal Ascendant and Square the Natal Descendant."

Transiting Neptune Square the Natal Nadir and Square the Natal Midheaven

See "Transiting Neptune Square the Natal Midheaven and Square the Natal Nadir."

Transit Neptune Trines

Transiting Neptune Trine the Natal Sun

See "Transiting Sun Trine Natal Neptune."

Transiting Neptune Trine the Natal Moon

See "Transiting Moon Trine Natal Neptune."

Transiting Neptune Trine Natal Mercury

See "Transiting Mercury Trine Natal Neptune."

Transiting Neptune Trine Natal Venus

See "Transiting Venus Trine Natal Neptune."

Transiting Neptune Trine Natal Mars

See "Transiting Mars Trine Natal Neptune."

Transiting Neptune Trine Natal Jupiter

See "Transiting Jupiter Trine Natal Neptune."

Transiting Neptune Trine Natal Saturn

See "Transiting Saturn Trine Natal Neptune."

Transiting Neptune Trine Natal Uranus

See "Transiting Uranus Trine Natal Neptune."

Transiting Neptune Trine Natal Neptune

Intuitive and creative artistic inspiration characterizes this transit. It is a favorable period for meditation and constructive spiritual practices and for dealings with hospitals and religious, cultural, educational, and psychiatric institutions.

Latent intuitive and clairvoyant faculties can be brought out by this transit, and the individual can gain a greater understanding of the long-range evolutionary processes of life.

Transiting Neptune Trine Natal Pluto

The individual can benefit personally through cultural and scientific advances during this transit. Often, there is an interest in regenerating existing social, cultural, and economic conditions. Individuals with this transit gain inspiration and intuitive guidance in whatever matter is of concern to them. Some individuals gain insights into scientific and spiritual laws and a greater understanding of the workings of the subconscious mind. An interest in parapsychology or the physics of paranormal phenomena sometimes develops. This is a favorable period for investigating previous incarnations, life after death, and spirit communication. It is also a good time to travel in pursuit of knowledge.

This is a good period to seek funding and financial support for worthwhile cultural projects. Benefits come through corporate money, government funding, joint finances, insurance, and inheritance.

Transiting Pluto trine natal Neptune has the same significance as transiting Neptune trine natal Pluto. Both transits occur, off and on, for a year or longer, and both indicate a sustained period of increased awareness of advanced scientific and occult aspects of life.

Transiting Neptune Trine the Natal North Node and Sextile the Natal South Node

See "Transiting Neptune Sextile the Natal South Node and Trine the Natal North Node."

Transiting Neptune Trine the Natal South Node and Sextile the Natal North Node

See "Transiting Neptune Sextile the Natal North Node and Trine the Natal South Node."

Transiting Neptune Trine the Natal Ascendant and Sextile the Natal Descendant

See "Transiting Neptune Sextile the Natal Descendant and Trine the Natal Ascendant."

Transiting Neptune Trine the Natal Midheaven and Sextile the Natal Nadir

See "Transiting Neptune Sextile the Natal Nadir and Trine the Natal Midheaven."

Transiting Neptune Trine the Natal Descendant and Sextile the Natal Ascendant

See "Transiting Neptune Sextile the Natal Ascendant and Trine the Natal Descendant."

Transiting Neptune Trine the Natal Nadir and Sextile the Natal Midheaven

See "Transiting Neptune Sextile the Natal Midheaven and Trine the Natal Nadir."

Transit Neptune Oppositions

Transiting Neptune Opposition the Natal Sun

See "Transiting Sun Opposition Natal Neptune."

Transiting Neptune Opposition the Natal Moon

See "Transiting Moon Opposition Natal Neptune."

Transiting Neptune Opposition Natal Mercury

See "Transiting Mercury Opposition Natal Neptune."

Transiting Neptune Opposition Natal Venus

See "Transiting Venus Opposition Natal Neptune."

Transiting Neptune Opposition Natal Mars

See "Transiting Mars Opposition Natal Neptune."

Transiting Neptune Opposition Natal Jupiter

See "Transiting Jupiter Opposition Natal Neptune."

Transiting Neptune Opposition Natal Saturn

See "Transiting Saturn Opposition Natal Neptune."

Transiting Neptune Opposition Natal Uranus

See "Transiting Uranus Opposition Natal Neptune."

Transiting Neptune Opposition Natal Neptune

The need to develop an attitude of spiritual serenity characterizes this transit. The individual generally goes through a psychological withdrawal from worldly affairs. There is likely to be a dependency on the family or close personal relationships for physical needs or for psychological support. This transit occurs toward the end of life.

Transiting Neptune Opposition Natal Pluto

The potential for increased intuitive spiritual awareness characterizes this transit.

This transit does not occur in the present generation, except among those who have reached an advanced age, such as our distinguished colleagues Dane Rudhyar and Marc Edmund Jones; however, it can occur in future generations, and has occurred in past generations.

This transit has the potential for producing profound and far-reaching cultural awareness which enables the individual to understand broad, long-term cultural evolutionary unfoldment. Normal life routines can be disrupted by large-scale political, economic, and social upheavals, as well as natural disasters.

Mysteries and intrigues can arise concerning relationships that are important to the individual. The individual may have to cope with difficult psychic experiences and problems that are based on the stimulation of painful subconscious memories. Some individuals may be subjected to, or themselves perpetrate, psychological manipulation or coercion—this should be avoided at all costs.

Problems may arise with corporate money, taxes, joint money, insurance, and goods of the dead.

Transiting Pluto opposition natal Neptune has the same significance as transiting Neptune opposition natal Pluto. Both transits last, off and on, for a year or longer and indicate a sustained period of spiritual and psychological tension and awareness.

Transiting Neptune Opposition the Natal North Node and Conjunct the Natal South Node

See "Transiting Neptune Conjunct the Natal South Node and Opposition the Natal North Node."

Transiting Neptune Opposition the Natal South Node and Conjunct the Natal North Node

See "Transiting Neptune Conjunct the Natal North Node and Opposition the Natal South Node."

Transiting Neptune Opposition the Natal Ascendant and Conjunct the Natal Descendant

See "Transiting Neptune Conjunct the Natal Descendant and Opposition the Natal Ascendant."

Transiting Neptune Opposition the Natal Midheaven and Conjunct the Natal Nadir

See "Transiting Neptune Conjunct the Natal Nadir and Opposition the Natal Midheaven."

Transiting Neptune Opposition the Natal Descendant and Conjunct the Natal Ascendant

See "Transiting Neptune Conjunct the Natal Ascendant and Opposition the Natal Descendant."

Transiting Neptune Opposition the Natal Nadir and Conjunct the Natal Midheaven

See "Transiting Neptune Conjunct the Natal Midheaven and Opposition the Natal Nadir."

28 Transits of Pluto

Transit Pluto Through the Houses

Transiting Pluto Through the Natal First House

Stimulation of intuitive clairvoyant faculties along with fundamental changes in the individual's basic consciousness and self-awareness characterize this transit. The individual will develop increased will power for self-improvement on all levels.

The fundamental and major changes in the individual's self-image and manner of personal expression which can result from this transit are often reflected in the personal appearance.

The individual expresses greater personal resourcefulness in many ways. There is increased will power in general, and a determination to bring about constructive change. This is a favorable period for constructive occult and spiritual practices.

During this period, there is also a greater desire for personal power and authority. However, if Pluto makes stress aspects to other planets while transiting the natal First House, the individual can tend to domineering, headstrong attitudes. The individual's attitudes toward the values of others can undergo a change.

Interest in advanced scientific subjects is often stimulated, and there may be personal involvement with joint finances and corporate business enterprises.

Transiting Pluto Through the Natal Second House

Resourceful use of money and possessions characterizes this transit. The individual finds new uses for or ways of recycling old or discarded items. An ambition for wealth and financial power often arises, and major changes can occur in one's business and financial relationships.

The individual may have serious responsibilities for handling other people's money. Often, there is involvement in some way in businesses related to occult interests, advanced technology, financial investments, corporate money, insurance, taxes, inheritances, alimony, and goods of the dead.

Financial loss, destruction, or theft of personal property or reversals of financial fortune can occur if Pluto makes stress aspects while transiting the natal Second House. If Pluto is afflicted while transiting the natal Second House, one can be tempted to use dishonest means or coercive tactics in business and financial affairs, or be subjected to such tactics oneself.

Transiting Pluto Through the Natal Third House

Important changes in one's intellectual concepts and manner of communication characterize this transit. In some cases, irrevocable changes in mental outlook occur. There can be major changes in attitude toward brothers, sisters, neighbors, and friends. There is a need for regeneration of personal thinking patterns.

The individual may be entrusted with secret information, or engage in secret communications during this transit. Some individuals experience telepathic communication.

The individual can develop an intellectual interest in occult or advanced scientific subjects, such as parapsychology, life after death, reincarnation, unexplained phenomena, ecology, economics, physics, or genetics. There may also be a strong concern with environmental, ecological issues.

Caution should be exercised in signing important documents and agreements, as such actions can have far-reaching consequences.

If Pluto makes stress aspects while transiting the natal Third House, there can be danger through short trips and traffic accidents.

Transiting Pluto Through the Natal Fourth House

Occult experiences which affect the deepest levels of consciousness characterize this transit. Some individuals seek to free themselves from family ties or seek to reform their family affairs. Financial affairs affecting the family may be of major concern. This is a favorable time for home-improvement projects.

Drastic changes can occur in home and family affairs. If Pluto makes stress aspects while transiting the natal Fourth House, one's home or family may be disrupted or destroyed by forces beyond one's personal control, such as earthquakes and other natural disasters, wars, and revolutions. There may also be the death of a parent or family member.

The individual may develop an interest in earth sciences and ecological issues during this transit.

Transiting Pluto Through the Natal Fifth House

Intensified personal charisma and dramatic appeal characterize this transit. Major changes can occur in the individual's creative self-expression, social activities, and pursuit of pleasure.

There can be an intensified sex drive and intense romantic involvements during this period. However, if Pluto makes stress aspects to other planets while transiting the natal Fifth House, romantic intrigues and sexual jealousy can present a problem.

The individual tends to express resourcefulness and inspiration in his or her creative artistic endeavors. There may also be an interest in improving affairs related to children. Some individuals become interested in corporate financial speculation during this transit. If Pluto makes stress aspects to other planets during this transit, there can be losses through financial speculation.

Transiting Pluto Through the Natal Sixth House

Interest in improving work methodologies characterizes this transit. The individual displays intensified will power in regard to his or her work. One's work is often related in some way to such fields as corporate business, insurance, taxes, occult studies, or advanced science. Work may also involve secrecy and matters which have important and irreversible long-range consequences; such work often relates to advanced technology.

Major changes can occur, for better or worse, in the individual's health and job situation, and in his or her manner of dress and personal hygiene.

If Pluto makes stress aspects while transiting the natal Sixth House, occupational hazards are a threat to the individual's health and safety. In extreme cases, disease can lead to death.

Transiting Pluto Through the Natal Seventh House

Major changes in one's important personal relationships and in one's attitudes toward others characterize this transit. Old marriages, partnerships, or close relationships are often terminated and new ones begun.

The individual can come into contact with strong-willed, dynamic, and sometimes occult, mysterious, or secretive individuals. A power struggle for supremacy can ensue in such relationships. Individuals with this transit should avoid dominating or coercing others and allowing others to dominate or coerce them.

The individual may become involved in corporate legal affairs or public relations strategies during this period.

If Pluto makes stress aspects to natal or other transiting planets while in the natal Seventh House, conflicts or lawsuits may arise over joint finances, corporate money, insurance, taxes, inheritance, alimony, or goods of the dead. Sexual problems or sexual jealousy can arise in marriage if Pluto is afflicted.

Transiting Pluto Through the Natal Eighth House

The destruction of old conditions in preparation for the influx of new ones characterizes this transit.

Latent clairvoyant faculties and occult abilities may be stimulated at this time. Some individuals develop an interest in reincarnation, life after death, parapsychology, spirit communication, and other occult subjects. There may also be involvement with joint finances, corporate business, inheritance, taxes, insurance, alimony, and goods of the dead. This transit is likely to stimulate the sex drive.

If Pluto makes stress aspects while transiting the natal Eighth House, there may be danger to the life of the individual, or someone of consequence to the individual may die. There is also the danger of involvement with underworld elements or corporate power struggles. The individual's life may be disrupted by natural disasters or by large-scale economic, political, or military forces beyond his or her personal control.

Transiting Pluto Through the Natal Ninth House

An interest in metaphysical and scientific approaches to education, religion, and philosophy characterizes this transit. Drastic and irrevocable changes can occur in the individual's religious, cultural, and philosophical convictions, often as the result of direct intuitive experiences affecting the individual's religious outlook and a personal encounter with inner spiritual realities.

Some individuals develop a desire to reform existing educational, legal, religious, and cultural institutions. Financial support, grants, or government funding for higher education may be forthcoming during this transit. Profound experiences and changes in philosophic outlook can come about through education, travel, and the development of clairvoyant faculties.

The individual may travel in relation to corporate business or business involvement with foreigners or with people in distant places, especially for the purpose of introducing scientific technology to other countries.

If Pluto makes stress aspects while transiting the natal Ninth House, the individual can adopt extreme or fanatical religious, educational, cultural, or philosophic viewpoints. The individual may be exposed to danger while traveling or visiting foreign countries. In extreme cases, this can mean involvement in foreign wars.

Transiting Pluto Through the Natal Tenth House

Increased will power and an ambition to succeed in one's professional affairs characterize this transit. There may be involvement in professional or political intrigues and power struggles.

This transit often indicates major, irrevocable changes in one's professional status and reputation, for better or worse. The individual experiences a desire to improve professional efficiency and methodologies. Business contacts with people of great wealth or power tend to be established at this time.

There is often professional involvement with corporate business and matters related to joint finances, corporate money, insurance, taxes, inheritance, and goods of the dead. Such activities can also involve advanced technology and corporate, military, or government secrecy. In some cases, professional activity or public status is related to the occult in some way.

If Pluto makes stress aspects while transiting the natal Tenth House, the individual can develop a power complex, and some individuals undergo major reversals in fortune.

Transiting Pluto Through the Natal Eleventh House

Transformation of personal goals and objectives characterizes this transit. The individual may develop friendships with powerful, influential people during this transit or become involved with occult, sometimes secret, friendships, groups, and organizations. There is a tendency to sever old, outworn friendships and group affiliations and establish new ones. The individual and his or her friends can exert a powerful, transforming influence upon each other's lives, for good or ill.

A desire to reform, transform or, in extreme cases, overthrow the existing social order is also a characteristic of this transit.

The individual can develop an intellectual interest in science, advanced technology, metaphysics, parapsychology, or occult pursuits. Some individuals receive grants or government funding for scientific work under this transit.

If Pluto makes stress aspects while transiting the natal Eleventh House, the individual may attempt to coerce or remake his or her friends, or vice versa. If Pluto is afflicted, the individual can become involved in power struggles in groups or organizations.

Transiting Pluto Through the Natal Twelfth House

The need to regenerate the contents of the subconscious mind characterizes this transit. The individual can make use of the resources of the subconscious and gain penetrating insights into its functioning.

If Pluto makes favorable aspects, this is an excellent time for meditation and the unfolding of intuitive, clairvoyant faculties, or for investigating previous lives. The individual can have some profound spiritual insights during this transit. In any event, the individual is likely to develop an interest in meditation, mysticism, or occult practices.

If Pluto makes stress aspects while transiting the natal Twelfth House, the individual can become involved in secret intrigues, secret sexual involvements, or behind-the-scenes power struggles. Dangers can arise from secret enemies or negative psychic practices. In extreme cases, the individual is imprisoned, institutionalized, or incarcerated in some way.

Transit Pluto Conjunctions

Transiting Pluto Conjunct the Natal Sun

See "Transiting Sun Conjunct Natal Pluto."

Transiting Pluto Conjunct the Natal Moon

See "Transiting Moon Conjunct Natal Pluto."

Transiting Pluto Conjunct Natal Mercury

See "Transiting Mercury Conjunct Natal Pluto."

Transiting Pluto Conjunct Natal Venus

See "Transiting Venus Conjunct Natal Pluto."

Transiting Pluto Conjunct Natal Mars

See "Transiting Mars Conjunct Natal Pluto."

Transiting Pluto Conjunct Natal Jupiter

See "Transiting Jupiter Conjunct Natal Pluto."

Transiting Pluto Conjunct Natal Saturn

See "Transiting Saturn Conjunct Natal Pluto."

Transiting Pluto Conjunct Natal Uranus

See "Transiting Uranus Conjunct Natal Pluto."

Transiting Pluto Conjunct Natal Neptune

See "Transiting Neptune Conjunct Natal Pluto."

Transiting Pluto Conjunct Natal Pluto

This transit does not occur in a normal life span, except, on occasion, during infancy, when Pluto can turn retrograde, then direct in motion. In this case, forces beyond the baby's or his or her family's personal control can endanger or alter the infant's future course. In political charts, there can be the death of old conditions and the beginning of new ones.

Transiting Pluto Conjunct the Natal North Node and Opposition the Natal South Node

Penetrating insights into the motivating forces behind popular beliefs and cultural trends characterize this transit. There can be a desire to transform existing trends and popular beliefs or, conversely, an attempt to exploit them, depending upon the general disposition of the individual concerned.

Transiting North Node conjunct natal Pluto and transiting South Node opposition natal Pluto has the same significance as transiting Pluto conjunct the natal North Node and opposition the natal South Node; however, it is of shorter duration.

Transiting Pluto Conjunct the Natal South Node and Opposition the Natal North Node

Penetrating insight into the historical development of cultural evolution characterizes this transit. There is often rebellion against traditional standards and mores.

The individual may engage in business related to the reuse or recycling of old, discarded items; some individuals go into the antique business.

Transiting South Node conjunct natal Pluto and transiting North Node opposition natal Pluto has the same significance as transiting Pluto conjunct the natal South Node and opposition the natal North Node; however, it is of shorter duration.

Transiting Pluto Conjunct the Natal Ascendant and Opposition the Natal Descendant

A desire for change in one's personal life style characterizes this transit.

The individual's personal mannerisms and appearance often undergo a transformation, and a new self-image develops. There is increased will power and greater self-awareness.

This transit can stimulate intuitive awareness, as well as latent clairvoyant faculties. The individual may develop an interest in occult, scientific subjects. There may be personal involvement in corporate business or matters related to insurance, taxes, alimony, or goods of the dead. In some cases, there is involvement with secrecy and advanced technology.

Transiting Pluto Conjunct the Natal Midheaven and Opposition the Natal Nadir

Intuitive insights into professional affairs characterize this transit.

The individual may adopt new methods and procedures in professional activities. This transit can also bring involvement in professional or political power struggles. In some cases, it indicates involvement with professional or governmental secrecy and intrigues. The individual's professional activities during this period tend to be related to corporate business, insurance, taxes, goods of the dead, advanced technologies, or occult activities in some way.

Important changes with far-reaching consequences in the career and status of the individual can develop at this time.

Transiting Pluto Conjunct the Natal Descendant and Opposition the Natal Ascendant

Discontinuation of old relationships and the formation of new ones characterize this transit. The individual may become involved with powerful or intuitively gifted people. In some cases, there is a struggle for supremacy or dominance in a relationship. There can be conflicts and secret intrigues involving secret enemies and opponents.

Improved methods in dealing with the public contribute to the individual's success.

If this transiting conjunction receives stress aspects from other planets, sexual problems may arise in marriage. There may also be lawsuits related to corporate money, insurance, taxes, alimony, or goods of the dead.

Transiting Pluto Conjunct the Natal Nadir and Opposition the Natal Midheaven

Stimulation of deep-seated psychological tendencies and subconscious memories characterizes this transit. There is a need to regenerate one's subconscious habit patterns and emotional attitudes toward family affairs.

The individual may change residences or renovate his or her home at this time. Occult activities may take place in the home and involve family members.

The individual is also likely to become involved with ecological issues at this time, and there can be business involvement with mining, geology, farming, real estate, or home and domestic products and services.

Transit Pluto Sextiles

Transiting Pluto Sextile the Natal Sun

See "Transiting Sun Sextile Natal Pluto."

Transiting Pluto Sextile the Natal Moon

See "Transiting Moon Sextile Natal Pluto."

Transiting Pluto Sextile Natal Mercury

See "Transiting Mercury Sextile Natal Pluto."

Transiting Pluto Sextile Natal Venus

See "Transiting Venus Sextile Natal Pluto."

Transiting Pluto Sextile Natal Mars

See "Transiting Mars Sextile Natal Pluto."

Transiting Pluto Sextile Natal Jupiter

See "Transiting Jupiter Sextile Natal Pluto."

Transiting Pluto Sextile Natal Saturn

See "Transiting Saturn Sextile Natal Pluto."

Transiting Pluto Sextile Natal Uranus

See "Transiting Uranus Sextile Natal Pluto."

Transiting Pluto Sextile Natal Neptune

See "Transiting Neptune Sextile Natal Pluto."

Transiting Pluto Sextile Natal Pluto

Increased will power, self-awareness, and opportunities for self-improvement characterize this transit. The intuitive and clairvoyant abilities are often stimulated.

The individual finds new uses for old, discarded items and resources, and displays resourcefulness in finding solutions to business and financial problems.

Transiting Pluto Sextile the Natal North Node and Trine the Natal South Node

Penetrating insights into cultural trends and developments, as well as opportunities to make use of them in some manner, characterize this transit.

The individual can develop an interest in influencing or reforming popular cultural trends and beliefs and a skill in the business exploitation of mass psychology.

Transiting North Node sextile natal Pluto and transiting South Node trine natal Pluto has the same significance as transiting Pluto sextile the natal North Node and trine the natal South Node; however, it lasts for a shorter period of time.

Transiting Pluto Sextile the Natal South Node and Trine the Natal North Node

This transit has basically the same significance as transiting Pluto sextile the natal North Node and trine the natal South Node; however, it confers a greater intellectual awareness of cultural tradition and prophetic insight into future cultural trends.

Transiting South Node sextile natal Pluto and transiting North Node trine natal Pluto has the same significance as transiting Pluto sextile the natal South Node and trine the natal North Node; however, it lasts for a shorter period of time.

Transiting Pluto Sextile the Natal Ascendant and Trine the Natal Descendant

Increased will power and resourcefulness in one's self-expression characterize this transit. It can help the individual to achieve a higher level of awareness. The individual becomes increasingly intuitive where important relationships are concerned. Relationships are often established with unusual and resourceful individuals. Many people change and improve their personal appearance and mannerisms during this transit.

This is a favorable time for involvement in business and corporate partnerships.

Transiting Pluto Sextile the Natal Midheaven and Trine the Natal Nadir

A desire for increased power and status characterizes this transit.

One can use the resources of one's unconscious mind effectively to uncover information that is valuable in realizing one's goals. This increased insight is accompanied by will power to overcome negative emotional conditionings and habit patterns.

This transit favors resourcefulness in both professional and domestic matters.

It is a favorable time for formulating business and professional strategy. There may be professional involvement with advanced technology, corporate business, taxes, joint finances, goods of the dead, or the occult. Some individuals become interested in improved methodology in the handling of dietary matters, farming, building, or construction. An interest in geology, archaeology, ecology, and the recycling of resources may also develop. Occult or scientific activities sometimes take place in the home. This is a favorable time for home-renovation projects.

Transiting Pluto Sextile the Natal Descendant and Trine the Natal Ascendant

This transit has basically the same significance as transiting Pluto sextile the natal Ascendant and trine the natal Descendant; however, there will be intellectual perception regarding one's relationships and ease in both self-regeneration and the expression of personal creativity.

Transiting Pluto Sextile the Natal Nadir and Trine the Natal Midheaven

This transit has basically the same significance as transiting Pluto sextile the natal Midheaven and trine the natal Nadir; however, there is an intensified intellectual awareness of family and ecological issues and an ease in improving professional methodologies.

Transit Pluto Squares

Transiting Pluto Square the Natal Sun

See "Transiting Sun Square Natal Pluto."

Transiting Pluto Square the Natal Moon

See "Transiting Moon Square Natal Pluto."

Transiting Pluto Square Natal Mercury

See "Transiting Mercury Square Natal Pluto."

Transiting Pluto Square Natal Venus

See "Transiting Venus Square Natal Pluto."

Transiting Pluto Square Natal Mars

See "Transiting Mars Square Natal Pluto."

Transiting Pluto Square Natal Jupiter

See "Transiting Jupiter Square Natal Pluto."

Transiting Pluto Square Natal Saturn

See "Transiting Saturn Square Natal Pluto."

Transiting Pluto Square Natal Uranus

See "Transiting Uranus Square Natal Pluto."

Transiting Pluto Square Natal Neptune

See "Transiting Neptune Square Natal Pluto."

Transiting Pluto Square Natal Pluto

The need to eliminate outworn ideas, conditions, and possessions, plus a forced realization of spiritual realities, characterize this transit.

Life-and-death issues may arise under this transit. The individual may be subjected to disturbing psychic influences.

Problems may arise in relation to insurance, taxes, corporate money, inheritance, joint finances, alimony, and ecological issues.

Financial problems can be brought on by forces beyond the individual's control. There is also the danger of business and political power struggles. The individual's employment and professional position may undergo drastic changes.

Caution should be exercised where sex is concerned: the individual can be subject to venereal disease during this transit.

Transiting Pluto Square the Natal North Node and Square the Natal South Node

The stimulation of unpleasant subconscious memories and the need to overcome negative emotional conditioning characterize this transit.

Conflicts can arise with parents, authority figures, or the government, and the individual is likely to rebel against currently popular social attitudes and beliefs. Should the individual blindly adhere to these attitudes and beliefs, especially where sex and money are concerned, he or she may be subjected to some kind of danger. A critical appraisal, without antisocial behavior, is demanded at this time.

Transiting North and South Nodes square natal Pluto has the same significance as transiting Pluto square the natal North Node and square the natal South Node; however, it lasts for a shorter period of time.

Transiting Pluto Square the Natal South Node and Square the Natal North Node

See "Transiting Pluto Square the Natal North Node and Square the Natal South Node."

Transiting Pluto Square the Natal Ascendant and Square the Natal Descendant

Power struggles in important relationships characterize this transit. Conflicts and lawsuits may arise over joint monies, corporate money, taxes, goods of the dead, insurance, and alimony. Serious problems can arise from the individual's attempts to remake or reform others or attempts of others to remake or reform the individual.

In general, individuals with this transit need to regenerate their manner of personal expression and their dealings with others. They should take special care to avoid situations of potential danger and violence.

Transiting Pluto Square the Natal Midheaven and Square the Natal Nadir

The need for regeneration of one's professional and domestic affairs characterizes this transit.

The individual may be subjected to professional and family power struggles. The individual may be subject to drastic changes affecting home, profession, or job. Both professional and family life can be disrupted by forces beyond the individual's personal control; sometimes these are ecological problems or natural disasters. Emergency conditions can create conflict between professional and domestic responsibilities. New methods will be required to cope with new situations in this regard.

Transiting Pluto Square the Natal Descendant and Square the Natal Ascendant

See "Transiting Pluto Square the Natal Ascendant and Square the Natal Descendant."

Transiting Pluto Square the Natal Nadir and Square the Natal Midheaven

See "Transiting Pluto Square the Natal Midheaven and Square the Natal Nadir."

Transit Pluto Trines

Transiting Pluto Trine the Natal Sun

See "Transiting Sun Trine Natal Pluto."

Transiting Pluto Trine the Natal Moon

See "Transiting Moon Trine Natal Pluto."

Transiting Pluto Trine Natal Mercury

See "Transiting Mercury Trine Natal Pluto."

Transiting Pluto Trine Natal Venus

See "Transiting Venus Trine Natal Pluto."

Transiting Pluto Trine Natal Mars

See "Transiting Mars Trine Natal Pluto."

Transiting Pluto Trine Natal Jupiter

See "Transiting Jupiter Trine Natal Pluto."

Transiting Pluto Trine Natal Saturn

See "Transiting Saturn Trine Natal Pluto."

Transiting Pluto Trine Natal Uranus

See "Transiting Uranus Trine Natal Pluto."

Transiting Pluto Trine Natal Neptune

See "Transiting Neptune Trine Natal Pluto."

Transiting Pluto Trine Natal Pluto

Wisdom and insight into the spiritual purpose of evolution characterize this transit. Because this transit occurs late in life, it marks a period during which the individual gains a deeper understanding of life and death.

Transiting Pluto Trine the Natal North Node and Sextile the Natal South Node

See "Transiting Pluto Sextile the Natal South Node and Trine the Natal North Node."

Transiting Pluto Trine the Natal South Node and Sextile the Natal North Node

See "Transiting Pluto Sextile the Natal North Node and Trine the Natal South Node."

Transiting Pluto Trine the Natal Ascendant and Sextile the Natal Descendant

See "Transiting Pluto Sextile the Natal Descendant and Trine the Natal Ascendant."

Transiting Pluto Trine the Natal Midheaven and Sextile the Natal Nadir

See "Transiting Pluto Sextile the Natal Nadir and Trine the Natal Midheaven."

Transiting Pluto Trine the Natal Descendant and Sextile the Natal Ascendant

See "Transiting Pluto Sextile the Natal Ascendant and Trine the Natal Descendant."

Transiting Pluto Trine the Natal Nadir and Sextile the Natal Midheaven

See "Transiting Pluto Sextile the Natal Midheaven and Trine the Natal Nadir."

Transit Pluto Oppositions

Transiting Pluto Opposition the Natal Sun

See "Transiting Sun Opposition Natal Pluto."

Transiting Pluto Opposition the Natal Moon

See "Transiting Moon Opposition Natal Pluto."

Transiting Pluto Opposition Natal Mercury

See "Transiting Mercury Opposition Natal Pluto."

Transiting Pluto Opposition Natal Venus

See "Transiting Venus Opposition Natal Pluto."

Transiting Pluto Opposition Natal Mars

See "Transiting Mars Opposition Natal Pluto."

Transiting Pluto Opposition Natal Jupiter

See "Transiting Jupiter Opposition Natal Pluto."

Transiting Pluto Opposition Natal Saturn

See "Transiting Saturn Opposition Natal Pluto."

Transiting Pluto Opposition Natal Uranus

See "Transiting Uranus Opposition Natal Pluto."

Transiting Pluto Opposition Natal Neptune

See "Transiting Neptune Opposition Natal Pluto."

Transiting Pluto Opposition Natal Pluto

This transit does not occur in a normal life span.

In a political chart, it indicates a period of economic difficulty, major power struggles, and ecological crisis.

Transiting Pluto Opposition the Natal North Node and Conjunct the Natal South Node

See "Transiting Pluto Conjunct the Natal South Node and Opposition the Natal North Node."

Transiting Pluto Opposition the Natal South Node and Conjunct the Natal North Node

See "Transiting Pluto Conjunct the Natal North Node and Opposition the Natal South Node."

Transiting Pluto Opposition the Natal Ascendant and Conjunct the Natal Descendant

See "Transiting Pluto Conjunct the Natal Descendant and Opposition the Natal Ascendant."

Transiting Pluto Opposition the Natal Midheaven and Conjunct the Natal Nadir

See "Transiting Pluto Conjunct the Natal Nadir and Opposition the Natal Midheaven."

Transiting Pluto Opposition the Natal Descendant and Conjunct the Natal Ascendant

See "Transiting Pluto Conjunct the Natal Ascendant and Opposition the Natal Descendant."

Transiting Pluto Opposition the Natal Nadir and Conjunct the Natal Midheaven

See "Transiting Pluto Conjunct the Natal Midheaven and Opposition the Natal Nadir."

29 Transits of the the Moon's Nodes to the Planets

Transit Node Conjunctions

Transiting North Node Conjunct the Natal Sun and
Transiting South Node Opposition the Natal Sun

See "Transiting Sun Conjunct North Node, Opposition South Node."

Transiting South Node Conjunct the Natal Sun and
Transiting North Node Opposition the Natal Sun

See "Transiting Sun Conjunct the Natal South Node and Opposition the Natal North Node."

Transiting North Node Conjunct the Natal Moon and
Transiting South Node Opposition the Natal Moon

See "Transiting Moon Conjunct the Natal North Node and Opposition the Natal South Node."

Transiting South Node Conjunct the Natal Moon and
Transiting North Node Opposition the Natal Moon

See "Transiting Moon Conjunct the Natal South Node and Opposition the Natal North Node."

Transiting North Node Conjunct Natal Mercury and
Transiting South Node Opposition Natal Mercury

See "Transiting Mercury Conjunct the Natal North Node and Opposition the Natal South Node."

Transiting South Node Conjunct Natal Mercury and
Transiting North Node Opposition Natal Mercury

See "Transiting Mercury Conjunct the Natal South Node and Opposition the Natal North Node."

Transiting North Node Conjunct Natal Venus and
Transiting South Node Opposition Natal Venus

See "Transiting Venus Conjunct the Natal North Node and Opposition the Natal South Node."

Transiting South Node Conjunct Natal Venus and
Transiting North Node Opposition Natal Venus

See "Transiting Venus Conjunct the Natal South Node and Opposition the Natal North Node."

Transiting North Node Conjunct Natal Mars and
Transiting South Node Opposition Natal Mars

See "Transiting Mars Conjunct the Natal North Node and Opposition the Natal South Node."

Transiting South Node Conjunct Natal Mars and
Transiting North Node Opposition Natal Mars

See "Transiting Mars Conjunct the Natal South Node and Opposition the Natal North Node."

Transiting North Node Conjunct Natal Jupiter and
Transiting South Node Opposition Natal Jupiter

See "Transiting Jupiter Conjunct the Natal North Node and Opposition the Natal South Node."

Transiting South Node Conjunct Natal Jupiter and
Transiting North Node Opposition Natal Jupiter

See "Transiting Jupiter Conjunct the Natal South Node and Opposition the Natal North Node."

Transiting North Node Conjunct Natal Saturn and
Transiting South Node Opposition Natal Saturn

See "Transiting Saturn Conjunct the Natal North Node and Opposition the Natal South Node."

Transiting South Node Conjunct Natal Saturn and
Transiting North Node Opposition Natal Saturn

See "Transiting Saturn Conjunct the Natal South Node and Opposition the Natal North Node."

Transiting North Node Conjunct Natal Uranus and
Transiting South Node Opposition Natal Uranus

See "Transiting Uranus Conjunct the Natal North Node and Opposition the Natal South Node."

Transiting South Node Conjunct Natal Uranus and
Transiting North Node Opposition Natal Uranus

See "Transiting Uranus Conjunct the Natal South Node and Opposition the Natal North Node."

Transiting North Node Conjunct Natal Neptune and
Transiting South Node Opposition Natal Neptune

See "Transiting Neptune Conjunct the Natal North Node and Opposition the Natal South Ncde."

Transiting South Node Conjunct Natal Neptune and
Transiting North Node Opposition Natal Neptune

See "Transiting Neptune Conjunct the Natal South Node and Opposition the Natal North Node."

Transiting North Node Conjunct Natal Pluto and
Transiting South Node Opposition Natal Pluto

See "Transiting Pluto Conjunct the Natal North Node and Opposition the Natal South Node."

Transiting South Node Conjunct Natal Pluto and
Transiting North Node Opposition Natal Pluto

See "Transiting Pluto Conjunct the Natal South Node and Opposition the Natal North Node."

Transit Node Sextiles

Transiting North Node Sextile the Natal Sun and
Transiting South Node Trine the Natal Sun

See "Transiting Sun Sextile the Natal North Node and Trine the Natal South Node."

Transiting South Node Sextile the Natal Sun and
Transiting North Node Trine the Natal Sun

See "Transiting Sun Sextile the Natal South Node and Trine the Natal North Node."

Transiting North Node Sextile the Natal Moon and
Transiting South Node Trine the Natal Moon

See "Transiting Moon Sextile the Natal North Node and Trine the Natal South Node."

Transiting South Node Sextile the Natal Moon and
Transiting North Node Trine the Natal Moon

See "Transiting Moon Sextile the Natal South Node and Trine the Natal North Node."

Transiting North Node Sextile Natal Mercury and
Transiting South Node Trine Natal Mercury

See "Transiting Mercury Sextile the Natal North Node and Trine the Natal South Node."

Transiting South Node Sextile Natal Mercury and
Transiting North Node Trine Natal Mercury

See "Transiting Mercury Sextile the Natal South Node and Trine the Natal North Node."

Transiting North Node Sextile Natal Venus and
Transiting South Node Trine Natal Venus

See "Transiting Venus Sextile the Natal North Node and Trine the Natal South Node."

Transiting South Node Sextile Natal Venus and
Transiting North Node Trine Natal Venus

See "Transiting Venus Sextile the Natal South Node and Trine the Natal North Node."

Transiting North Node Sextile Natal Mars and
Transiting South Node Trine Natal Mars

See "Transiting Mars Sextile the Natal North Node and Trine the Natal South Node."

Transiting South Node Sextile Natal Mars and
Transiting North Node Trine Natal Mars

See "Transiting Mars Sextile the Natal South Node and Trine the Natal North Node."

Transiting North Node Sextile Natal Jupiter and
Transiting South Node Trine Natal Jupiter

See "Transiting Jupiter Sextile the Natal North Node and Trine the Natal South Node."

Transiting South Node Sextile Natal Jupiter and
Transiting North Node Trine Natal Jupiter

See "Transiting Jupiter Sextile the Natal South Node and Trine the Natal North Node."

Transiting North Node Sextile Natal Saturn and
Transiting South Node Trine Natal Saturn

See "Transiting Saturn Sextile the Natal North Node and Trine the Natal South Node."

Transiting South Node Sextile Natal Saturn and
Transiting North Node Trine Natal Saturn

See "Transiting Saturn Sextile the Natal South Node and Trine the Natal North Node."

Transiting North Node Sextile Natal Uranus and
Transiting South Node Trine Natal Uranus

See "Transiting Uranus Sextile the Natal North Node and Trine the Natal South Node."

Transiting South Node Sextile Natal Uranus and
Transiting North Node Trine Natal Uranus

See "Transiting Uranus Sextile the Natal South Node and Trine the Natal North Node."

Transiting North Node Sextile Natal Neptune and
Transiting South Node Trine Natal Neptune

See "Transiting Neptune Sextile the Natal North Node and Trine the Natal South Node."

Transiting South Node Sextile Natal Neptune and
Transiting North Node Trine Natal Neptune

See "Transiting Neptune Sextile the Natal South Node and Trine the Natal North Node."

Transiting North Node Sextile Natal Pluto and
Transiting South Node Trine Natal Pluto

See "Transiting Pluto Sextile the Natal North Node and Trine the Natal South Node."

Transiting South Node Sextile Natal Pluto and
Transiting North Node Trine Natal Pluto

See "Transiting Pluto Sextile the Natal South Node and Trine the Natal North Node."

Transit Node Squares

Transiting North and South Nodes Square the Natal Sun

See "Transiting Sun Square the Natal North Node and Square the Natal South Node."

Transiting North and South Nodes Square the Natal Moon

See "Transiting Moon Square the Natal North Node and Square the Natal South Node."

Transiting North and South Nodes Square Natal Mercury

See "Transiting Mercury Square the Natal North Node and Square the Natal South Node."

Transiting North and South Nodes Square Natal Venus

See "Transiting Venus Square the Natal North Node and Square the Natal South Node."

Transiting North and South Nodes Square Natal Mars

See "Transiting Mars Square the Natal North Node and Square the Natal South Node."

Transiting North and South Nodes Square Natal Jupiter

See "Transiting Jupiter Square the Natal North Node and Square the Natal South Node."

Transiting North and South Nodes Square Natal Saturn

See "Transiting Saturn Square the Natal North Node and Square the Natal South Node."

Transiting North and South Nodes Square Natal Uranus

See "Transiting Uranus Square the Natal North Node and Square the Natal South Node."

Transiting North and South Nodes Square Natal Neptune

See "Transiting Neptune Square the Natal North Node and Square the Natal South Node."

Transiting North and South Nodes Square Natal Pluto

See "Transiting Pluto Square the Natal North Node and Square the Natal South Node."

Transit Node Trines

Transiting North Node Trine the Natal Sun and
Transiting South Node Sextile the Natal Sun

See "Transiting Sun Sextile the Natal South Node and Trine the Natal North Node."

Transiting South Node Trine the Natal Sun and
Transiting North Node Sextile the Natal Sun

See "Transiting Sun Sextile the Natal North Node and Trine the Natal South Node."

Transiting North Node Trine the Natal Moon and
Transiting South Node Sextile the Natal Moon

See "Transiting Moon Sextile the Natal South Node and Trine the Natal North Node."

Transiting South Node Trine the Natal Moon and
Transiting North Node Sextile the Natal Moon

See "Transiting Moon Sextile the Natal North Node and Trine the Natal South Node."

Transiting North Node Trine Natal Mercury and
Transiting South Node Sextile Natal Mercury

See "Transiting Mercury Sextile the Natal South Node and Trine the Natal North Node."

Transiting South Node Trine Natal Mercury and
Transiting North Node Sextile Natal Mercury

See "Transiting Mercury Sextile the Natal North Node and Trine the Natal South Node."

Transiting North Node Trine Natal Venus and
Transiting South Node Sextile Natal Venus

See "Transiting Venus Sextile the Natal South Node and Trine the Natal North Node."

Transiting South Node Trine Natal Venus and
Transiting North Node Sextile Natal Venus

See "Transiting Venus Sextile the Natal North Node and Trine the Natal South Node."

Transiting North Node Trine Natal Mars and
Transiting South Node Sextile Natal Mars

See "Transiting Mars Sextile the Natal South Node and Trine the Natal North Node."

Transiting South Node Trine Natal Mars and
Transiting North Node Sextile Natal Mars

See "Transiting Mars Sextile the Natal North Node and Trine the Natal South Node."

Transiting North Node Trine Natal Jupiter and
Transiting South Node Sextile Natal Jupiter

See "Transiting Jupiter Sextile the Natal South Node and Trine the Natal North Node."

Transiting South Node Trine Natal Jupiter and
Transiting North Node Sextile Natal Jupiter

See "Transiting Jupiter Sextile the Natal North Node and Trine the Natal South Node."

Transiting North Node Trine Natal Saturn and
Transiting South Node Sextile Natal Saturn

See "Transiting Saturn Sextile the Natal South Node and Trine the Natal North Node."

Transiting South Node Trine Natal Saturn and
Transiting North Node Sextile Natal Saturn

See "Transiting Saturn Sextile the Natal North Node and Trine the Natal South Node."

Transiting North Node Trine Natal Uranus and
Transiting South Node Sextile Natal Uranus

See "Transiting Uranus Sextile the Natal South Node and Trine the Natal North Node."

Transiting South Node Trine Natal Uranus and
Transiting North Node Sextile Natal Uranus

See "Transiting Uranus Sextile the Natal North Node and Trine the Natal South Node."

Transiting North Node Trine Natal Neptune and
Transiting South Node Sextile Natal Neptune

See "Transiting Neptune Sextile the Natal South Node and Trine the Natal North Node."

Transiting South Node Trine Natal Neptune and
Transiting North Node Sextile Natal Neptune

See "Transiting Neptune Sextile the Natal North Node and Trine the Natal South Node."

Transiting North Node Trine Natal Pluto and
Transiting South Node Sextile Natal Pluto

See "Transiting Pluto Sextile the Natal South Node and Trine the Natal North Node."

Transiting South Node Trine Natal Pluto and
Transiting North Node Sextile Natal Pluto

See "Transiting Pluto Sextile the Natal North Node and Trine the Natal South Node."

Transit Node Oppositions

Transiting North Node Opposition the Natal Sun and
Transiting South Node Conjunct the Natal Sun

See "Transiting Sun Conjunct the Natal South Node and Opposition the Natal North Node."

Transiting South Node Opposition the Natal Sun and
Transiting North Node Conjunct the Natal Sun

See "Transiting Sun Conjunct the Natal North Node and Opposition the Natal South Node."

Transiting North Node Opposition the Natal Moon and
Transiting South Node Conjunct the Natal Moon

See "Transiting Moon Conjunct the Natal South Node and Opposition the Natal North Node."

Transiting South Node Opposition the Natal Moon and
Transiting North Node Conjunct the Natal Moon

See "Transiting Moon Conjunct the Natal North Node and Opposition the Natal South Node."

Transiting North Node Opposition Natal Mercury and
Transiting South Node Conjunct Natal Mercury

See "Transiting Mercury Conjunct the Natal South Node and Opposition the Natal North Node."

Transiting South Node Opposition Natal Mercury and
Transiting North Node Conjunct Natal Mercury

See "Transiting Mercury Conjunct the Natal North Node and Opposition the Natal South Node."

Transiting North Node Opposition Natal Venus and
Transiting South Node Conjunct Natal Venus

See "Transiting Venus Conjunct the Natal South Node and Opposition the Natal North Node."

Transiting South Node Opposition Natal Venus and
Transiting North Node Conjunct Natal Venus

See "Transiting Venus Conjunct the Natal North Node and Opposition the Natal South Node."

Transiting North Node Opposition Natal Mars and
Transiting South Node Conjunct Natal Mars

See "Transiting Mars Conjunct the Natal South Node and Opposition the Natal North Node."

Transiting South Node Opposition Natal Mars and
Transiting North Node Conjunct Natal Mars

See "Transiting Mars Conjunct the Natal North Node and Opposition the Natal South Node."

Transiting North Node Opposition Natal Jupiter and
Transiting South Node Conjunct Natal Jupiter

See "Transiting Jupiter Conjunct the Natal South Node and Opposition the Natal North Node."

Transiting South Node Opposition Natal Jupiter and
Transiting North Node Conjunct Natal Jupiter

See "Transiting Jupiter Conjunct the Natal North Node and Opposition the Natal South Node."

Transiting North Node Opposition Natal Saturn and
Transiting South Node Conjunct Natal Saturn

See "Transiting Saturn Conjunct the Natal South Node and Opposition the Natal North Node."

Transiting South Node Opposition Natal Saturn and
Transiting North Node Conjunct Natal Saturn

See "Transiting Saturn Conjunct the Natal North Node and Opposition the Natal South Node."

Transiting North Node Opposition Natal Uranus and
Transiting South Node Conjunct Natal Uranus

See "Transiting Uranus Conjunct the Natal South Node and Opposition the Natal North Node."

Transiting South Node Opposition Natal Uranus and
Transiting North Node Conjunct Natal Uranus

See "Transiting Uranus Conjunct the Natal North Node and Opposition the Natal South Node."

Transiting North Node Opposition Natal Neptune and
Transiting South Node Conjunct Natal Neptune

See "Transiting Neptune Conjunct the Natal South Node and Opposition the Natal North Node."

Transiting South Node Opposition Natal Neptune and
Transiting North Node Conjunct Natal Neptune

See "Transiting Neptune Conjunct the Natal North Node and Opposition the Natal South Node."

Transiting North Node Opposition Natal Pluto and
Transiting South Node Conjunct Natal Pluto

See "Transiting Pluto Conjunct the Natal South Node and Opposition the Natal North Node."

Transiting South Node Opposition Natal Pluto and
Transiting North Node Conjunct Natal Pluto

See "Transiting Pluto Conjunct the Natal North Node and Opposition the Natal South Node."

Glossary

Ascendant   The point at which the eastern horizon intersects the ecliptic. The First House cusp or rising sign.

Aspect   The angle formed between two imaginary lines connecting two celestial bodies or points with the Earth.

Conjunction   The occurrence of a direct or nearly direct line-up of two planets as seen from the Earth.

Cusp   The line of division between two houses. The cusps are normally named for the line between a house and the house below it. Thus, the Seventh House cusp is the line between the Seventh and Sixth houses.

Descendant   The point at which the western horizon intersects the ecliptic. It is also the cusp between the Sixth and Seventh houses.

Ecliptic   The plane of the Earth's orbit around the Sun extended into space to meet the celestial sphere. From the Earth, the ecliptic appears to be the path the Sun follows around the Earth in a year's time.

Hidden Aspect   This occurs when one planet involved in an aspect is in the early degrees of one sign and the other planet involved is in the last degrees of another sign. Hidden aspects can occur in all the major aspects as well as in the semi sextile and inconjunct in the family of minor aspects.

Horoscope   A map or chart of the position of the planets in the heavens at the exact time and place of one's birth. The map covers the entire sky, a full circle of 360°. Also called a' *natal chart* or *map*.

House   One of twelve divisions made in the cycle of the Earth's daily rotation. Each house represents an approximate two-hour period during which approximately one-twelfth of the Zodiac appears to pass over the horizon. The houses are named in order, beginning with the First House and continuing through to the Twelfth House. Each house presides over a different department of practical affairs and is associated with a specific sign of the Zodiac.

Meridian   A great circle on the celestial sphere passing through the north and south points of the horizon and the zenith, which is directly above the observer.

Midheaven (also written *M.C.* from the Latin *medium coeli*)   The point at which the meridian intersects the ecliptic above the earth.

Nadir   The point on the ecliptic directly opposite the Midheaven looking downward from the observer. Also called the Fourth House cusp.

Node   Each of the two points at which a planet's orbit intersects the ecliptic: once when the planet moves north across the ecliptic, and once again when it moves south. In astrology, the Nodes of the Moon are especially significant.

Opposition   An aspect representing an angular relationship of 180° between two planets. Planets in opposition generally occupy approximately the same number of degrees in two signs directly across the Zodiac from each other, unless there is a hidden aspect.

Quadruplicity   One of three fixed groups of signs, each containing four signs. The three quadruplicities relate to three characteristics—Cardinal, Fixed, and Mutable—and are concerned with basic modes of activities.

Sextile   That aspect representing an angular relationship of 60°, or one-sixth of a circle. Planets in sextile aspect are placed two signs apart and occupy approximately the same number of degrees in these signs, plus or minus 6°, unless there is a hidden aspect.

Square   That aspect representing an angular relationship of 90°. Planets in square aspect generally occupy the same number of degrees in signs which are three signs apart, unless there is a hidden aspect.

Sun signs   The twelve traditional signs of the Zodiac. They are Aries (the Ram), Taurus (the Bull), Gemini (the Twins), Cancer (the Crab), Leo (the Lion), Virgo (the Virgin), Libra (the Scales),

Scorpio (the Scorpion), Sagittarius (the Archer), Capricorn (the Goat), Aquarius (the Water-bearer), and Pisces (the Fishes).

Trine   That aspect representing an angular relationship of 120° or one-third of a circle between two planets. Planets in trine aspect generally occupy the same number of degrees in signs four signs apart, unless there is a hidden aspect.

Triplicity   One of four fixed groups of signs, each containing three planets. The four triplicities relate to the four elements earth, air, fire, and water. They are concerned with tendencies of the temperament.

Vernal equinox   The intersection of the plane of the ecliptic with the celestial equator. This intersection occurs once a year, at the moment the Sun crosses the celestial equator moving from south to north.

Zenith   That point in the celestial sphere directly above the observer.

Zodiac   The band of sky 18° wide having the ecliptic as its central line. It consists of twelve parts, each 30° wide, which represent the twelve signs of the Zodiac.

Index

ACA, Inc., Box 395, Weston, Massachusetts 02193

Please send me the personalized computer printout of four months' transits and cross-reference index offered in *Predictive Astrology*. I am enclosing $4.50 (check or money order—do not send cash). I want my transits to start with the first day of the month and year indicated: month_____
year_____

Mailing Information

Name_____

Address_____

City_____State_____Zip Code_____

Birth Information

Name_____

Date of birth: Month_____Day_____Year_____

Time of birth: (exact local time if known)_____A.M. ( ) P.M. ( )

Time of birth unknown ( )

Place of birth:
Town or nearest large city_____

State_____Country_____

IF YOU DO NOT WISH TO REMOVE THIS PAGE, INFORMATION MAY BE SUPPLIED ON A PLAIN SHEET OF PAPER. DO NOT FORGET TO PROVIDE ALL INFORMATION.

Note: The price guarantee of $4.50 per complete transit chart expires December 31, 1979. After that date write ACA for price information.